THE ONLY WAY TO FLY

Books by Robert J. Serling

ROBERT J. SERLING

THE ONLY WAY TO FLY

THE STORY OF WESTERN AIRLINES, AMERICA'S SENIOR AIR CARRIER

DOUBLEDAY & COMPANY, INC., GARDEN CITY, NEW YORK

All photographs courtesy of Western Airlines

Library of Congress Cataloging in Publication Data

Serling, Robert J
The only way to fly.

Includes index.
1. Western Air Lines, Inc. I. Title.
HE9803.W47S47   387.7'06'578
ISBN 0-385-01342-6
Library of Congress Catalog Card Number 75-40744

To the memory of my brother Rod

FOREWORD

This is a story of men and machines, a tale that took fifty years to unfold and is still being written.

As in all stories of men, it includes heroes and villains, generals and spear carriers, success and failure, happiness and tragedy. Its machines range from the incredibly primitive to the incredibly complex; they, too, are characters in this half-century chronicle, for the airplane is an extension of man himself—his strengths and his weaknesses, his vision and his mistakes, his dreams and his nightmares, his pride and his humility.

In essence, this is the history of an airline, one that proudly claims the honor of being the nation's oldest scheduled air carrier. It was not the first, definitely it is not the biggest, and no airline can unqualifiedly boast of being the best. It does not even like to be called "America's Oldest Airline," preferring the title of "America's Senior Airline," as if "oldest" might be construed as ancient, antiquated, or, perhaps, doddering.

But longevity is not the prime point of this book's conception and writing, for this is far more than just the story of a single airline. What the company did in the past fifty years is what every airline has done over approximately the same time span; no carrier, including this one, has a monopoly on overcoming adversity through sheer determination. Or on rising from the scorned status of a transportation midget to an ocean-flying giant. Or achieving success in spite of, and sometimes because of, top-level feuds that stained corporate carpets with executive blood.

You are about to read, in effect, the history of U.S. commercial aviation told: it is one through the eyes of one airline that in 1976 celebrated fifty years of unbroken operation under the same name. It is a happy coincidence that its Golden Anniversary occurred in the same year the industry observed its bicentennial; just as this one airline reflects the experiences and accomplishments of the air transportation industry, so does that industry itself symbolize what America has achieved in terms of human and technological progress.

In many respects, however, this tale is as unique as it is representative. It concerns a carrier that once was the nation's biggest, only to dwindle virtually overnight to an airline serving just four cities. It is a company that has had six presidents over its first five decades—including one who died of a broken heart after he was forced out, one who knew a lot about coal mining and nothing about aviation, and one who defied the President of the United States on a matter of principle. It is an airline that almost went out of existence on three separate occasions, twice through merger and once through near-bankruptcy. It is a carrier that today is one of the most prosperous and well-run in the world, yet until mid-1976 was the only U.S. trunk airline that did not fly transcontinentally.

It was born April 17, 1926. Its most prized possession was a brand-new airmail contract authorizing daily flights between Los Angeles and Salt Lake City. Its major physical assets consisted of six wood-and-fabric biplanes and an old hangar that had once been a movie studio. Its payroll on the first day of operation numbered exactly twenty-four persons—five executives and nineteen employees, four of them full-time pilots.

Today it is known as Western Airlines.

                                        Robert J. Serling

PROLOGUE

Los Angeles in 1926 was known primarily for two things, neither connected with aviation.

Its principal products were oranges and motion pictures, the former with somewhat more seniority; local growers had begun shipping the citrus fruit to the East in 1877 via train; most of the vast acreage now saturated with industrial and residential complexes was, fifty years ago, a warm, lush, gold and green blanket of orange groves.

The same colors could be applied to the relatively infant movie industry—in a financial sense. By 1926 Hollywood was turning out approximately 80 per cent of the world's motion-picture productions. The major films of that day were the epics, featuring mammoth sets and casts of thousands. MGM's *Ben Hur* was 1926's biggest picture and a legitimate movie classic. So was Paramount's *Wings*, a film that the following year was to win the industry's first Academy Award. It starred Charles "Buddy" Rogers, Richard Arlen, and Clara Bow, but the real stars were the airmen who filmed the exciting, truly dangerous dogfights and crashes.

Wings, one of the best airplane movies ever made, was only too typical of 1926 aviation in that stunt flying, barnstorming, and intentional crashes to provide thrills for moviegoers were a pilot's major source of employment. And, for that matter, that his prime source of flight equipment consisted of worn-out surplus aircraft from World War I.

Not that there was a scarcity of aircraft manufacturers; there were, in fact, too many of them competing precariously in an extremely limited market. Airplanes were not only relatively expensive but, as far as the public was concerned, they were also symbols of dangerous living. The fatality rate among the companies building them was somewhat higher than the fatality rate of their products—a dubious accomplishment.

A few were to become giants in the airframe manufacturing industry. Sikorsky, for example; in 1926, Sikorsky was primarily building landplanes—such as a giant two-engine bomber that eventually was sold to Howard Hughes and used in *Hell's Angels,* disguised as a German Gotha. But on the Sikorsky drawing boards was a new amphibian, forerunner of the great flying boats that would someday make Pan American one of the world's most powerful airlines.

Up in Seattle, Boeing had just sold an experimental mailplane known as the Model 40 to the U. S. Post Office Department and was thinking about enlarging it so it could carry passengers. Ford was testing a single-engine, all-metal transport—ordained to be a financial flop but a technological advance that was to spawn, only a year later, the Ford trimotor.

In San Diego, Claude Ryan was not only building a small, beautifully performing high-wing cabin monoplane but operating an airline as well—Ryan Airlines, which flew between San Diego and Los Angeles in 90 minutes, charging $17.50 for a one-way trip and $26.50 for a round trip. More than 5,600 passengers used this service in 1926, a traffic volume encouraging Ryan to buy a large biplane that was modified into an 11-passenger transport.

A Hollywood garage was the site chosen by another airplane builder. He was a self-taught barnstormer and a native Californian who had been in aviation since 1913, when he built one of the first successful seaplanes in the United States. In 1916, with his brother Malcolm, he founded a company in Santa Barbara, California, which over the next four years turned out a ten-passenger flying boat, two Navy seaplanes, and a small sport biplane. The firm folded in 1920, and the brothers went their separate ways. Malcolm invented a four-wheel braking system for automobiles, and the other brother—Allan Haines Lockheed —formed the Lockheed Aircraft Company. In that ramshackle garage was built the first Lockheed Vega, a plane that was to break virtually every speed and distance record on the books and write new chapters in the annals of aviation.

Even more successful was the tiny Santa Monica company that originally built the plane Ryan had converted into a transport aircraft. The airplane was the Cloudster, and its designer was Donald Douglas; it happened to be the first airplane ever built that could carry a payload equal to its own weight.

It was the success of one of his military models that led Douglas into his first real commercial venture. He had sold the Army a twin-place observation plane that he figured easily could be turned into a mail-carrying plane. The most obvious customer for the civilian version was the U. S. Post Office Department, which had been flying the mail exclusively since May 15, 1918. The Post Office had operated a hodgepodge of a fleet from the inception of air mail service before standardizing on a single type—the old World War I de Havilland DH-4, a British-built biplane powered by U.S.-designed Liberty engines. Ancient Curtiss Jennies, Standard JR-1Bs, Martins, and other assorted aircraft comprised the mail-carrying armada; at one time, the Post Office even bought eight all-metal, single-engine German Junkers, which could haul five passengers as well as mail.

With its DH-4s gradually wearing out, the Post Office announced competition for bids on a new mailplane. Douglas entered its redesigned observation plane, the M-1; the government ordered one of them, plus a number of two improved models—ten M-3s and forty M-4s. But they were to fly for Uncle Sam only briefly—the dramatic story of the U. S. Air Mail Service was nearing its end.

That story is fascinating on its own. It is sufficient herein to trace the background that led to the metamorphosis of the government-owned civil air operations into a system run entirely by private industry. Foremost was the growing realization that U.S. commercial aviation had fallen far behind European progress. As far back as 1919, Britain and France were operating scheduled flights between London and Paris. Ten years before inventor William Stout talked Henry Ford into backing an all-metal monoplane, Junkers of Germany was flying an all-metal transport with internally braced wings and stressed skin—a con cept in which the wing covering adds to both strength and load-carrying ability; the principle is still employed in today's jet airliners. In 1923, when the only U.S. airline operating a regular passenger service folded ignominiously, Britain was sending thirty scheduled flights daily across the Channel, in aircraft that featured upholstered chairs, bar service, and champagne lunches served by jacketed stewards. Russia's Igor Sikorsky in 1913 built a four-engine airliner with an enclosed cockpit and cabin, accommodations for two pilots and four passengers, electric lights, and a washroom. French air mail service dwarfed America's in route length, flight frequency, and equipment during the early twenties. Even in Italy, not a technologically minded nation, an aeronautical engineer named Caproni had built a hundred-passenger flying boat with eight engines, nine wings, and a gross weight of thirty thousand pounds.

Compared to such achievements, U.S. aviation wasn't even in rompers; it was more like diaper-clad. This is not to disparage what our early air mail pilots did for aviation in their own country; they blazed aerial trails with obsolete, often dangerous equipment, in an atmosphere of general indifference and lethargy. Of the first forty pilots hired by the Post Office Department in 1919, thirty-one had been killed in crashes by 1925. During the less than ten years the government flew the mail, there were two hundred crashes and eighty pilots killed or seriously injured.

Yet far outweighing these setbacks and tragedies were the solid accomplishments. The air mail pilots in just short of a decade flew fifteen million miles and completed 90 per cent of their trips, carrying more than three hundred million letters. Most of them formed the nucleus of the crews that were to fly for the airlines, who seized eagerly on their hard-won knowledge. As R. E. G. Davies, in his *Airlines of the United States* (New York: Putnam, 1972) put it:

> The accumulated experience in flying techniques, especially at night, and the ground organization of aerodromes and lighted airways, gave the first private operators a priceless asset. The aggregate effect was to give the United States a flying start in the field of commercial aviation, enabling it to overhaul Europe, in

spite of the latter's eight-year head start, within two years of spectacular growth.

It is only fair to point out that the U. S. Government itself opened the doors for private operation of the airways. The Post Office Department, which never intended to fly the mail permanently, nevertheless recognized from the start that private industry lacked the financial resources. Appropriations for the air mail service totaled some seventeen million dollars and income only about three million over a 9½-year period. But by the midtwenties, it had become very apparent that the only way to revitalize sagging U.S. commercial aviation was to give private operators a crack at what was virtually the sole revenue source from flying: namely, the mail. There were some feeble arguments advanced to the effect that if private industry wanted to get into the aviation act, it could carry passengers. This was patently ridiculous, inasmuch as the average American of 1925 would have preferred facing a hungry lion to stepping into an airplane. As a matter of fact, it would take fifteen years—from 1926 to 1941—before airline passenger traffic would start surpassing mail in terms of revenue. It was clear that the only way to get U.S. commercial aviation off the ground was through a mail-carrying subsidy; development of passenger business would have to come later.

There had been, prior to 1926, a few attempts to operate all-passenger airlines, without mail income. Most of them drowned in a sky of red ink, including the very first—a scheduled passenger service begun in 1913 between St. Petersburg and Tampa, Florida, using flying boats; it lasted less than five months.

In 1919, two new airlines began operating: Aero Limited, which flew surplus wartime flying boats between New York and Atlantic City, and Florida West Indies Airways, Inc., which started passenger service in the Caribbean out of Florida. The latter was purely the product of the new Prohibition Act, the bulk of its traffic consisting of Americans after legal drinks in Havana and Bahamas bars. Aero took due note of this lucrative business and transferred its entire fleet to Miami, from where it flew frequent trips to Nassau. Both were rather hit-and-miss, more like sporadic air taxi services than regularly scheduled operations.

Aero Limited gradually faded into obscurity, but Florida West

Indies became part of a new venture masterminded by Inglis Uppercu, a New York automobile dealer who was the chief backer of Aeromarine Airways which established flying-boat service between New York and Havana via Atlantic City, Beaufort (S.C.) and Key West in 1921, adding Miami–Havana flights the same year.

Aeromarine's next move was to counteract the seasonal nature of these southern operations. It followed Aero Limited's strategy in reverse, moving all its planes North in May of 1922 and inaugurating scheduled service across Lake Erie between Detroit and Cleveland. This was followed by further expansion to such cities as Buffalo, various coastal cities in New England, Montreal, and Cleveland—all via flying boat. It was a case of overexpansion, however; Aeromarine, although it operated for three years carrying more than seventeen thousand passengers with a perfect safety record, went out of business in September 1923, made an abortive attempt to reorganize the next year, and then died for keeps. Its subsidiary, Florida West Indies Airways, also went under eventually and was absorbed in 1927 by a new firm headed by an ex-Navy pilot. His name was Juan Trippe.

Three other companies dipped their corporate feet into the very muddy waters of the airline business in this period. American Trans Oceanic started flying between Miami and the British island of South Bimini in 1919 but operated only for a short time. That was the same year Eddie Hubbard, an Army flight instructor, began flying mail between Seattle and Vancouver under a Post Office foreign mail contract. Hubbard, who later was to become a key official at Boeing, did business under the name of Seattle–Victoria Air Mail Line and utilized the Boeing B-1 flying boat, the first commercial aircraft Boeing ever built. When he left to go with Boeing, the route was flown under various names for another seventeen years.

There also was a Gulf Coast Airline, begun in 1923 to provide flying-boat service between New Orleans and Pilottown at the tip of the Mississippi Delta. History does not record the exact date of its demise, but there is one thing to be noted about all these early airline efforts—every one involved the use of flying boats, not landplanes. Airfields throughout the United States, with few exceptions, were too primitive, inadequate, and actually dangerous to warrant confidence on the part of the public or airmen themselves. Not until the government—prodded by the growing demand for regular air mail service—established lighted airways and modest airport improvements did scheduled air transportation become feasible between inland cities.

The only outfit to try it on a scheduled basis was none other than the United States Army Air Service. In June 1922, it launched air service between Washington, D.C., and Dayton, Ohio, using DH-4s on a schedule of four weekly flights. It was more or less of an experimental nature and actually was called the U. S. Army Model Airway. The initial purpose was to test and develop air navigation facilities and promote airport development, and the few passengers carried were limited to military and government personnel. Not more than three hundred a year boarded the Army planes, even when the route was extended first to San Antonio and later—in 1926—to Los Angeles. The Model Airway was phased out when the private airlines took over the airway system, thanks to a legislative event that occurred on February 2, 1925.

Known officially as the Contract Air Mail Act, it bore the more familiar title of the Kelly Act, after Representative Clarence Kelly of Pennsylvania, who was its chief sponsor and proponent. In actuality, it was more of an aviation Magna Carta, for the bill turned virtually the entire job of flying the mail over to private contractors, who would bid for the various routes; the one exception, temporarily, was transcontinental authority.

Ironically, Congressman Kelly was no great aviation supporter; he was a spokesman for and loyal advocate of the railroads, which lobbied hard for the act in order to get the Post Office Department out of the business of carrying the mail. Not by the farthest stretch of the imagination did Kelly or any of the railroad lobbyists foresee the day when the Frankenstein monster he unwittingly created would be carrying 80 per cent of the nation's first-class mail. On Capitol Hill, in fact, Kelly was known as "the voice of the railway mail clerks."

Kelly's success was followed by another beneficial event tied into the unhappy fate of General Billy Mitchell, whose court-martial and subsequent conviction disturbed many farsighted Americans. Mitchell was brash, intemperate, and uncompro mising, but many of his overly shrill claims and charges about the sad state of American aviation bore a ring of sincerity and accuracy. While they goaded President Coolidge into finally approving the court-martial verdict (although he did soften the monetary punitive provisions), they also convinced Coolidge that something more practical than making a martyr out of Mitchell had to be done.

Fortunately for aviation, the Coolidge cabinet included a man inherited from the Harding administration, one of tremendous integrity and intelligence; as politically conservative as the President but with far more vision, compassion, and practicality was Herbert Clark Hoover, the Secretary of Commerce. Long before Mitchell was court-martialed in the fall of 1925, Hoover had established the Joint Committee of Civil Aviation—a distinguished group composed of key officials within the Commerce Department who were devoted to furtherment of civil aeronautics, and equally prestigious representatives from the American Engineering Council. The committee began work one month after the Kelly Act was passed, and the group's main accomplishment was a thorough survey of various aviation problems—safety, equipment, finance, regulatory status, and technological needs. The gist of its final report was a blunt confirmation of fears that U.S. aviation was years behind Europe, and that what was needed was a new national aviation policy enabling civil aeronautics to grow and prosper.

Hoover kept plugging away and finally hit something of a jackpot after his own special committee had concluded its work —a job that might have been the usual exercise in futility were it not for history's giving the Secretary of Commerce unexpected if tragic support. The destruction of the dirigible *Shenandoah* furnished more than mere ammunition for Billy Mitchell; while it led to his ultimate court-martial, it also added credence to what he had been saying about American aviation in general. There were several bad military crashes occurring at about the same time, and Coolidge—who might have ignored the Hoover group's report—was forced to take some action. While the Post Office Department was still wading through an unexpected avalanche of bids for private air mail contracts, Coolidge told a well-known financier to be prepared to head a study of the whole aviation picture, civil as well as military. This was in March 1925; on September 13, the financier picked up a newspaper and read that he was to be chairman of a special aviation inquiry board of eight members, including himself. It was the first time Dwight Morrow, one of the most highly regarded financial and industrial figures in the United States, had heard from the White House since Coolidge's call the previous March; Morrow (who was to become the father-in-law of Charles A. Lindbergh) received official word via a presidential letter the next day.

The Morrow board, leaning heavily on what the Hoover committee already had unearthed but also doing considerable investigative work of its own, wound up giving commercial aviation a boost as significant as what the Kelly Act had provided. Its final report was issued November 30, 1925, soon enough for Coolidge to insert the recommendations into his December 8 annual message to Congress; by then, Coolidge was only too anxious to get away from the heat of the court-martial verdict. The Morrow report urged the separation of civil aviation from military aviation, and the establishment of a Bureau of Aeronautics within the Commerce Department—the latter recommendation favored strongly by Hoover. It fell short of what some aviation enthusiasts were proposing—a Department of Air, which would be an independent agency—but it still was a long step forward for civil aviation. On May 20, 1926, Coolidge signed the Air Commerce Act, creating an Aeronautics Branch within Commerce.

In broad terms, the act gave the Secretary of Commerce authority to designate and establish federal airways; install, operate, and maintain air navigation aids, excluding those established at airports; encourage and support research for improving such aids; license pilots; issue airworthiness certificates for aircraft and their major components, and investigate accidents. More specifically, it put the Aeronautics Branch (the name was changed later to Bureau of Air Commerce) in charge of two new divisions: Air Regulation and Air Information. In addition, Commerce's Bureau of Lighthouses was instructed to set up an airways division for coastal operations; the Bureau of Standards had to organize an aeronautical research division; and the Coast

and Geodetic Survey was told to establish an air-mapping section—a task it still performs to this day.

At the same time as the Kelly Act went into effect, there were
just three passenger-carrying airlines flying in the United States.
Ryan's previously mentioned Los Angeles–San Diego airline was
one, although Ryan terminated its operations without even
bothering to bid on a mail contract. Apparently his heart was
never in the business of carrying passengers, and he figuratively
threw away a gold-plated key to the door of a new industry.

The second carrier had even more impressive credentials than
Ryan's small but prosperous outfit: It was owned by none other
than Henry Ford, who had been talked into aviation (some accounts claim that "dragged into" would be more accurate) by
Harry Brooks, the son of a close friend, and by Ford's own chief
engineer, William B. Mayo, whom Ford greatly respected.
Brooks and Mayo were instrumental in convincing Ford that he
should back Bill Stout's new all-metal transport, using the plane
to fly regularly scheduled trips between Detroit and Chicago.
The operation, strictly private, began early in April 1925, and
was successful enough to warrant Ford's bidding for an air mail
contract over the same route. In typical Ford fashion, once
Henry bought the idea he went whole hog—building a factory
for Stout at Dearborn along with a modern airfield, which featured the nation's first airport hotel. A second route, also restricted to traffic composed of Ford officials and occasional priority cargo, was opened in July between Detroit and Cleveland.

The third was a minuscule, one-plane affair operated under the
name Pacific Marine Airways. Its founder was Sid Chaplin,
brother of renowned movie comedian Charlie Chaplin, and its
lone piece of equipment—an old flying boat—started making excursion flights in 1922 between Wilmington, California, and
Catalina Island.

The three airlines' combined routes totaled approximately
three hundred miles; one was not even an airline but what today
would be called a business aircraft fleet, the second flew less
than six thousand passengers in calendar 1925, and the third was
more in the nature of a sightseeing operation. In that same year,
a German airline carried more than fifty thousand passengers.
Britain's Imperial Airways flew some fifteen thousand persons

nearly seven hundred thousand miles. France was operating regular passenger service between Paris and London, and from Paris to Brussels, Berlin, Rotterdam, Warsaw, Constantinople, and Casablanca. Among the other nations operating scheduled air service were Finland, Switzerland, Denmark, Hungary, Poland, and Austria.

The chief reason for America's backwardness was not lack of technical skill but attitude. To most Americans, the airplane was a toy that often approached the status of romantic fiction. It was something to be enjoyed vicariously—in pulp magazines recounting the make-believe exploits of World War I fighter pilots, in movies like *Wings,* in barnstorming appearances at county and state fairs. It was something to be read about—usually with much head-shaking, raised eyebrows, and clucks of pity, for most newspaper stories concerning aviation dealt with death.

It was different in Europe, where the airplane was not a toy but a real instrument. On the war-ravaged Continent, its power had been seen and felt, not just read about. And when peace came, the transition from military to civil use was accepted as a logical, inevitable fact. The United States, not especially embarrassed at its failure to put a single American-built aircraft into actual combat despite its vast industrial prowess, regarded aviation with either fond amusement or outright contempt. A returning U.S. war flier had two choices if he wanted to stay in aviation: barnstorm or fly the mail.

Aviation was no prime labor market; by Armistice Day, the Army Air Service had almost three thousand trained pilots and some fifteen thousand skilled mechanics. It is, of course, impossible to estimate how many would have chosen careers in commercial aviation if there had been job opportunities, but even a small percentage would have had trouble finding work. At the height of its air mail service, the Post Office Department was operating just under a hundred planes—no small fleet by the standards of the day, but it was just about the only game in town and certainly not large enough to offer many employment chances for those wanting to get into civil aviation.

And there were plenty in that category, not only pilots and mechanics but also entrepreneurs who greeted passage and signing of the Kelly Act with avid glee. Within weeks after the measure became law, the Post Office Department was buried under an avalanche of more than five thousand inquiries from would-be airline tycoons. If all five thousand actually had submitted bids, it probably would have taken another year to get the embryonic industry out of its womb. As it was, the bona fide applicants were sufficiently small in number for the Post Office to award its coveted mail routes with relative speed—for any government agency, that is. The first of several hundred bids were opened on September 15, 1925—7½ months from the day President Coolidge made civil operation of the air mail a legal reality. The initial contracts were awarded only three weeks later, covering air mail service to be flown over five segments designated officially as Civil Air Mail routes, or CAMs, as they became more familiarly known.

Another seven contracts were let later, the Post Office Department retaining its authority to fly the mail between New York and San Francisco via Chicago; the twelve CAM routes were, in essence, set up to feed the main transcontinental or "Columbia" route, which the government eventually was to relinquish by the fall of 1927. To the Ford Motor Company went the honor of being the first to start scheduled, privately operated air mail service—over CAM-6 and 7, the Detroit–Cleveland and Detroit–Chicago routes it already had been flying. The date was February 15, 1926, and next in line was Florida Airways between Jacksonville and Miami, which was part of CAM-10, Atlanta–Miami. That was April 1, and five days later, Walter T. Varney began service on CAM-5 between Pasco, Washington, and Elko, Nevada. CAM-2, Chicago–St. Louis, was inaugurated April 15 by Robertson Aircraft Corporation. By the end of the year, all twelve successful bidders were in full or partial operation. It is significant to observe, however, that by 1931 not one of those original four operators were flying the CAMs they so bravely began. Ford discontinued service in mid-1928, Florida Airways did likewise even earlier, Varney sold out to start an airline elsewhere, and Robertson faded from the picture when it sublet CAM-2 to American Airways. Only one of the original twelve, in fact, has survived as the same corporate entity it was when launched a half century ago.

This was the company awarded CAM-4, Los Angeles–Salt Lake City.

It was called Western Air Express, and its president was a stocky ex-racing driver named Harris M. Hanshue.

CHAPTER ONE

"There Have Been Four Hundred Failures in This Damned Business. . . ."

Precisely who thought up the idea of starting Western Air Express would have to be resolved through a spiritualism session—all the principals involved in its creation are dead, and the dusty, yellowing clippings in Western's archives provide a half-dozen versions.

All the evidence, however, points to Harris Hanshue as at least one of the chief founders, and if he was not the one who actually proposed bidding for an air mail contract, he did most of the spadework—including several trips to Washington for information on how to submit a formal bid, what data would impress the Post Office Department to the greatest extent, and establishing personal contacts with various government officials.

The real father of WAE, however, was not one or several individuals; it was a state of mind—civic pride. And it might be said that the mother was civic jealousy. For years, Los Angeles had looked northward to San Francisco with a collective feeling of envy that could be classed as a municipal inferiority complex. San Francisco had a kind of cosmopolitan class; by contrast, Los Angeles was somewhat akin to a gawky, gangling, awkward teen-ager with growing pains and acne on its community face. Even in those days, the City of Angels was a sprawling metropolis, swelling in population and development without apparent purpose or plan. "Six suburbs in search of a city" was the apt description given it by one writer.

It was big and getting bigger daily; by 1926, the population of Los Angeles County had reached more than 1.8 million. But Los

Angeles seemed to lack the almost human personality of a San Francisco, a New Orleans, or a New York; it was like a *nouveau riche* millionaire, whose mushrooming affluence cannot hide crudeness nor command respect. It was in this atmosphere that Los Angeles suffered the cruelest blow of all—the naming of San Francisco as the West Coast terminus of the first transcontinental air mail route, inaugurated in 1920. For almost five years, Los Angeles chafed under the ignominy of sending or receiving air mail via train to and from San Francisco. But when it became apparent long before the Kelly Act was introduced that the government was going to get out of the air mail business, a handful of Los Angeles civic leaders—Hanshue included—saw their opportunity.

There are two versions of what exactly transpired. One is that an official of the Post Office Department visited Los Angeles early in 1925, got a group of bankers together, and discussed the value of air mail to West Coast business and industry. From that meeting, he got the definite impression they already were sold on air mail and needed only an airline. He made no suggestions on the latter subject, but his talk, so the story goes, stirred up such interest that the bankers set about finding someone to organize and manage an air carrier company. They picked Hanshue, who at the time was Pacific Coast distributor for the Apperson Automobile Company—selling the Apperson successfully even though the firm itself was sliding toward bankruptcy. The bankers were said to feel that if anyone could sell the product of a failing company, he must have the ability to tackle a brand new industry, fraught with physical as well as financial risk. Hanshue reportedly went to Washington, scouted the situation, and returned to announce, "I'll take the job."

Version II holds that the Post Office Department official's talk to the bankers played no role in the formation of a new airline. According to the second account, Hanshue himself conceived the idea for a private air mail company and went to Harry Chandler, publisher of the Los Angeles *Times,* to get his advice and support. Chandler was interested immediately and suggested "let's go see Bill Garland"—Garland being a prominent Los Angeles realtor.

Garland recounted many years later that the three of them

spent an entire afternoon talking about ways to raise money and organize the airline. The fourth partner/ally was James Talbot of Richfield Oil, and on July 15, 1925—two days before the first CAM routes were opened to bids—Chandler and Talbot filed articles of incorporation in Sacramento under the name Western Air Express, listing Hanshue as the president; whatever version is right, and the weight of evidence leans toward II, Hanshue definitely was in the driver's seat from the start. He was in Washington when the WAE bid was accepted November 7, and returned triumphantly to Los Angeles with the contract in his briefcase. What went with the contract, of course, was an Everest-sized mountain of problems still ahead. All he and his associates possessed at this point was authorization for an airline existing solely on paper.

Yet adversity was nothing but a challenge for this burly, abrupt, generally self-effacing native of Michigan who had taken his first lumps on the gridiron. He had played center at Michigan under the football genius that was Fielding Yost; never a true star nor even a first-stringer, Hanshue nevertheless had a dogged tenacity and special brand of courage that marked both his personality and his philosophy. Forty years old when he became Western's first president, he bore a striking physical resemblance to the late Vince Lombardi—they had the same sturdy, stocky build, that ingratiatingly warm if rare smile, and an air of command authority that earned instant respect. Hanshue had one more thing in common with Lombardi—Hanshue seemed to exude unconsciously a kind of natural "father image"; it was neither by whim nor in jest that fairly early in his life he acquired the nickname "Pop," which he bore to the day he died.

It was not just these qualities that impressed men like Chandler, Garland, and Talbot. Hanshue also happened to be a successful businessman, attaining moderate wealth the hard way —from the bottom up. After he graduated from Michigan in 1903, he came to California with a job of demonstrating automobiles for the Olds Motor Company. It was typical of Hanshue that he regarded the hazards of racing as the best way to display the car's virtues. For six years, he squirmed unhappily under orders to demonstrate the Olds with conventional methods—such as driving prospects around the block. He finally convinced somebody at the home office to let him enter the car in California racing competition, and from 1909 to 1914, Pop Hanshue hung up quite a few speed records—mostly roaring over the road between Los Angeles and Sacramento.

It was his wife who finally talked him into a more prosaic way of life. He put away his leather jacket, helmet, and goggles in favor of business suits—in the process selling enough cars to make possible the opening of his own agency and later becoming a West Coast distributor. He was serving in that latter capacity when he was bitten by the aviation bug, having made enough money to become a major investor in the airline venture, and there was no doubt from the start who was going to lead it; while he knew nothing about airline operations, neither did any of his colleagues, and his own dominant, aggressive personality was such that he appears to have been the only one considered as Western's first president.

The list of original stockholders read like a western edition of *Who's Who*. Unlike one recalcitrant potential investor, who warned the soliciting Hanshue "there have been four hundred failures in this damned business," they shared a common faith in aviation's future. The names included Los Angeles *Times* columnist Bill Henry; Harold Janss, a Los Angeles financier; K. R. Kingsley, former president of Standard Oil of California; William Wrigley, Jr.; department store magnate John G. Bullock; Fred Bonfils, colorful publisher of the Denver *Post;* and the Mormon Church (Church of Jesus Christ of Latter-day Saints, in Salt Lake City, and the head of that church, Heber J. Grant; consistent support by the powerful Utah-based religious sect would be no small factor in Western's future development).

That impressive list of stockholder names contained one flaw: Most of the men mentioned bought relatively few shares, supplying more morale than financial aid. The bulk of the financing came from Ford dealers throughout Southern California, and this was achieved largely through the efforts of Major Corliss C. Moseley, whom Hanshue selected to be vice president of operations well in advance of the route award.

Moseley was a well-known figure in West Coast aviation, although most of his experience had been military. He flew combat missions in World War I, tested planes for the Army, and after

the war became commandant and instructor of the National
Guard squadron at Griffith Park, Los Angeles. Hanshue chose him
mostly on Chandler's recommendation, not only because of his
aviation background, but also because Moseley knew quite a few
ex-Army and air mail pilots who might be looking for new jobs.
Before "Mose," as everyone called him, could dredge up a few
men with wings, however, his first task was to help Hanshue
raise money—taking a year's leave of absence from the National
Guard to help the prospective airline get organized.

Moseley and Bill Henry happened to be friends, and Henry
proposed that they approach Bryon L. Graves, Southern California distributor for the Ford Motor Company. They went to see
him, and Graves expressed immediate interest.

"Mr. Ford's got an airplane he's trying to sell," Graves observed cautiously. "I think I could raise you some dough among
our dealers if Western became a Ford customer."

The airplane was the single-engine Stout, whose chief virture
was its all-metal construction; the airplane actually was a dog,
but Moseley didn't know that at the time.

"If you can raise a good chunk of cash," he promised Graves,
"we'll buy seven Ford-Stouts."

It was a pledge Moseley was to regret later, but Hanshue had
given the major his orders: Get some money and buy some airplanes for delivery before the air mail contract was issued.
Graves kept his promise and solicited most of the $360,000 it
took to get Western Air Express into business.

With financing out of the way, Moseley turned to manpower.
The supply was unlimited, and the major was choosy. The first
pilot he hired he knew from his college days at the University of
Southern California—a slim ex-Army flier who had been one of
USC's greatest athletes. He was Fred W. Kelly, who had been on
the same football team as Moseley. Football, though, was not
Kelly's major sport; in 1912, when he still was a freshman, he
was picked to represent the United States in the Olympic Games
at Stockholm and won a gold medal by winning the 110-meter
high hurdles in the then-record time of 15.1 seconds. When he
returned, the Los Angeles *Times* gave him a scholarship to finish
college, and he continued to set track records. Dean Cromwell,

the Knute Rockne of college track and field coaches in those days, called him "the greatest athlete I've ever coached."

Kelly, who in his more mature years bore some resemblance to movie star David Niven, became interested in flying while he was in Europe for the Olympic competition. Before going home, he agreed to a match race against the great Jim Thorpe in a special track meet at Rheims, France. Just as the starting gun went off, an airplane began circling the field. Foolishly—as far as the race was concerned—Fred looked up, and the distraction cost him whatever chance he had to beat the swift Indian. Fifty years later he was to tell an interviewer that momentary lapse in concentration changed his life. When he saw the plane, he reminisced, "I knew that was what I wanted to do."

The *Times* scholarship aid notwithstanding, Kelly left college in 1916 and enlisted in the U. S. Army Signal Corps' Aviation Section. He learned to fly at Gerstner Field, Lake Charles, Louisiana—in a Jenny—and waited to be shipped to France. The overseas assignment never materialized, and Kelly spent most of the war as a flight instructor—although he had only twenty-five hours of flight time logged himself. His sole exploit got him into a large tub of hot water; it occurred shortly after he was transferred to a squadron at Mitchell Field, Long Island, and Kelly—an inveterate prankster—read in the newspapers that President Wilson was leaving New York by ship for the Paris peace talks that very day.

"I need some flight time," Kelly informed his commanding officer. "Can I take a Jenny up for an hour or so?"

Permission was granted, the unsuspecting officer never dreaming what Kelly's flight plan entailed. Accompanied by an Army buddy, Fred took off, thundered over Riverside Drive, and headed down the Hudson River toward the huge New York pier complex where the President's ship had just left its dock. The vessel was the liner *George Washington,* surrounded by tugs and its stacks belching columns of black smoke as it prepared to get under way. For some unknown reason, Kelly had an irresistible urge to mess up that smoke. He buzzed the ship so low that he not only left the smoke columns in swirling disintegration, but also almost hit the radio antenna suspended between the masts.

To compound this felony, Kelly proceeded to fly under every

bridge on the East River, and if no one on the *George Washington* spotted the Jenny's wing numerals, pop-eyed witnesses near the bridges evidently did. Kelly was greeted back at Mitchell by an apoplectic officer of the day.

"You stupid sonofabitch!" he screamed before Kelly could turn off the engine. "You're confined to post for two weeks!"

"I just wanted to say good-bye to the President," Fred explained lamely.

The punishment, Kelly readily conceded, was lenient in light of the offense. He heard later that Woodrow Wilson himself told the liner's captain, "Find out who that pilot was and give him the works!" The commanding officer at Mitchell must have been a Republican.

Confinement to post meant Kelly still could fly, which was the only thing he wanted. When the Armistice was signed, he found himself an unwilling member of that army of restless, frustrating airmen who had no outlet for the love of flight they had acquired. Like malaria, it refused to go away. Kelly tried hard to stay in aviation, but he had to eat and he took a job as salesman for a water boiler firm in New York.

"I sold one boiler," he was to recall in subsequent years. "It blew up, so I quit."

For a time, he barnstormed in Cuba, and worked as an airplane mechanic there while mending a broken arm suffered in his first crash landing; generated some modest headlines when he became the first man to fly between Havana and Santiago, Cuba; carried an occasional illegal load of rum back to the Prohibition-plagued States; and eventually drifted back to California, where he worked on his father's barley farm at El Toro. Coach Cromwell came to his rescue, offering Kelly a job as assistant track coach at USC, but this lasted only one year, and Kelly went from one job to another, still seeking that elusive aviation career.

It was at this stage of his life, about a year before Western's corporate gestation, that he joined the Los Angeles National Guard squadron and was reunited with his former football teammate. Moseley did not confide his dealings with the airline's founders, and Fred renewed his flying skills at the Guard field while going to work for a company producing a variety of industrial machines. When Moseley was asked to join Western Air Express and to line up some pilots, his first thought was of the wiry, happy-go-lucky Kelly.

At first Moseley had a tough time locating him; Fred was on the road constantly, and Moseley finally tracked him down in Chicago, where he was supervising installation of a glass-grinding machine in some factory. Moseley took him out to dinner that night, discussing Hanshue's plans for an airline and his own role in its formation.

"We need pilots—good pilots," he said. "You interested?"

"I sure am," Kelly responded enthusiastically—adding, however, with typical airman caution, "What equipment will we be flying?"

"That all-metal plane Bill Stout's been building for Henry Ford."

"I don't know a damned thing about it," Kelly confessed.

"Neither do I. If you come with us, your first job will be to go to Detroit and check it out. All I know is that it's Liberty-powered like the Guard's DH-4s. When you get back to Los Angeles, I'll give you a crash course on the Liberty so you'll know what the hell you're looking at on the Stout."

Kelly didn't become Western's first pilot officially until December 1, 1925—the date his seniority began. But long before he went on Western's payroll, Moseley dispatched him to Detroit, where—through the courtesy of Bryon Graves—he went on the Ford payroll for five dollars a day while Western paid his expenses. He was there for several months, a period in which he thoroughly inspected the 2-AT "Air Transport" designed by William Bushnell Stout, which already was flying between Detroit and Chicago/Cleveland.

Yet while it looked like the later trimotor, the 2-AT came nowhere close to its successor in performance and stability. It was big for its day, with a capacity of eight passengers, but Kelly recognized quickly that size was one of its chief drawbacks. He knew Western needed an efficient mail-carrying plane and that employing an eight-passenger transport was like assigning an Army division to wipe out a lone machine-gun nest. More important, the 2-AT was too heavy for the single Liberty engine that powered it.

For some strange reason Kelly never could explain, he did not fly the Stout plane himself. But he did rely heavily on the opinion of one of Ford's crack test pilots, Larry Fritz, with whom he became close friends.

"You don't want that plane," Fritz told him candidly. "It'll never get over the Rockies."

Privately, other Ford test pilots gave Kelly the same verdict. He wrote Moseley that Western would be buying a turkey in the 2-AT. Mose ordered him back to Los Angeles and broke the sad news to Hanshue.

"Maybe the guy's wrong," Pop insisted. "That's only one man's opinion on that airplane; how about seeing for yourself? Hell, Mose, you used to be an Army test pilot. We promised Graves we'd buy the goddamned thing, and we're in trouble if we renege."

"We're in trouble if we buy it and it turns out to be a lemon," Moseley warned. "Okay, Pop, I'll test-fly it myself."

"When?" Hanshue worried. "We're running out of time."

"I've got to attend a conference the Air Force has called on National Guard matters. I'll fly one of my DH-4s to Dayton for the conference and go up to Detroit as soon as the meeting's over."

In Dayton, Moseley called the Ford airplane plant and obtained permission to fly there for the purpose of testing the 2-AT. It took only one flight to confirm Kelly's fears. The Stout plane was even worse than Fred had described it, needing almost a mile for takeoff at nearly sea level, not to mention its over-all performance and construction, which Moseley later termed "actually pitiful."

But now he was in a real dilemma. He himself had been responsible for the terms under which Graves and his network of dealers had invested in Western Air Express. That rash, impulsive promise had put him in the position of threatening destruction of the airline before it could get off the ground. There might not be enough new stockholders to fill the gap if Graves yanked out what he and so many others had put in. Then it occurred to him that one of the original stockholders was in Detroit—George Holley of the Holley Carburetor Company, whose product was used on Ford cars. Holley had not only invested ten thousand dollars in WAE but also had talked ten other men into buying

Western stock. Moseley called him, was granted an immediate appointment, and laid his cards right on the table.

"It's just this simple," he said. "The airplane is no good. It can't operate from the altitude at Salt Lake City with any kind of a load, and it would have one hell of a time getting over the Rockies."

"What do you want me to do?" Holley asked. "Graves and his dealers invested in good faith. You were the one who ordered the plane without even knowing what you'd be buying."

"But I do know," Mose insisted, "that if we go ahead and do buy it, we'd end up in disaster for all stockholders—including Graves and the others. We're going to have crashes, and we'll probably lose the route for failure to perform under the terms of the air mail contract."

That was enough to convince Holley. Moseley composed a telegram to be sent to Hanshue and Graves, over Holley's name, supporting the thumbs-down verdict on the Ford-Stout aircraft. Then he went back to his hotel and waited nervously for a wire informing him that his services at Western Air Express were no longer needed. What he got back was indeed a telegram—from Hanshue and Graves, telling him to proceed to choose another airplane.

He did, while simultaneously choosing four more pilots, all from his National Guard outfit and men whose flying ability he respected. They included:

• Charles "Jimmie" James, a former Army pilot who was working for Standard Oil of California with occasional leaves to perform patrol missions for the Forest Service.

• Al DeGarmo, like James a graduate of the Army's March Field training and a veteran of every kind of flying job, from charters to border patrol.

• Maurice "Maury" Graham, a World War I flier whom Moseley rescued from a job in a stationery store.

• Eldred Remelin, also ex-Army, who was hired as the lone reserve pilot with a post as station manager at Salt Lake City to hold down when all four regulars were flying.

That quartet of regulars—Kelly, James, DeGarmo, and Graham—promptly dubbed themselves "The Four Horsemen," and they were just as close as the famed Notre Dame backfield from whom they swiped the nickname. Inseparable friends as well as fellow pilots, they made life miserable for the fifth wheel —namely, Mr. Remelin. For the first two years Western operated, the Four Horsemen refused ever to let Remelin, or the two other reserve pilots eventually hired, fly a trip. When one of the Horsemen was on vacation or sick, the other three would apportion his schedule among them. Inevitably, Remelin got fed up and resigned, going over to United, where he rose to captain and later retired to culminate a long and honorable airline career.

Admittedly the Horsemen's lack of charity toward any reserve pilot was based on sheer avarice—the starting pay was only $150 a month plus $.05 a mile, and the latter amount wasn't paid unless trips were flown. But it also reflected a feeling of comradeship that none of them could put into words. They took immense pride in being Western's first pilots, and their common bond was the knowledge that the fledgling airline had emancipated them from ground jobs. James was the only one who was doing any flying when Moseley hired them, and that was sporadic. DeGarmo was working as a tool director on an oil rig in Palmdale when Moseley phoned him.

"How soon can you put down that sledgehammer and start flying?" Mose asked.

"Right away," DeGarmo barked—quitting his job in the next five minutes.

Even as he lined up airmen, Moseley settled on his choice of aircraft. He had test-flown the Douglas XO-2 at Wright Field, Dayton, and fell in love with the sturdy little plane. Basically it was the same as the M-3 and M-4 mailplanes the Post Office Department had been operating except for slightly shorter wings and a different landing gear. Moseley asked Douglas for two major modifications: a nose radiator, and steel-backed bearings to give the engine an estimated extra fifty hours of flight time between overhauls. Douglas agreed, and Mose recommended to Hanshue that Western purchase five M-2s. The price per plane was $11,000 plus optional equipment and spare parts, adding up to a total of $74,450. A sixth M-2 was ordered later. The contract for the initial five was signed November 12, 1925. Major Moseley now had his pilots and his planes.

Hanshue, meanwhile, had been hiring what *he* needed: executives. In Moseley, he had an ideal man for what he termed the technical side of an airline's operations. The other side was traffic, and one might wonder why it was necessary for anyone to handle traffic, inasmuch as Western Air Express was founded primarily to carry mail. The company seemed to have burned a few bridges when it rejected an eight-passenger airplane in favor of an aircraft that could carry only two customers—in total discomfort, it must be added. The Stout-Ford 2-AT was a cabin monoplane; the Douglas M-2 was an open-cockpit biplane.

But Pop Hanshue was far more visionary than his lack of aviation background would indicate. First, he had no illusions about air mail business falling into Western's lap simply because Los Angeles citizens had an airline to fly it. He knew the public still had to be sold on the advantages of sending mail by air, and that mail customers had to be cultivated. Thanks to a last-minute amendment to the Kelly Act, the Post Office would be paying the airlines by the weight of the mail they carried; originally, it was intended to give them a percentage of whatever postage was paid, which would have been not only cumbersome but also not nearly as lucrative as the weight method. The latter, of course, subsequently invited some ingenious devices by some airlines for cheating on weight—such as stuffing the bottom of mail sacks with bricks and sending wet blotters in envelopes—but in general it was a fair compensation procedure.

In addition to recognizing how essential it was to "sell" air mail to the Southern California populace, Hanshue, from the day he began dreaming about starting an airline, never envisioned a mail-only operation. He predicted on more than one occasion that a sizable chunk of Western's revenues would come someday from passenger business, and that when demand called for bigger, more comfortable planes, WAE would be ready. Thus he had more in mind than an air mail salesman when he told his associates he was going to recruit a traffic manager.

He found him quite by accident. Pop was returning to Los Angeles with the mail contract by train, and when it stopped in Salt Lake City, a young reporter from a Salt Lake City newspaper boarded to interview the new president of Western Air Express.

The reporter introduced himself as James G. Woolley and began asking questions without a pen, pencil, or piece of paper in sight.

"Aren't you going to take notes?" Hanshue asked suspiciously.

"I don't have to," the plump, pleasant-faced Woolley assured him. "I'll remember everything."

"Look, young man," Pop growled, "this award means a lot to me, and I want to make sure you get everything straight."

"It will be," the reporter said confidently. "I'll send you a copy of the story as soon as we run it."

Mollified but still uncertain as to the wisdom of this course, Hanshue began answering questions until the train was ready to pull out. A few days later, Woolley sent him a clipping of the interview, and Hanshue was more than impressed. Not only were the facts right, but also every quote was almost identical to what Hanshue remembered saying. Almost on impulse, he dictated a telegram offering Woolley not just a job but also the position of traffic manager—the title being considerably more persuasive than the salary, which wasn't much more than he was making at the newspaper.

Woolley came to Western one month before the scheduled start of service, joining an executive team that included Graves—who had been named treasurer—and Robert A. Morton, a Los Angeles lawyer who had agreed to serve as secretary. The office force consisted of two persons: Hugh W. Wright, the accountant, and Evelyn Hawley, stenographer. The rest of the first Western Air Express roster included five mechanics—Max Cornwell, L. F. Blunder, Clyde Reitz, James T. King, and Everett Drinkwater—all under the supervision of field manager C. C. Cole; radio operators E. A. Russell, W. L. Jepson, and E. M. Willis, and three night watchmen for the Los Angeles, Las Vegas, and Salt Lake City stations—John Coker, E. A. Blum, and Peter Stevenson, respectively.

Officers and employees . . . pilots and planes.

Next problem: ground facilities.

Executive office space was easy. Hanshue rented part of an office building at Ninth and Main streets in downtown Los Angeles; the official address was 117 West Ninth Street.

Noise nuisance suits not being even a minor aviation problem in those days, both Hanshue and Moseley also sought an airport location that wouldn't be too far from the city's center and the main post office. The National Guard field at Griffith Park was considered—Hanshue had listed it as one of Western's qualifications for flying the mail—but it was rather limited in size, and Moseley suspected the Army would take a dim view of sharing a military facility with civilian operations. A reconnaissance of all available sites centered on a large grain field at Telegraph Road and Santa Fe Crossing in the suburb of Montebello, owned by a couple of brothers named Vail, whose family had made a fortune in the cattle business. Dubious at first, they finally succumbed to a few sessions of persuasion, generally based on the argument that selling or leasing the property to Western Air Express was slightly more patriotic than financing restoration of the U.S.S. *Constitution,* "Old Ironsides." The Vails, in fact, went even farther than Hanshue or anyone else expected—they leased Western the land just for the taxes, an arrangement so generous that the Los Angeles City Council later adjusted the rent to a larger though still nominal amount.

Salt Lake City, which already had an airport of sorts, was no problem, but Las Vegas—which would be a refueling stop for the M-2s—was nothing but a way station on the Union Pacific Railroad. The town had only about four thousand residents in 1925, most of them employed by the railroad, and they would have been more surprised at the landing of an airplane than of a pterodactyl. Negotiations were launched with a certain Las Vegas couple named Rockwell, who agreed to provide Western with sufficient land adjoining Highway 91, about two miles west of the city; years later the Last Frontier Hotel was built on the site. It was not to be the Rockwell's last association with Western, for their son Leon eventually became a WAE pilot.

Moseley already had presented Hanshue with a final preservice problem: emergency landing fields, reminding the harassed new president of Western Air Express that airplane engines of 1925–26 vintage were as trustworthy as a nymphomaniacal wife. Any Liberty that ran for more than fifty hours without some kind of malfunction deserved display in the Smithsonian. Even with the engine modifications Moseley had ordered on Western's M-2 power plants, the required overhaul time for this improved version was every 150 hours—in dramatic comparison to the thousands of hours that elapse between overhauls on today's jet engines.

So Moseley and the Four Horsemen began a series of preliminary survey flights over the Los Angeles–Las Vegas portion of the route, using DH-4s borrowed from Mose's National Guard fleet. The Horsemen wanted to do an aerial inspection of the Las Vegas–Salt Lake City leg, too, but Moseley decided he didn't want to abuse the privilege. The rest of the projected 653-mile airway was surveyed on the ground, the entire route closely following the tracks of the Union Pacific. This was by intent; there were no radio beams or even beacons to serve as navigational aids, and the snaking tracks of the iron horse gave pilots an effective way in which to establish position and stay on course. To avoid the possibility of a midair collision between two converging pilots concentrating on following the rails, Moseley put in a simple rule: Stay on your right side of the tracks, like always driving on the right side of the road.

On one survey flight, Moseley had just taken off from Las Vegas and frowned at the de Havilland's odd behavior—it was pulling to the right, and the right wing felt heavy. His mechanic, sitting behind him, kept pounding him on the head with one hand and pointing frantically to the right with the other, but Moseley was too busy trying to gain some altitude to pay any attention. When the DH-4 finally staggered up to a respectable height, Mose finally looked in the direction in which the mechanic was wildly gesturing.

There was a hand, desperately clinging to the outer leading edge of the underwing. Gradually, a head appeared and then the whole body—of a sixteen-year-old boy, it turned out, who somehow had grasped the plane's underwing guard as it taxied toward the runway and refused to let go. Now he was hanging onto one of the outer struts between the wings, and Moseley motioned him to work his way toward the cockpit. The youngster flew all the way to Los Angeles, crouched by the side of the fuselage. Mose throttled down as much as he dared, but the windstream still exposed the boy to the equivalent of a ninety-mile-an-hour gale. When they landed, the young hitchhiker had been stripped of everything but a shirt collar and cuffs. Moseley scrounged up some clothes and shipped him home by train.

In February 1926, Moseley and four pilots—DeGarmo, James, Graham, and Remelin—left Los Angeles in two Dodge trucks and a 1924 Studebaker roadster that DeGarmo had contributed to the expedition, said expedition aimed at scouting emergency landing strips along the route. They were gone two weeks, Kelly joining the safari in Las Vegas and causing a minor railroad accident by the means of his arrival. He flew in on a Guard DH-4, accompanied by an Army pilot who would fly the plane back to Los Angeles after depositing Kelly. They came in over a rail yard where a freight engineer was switching cars. The engineer became so engrossed at the sight of the plane that he plowed into a boxcar, knocking it completely off the tracks.

The six men and their three-vehicle caravan rolled slowly across the rugged land that would soon be passing underneath their wings—deserts and mountains, valleys and plateaus, all wild and primitive and of indescribably deceptive beauty. They carried a huge roll of canvas twenty-four inches wide. Each chosen landing strip would be marked one of three ways: canvas laid down in the shape of a T meant "safe to land"; a V meant "land only in one direction," and a single strip warned "dangerous—you'd better be lucky." A marker was laid down approximately every twenty miles, and they installed some three hundred of them along the lone airway they would be flying.

All along the way, they introduced themselves to farmers, ranchers, and railroad clerks, making arrangements to have them phone in weather information to the nearest of Western's three stations. The Union Pacific already had promised to furnish pilots with keys to the UP telephone shacks that were spotted every five miles along the tracks; wisely, the survey team picked emergency landing sites as close to the tracks as possible.

During the whole two weeks, they only enjoyed the luxury of a warm hotel room when toward the end of the day they found themselves reasonably close to a town. On such occasions, they were greeted like visiting royalty; DeGarmo remembers that along with the proverbial red carpet went thick, succulent steaks (usually free), which Graham, a vegetarian, had to reject. More often they slept under the stars or inside the trucks and the Studebaker. A bond of chrome-steel friendship seems to have been forged among the Four Horsemen on that trip, as individual personalities and idiosyncrasies began to emerge in the crucible of daily proximity.

There was Kelly—quiet but with a devilish sense of humor. DeGarmo, rough-hewn, fiercely independent, and like so many strong men possessing a thick vein of sentimentalism and a heart as big as his burly frame. James, more mature than the others, a kind of natural leader. Graham, the most complex of them all, with a streak of stubbornness bordering on recklessness; a Christian Scientist and a health faddist.

They were a quartet of pilots typical of the early airmen, courageous to a degree that can only be appreciated if one understands the inadequacies of their tools and the Jekyll-Hyde nature of the environment in which they worked, changing from friend to killer in seconds; improvident, only too natural for men who lived from one paycheck to the next because they lived from one day to the next; fatalists, almost every one of them, which in some ways fueled their bravery; enormously skilled, not just as an essential of survival but also as a facet of their love of flying. It was not just a job but also a way of life.

For years, long after Western was operating dependable multi-engined aircraft over the original route, some of those canvas markers and the clearings so laboriously hacked out with pick and shovel were still visible from the air. According to one account, Hanshue himself accompanied the group on this mission, but there is no evidence to support the story and Hanshue would have been foolish even to consider going along. There was too much to do at the executive level prior to inauguration of service —such as selling air mail to the public. It was no minor task, because before Western began service, Los Angeles was sending out an average of only thirty-five pounds of air mail daily. Supposedly it was the government's function to promote air mail, but Uncle Sam was not, is not, and probably never will be an effective promoter or salesman—not without some professional help from private industry.

Hanshue wasn't about to wait for Uncle Sam in this vital area. Besides, he had in Woolley an ingenious, energetic, natural-born publicist who could have sold matzo ball soup in downtown Cairo. Woolley, aware that fast mail service would be useful, particularly in such business transactions as bank clearances, contracts, and negotiations, canvassed hundreds of business firms to determine how many of them already were using air mail and if they would utilize Western's service when it started.

He hired interviewers for this informal poll, and when some were barred from entering certain buildings on the ground that they were soliciting business, Woolley enlisted the power of the United States Government; he talked the Post Office Department into issuing air mail stickers for office building mail chutes, with Western employees designated as official agents. No pompous building manager had yet figured a way to ban entry by the federal government, so the stickers began appearing in impressive numbers.

Another Woolley idea was to set up booths manned by attractive girls in drugstores, markets, and Post Office branches, where pamphlets extolling the virtues of air mail were distributed.

"Fly Your Mail!" proclaimed one brochure. "Constant! Direct! Daily!"

"Los Angeles to New York in Thirty Hours!" it continued. "Beginning in April 1926, Transcontinental Air Mail Service for Southern California!

"Just Think!—forty-two hours saved between Los Angeles and Chicago. Proportionate time saving to and from all eastern points, whether on air mail routes or not.

"You should use the official 'Air Mail' envelope with red, white, and blue stripes similar to the design on the outside of this folder and the official 'Air Mail' stamp—but if these are not available, mark your letter plainly 'Air Mail' and affix the proper postage."

The same pamphlet described the M-2 as "the latest aircraft development of the famous 'Around-the-World' cruisers—built in Southern California and conceded to be the world's finest airplanes." Both statements might be challenged mildly by aviation historians. First, about the only thing the M-2 had in common with the Douglas "World Cruisers" that flew around the world in 1924 was the fact that both were biplanes; second, the M-2 was a capable little aircraft, but only the enthusiastic new traffic manager of Western Air Express would have classed it as the "finest." Like most of his counterparts in the infant industry, he could be forgiven for letting zeal occasionally collide with accuracy, such as bragging that the M-2 had a top speed of 145 miles per hour—which was true except that if it were maintained for any length of time, *sans* benefit of a tailwind, Western would go through the twenty-one spare Liberty engines it had ordered in a hurry. A more practical figure was the M-2's 115-mile-per-hour *cruising* speed capability, which any of the Four Horsemen would have been happy to average. But Woolley, like Hanshue, recognized the importance of instilling confidence in a public that had yet to appreciate what the dawn on aviation's horizon really meant. And in this case, the end truly justified the means for Woolley's efforts; the grandiose promotion, the glittering promises, and the high-flown assurances all resulted in not only an upsurge of interest but also positive support by Southern California businessmen and lay public alike. It wasn't easy, for the first air mail rates involved a complicated zone system with five different postage charges.

And now the M-2s began to arrive, flown to Vail Field from Santa Monica by Douglas test pilot Eric Springer. They were painted red and silver; reportedly Woolley wanted an all-red airplane but was talked out of it by Moseley, who pointed out that the solid red color scheme would add too much weight. Woolley did get approval for what he proposed as the first Western Air Express insignia—an Indian arrowhead on the tail. Before the planes went into service, however, mechanic Jim King in Salt Lake City added something else. He had heard that the brass hats in Los Angeles didn't think the arrowhead was distinctive enough, and one day, after swinging a hammer during construction of the WAE hangar at the Salt Lake City Airport, he got to thinking about the problem. The next time Hanshue was in town to check on airport progress, King approached him.

"Like to show you something, Mr. Hanshue," he offered.

"Sure," Hanshue said, puzzled.

King placed a buffalo nickel on a table, put a sheet of toilet paper over the head, and rubbed it with his greasy finger.

"How's that for an insignia?" King suggested.

"Interesting," allowed Hanshue. "I'll show this to Woolley."

He did, and Woolley jumped at it with the alacrity of a man who had just been offered the original "Mona Lisa" for fifty dollars.

"It needs a little refinement," he chortled, "but an Indian head is perfect for an airline serving the West."

What was added was a full-feathered bonnet replacing the nickel's single feather, plus an arrow. One of the most famous and long-lived airline symbols in history, the Indian head was to remain on all Western aircraft for another forty-five years, in varying versions but substantially with the same motif.

A new "hangar" went up at Vail Field, built largely of trusses from the old Charles Ray motion-picture studio that had once flourished on the fringe of the hayfield. A small operations office inside the hangar and a four-thousand-foot oiled runway completed Western's first major airport facility. Each of the Four Horsemen plus Remelin had his name painted on the side of an M-2. The sixth plane, ordered by Hanshue after the initial contract for five, was delivered shortly before the flights began.

Moseley sent the pilots on familiarization runs to and from Salt Lake City, twenty-five to thirty hours of checkrides per man. With Moseley flying the sixth plane, all the M-2s were flown to Salt Lake City in a final proving flight; James, DeGarmo, and Remelin stayed there while the others flew back to Los Angeles. A flip of the coin had decided who would fly the inaugural trips, Graham beating Kelly for the honor of taking out the first eastbound flight, and James outtossing DeGarmo for the westbound.

On the evening of April 16, 1926, all bets had been placed, personnel hired, aircraft readied—and quite possibly a few prayers were winging upward.

An airline had been conceived and was stirring in its corporate womb, nourished into sustained life by funding and smart exploitation and careful planning. Its genes were those of men like Hanshue . . . Moseley . . . Chandler . . . Graves . . . Talbot— for in its blood was vision, tenacity, and bravado. Its forebears were men who wore their wings in their hearts: the pioneer air mail pilots, young men with old faces, the skin around their eyes already crinkled from squinting at a thousand suns, a thousand approaching storms; the airmen of World War I, an oasis of braternal chivalry amid slaughter, adding bullets to the hazards of flying planes in themselves dangerous; aerial architects like Douglas . . . Martin . . . Curtiss . . . Lockheed . . . Boeing— blending dreams with genius.

And two brothers named Wright.

This was Western Air Express on the morning it was born.

CHAPTER TWO

"Neither Snow, nor Rain, nor Heat, nor Gloom of Night . . ."

April 17, 1926, was a Saturday—overcast and a bit chilly.

Vail Field looked like a De Mille production scene, crawling with spectators, reporters, and cameramen—both still and movie. For Los Angeles, anyway, it was a particularly newsworthy event, one deserving of the city's ultimate accolade to a newsworthy event: the presence of a movie celebrity. In this case it was actress Claire Windsor, presumably invited by the enterprising Woolley. She wasn't exactly a top star, but at least she was a screen personality, and Woolley would have settled for Rin-Tin-Tin at this point.

Stealing the show from Miss Windsor was Maury Graham, who showed up attired in the air mail pilot's traditional uniform of the day: coveralls with a battered helmet, businesslike goggles, and a .45 revolver strapped to his waist. In his pocket was something of equal importance to the goggles and gun—a memorandum from Moseley, with a duplicate sent to Jimmie James in Salt Lake City. It read:

> Best of luck to you both. Fly low and slow and always remember that a successful aerial journey consists of getting your ship to its destination and on the line, regardless of whether it is one day or one year. The main thing is to finally complete the trip with both yourself and your ship in good shape. Don't take any chances and play the game safely.

At a final briefing in Salt Lake City, before flying three of the planes back to Los Angeles for inaugural day, Moseley had given more specific oral instructions.

"Cruise around ninety," he told them. "By keeping the speed down, the engines will last longer."

"Ninety's pretty slow, Mose," Kelly objected. "That'll mean a schedule of more than eight hours."

"Let's try it for a while, anyway. If those Libertys seem to be holding up, we'll increase the speed. They won't last more than 600 hours at best, even with overhauls every 150 hours."

The schedule handed both Graham and James called for eight hours and twenty minutes elapsed time, including the refueling stop at Las Vegas. Hopefully, the eastbound flights, with some tailwinds normally expected, would cut this to some extent.

Pop Hanshue was at Vail to see Graham off, his coal-black eyes shining behind his tortoise-shell glasses. He formally greeted Los Angeles Postmaster P. P. O'Brien and, with cameras clicking and whirring, they supervised the weighing and loading of 256 pounds of mail—impressive compared to the previous 35-pound average but far short of the M-2's half-ton capacity. Even on this proud occasion, Hanshue kept glancing at the empty seat ahead of Graham's cockpit, Hanshue's busy mind touching base on all aspects of a problem far greater than getting people to send letters by air: getting them to fly.

Graham completed his inspection of the sleek, gleaming M-2 which, incidentally, lacked the new Indian head insignia. There hadn't been time to paint one on the fuselage; in its place was an ornate pair of wings with the letters "U.S. Air Mail" superimposed, and the Indian head would be added later. Maury shook hands with Hanshue and the postmaster, climbed into the cramped cockpit, and in a few minutes was roaring down the oiled runway. Looking on, pride and affection blending with envy, was Fred Kelly, who was all suited up ready to fly if Graham's ship had developed some malfunction.

The cheers of the crowd were being echoed more than six hundred miles away in Salt Lake City, where Jimmie James was set to take off on the westbound trip. James, disdaining the coveralls, wore faded khaki riding breeches, high-laced boots, a heavy pullover sweater, and the usual .45—the armament, standard paraphernalia for air mail pilots, was supposed to be used to guard the mail in the event of a forced landing, but its more practical purpose was as an instrument of survival.

Salt Lake City weather was sunny and clear, in contrast to the overcast skies at Los Angeles. James, with DeGarmo standing by as his alternate, waited impatiently for the local politicians to finish their inevitable oratory and was ready to start the engine when he felt a heavy thudding on the front of the plane. He leaned out and shook his head as he watched the pretty daughter of Utah's governor trying in vain to break a bottle of Salt Lake water against the propeller. He climbed out, worrying that she might have damaged the prop. Fortunately it still was unharmed, and Jimmie suggested that she hit a wheel hub cap instead. This done, he started the engine and some eight hours later was landing at Vail, tired and his face blackened with soot from the exhaust pipes.

While the welcoming committee was pawing eagerly through the first-flight souvenirs, Moseley was called to the phone: Graham had just landed on schedule in Salt Lake City. Western's first day was a success.

It was not nearly as successful as subsequent days, however. Only a little more than a month after operations began, the airline was averaging 245 pounds of mail daily—still far under the M-2's capacity but comfortably close to the first-day poundage, which was expected to be heavy out of sheer novelty. In six weeks, Western Air Express was flying 85 per cent of the volume that the government planes had been carrying between San Francisco and Salt Lake City; by every standard of measurement, Southern California indeed had been ready for direct air mail service. By August of 1926, in fact, Los Angeles had become the greatest user of air mail on the basis of pounds carried for every one thousand persons in a city's population. At the end of Western's first six months, LA was sending or receiving 40 per cent of the nation's air mail.

It seems pertinent at this point to discuss the historical significance of April 17, 1926, a date on which Western based its claim as the nation's senior scheduled carrier. That claim has been vigorously disputed by two other carriers—United and TWA.

TWA's argument is on rather tenuous ground. It, too, gives April 17, 1926, as its birthdate—even though it wasn't even in existence. In 1930, the government ordered the formation of a new airline under the name of Transcontinental and Western Air —composed of Transcontinental Air Transport and about three fourths of Western's assets in routes, planes, and personnel. TWA still contends it deserves to share the "senior airline" title with Western because of this affiliation.

United's claim is chronological seniority. Western, of course, was the fifth airline to start operations under the Kelly Act. But of those five, only Western survived. As previously recounted, Ford and Florida Airways dropped out, and both Varney and Robertson sold their routes to other carriers. United argues that Varney was a predecessor company; Varney, after extending his original CAM-5 east to Salt Lake City and to Seattle and Spokane, peddled the whole system to United in 1930 for one million dollars. In United's view, this established Varney's starting day of April 6, 1926, as its own date of birth—thus making it America's senior surviving air carrier by a margin of eleven days.

Western, on the other hand, points out that if United wants to pin its "senior" claim on its acquisition of Varney, it was a few years late. Two years after he launched WAE, Hanshue was to buy Pacific Marine Airways, which began operations in 1922; accepting United's predecessor line of argument, that would make Western four years older than UAL.

Western and United have been feuding about "who was first" since the early forties when the seniority issue first arose. The quarrel has simmered down considerably in recent years, but for a long time the various public-relations and advertising officials at Western used to exchange bitter correspondence with their counterparts at United.

Hanshue and his tiny band of pioneers were far more concerned with sheer survival than with establishing a place in history. Pop naturally was pleased at the avalanche of publicity given the start of service. The Los Angeles *Examiner*, for example, made the Graham/James inaugural flights the subject of a lead editorial the same day they flew. In a tone of provincial pride, it hailed the new air mail service "which puts Los Angeles wing to wing with points east and intermediate and applies an abbreviated measure to the intervening miles."

"When the people of the Atlantic Coast become sensible of the very greatly diminished width of the continent, perhaps they will feel that California is not a distant land after all," it continued. "They may at last come to experience a feeling of neighborliness toward this region, and follow that up by visiting here in large numbers."

The *Examiner's* two-column headline over the editorial read, "Make Air Mail Big Success and Speed Passenger Service." The newspaper remarked that "these initial operations of the Western Air Express, of course, will suggest passenger carrying along this route, at least as far as Salt Lake City. Bridging only this distance by air will reduce the trip East or West by one day. . . . The people of Los Angeles and Southern California . . . will be speeding the day of fast trains and passenger-carrying transcontinental planes by making the air mail a success."

To which Hanshue might have growled, "Fine—but where the hell are the passengers?"

He got his first one on a gusty day in May—specifically the twenty-third. And the first person to pay Western Air Express for passage between Salt Lake City and Los Angeles did so not with any feeling of confidence in the safety, reliability, and comfort of air travel, he did it because he had a hobby of collecting "firsts" —from stamps to steamship maiden voyages—and he wanted badly to be Western's first passenger.

His name was Ben Redman, and he owned fireproof storage warehouses in both Salt Lake City and Santa Monica. He also was one of the original fifty or so stockholders in Western Air Express, which gave him something of a priority status. Actually, he needed no such status; early in 1926, after buying WAE stock, he wrote Hanshue a note of congratulations on winning the mail contract and expressing the hope that he could become the first passenger. In effect, he made the airline's first advance reservation, for in the letter he enclosed a twenty-dollar check as a deposit on his ticket. Hanshue was so impressed that he gave orders that the check never be cashed—and it never was.

Redman showed up at the Salt Lake City airport that day, handed over seventy dollars (the ninety-dollar fare minus his deposit), and was outfitted in coveralls, parachute, helmet, and goggles. Also boarded was another Salt Lake City resident, J. A. Tomlinson. They sat on top of a mail sack, clutching box lunches, while Jimmie James explained how to work (1) the parachute if needed and (2) the M-2's toilet facilities if needed, said facilities consisting of a tin can. By comparison, the pilot had sheer luxury at his disposal: a tube stuck through the bottom of the cockpit.

They took off at 9:30 A.M. and five hours later landed at Las Vegas to refuel. Redman and Tomlinson staggered out of the plane to stretch their legs and would have been forgiven if they had refused to reboard; for a good portion of the trip they had flown through a dust storm, and both passengers were pale from fatigue and nervousness. But they also were game, and three hours later climbed more or less jauntily out of the M-2, waving to the crowd of photographers and reporters gathered at Vail Field to record the arrival. Although Western actually flew four passengers on May 23, Redman got most of the attention and the honors because he made the first reservation. In Western's small but nostalgia-crammed museum, there is displayed the certificate James handed Redman upon completion of the flight, along with that never-canceled check. The certificate recorded the total flying time of eight hours, the maximum altitude reached (12,000 feet), the maximum speed (130 mph), and the air mail carried (136 pounds). It also bore Western's first slogan, another product of Woolley's fertile mind: "Time Flies—Save Time."

The four intrepid men who flew Western Air Express that day were the forerunners of a slow but steady growth in the carrier's passenger traffic. By the end of 1926, WAE had carried more than two hundred customers, most of whom admittedly went for the sheer novelty of the experience and the opportunity to brag about it if they survived. Included was the first woman passenger, Maude Campbell of Salt Lake City. Two weeks after Ben Redman became a footnote in aviation history, Maude plunked down $180 for a trip from Salt Lake City to Los Angeles and return, and drew Al DeGarmo as her pilot for the westbound flight.

She had learned about Western when she was having a quiet

drink with a male friend. He was telling her that the airline was going to start a mail service to Salt Lake City, and Maude—an aviation buff from girlhood—was intrigued.

"Can they carry passengers on the mailplanes?" she asked.

"I understand they will, if anyone is damned fool enough . . ."

"I think I'd like to go," she announced.

When she made her reservations, the alert Woolley—no male chauvinist, he—noticed the name instantly, and his publicity oriented brain whirred like a computer. When the attractive young lady arrived at the airport for her flight, there was a special flying suit for her, not the greasy extra set of pilot coveralls usually furnished passengers. It so happened that Jimmie James was a member of the Black Falcons, otherwise known as the National Guard's 478th Pursuit Squadron at Griffith Park, and one of the outfit's sponsors was famed theater owner Sid Grauman. Sid had given James handsome new coveralls bearing the Black Falcon insignia, and Jimmie gallantly (either with Woolley's approval or connivance) offered them to Miss Campbell.

DeGarmo gruffly showed her what passed as toilet facilities and briefed her on use of the parachute: "If there's any trouble with the plane, jump out, count to three, and then pull the ripcord."

A Salt Lake City newsman wrote that Maude's cockpit accommodations were "fitted up like a boudoir." This had to be pure invention, or maybe the reporter had never been inside a boudoir. Except for the clean coveralls, Miss Campbell wasn't any better off than a male passenger and probably worse off—under the flying suit she wore a pair of plus-four knickers, which qualified in any case the practicality of that tin can. Maude remembers wryly that "I waited until we got to Las Vegas; there was no other way."

At Las Vegas, none other than Moseley took over the final leg to Los Angeles, where the resourceful Woolley had pulled out all the stops. A horde of newsmen and photographers almost as large as the one that witnessed the inaugural flight was present. So was Pop Hanshue, with an armful of gladiolas, which he handed Maude as she stepped out of the plane, windblown, her nose red from the cold, and slightly deaf even though she had stuffed her ears with cotton underneath the helmet. She stayed in Los Angeles a week and took the return flight home with a total lack of fanfare. For years she saved the scribbled notes the pilots kept passing up to her, pointing out items of interest along the route, and later presented them to Western for display in its flight museum.

Such notes were not only a form of in-flight entertainment, but also the *only* entertainment on the long, tedious flights—even the pilots welcomed them as a means of diversion. More than anyone else they appreciated what it meant for people to climb into an airplane they feared, mistrusted, and faced with a kind of masochistic bravery. The time-honored definition of aviation, "hours and hours of boredom punctuated by moments of stark terror," applied more to 1926 flying than it does now. So their equivalent of today's occasional remark over the PA system was a scrawled, handwritten note; even the usually taciturn DeGarmo enjoyed the practice, while the more extroverted pilots like James actually relished it.

Maude Campbell wasn't the only passenger who preserved those notes as treasured mementos. Another was Mrs. Ida Nichols, then Ida Larson of Moab, Utah, who on March 20, 1927, flew from Salt Lake City to Los Angeles with Jimmie James. Nearly forty years later, she sent Western her original ticket receipt, the flight certification form (numbered 103), and the sheaf of Jimmie's notes excerpted below—and note the flying time of only five hours; by then, Western's pilots and mechanics had convinced Moseley to lift the speed restriction:

6:30 A.M.—"The nippy air will give you a whiskey nose. We are at 8,000 feet above sea level and going 110 miles per hour . . . hope you are not too cold."

7:00 A.M.—"We are making excellent time but not close to record time. We have a 15-mile tailwind. You can get direction and velocity of wind by looking at steam coming out of locomotive at Lynndyl on left. Taken us 45 min. so far and train time is 4 hours."

7:25 A.M.—"We will see some wild horses soon, sometimes several hundred, sometimes just a few. We keep them pretty well worried."

8:18 A.M.—"We climb up over the Mormon Range now. Cedar City up against mountains on the left. Don't know if you can see it or not. We get 10,000 ft. again to go over this range. It is the highest and roughest spot on this trip. If you feel a bump in a few minutes you will know that you have crossed the Utah-Nevada line. If you get bumped out, don't forget to pull ripcord in chute and if it doesn't work bring it back. They are guaranteed. Cedar Breaks, Bryce Canyon, Zion, Kaibab Forest and the whole works are about 40 miles to the left."

9:45 A.M.—"One more hour of slavery . . . See that dust storm. Here comes gloom again. I can foresee some rough air just as we go over these mountains into Los Angeles valley. However it won't last long. This is Cajon Pass."

10:15 A.M.—"Big Bear Lake is on top of snow-covered mountain on left. Victorville is on right where you can see the smoke coming out of cement plant. Forget you are hors de combat because from now on everything is green and pretty. Springtime. 30–35 minutes to LA."

Maury Graham was another pilot who loved "talking" to passengers. He took particular delight in pointing out the advantages of air over train travel. A newspaperwoman who flew with him from Los Angeles to Salt Lake City recalled in a subsequent article that while he provided the usual notes, calling her attention to various points of interest, he became positively verbose when he spotted a train. She quoted one such note:

"There's the train that left LA at 11 last night and is due in Salt Lake City at 5 tomorrow morning. You see, the air mail beats everything on speed—we're doing in six hours what the train takes twenty-seven to achieve!"

Kelly, for all his good humor and carefree attitude, varied in his relations with the customers. He could be as friendly as James on one flight and positively brusque on the next. Long after Kelly retired as a Western captain, the airline received a letter from a passenger who recalled flying with him in 1928. His description of Fred was not one of all-out charm.

> He was tall, dark, grim and begrudgingly civil. . . . The ship was an open biplane and the passenger took in the same amount of fresh air as did the pilot. This was really living it up—especially when Kelly gave me the instructions regarding the use of the 'chute: "You're supposed to count to three before pulling the ripcord but my advice is that if we have to leave this ship, count to at least six and be damned sure you're free of the ship. I'll do my best to see you're out of the cockpit but use your head."

But they all were heroes to the public—personifications of the father image and Greek god aura that passengers have bestowed on pilots for so long. When Maury Graham bought a new Jordan automobile from a San Diego dealer, the latter ecstatically contacted the local paper, which ran a full-column article on the event. "HIGH FLYER PURCHASES JORDAN," ran the headline over a story beginning, "After 10 years' experience in the highest development of motorized transportation, that of flying, Capt. Maurice Graham, air mail pilot, has selected a Jordan sedan for his personal use when not on duty." One wonders if Maury got a discount.

Speed gradually began selling air travel to the public. Even the fastest train took some twenty-four hours between Salt Lake City and Los Angeles, and by automobile, it was at best a two-day trip and usually three days. By contrast, Western's planes were averaging six hours, while both Graham and James, benefiting from tailwinds, flew the route on two occasions in less than 4½ hours. Nevertheless, it was hard for even the wily Woolley to drum up passenger business when all he had to offer was the cramped M-2; technically it was a two-passenger airplane, but carrying two persons in that cramped front cockpit was not air travel at its finest. More often than not, the flights deliberately were restricted to a single passenger, because mail had priority—on one day in August 1926, the WAE fleet hauled more than thirty-three thousand pieces of mail.

Some of the earliest passengers were movie celebrities. DeGarmo, for example, struck up a friendship with Wallace Beery, who loved flying and enjoyed companionship with the pilots. Beery was one of the few stars whose real-life personality duplicated the roles he played on the screen; he was tough, crude, and profane, with the disconcerting habit of removing his shoes as soon as he settled down in the M-2's passenger seat. More was involved than the danger of potential frostbite—it seems Beery had an aversion to regular changes of socks, and the pilots could have used smoke masks along with their goggles.

"When his shoes were off," DeGarmo remembers with a chuckle, "the engine seemed to pick up speed just to get away from the odor. I had to sit in the slipstream behind him, and even at five thousand feet, I could smell those feet. But he was one hell of a guy. I still can see him strapped in his parachute, dancing around the ready room, always clowning."

Will Rogers was another frequent Western passenger and a close friend of all the Four Horsemen. James got to know the versatile humorist first, but Kelly and DeGarmo flew him more frequently. Rogers, in fact, once offered DeGarmo a job as his personal pilot around the time he got interested in a new Lockheed monoplane Western had just bought. Rogers fell in love with it and asked Al what he thought of it. DeGarmo took one look at its unusual parasol-wing construction and shook his head. He just didn't like that particular Lockheed, and told Rogers the wing structure seemed too flimsy.

Graham agreed with the verdict after a test flight. Maury took it up, pulled into a steep climb, and heard at least one wing strut crack ominously. After Lockheed repaired the damage, the cowboy philosopher chartered the plane and hired Kelly to fly him to the 1928 Republican National Convention in Kansas City— DeGarmo and Graham politely but adamantly declining the assignment. As they were landing to refuel at Las Vegas, a wheel hit a bump and the gear collapsed, flipping the plane on its back. Kelly and Rogers climbed out unhurt, Will muttering, "This never would have happened if I had been going to a Democratic convention." It was the only flight the Lockheed made for Western.

Jimmie James was sitting around the Salt Lake City terminal one day when actor Ben Lyons walked in.

"I have to get on your next flight to Los Angeles," Lyons pleaded. "They tell me there's no space, but this is an emergency."

James said he'd try, and somehow squeezed Lyons in between mail sacks. The next day he found out why the actor had been in such a hurry; as soon as he arrived in Los Angeles, he married Bebe Daniels, whom at least two of the Four Horsemen already knew. The actress had been a passenger on James' plane a few weeks earlier, heading from Salt Lake City to Los Angeles. En route, Jimmie spotted Kelly's approaching eastbound flight and waggled his wings in their prearranged signal to land.

Mystified, Kelly complied, thinking James must be in some kind of dire trouble. They both landed on a desert strip, where James introduced his famous passenger. Neither took notice of the time that elapsed while they chatted, and both pilots were about an hour late arriving at their respective destinations— much to the concern of the worried Moseley, who feared they had crashed.

"What happened?" he asked James. "You're an hour late."

"Headwinds," Jimmie explained laconically.

Just then the telephone rang; it was Kelly reporting his own safe but very tardy arrival.

"And just what the hell went wrong with your flight?" Mose demanded.

"Headwinds," said Kelly.

Apparently passing notes to passengers was not enough to relieve the monotony of a routine flight, not to mention the fact that usually there were no passengers. On some of the latter occasions, the boys used to buzz herds of wild horses and deer, or shoot at coyotes with their .45s—seldom coming close to hitting one. Chasing locomotives was another popular sport, especially when there was any kind of stiff headwind. The technique was to overtake a train doing about sixty miles an hour, fly low and slow until they were abreast of the engine cab, and wave at the startled engineer and fireman. A variation of this stunt, supposedly conceived by Kelly, was to approach a train head on at night with all wing lights out. When plane and locomotive were only a few yards apart on a direct collision course, the pilot suddenly would turn on all his lights and zoom up at the last second.

Moseley sternly forbade such shenanigans, knowing full well he might as well have been talking to himself. The pilots needed such antics not only to combat boredom but also to offset the tensions of the very real dangers they faced with alarming frequency. In the first year of Western's operations, the Four Horsemen had thirty-eight forced landings—twenty-five due to bad weather and thirteen because of mechanical troubles. Moseley never did hear about a near disaster involving Kelly and De-Garmo, a hair-raising escape from a midair collision. Kelly was coming from Salt Lake City and DeGarmo was heading east, both virtually at the same altitude.

They should have been ten miles apart, but Kelly was busy eating lunch and unwittingly strayed off course smack into DeGarmo's path. Fred never saw the oncoming plane, and DeGarmo spotted Kelly so late that if he had pulled up, he probably would have stalled. They passed so close that, in Al's words, "you couldn't have put a hand between my tailskid and the center section of his wing."

"I turned around and tried to follow him to get his attention. When I finally caught up to him, he was still eating and never saw me. I gave up and headed back toward Salt Lake City. Later I called him and told him what had happened. To the day he died, he never believed me."

All the pilots had their share of emergency landings. Weather, far more than the temperamental Libertys, always was the biggest problem. The Union Pacific supplied whatever weather information it could, but what were acceptable conditions to a railroad often were lethal to a pilot. Farmers and ranchers along the way provided their share of weather data, too, and while these were preferable to no data at all, they still were woefully inadequate.

It was only natural that a special kind of relationship developed between the hardy, often lonely inhabitants of the farms and ranches on CAM-4 and the pilots who flew the route daily. In a sense, many of these rural folk were part of the air mail system; they provided food and shelter to airmen forced down near their homes, and a few tended the relative handful of emergency fields equipped with government-purchased beacons. One such family was the Bonners, who operated a farm on the edge of a desert in southern Utah. An emergency strip was located nearby, and Bonner would dutifully turn on the lights at dusk and turn them off at dawn.

Western's pilots knew such families by location rather than by name, often establishing them as individuals by the number of children coming out to wave at the mailplanes roaring overhead. But the Bonners were something special.

When Bonner was killed in an accident, the pilots somehow found out and began collecting a Christmas fund. They had counted the children in the family—eight—and they were touched by Mrs. Bonner's continuing to maintain those lights faithfully after her husband's death. Kelly was appointed vice president in charge of ascertaining the kids' sizes—which he accomplished by flying low over the Bonner home and dropping a camera and a note asking the mother to take a picture of the children and send them to Western's home office.

She mailed the requested snapshot, from which the pilots figured out the children's sizes. A few days later, shortly before Christmas, Kelly flew over the house again and blinked. There on the roof were painted words:

"Merry Xmas Western Air Express Pilots."

Kelly returned Christmas Day, roared low over the Bonner residence, dropped several packages of gifts for the children plus an envelope stuffed with money for Mrs. Bonner, waved good-bye, and flew off again. But he had flown low enough for all the Bonners to see what he was wearing over his coveralls—a Santa Claus suit.

Drunks and dogs furnished occasional respite from routine. DeGarmo took on a passenger in Salt Lake City, choosing to ignore what he lugged aboard the plane: a bottle of whiskey. Al figured he'd drink himself into merciful oblivion, which wasn't a bad idea because the official weather report—relayed from the Weather Bureau in San Francisco, which was 350 miles from the nearest point on Western's route—called for stormy skies. This time the prediction was only too accurate, and DeGarmo ran into turbulence and thick overcast. He was too busy concentrating on his handful of instruments and trying to keep the plane level to pay much attention to his passenger—until he felt a strange vibration and a heaviness on the controls. He looked up to find the front cockpit empty.

The crazy bastard must have jumped, DeGarmo thought with sinking heart; how do I explain this to Moseley? Then he happened to glance out at the right wings. There was the passenger, clinging to a strut, waving happily. Al managed to coax him back to the cockpit via hand signals and the power of prayer.

For some reason, probably the unfamiliar noise of airplane engines, dogs seemed to flock to Vail Field, where they could bark at the planes and scrounge free meals! On more than one occasion, pilots were startled to hear barking after they had taken off—only to discover that the mechanics had figured out a way to reduce the canine population at Vail. They merely sneaked various Rovers into the mail compartments and sent them to Las Vegas.

People as well as dogs invariably showed up when a mailplane arrived, particularly at Vegas and Salt Lake City, not unlike the old days when an entire town would greet each incoming stagecoach. And the pilots picked up a number of interesting friends this way—such as the Las Vegas businessman who would meet every Jimmie James flight and shoot craps with him until he was ready to take off on the next leg. Kelly made friends with a small, admiring youngster named Ted Homan, who haunted the Las Vegas airport almost daily. The boy didn't just like airplanes—he loved them. He didn't just admire Kelly— he worshiped him. In 1927, Kelly talked Ted's parents into letting him fly the youngster to Salt Lake City.

That gesture paid off not merely in a lasting friendship between a pilot and a little boy, but also in furnishing Western with one of its finest airmen. Homan was to become a senior captain, respected and liked by all, and against considerable odds. When he reached manhood, Homan was less than five feet, five inches in height and probably would have been rejected if it had not been for his long involvement with Western itself; in his teens, he used to go out to the Vegas airport, help unload the planes, and run errands for the crews.

DeGarmo even wound up delivering newspapers by air.

Through Rogers, he had met a reporter for the Los Angeles *Herald Examiner* whose home was at Victorville, on the mailplane route and some distance from the normal newspaper delivery point. So Al would drop the daily paper in the reporter's tennis court everytime he flew out of Vail and over Victorville. Low-altitude flying was an accepted procedure in those radioless days; in really soupy weather, the M-2s were flown so close to the ground that the landing-gear wheels almost touched the sage-brush along the rail tracks. Often the eastbound plane on the right side of the tracks never saw the westbound flight passing on the left.

The sturdy little Douglas was no dream to fly. It was a ground-loving bitch when the load was even moderately heavy, especially during hot weather at Vegas and Salt Lake City. The first planes Western bought had short exhaust stacks, and the glare generated by those twelve pounding cylinders was so bright that it was hard to see. The truncated stacks also increased the noise level, and many of the early M-2 pilots developed hearing problems in later years. Eventually, Western installed longer stacks, which helped somewhat, but the M-2 was never any docile beast of burden—it had to be wrestled as much as flown, like most aircraft of its day. That it turned out to be reliable was due to the dedication and skill of Western's platoon of mechanics—they coddled, nursed, pampered, and scrubbed the balky Libertys, and every malfunction was a personal affront. By coincidence, the airline's first superintendent of maintenance was Everett Drinkwater; another Drinkwater, no relation, would someday become Western's fourth president.

The dangers were offset—sometimes—with laughs. James had an engine quit on him over some rugged territory and dropped three-minute flares to illuminate an emergency strip below. He managed to land while flares were still coming down and was immediately accosted by a woman from a nearby ranch.

"You coward!" she screamed. "You left your passengers up there while you saved your own neck!"

"What passengers?" Jimmie yelled back.

"Those poor souls floating down with the lanterns in their hands!"

The mail business was good enough for Hanshue to expand

the fleet in a modest way. Less than four months after service started, he ordered a seventh plane—this time a modified M-4. It had the M-2 landing gear and a reserve gasoline tank carrying eighty gallons, plus a larger oil tank. The price tag was $13,576, which included $310 for the reserve tank; that was more than $2,500 above what Western had paid for the original six M-2s, but the more modern M-4 was worth the difference.

Sometimes the government was slow in making its mail payments of three dollars per pound carried, and Hanshue had to scramble for cash during the first few months. When a prominent evangelist staged a fake kidnaping in 1926, the press came close to outnumbering the police in the search for the supposedly missing lady preacher. It was never recorded who originated the idea of chartering planes to the newspapers and wire services, but someone at Western did just that—the airline was about three months behind on its fuel bills and needed a financial transfusion. Sufficient search flights were flown to pay off the back bills.

Actually, the revenue deficiency was temporary; for a participant in a brand-new, uncertain, inexperienced, and risky industry, Western Air Express was doing fine, well enough to start hiring a few additional pilots and ground personnel, and well enough to do something no airline of today can afford—Hanshue set up a crash insurance reserve fund, necessitated by the fact that in 1926 insurance underwriters charged prohibitive premiums for air travel.

Within six months from the start of operations, WAE was more than breaking even, and by the end of 1926, it showed a profit of $28,674.19—an infinitesimal sum by modern standards but a tremendous accomplishment fifty years ago. Western, in fact, was the first airline to make a scheduled air mail operation a paying proposition. And as the red ink darkened into black throughout that first year, Hanshue began to plan expansion.

On October 15, 1926, the Post Office Department put its coveted transcontinental air mail route—the so-called Columbia Line—up for bids. The route was broken into two segments: Newark–Chicago, and Chicago–San Francisco. Hanshue, with approval of Western's directors, filed his bid for the latter route. His confidence was so high that it infected the board of directors, which voted to increase the airline's capitalization to $2 million if the new route (redesignated CAM-18) was won.

There was solid reason for Pop's optimism. He wasn't worried about anyone underbidding him, because he already had met that challenge when he won Western Air Express its first mail contract. Another group actually submitted a lower bid than Western's for the Los Angeles–Salt Lake City route but was disqualified for lack of adequate financial backing and experience. If the Post Office Department was giving such qualifications priority over the bid itself, Hanshue felt, Western held the high cards for the new route. Between April 17 and October 15, the airline had achieved a perfect safety record, surprising reliability despite the rugged terrain and frequently miserable weather, and an impressive upsurge in air mail volume thanks to efficient promotion. As for respectable financial support, there was nothing small-time in names like the Los Angeles *Times*, Ford, the Mormon Church, and Richfield Oil.

What Pop didn't count on, however, was the quality of the opposition—smart, enterprising, and with a trump card Hanshue didn't have. At its core was Eddie Hubbard, at the time still operating a foreign mail route between Seattle and Victoria in Boeing flying boats. That connection with Boeing was to be the chief instrument in Western's eventual defeat; Hubbard was a close friend of William Boeing, and when Eddie heard about the Chicago–San Francisco bid, he went right to the Boeing factory. His idea was simple, but devastating as far as Western was concerned: Build a new mailplane with enough room to carry at least two passengers in relative interior comfort. He took his plan to Clair Egtvedt, Boeing's chief designer, arguing that such a plane could be profitable enough to permit submission of an extremely low bid.

Egtvedt was sufficiently intrigued to discuss the proposal with Boeing himself, who promised financial support. Out of all this came the brilliantly conceived Boeing 40A, a biplane with an exterior pilot's cockpit but a cabin in the large fuselage, and a new airline: Boeing Air Transport. Hubbard organized the airline, working out of Salt Lake City, which was the junction point connecting the Columbia Line to the two feeder lines serving it— Varney from Seattle and Western from Los Angeles.

Hubbard's air mail experience and the excellent financial reputation of the fast-growing Boeing Company supplied qualifications as good as Western's; the 40A, powered by a new Pratt & Whitney engine far superior to the Liberty, supplied the means by which Boeing Air Transport not only could underbid Hanshue but by such a wide margin that he wasn't even in the running. Boeing submitted a bid of $2.88 per pound of mail for the entire route of nearly two thousand miles, a figure based on calculating $1.50 for the first thousand miles and $.15 for every hundred miles thereafter. Western's bid was $4.25–$2.24 for the first thousand miles and $.224 for each hundred miles more.

Hanshue was more than disappointed; he was angry, arguing that the winning Boeing bid was so low that Boeing couldn't possibly operate profitably. Yet it did just that, carrying thirteen hundred tons of mail and more than six thousand passengers in its first two years, thanks mainly to the 40A and an engine that put the Liberty to shame in terms of reliability, economy, and efficiency.

For Hanshue, however, failure to gain the coveted CAM-18 was merely a lost battle in a long war. What he regretted more than loss of a lucrative mail route was CAM-18's potentiality for passenger traffic. Pop was one of a handful of airline management pioneers who welcomed mail revenues yet hated to depend on the government's coffers as the major source of income. Western's intake from mail pay during its first 8½ months came to nearly $200,000; that from passenger traffic amounted to slightly over $9,000, with another $3,600 derived from "special service"—mostly charter flights. This imbalance was true throughout the industry, but Hanshue more than most of his fellow airline executives squirmed under the necessity of relying almost entirely on mail payments.

He was no blind optimist in his belief that passenger traffic eventually had to outstrip mail in making any airline viable. For one thing, he was encouraged by the gradual increase in Western's passenger traffic—achieved despite the World War I accommodations on the M-2. Along with the lack of comfortable aircraft went the even greater detriment of widespread fear of flying. Hanshue had laughed wryly when he heard that a fair-sized proportion of passengers were handing his pilots tips ranging from twenty to fifty dollars at the end of a flight—only too obviously a gesture of pure gratitude, of enormous relief that they had gotten down in one piece. If there had been any such gimmick as a psychological motivation survey done on passengers in those days, it would have shown that the majority flew for the same reason they climbed on roller coasters—the excitement of facing danger with the odds somewhat in their favor.

Hanshue sensed that the nonflying segment of the population had to be approached not from the standpoint of selling flying's excitement but its advantages—starting with the prime advantage of all: speed. The automobile was no real competitor—not in the midtwenties, when the intercity highway system was a joke and cars themselves were technological adolescents. Trains carried the overwhelming bulk of intercity traffic in relative swiftness—nothing to match that of the airplane, but with the added inducement of far greater comfort, reliability, and safety.

This, in Hanshue's mind, was aviation's major challenge: Add the elements of comfort and safety to the airplane's speed and you'd have a way to sell air travel. And with an airline created to serve the West, he had a natural market—an area where cities were farther apart, travel distances greater, roads more primitive, trains less frequent.

He was a dreamer, but a dreamer with a sense of practicality and an intuitive opportunism running through his chunky body. Impulsive, yet patient when he had to be, he knew what he wanted, what Western and all aviation needed; he bided his time, moving cautiously in one direction even as he struck suddenly in another.

In 1927, a little more than a year after the first Western Air Express mailplanes had inaugurated service, an event occurred that revolutionized U.S. aviation. The date was May 21—when a lone pilot named Charles A. Lindbergh flew nonstop from New York to Paris, thus creating not only a legendary national hero, but also an upsurge of confidence and interest in aviation that was and still is difficult to measure. How many youngsters were inspired to become pilots by Lindbergh's feat will never be known. How many ordinary Americans whose decision at least to try flying stemmed from Lindy's exploit is impossible to judge. It is certain, however, that commercial aviation derived enormous benefits from a flight that combined pure luck with magnificent skill, recognized danger mitigated by careful planning.

Western was one of the inheritors of that Lindbergh legacy. What the Lone Eagle achieved in 33½ dramatic hours seemed to wipe out all the previous years of aviation's immaturity and the public's indifference. It was followed in rapid succession by Byrd's and Chamberlain's successful transatlantic flights, Maitland's and Hegenberger's Oakland-to-Honolulu jaunt, and a host of lesser headline-grabbing ventures giving the airplane a reputation for safety which, while it was not really deserved, furnished a welcome stimulant to the commercial carriers.

Another event took place several months before the tiny *Spirit of St. Louis* flew its way into the nation's heart and made aviation respectable overnight. It earned few headlines, attracted comparatively little public attention, and had all the dramatic impact of a marshmallow dropped into cotton. But to the future of Western Air Express, it meant even more than the Lindbergh flight.

Late in 1926, multimillionaire Daniel Guggenheim—a man who had made a fortune in mining—summoned his lawyers to a conference. He informed them that he wanted to establish a fund for the promotion of commercial aviation. They weren't one whit surprised; he already had given New York University five hundred thousand dollars for the establishment of a school of aeronautics.

"What sum do you have in mind, Mr. Guggenheim?" an attorney asked politely.

"Two and a half million dollars," was his unblinking answer.

Eventually, word of the new Guggenheim Fund trickled out to the West Coast, and Pop Hanshue read the skimpy details. He was a man whose eyes smiled more than his lips, and his eyes now were aglow with the fires of sudden vision.

CHAPTER THREE

"The Mail Comes First"—but Not for Long

Outwardly, 1927 was the pioneer year of 1926 in repetition: the same M-2s, the same suffering passengers carried more as extra cargo on a space-available basis than as valued customers, the same desperation-tinged Woolley promotion schemes, and the same overexposure to danger that made Western's perfect safety record more of a miracle than a positive accomplishment.

Already the crews' experiences were taking on the substance of potential legends, stories that would be told throughout the years—acquiring a few harmless embellishments along the way. Typically, the pilots remembered the humorous aspects while forgetting the less pleasant, such as the fact that in many instances they came close to buying the farm. ("Buying the farm" is an expression believed to have come from the days when pilots who made forced landings had to pay for damage to fields and crops; the phrase became the airman's synonym for a fatal crash.)

Jimmie James always loved to kid Kelly about the time Fred's M-2 had engine trouble and he came down on one of the original emergency strips. Aboard were two passengers, a man and woman, and some 150 pounds of mail. Kelly hiked to a nearby ranch, introduced himself officiously as a United States air mail carrier, and commandeered a horse. The nag's only resemblance to a healthy, normal equine was its four legs; it was so swaybacked that when Kelly gingerly mounted it, his long legs touched the ground.

He coaxed this pale facsimile of Man o' War back to where

the M-2 sat, the two passengers welcoming him eagerly and nodding with great satisfaction when Kelly informed them, "We'll
have to use the horse to reach a Union Pacific station."

"I don't mind," the man assured Fred. "You and I can walk
while the lady . . ."

"The mail comes first," Kelly said sternly. "You and the lady
will have to wait here until I get back."

He rode away, looking like Matt Dillon astride a Shetland
pony, while behind him the two marooned passengers heated the
air with profanity. Kelly didn't return for them until he had
safely delivered the mail to the Union Pacific.

Pilots might have been tempted to ignore the rules out of sympathy, but they had to remember that mail revenue furnished
about 93 per cent of their salary. Every airline lived in mortal
fear of having a mail contract canceled for nonperformance; this
was the reason Western, when it began service on CAM-4,
bought six planes to handle two daily flights, one in each direction. Hanshue needed backup equipment in the early stages,
knowing he could not afford the luxury of increased schedules
until pilots, planes, and engines gained some operating experience.

As of January 1, 1927, Western had flown almost sixty-six
thousand pounds of mail, and the average poundage per flight
was increasing daily. Unfortunately, the passenger count was not
accelerating with anywhere near the pace of the mail. During
the entire year of 1927, only four hundred persons were carried.
That was almost double the 1926 total, true, but far short of
what Hanshue not only hoped but also expected—not when he
considered the growing interest in commercial aviation, the success of privately operated mail service, and the recognized promotion abilities of one James Woolley. Hanshue knew why only
too well; not even Woolley could sell the M-2 to passengers
once the sales pitch of "Fly with the U.S. Mail" had lost its appeal.

Pop liked and respected Woolley enough to make him a vice
president of traffic, but to the ex-newspaperman it was like being
named vice president of precisely nothing. His public-relations
duties were relatively simple; after the Lindbergh flight, news-

papers would print anything if it concerned aviation. And promoting mail seemed to lack the challenge it once had.

Prominent people, from movie stars to politicians, gave Woolley about his only chance to push passenger service as he did air mail. A booking by even a minor actor or eager starlet was enough to have the vice president of traffic rush a photographer to Vail Field. A well-known political figure was a greater bonanza; when Senator Reed Smoot of Utah flew WAE, trying manfully to look simultaneously brave and relaxed after a rough flight from Salt Lake City, Woolley made sure there were cameras to record a United States senator's patronage of Western's superb service. Publicly Woolley extolled the virtues of the airline's equipment, personnel, and safety philosophy; privately he complained bitterly that he might as well have been trying to sell space on the *Titanic*'s second voyage. All Hanshue could tell his frustrated vice president of traffic was to be patient—some irons were about to go into the fire.

Hanshue himself was working as hard as anyone else. He found little time for his favorite recreations, golf and handball. He feuded almost daily with Moseley. While Pop had picked the major to head operations, Moseley actually got the job thanks to Harry Chandler's recommendation, and there seems to have been no love lost between Hanshue and his operations chief. Moseley reportedly didn't like taking orders from a man with absolutely no aviation background, and Hanshue was the kind of man who expected orders to be obeyed, not debated. There is some suspicion that the ill feeling between these two fine men may have started during the organizational days, when Moseley committed the airline to buy the Ford-Stout 2-AT and almost got stuck with it. There may be a smidgen of truth in this, but it is far more likely that their differences were more in the nature of a personality clash; both were strong, obstinate, domineering men, and while Moseley might complain that Hanshue didn't know the front end of an airplane from the rear (according to some accounts, Pop was afraid to fly), the latter in turn could point out that Mose knew little about the airline's business side, such as financing and route development.

While they didn't hit it off, however, they tried hard to work together in a common cause—namely, constantly improving the profit picture with an eye to future expansion. Both realized, for example, that the M-2 was no better than the engines that powered it, and the Liberty was like an ailing heart in the body of an otherwise healthy man. Hanshue had more on his mind than obtaining an aircraft with larger passenger capacity; he realized he might need a new mailplane as well, particularly if the airline obtained additional mail authority. The equipment dilemma was common throughout the industry. The only justification for buying airplanes with adequate passenger capacity was to operate them over routes blessed with mail contracts; without mail revenue, no one figured to make money carrying only people. This applied to Hanshue, too, for he had his doubts about the potentiality of passenger traffic between Los Angeles and Salt Lake City. If he had won the Chicago–San Francisco route, it would have been a different ball game: Salt Lake City would have been fed by traffic from both of the two biggest West Coast cities.

But Pop was only temporarily thwarted, not licked, by the CAM-18 defeat. He moved cautiously through the first half of 1927, concentrating on increased efficiency in the mail service and dipping Western's toes most tentatively in the waters of expansion. He tried, for example, several fare-reduction plans—first a special half-price summer rate, then cutting the one-way tariff between Los Angeles and Salt Lake City from ninety dollars to seventy-five dollars and finally down to sixty dollars (roughly the same fare that exists today). He signed, along with three other airlines, a contract with the American Railway Express Company to fly small express shipments. The terms were generous, the airline getting 75 per cent of the revenue from each shipment, but the volume of parcels carried was small—in 1928, the first full year of express service, Western grossed slightly more than five thousand dollars, compared to mail revenues of more than a million.

While neither the various fare-reduction schemes nor the new express service resulted in much more than a trickle of fresh income, mail profits soared higher than the planes flying the bulging sacks. The Post Office Department itself contributed to the increasing popularity of air mail by abolishing, early in 1927, the cumbersome zone system for postage, replacing it with a flat nationwide rate of ten cents for every half ounce. No one, Hanshue included, could believe the black-ink figures pouring in daily. It cost Western less than four hundred dollars to operate a single flight between California and Utah, but it was grossing up to fifteen hundred dollars per trip.

In September, the Post Office announced it would accept bids on CAM-12, a north-to-south spur route between Cheyenne, Wyoming, and Pueblo, Colorado, via Denver and Colorado Springs. Originally, CAM-12 had been operated by Colorado Airways, headed by Anthony F. Joseph, but the route involved treacherous and difficult terrain which, combined with Joseph's inexperience, led to Colorado's early demise. At this point, Hanshue was bating only .333 in his route applications. When he successfully bid on CAM-4, he also put in a halfhearted offer to operate CAM-8 between Los Angeles and Seattle—a route that Western flies today in competition with United. He was easily outbid by Vern C. Gorst, an Oregon bus operator who decided to get into the airline business because he didn't want planes competing with his buses; Gorst started Pacific Air Transport, which eventually was merged into United.

Western's second CAM defeat had involved the Chicago–San Francisco route, but Hanshue now was ready to raise his average to an even .500. His bid for CAM-12 was accepted, and Hanshue then made his second major aircraft purchase, ordering three Stearman open-cockpit biplanes for delivery in time to start service on the newly acquired route by mid-December. Woolley dutifully plugged the Stearmans as glowing examples of aeronautical engineering genius and, along with numerous other Western officials and employees, wondered when they were going to get some bigger airplanes.

The time was coming.

On September 30, Hanshue mailed a letter to every Western Air Express stockholder, brief but in significance amounting to an opus of financial and future import.

> There is inclosed herewith a check in the amount of your participation in what is believed to be the first earned dividend ever distributed by a company en-

gaged solely in transportation by airplane and entirely dependent for its revenue upon patronage of the service offered. . . .

Hanshue's additional reference to "furtherance of an expansion policy immediately impending" was no idle boast nor promise. He already had been to New York where, with a number of other airline executives, he had met with Harry Guggenheim, who was administering his father's Fund for the Promotion of Aeronautics. The sober-faced assembly of air carrier operators listened as Guggenheim read the fund's objectives: ". . . to promote aeronautical education throughout the country, to assist in the extension of aeronautical science, and to further the development of commercial aircraft, particularly in its use as a regular means of transportation of both goods and people."

Guggenheim had his doubts about the fund's prospects even before the airline participants arrived. Most of them had received invitations accompanied by railroad tickets—they had passed the word that if they had to fly to New York, no thanks. And at the meeting, Guggenheim took due note of the fact that only two of those who showed up displayed any interest. They were Walter Varney and Harris Hanshue.

Hanshue returned to Los Angeles and continued to correspond with the Guggenheims, who were impressed not only by Western's record but also by the bluff, open personality of its president. Of all the grants and loans the fund was to make throughout the aviation and educational systems, none carried the historical importance of what Western Air Express received before 1927 was over, for Harry Guggenheim and Pop Hanshue shared a mutual conviction: that the airlines could not progress if almost totally dependent on mail pay. And accompanying that mutual conviction was a mutual belief: The future of commercial aviation lay in the development of passenger traffic.

The fund's offer to Western Air Express was simple but vital in its long-range consequences. Guggenheim would lend the airline $180,000 to launch a "Model Airway" between Los Angeles and San Francisco, the money to be used for the purchase of suitable passenger-carrying aircraft for the airway's operation. The only stipulation was that the planes could haul only passengers—which wasn't much of a stipulation, inasmuch as WAE couldn't fly mail over a route for which it held no air mail contract. Nevertheless, in a financial sense, this was akin to telling Western it had to fly the airplanes without fuel. An outright grant of $60,000 was made for purchase of ground facilities.

There were no strings attached to the loan, mainly because Guggenheim didn't expect to be paid back and frankly told Hanshue the $180,000 was more in the nature of an outright grant. Typically, Hanshue refused to accept the money as a gift. He insisted on inserting into an official agreement a clause requiring that the loan be repaid within eighteen months, and that Western Air Express would pay 5 per cent interest per annum on the amount. Hanshue also put up some $100,000 in public-utilities securities to guarantee the loan. The surprised fund officials accepted this proviso, still expecting Western to default; it didn't, and repaid the $180,000 before the end of 1929.

Just as he once had organized an airline on paper, with no planes and no employees, now Hanshue had himself a new 365-mile route between California's two biggest cities—and no aircraft to fly it. The ink was scarcely dry on the Guggenheim contract when Pop went shopping—with a list of specifications for the airplane he wanted: a cruising speed of at least 120 miles an hour; multi-engined for safety; capacity for ten or more passengers and one thousand pounds of cargo; a range of six hours' flying time without refueling; a ceiling of sixteen thousand feet.

He circulated the specifications among airframe and engine manufacturers not only in the United States but also abroad, but his first inspection stop was virtually in his own backyard—the Douglas plant in Santa Monica. It was only too natural for him to turn to the builders of the gallant M-2, but this time Donald Douglas had nothing satisfactory either on the shelf or on the drawing board. Douglas did offer Western two airplanes that had just barely reached the blueprint stage—a twin-engine airliner called the Wasp, and a trimotor. Neither was ever built, although the price tags were attractive: $34,000 for the Wasp and $44,500 for the trimotor. Douglas might have built the trimotor if Western had shown interest, but both designs were too far away from actual construction to be practical, and their projected specifications fell short of what Hanshue was seeking.

There was a U.S. transport plane available when Hanshue began his search for the Model Airway's flight equipment—and that was the redoubtable Ford trimotor. The initial version, called the 4-AT, was designed and built in the unheard-of time of four months; the first one to come off the assembly line had an open cockpit, demanded by Ford test pilots who claimed a closed cockpit wasn't safe because they couldn't feel the wind on their faces! This pilot-dictated deficiency was corrected quickly in subsequent models which, it must be pointed out, met many of Hanshue's specifications. The new Ford was enormously strong with its all-metal construction, carried twelve passengers, climbed nine hundred feet a minute to a maximum ceiling of sixteen thousand feet, hauled a ton of payload on a six-hour flight without refueling, cruised in excess of one hundred miles an hour, could become airborne in three plane lengths, climbed on two engines, and could maintain level flight on one engine.

It probably always will be a mystery why Hanshue rejected the Ford or, for that matter, why he evidently never even considered it seriously. One possible though not entirely plausible explanation is that he was prejudiced against the airplane because of the bad experience with the Stout.

Possibly, Hanshue may have been wary about the Ford's metal construction, which was a relatively new development in the United States. Junkers long ago had proved that an all-metal plane was not only practical but also safer, but there was widespread suspicion in the United States—to such an extent that one top airline official was quoted in the press as declaring that "the fabric-covered plane can be maintained over a long period much more economically than the all-metal plane." Hanshue wasn't the executive who offered this dubious assessment, but he may very well have believed it at the time; he was a businessman, not an aeronautical engineer, and as a businessman he turned not to the relatively new Ford but to a well-tested aircraft with a proud lineage.

He ordered three new Fokker F-10s, designed and built by the renowned Anthony Fokker of the Netherlands. The $70,000 base price was much higher than that of the Ford, which was being offered at $50,000, but the F-10 was superior in several respects with one key exception: It was built primarily of wood, and it lacked the American plane's incredible sturdiness. On the other hand, the Fokker predated the 4-AT by almost two years and was a more proven airplane. It cruised just under 120 miles per hour, 20 miles per hour faster than the Ford. Its payload was greater, nearly 2,500 pounds, with a service ceiling of 18,000 feet and as high as 7,000 feet on two engines. Its climb rate of 1,400 feet a minute far exceeded the Ford's.

As a matter of fact, there was a good deal of Fokker in the Ford. The very concept of a three-engine transport plane came from Tony Fokker, and externally the two trimotors were virtual twins—a layman could tell them apart only by the Ford's "washboard" corrugated aluminum skin (which, in turn, was borrowed from the Junkers). Fokker brought his trimotor to the United States in 1925 for demonstration purposes, a year before the 4-AT made its first flight. It would be unfair, of course, to accuse Ford of copying the Dutch plane, because the internal differences were far more important than the external resemblance, but Fokker himself always thought the Ford was more imitation than innovation.

The Ford's all-metal construction was largely responsible for the Fokker's over-all superiority in many areas of performance. The former weighed 6,500 pounds empty, compared to the slightly larger Fokker's 2,000 pounds: Tony Fokker's plane had a tubular steel fuselage, but the rest of the aircraft was wood and fabric. It was much quieter than the Ford, too, with better soundproofing and less vibration—even the Ford's most vociferous supporters concede it probably was the noisiest airplane ever built.

The Fokker's American-made engines were a decided asset in overcoming any prejudice passengers might have against a foreign-designed airplane, and the F-10 itself was built in the United States—Fokker had established the Fokker Aircraft Corporation of America, with factories in West Virginia and New Jersey. Curiously enough, though, there never seemed to be any bias involving the Fokker's foreign bloodlines; Fokker's own brilliant reputation was the main antidote, and so was the F-10's immense size for those days. Its wingspan of 79 feet and fuselage length of 50 feet (the comparative wingspan and fuselage dimensions of Western's smallest jet, the Boeing 737, are 93 feet and 94 feet, respectively) imparted a feeling of security and safety. After all, few Americans had ever seen a plane of this size, and if Lindbergh could fly the Atlantic in a tiny single-engine ship, this giant *had* to be three times safer.

These were busy and hectic times for Pop Hanshue, who had confided to a friend, when Hanshue was organizing Western Air Express, "I'll stay in this business a year and if things don't work out, I'll quit." Now he was up to the proverbial armpits with assorted projects, plans, and problems—the major one being the launching of the Model Airway, as early in 1928 as possible. Simultaneously with this massive advance preparation went the task of taking over CAM-12. December 10, 1927, was the starting date for service, and Hanshue, accompanied by Moseley, was in Denver to await arrival of the first flight from Pueblo in one of the new Stearmans. Western by then had added a number of new pilots to the roster, and the Four Horsemen weren't involved in this inaugural. The pilot who brought the ship into Denver drew Moseley to one side.

"I ran into a lot of snow," he reported. "It's murder up there."

Moseley turned to the airman scheduled to fly the Denver–Cheyenne leg, a young pilot named Taylor.

"If it looks too bad, come back," Moseley cautioned. "And whatever you do, don't get into the overcast, stay underneath."

Taylor nodded, climbed into the Stearman, and took off. Moseley, Hanshue, and the small crowd that had come out to welcome the mail flight watched the plane circle the field and then disappear as it headed north. A few minutes later they heard its engine, throbbing gradually louder as Taylor apparently was following Moseley's orders and returning. No one could see the plane through the thick overcast, and suddenly the growl of the engine began diminishing, again fading to the north.

"He must have changed his mind and gone on," Moseley worried out loud. Hanshue said nothing, his heavy face frowning. They were talking to some Denver city officials when Moseley was called to the phone. A reporter told him that Taylor had crashed.

"Is he . . . ?" Moseley started to ask.

"He's dead," the reporter said.

Western had suffered its first crash. Fortunately, Taylor was the only one aboard the mailplane, but his fate got Hanshue to thinking about his pilots' happy-go-lucky attitude when it came to financial security. What with mail pay added to their base wages and frequent tips from grateful passengers, the senior airmen like the Four Horsemen sometimes seemed to have more ready cash than Hanshue himself, who was making a modest $12,000 a year as president. But most of them were incapable of hanging onto it for any length of time, and Pop, very paternalistic in his gruff way, knew that a fatal accident could leave a pilot's family destitute.

It was then that he gave Western's flight crews their first fringe benefit: He bought life insurance policies for all of them, listing their families as the beneficiaries. It was a generous and welcome gesture that assured pilot loyalty toward the company —although it came just too late to keep DeGarmo from reducing the Four Horsemen to the Three Horsemen.

DeGarmo was making $150 a month plus one and a half cents a mile in mail pay when Boeing Air Transport, seeking experienced pilots, offered him the same base salary and $.05 a mile. Al wanted to stay with Western and asked Moseley for a raise. Mose, a tight man with a company buck, flatly refused. A few weeks later DeGarmo walked into Moseley's office.

"I'm going to work for Boeing," he announced.

"When?" Moseley demanded.

"As of right now."

"The hell you are," Moseley shouted. "You're flying the first run today."

"The hell I am," DeGarmo said calmly. "I quit."

Years later, DeGarmo was to confess, "I should have stayed with Western," but at the time all he regretted was breaking up the Four Horsemen. He always kept in touch and maintained the close friendship, and even today is openly and touchingly proud that he was one of Western's original pilots. Moseley's stiff rejection hurt him, not merely because it forced him to leave the airline but also because they were good friends.

It might be speculated what would have happened if DeGarmo had gone over Moseley's head—right up to Hanshue, whom the pilots liked even though they never got particularly close to him. As far as is known, DeGarmo left before Hanshue found out about it, which was unfortunate; Pop, already arguing frequently with Moseley, might have overruled him in DeGarmo's case.

Hanshue, of course, was embroiled in too many major demands on his time to worry about a single pilot. He was able to tell stockholders at the end of 1927 that Western Air Express had netted almost $307,000 during the year—amounting to $72.60 per share of stock issued and outstanding; the original shareholders had tripled the value of their investment in less than two years. It was an auspicious ending for the year just past, and an equally auspicious start for the critical twelve months ahead—the year of the Model Airway.

Salesman Hanshue and promoter Woolley formed a two-man team loaded with ingenuity, imagination, and perseverance, which is exactly what the Model Airway demanded if there was to be any chance of success.

For Woolley, the chance to sell air travel was like elevating a Los Angeles Coliseum gate guard to first-string quarterback on the Rams. Gone were the days when his proudest accomplishment was to tie in the exploits of Western Air Express to the consumption of California orange juice. This involved a joint advertising project extolling the virtues of the airline and the juice firm; the ad carried the headline, SIPPING AND ZIPPING THROUGH THE AIR, followed by this text:

> Passengers and pilots of the Western Air Express flying 600 miles between Los Angeles and Salt Lake City in six hours carry luncheons including Mission Orange Juice in Thermos bottles. Since its first flight seven months ago, Western Air Express has carried more than 200 passengers and 25 per cent of all U.S. Air Mail.

Naturally, the ad refrained from mentioning that in most cases, the passengers were forced to savor the delicious beverage while sitting uncomfortably atop a mail sack. Now, however, Woolley had something legitimate to brag about—the plans he and Hanshue were drawing up for the Model Airway called for standards of service and safety not only nonexistent in the

United States but also exceeding anything developed to date in Europe. To handle the promotion/advertising workload, Hanshue let Woolley hire four public-relations assistants—one of them a young newspaperman from Montana, Clancy Dayhoff, who was to become something of an airline legend in his own right.

The fact that Western took on as many PR types to help launch the Model Airway as the number of pilots it hired to start the airline itself was indicative of the importance Hanshue attached to the public-relations operation. The pilot force, of course, had been greatly expanded by this time—and no one could complain about the quality of the new airmen joining the WAE roster.

There was Silas "Si" Morehouse, one of Fokker's best test pilots . . . colorful Royal Leonard, who would someday become Chiang Kai-shek's personal pilot . . . Ralph Montee, a barnstorming veteran who knew California's varied terrain better than he did the rooms in his own house . . . George Rice, a camera nut whose most prized picture was a snapshot of a mailplane's smoking wreckage—the same aircraft he had just evacuated, unhurt . . . H. H. "Dutch" Holloway, another barnstormer but an unusual one in that he had made his precarious living in a flying boat around the San Francisco Bay area.

More than six months' preparation went into the actual start of Los Angeles–San Francisco service. Woolley and his quartet of youthful assistants, with Hanshue contributing his own share of ideas, went all-out. As the various plans and schemes sifted through gestation, discussion, approval, and finally implementation, Woolley's initial major effort was distribution of thousands of attractive little brochures describing the upcoming joys to be experienced on the Model Airway. One cannot resist quoting a few paragraphs, along with some gentle observations as to the accuracy of a few of Woolley's claims—remembering that the pamphlet was written long before the first passenger was booked and the first flight took off.

"Western Air Liners are all of the tri-motored salon type, insulated and upholstered. All engine noises and vibrations are eliminated." (The second sentence has to be questioned; the Fokker *was* relatively quiet, easily the quietest airliner then in service, but it was by no means free of all noise and vibration, and by today's standards it would be unbearable.)

"The Express Cruisers accommodate 15 passengers, individually seated in upholstered lounge-type chairs beside windows which can be opened or shut at pleasure." (Woolley was being either overoptimistic or was badly informed when he boasted of a 15-passenger capacity for the F-10. Western ordered the aircraft with 12 seats, and where the vice president of traffic got the figure 15 wasn't clear; he probably included the three-man crew —two pilots and a steward.)

"Stewards are constantly in attendance and are capable pilots themselves." (There is no record of any early WAE steward being a qualified transport pilot, although a few may have had some flying lessons and might even have earned a limited license. Woolley apparently was referring to the initial practice of having the copilot double as a flight attendant.)

"Most insurance companies include air travel risks on regular air lines in ordinary policies. Special insurance, if desired, can be arranged on booking transportation." (The word "most" was stretching the truth a bit; in 1928, only a handful of insurance underwriters included air travel in regular policies, and then only when stiff additional premiums were paid. Many policies, in fact, were voided once a policyholder stepped aboard a plane and were not actuated again until the air trip was over. It was 1937 before air travel insurance became available to the general public at reasonable rates—$.25 for $5,000 worth of protection. The "special insurance" mentioned in the brochure was, indeed, available, but at such prohibitive cost that few ever bought it. It already has been pointed out that Hanshue was forced to set up Western's own crash insurance reserve because of the high premium rates, and the insurance he bought for pilots was equally exorbitant.)

Woolley's promotion copy invariably referred to the F-10's interior as "equaling the appointments of the most modern Pullman." It fell far short of that boast, but for its day it wasn't any slum area. The Fokker's cabin was finished in mahogany and light pile fabric—far plusher than any of the early Fords that went into airline service. There were cabin dome lights for reading, and overhead baggage racks, a wide aisle with six feet of headroom floor to ceiling, and the rather thickly upholstered seats with full armrests plus ashtrays were vastly superior to the wicker spine-torturers on the initial Fords. "Leviathan of the Air," a Fokker advertisement described the F-10, and the plane really was a giant in those days. Actually, it was too much aircraft for a single pilot, who would have needed the physical endowments of an octopus to cope with all the new cockpit gimmicks.

The F-10's size, in fact, is believed to have led to the first designation of the pilot-in-command as "captain," although the man in the right seat wasn't called "copilot" until a few years later. Pan American and Western began referring to the commanding pilot as captains at about the same time, the former also acquiring Fokker trimotors. Because Juan Trippe insisted on using nautical terms, Pan Am's copilots were called "first officers"—something the airline industry wasn't to adopt for a long time. Woolley's aforementioned brochure listed the left-seat occupant as "pilot captain" and his colleague as "pilot mate."

The WAE Fokker pilots had it almost as good as the passengers, with such innovations as landing-gear brakes and a lighted instrument panel in which were set no less than twenty-two instruments and switches. What they liked most of all was the F-10's speed; what they disliked was its tendency to roll in turbulence, attributed mostly to its relatively light weight for a plane of its dimensions. This was one of the few problems Hanshue couldn't foresee in his advance planning; the airsickness "burp" bags he ordered were so small a passenger had trouble spitting into one. For as long as Western flew the Fokkers, passengers were grateful for those "windows which can be opened or shut at pleasure." It was easier to open a window and heave than throw up in a burp bag. Airsickness on the F-10 was so prevalent that planes frequently had to be hosed out after landing, and one later-day pilot named Ed Chapman invented a spray deodorizer on which he reportedly made a modest fortune. (Pop's mistake in ordering undersized bags didn't match the boner pulled by American Airlines some years later. The airline bought a few hundred thousand ice cream containers, which would have made excellent burp bags except for one tiny item—no one at American noticed that each container carried the imprinted message: "Thank You—Come Again.")

Western's Fokkers amounted to a deluxe version, including

twelve seats made-to-order with extra padding. The whole package upped the price to some $80,000 per plane, Western using
the entire amount of the $180,000 loan toward the F-10 purchase
and paying the remaining $60,000 from its own cash reserves.

The F-10's rough-weather idiosyncrasies didn't show up to any
great extent on the Model Airway, and for a very good reason.
The Guggenheim Fund insisted on assigning a prominent meteorologist, Sweden's Dr. Carl Gustav-Rossby, to Western, and this
expert established a network of 37 weather-observation stations
between Los Angeles and San Francisco, which ate up most of
the $60,000 grant for ground facilities. Many were in remote
areas and could have been mistaken for forest ranger fire-lookout
installations. They all employed the latest scientific weather-observation equipment, including instrumented balloons sent aloft
to measure winds and visibility. The data the stations submitted
were telegraphed or phoned to Gustav-Rossby in Los Angeles;
Gustav-Rossby would issue the weather advisories to pilots at
both ends of the Model Airway, giving them a choice of five
already-surveyed routes, and the crews selected the one with the
most favorable weather conditions. Also set up before the airway
opened were a number of intermediate landing fields, most of
them close to the primary route, which was laid out rather informally. A group of pilots were sitting around one day and got to
discussing the various routes they might follow. Dutch Holloway
whipped out a ruler, lined it up between Los Angeles and the
Bay cities on a map, and drew a straight line. That was the
course Western's pilots flew most frequently, weather permitting,
not only when the Model Airway was in operation but even
today.

The emphasis on weather reporting reflected Guggenheim's
and Hanshue's priority to safety. The experiment was aimed at
learning whether an airline could make money without mail pay.
It was not enough to talk the fearful into luxurious planes; the
public also had to be convinced it was safe to fly, and accurate
weather forecasts were a prime factor. Hanshue knew that one
bad crash would offset all the fancy services, plush cabin inte-
riors, and glowing reassurances pouring out of the typewriters of
Woolley and his eager associates.

If safety received No. 1 priority, however, service came in a close second. The first really palatable in-flight meals became a feature on the Model Airway—thick, succulent sandwiches and hot coffee prepared by a well-known Los Angeles restaurant called the Pig 'n Whistle, which charged Western $1.50 per sandwich. With the food went a Woolley literary masterpiece—an elaborate booklet titled *The Log of My Flight Between Los Angeles and San Francisco Via Western Air Express*. The verbose title did nothing to detract from the publication's quality; handsomely bound in birchwood parchment, it included space for entering statistical data on the flight, a history of California, a detailed map of the route, aerial views of the terminal cities, information on both Western and the F-10, and a few aviation facts and figures. The booklet cost the airline considerably more per copy than what the Pig 'n Whistle was getting for each sandwich, but the salesman in Hanshue loved it and considered the expenditure worthwhile.

From the standpoint of service, the outstanding innovation was the employment of the nation's first cabin attendants—all men. Stewards were nothing new in commercial aviation—some European airlines had flight attendants as far back as 1919—but Western became the first U.S. carrier to hire them. With a bit more foresight in those male chauvinist days, it also could have become the first airline in the world to employ stewardesses, but not even Woolley thought of this gimmick—which wasn't surprising, inasmuch as some of the pilots even objected to women passengers. By passing up this chance to make some additional aviation history on the precedent-breaking Model Airway, Western surrendered the honor of putting the first stewardesses on airplanes to Boeing Air Transport, a United predecessor; Boeing in 1930 assigned eight registered nurses to its flight, and Western was not to hire female flight attendants until 1935.

The new stewards served meals, handed out free daily newspapers, answered questions, and fulfilled the chief duty of all early-day cabin attendants: Look happy, no matter what. Ground service matched in-flight service in pampering the customers. Western shelled out two thousand dollars for a Cadillac, which it leased to a young driver for fifty dollars a week. The driver, Joe Ferrante, eventually parlayed this single-car operation into a fleet of airport limousines, but while the Model Airway existed, he ran the Cadillac for the exclusive—and free—use of Western's passengers. Another car was based at the Oakland airport, the airway's northern terminus.

Hanshue was shooting for a starting date of around May 1, 1928, but there were too many uncompleted details, too many last-minute problems, too many unexpected difficulties to meet this deadline. Fokker's aircraft deliveries were delayed, not by much but enough to set the inaugural date back a few weeks. The three red Fokkers, each carrying the Indian head on its fuselages, left New York May 13 on a nationwide goodwill tour, stopped at forty cities in six days, and reached the West Coast only a week before the inaugural northbound and southbound flights.

It might have been expected that a couple of Horsemen would take out the first trips, but the delivery delays plus the publicity tour made it impossible for them to be checked out in the F-10 and go through the route familiarization routine in one week. Hanshue yielded to no man in sentimentality, but the stakes in the Model Airway were too high to take any chances on pilots inexperienced in handling an aircraft as large as the Fokker. The two pilots given the honor had several hundred hours on Fokkers. And that was typical of Pop, a remarkable figure among those airline pioneers. Essentially a promoter/salesman at heart, he bowed with instinctive alacrity to safety as the cornerstone of any successful airline operation.

Safety was not just a creed but also a religion to this man who launched Western Air Express as an aviation neophyte, yet was blessed with farsighted wisdom. He assigned to the Model Airway "ground operators" who today would be called flight dispatchers, and he laid down a strict rule: A ground operator could order a pilot not to take off, but he never could order him into the air.

"It is far more important," Hanshue told them, "to reach a destination than merely to keep operating efficiency at 100 per cent."

This was the philosophy he had injected into the minds and hearts of every Western employee by May 26, 1928—inaugural day for the Model Airway and the beginning of a daring and gallant experiment. A nation would be watching its success or

failure, and so would Hanshue's colleagues in the airline industry, who already had demonstrated their respect for him by
electing him president of their newly formed trade organization,
the American Air Transport Association. Tingeing the respect,
however, was an element of covetous envy, a kind of wary suspicion that this upstart from the West had to be watched. They
were something of pirates in those days, Hanshue included—a
brotherhood of buccaneers whose common bond was adversity
but with fragile loyalties that lasted only until the next raid into
another man's domain. It was a loosely regulated industry at
best, the limited number of government air mail contracts
(thirty-two in all) being the only federal club held over their
heads. In this permissive atmosphere, territorial invasion was
natural strategy, merger a frequently used device, backroom
deals a way of life. Because only the mail routes were inviolate
jurisdictions, development of all-passenger markets beckoned
every entrepreneur owning more than one airplane.

And this gave the forthcoming Western/Guggenheim experiment the status of a giant test tube.

CHAPTER FOUR

"The Only Way to Travel . . ."

All the fanfare whipped up by Woolley and his ballyhooing cohorts made May 26, 1928, a major event, with wide press coverage and a highly satisfying public response.

Thousands of spectators turned out at the Los Angeles and Oakland airports to witness the simultaneous 10:30 A.M. takeoffs. In only one respect had Woolley failed to live up to his advance blurbs: There was no special "steward" aboard either plane, for the respective copilots were to serve the lunch. There hadn't been enough time to interview, hire, and train flight attendants; stewards would be working the trips in a short time, but on Inaugural Day and for a short time thereafter, the "pilot mates," as Woolley had ingloriously dubbed them, would serve the cold fried chicken, sandwiches, fruit, cake, and coffee. One of the Model Airway's quickest revelations was the impossibility of assigning cabin duties to the copilot—the F-10 was too big an airplane to warrant the luxury of keeping the second pilot "constantly in attendance," as Woolley had so rashly promised.

The two Fokkers passed each other at precisely the halfway point, and both landed on schedule. The passengers, who had paid fifty dollars apiece for the three-hour flight, all expressed delight with their experience.

"The only way to travel," one beamed—unknowingly coming close to what four decades later would be Western's advertising slogan.

A more pertinent comment on the opening of the Model Airway came from Howard Waldorf, aviation editor of the Oakland

Post-Enquirer, one of the earliest and best of what is now a fast-vanishing breed of aviation writing specialists. He covered the takeoff of the first northbound flight, commanded by ex-Fokker test pilot Si Morehouse, and some seventeen years later Waldorf wrote this recollection of May 26:

"To me, the outstanding picture of the event was seeing the pilot go on board with a weather report and forecast in his hand. It was truly the launching of a new era in air transportation."

Waldorf took at least one of the pre-inaugural demonstration flights that Woolley staged for the benefit of the press and city officials.

"Seats so comfortable you could loll back and go to sleep to the restful drone of the three engines," he remembered. "Plenty of leg room and an aisle you could walk up and down while the ship was in the air."

The so-called Model Airway experiment never really ended; rather, it gradually was absorbed into Western's normal operations, and the lessons learned were incorporated into the airline's procedures and policies. In a technical sense, it terminated when Hanshue repaid the Guggenheim loan in full before 1929 was over. There is some dispute as to how many passengers the Model Airway innovation attracted. From all available evidence, the Los Angeles–San Francisco traffic in the first year probably totaled about five thousand passengers—not a bad showing, but insufficient to put the Model Airway in the black. In other words, judged solely by a financial yardstick, the experiment failed in that it demonstrated the futility of trying to make money with an all-passenger operation.

But more was involved than cold profit-vs.-loss figures, and in all other respects the Model Airway was a smash hit. Financial flop, yes—it literally was subsidized by Western's profits from the two air mail routes, profits so huge that Hanshue not only was able to repay Guggenheim but still reported a 1928 net of nearly $700,000 from revenues of some $1.4 million. Mail payments accounted for more than $1.2 million of the gross, passenger revenue about $133,000, and charters made up the rest (plus a modest $177 from excess baggage charges, a pretty good indication that businessmen made up the bulk of passenger volume, with vacation and pleasure trips by air extremely rare).

Disappointed though he was at the Model Airway's deficit, Hanshue still insisted that passenger traffic was the wave of the future. Unlike many industry executives who would have tossed nonmail expansion in the nearest wastebasket after that Model Airway experiment, Pop grasped its far greater implications. The Fokkers had achieved an almost unbelievable on-time performance of 99 per cent, with a perfect safety record; obviously the expensive but valuable weather network had paid off in establishing crew and public confidence alike. The stations were reporting weather conditions covering forty miles on each side of the route flown. The system's only weakness was that the reports had to be transmitted either to Oakland or Los Angeles, and if conditions changed drastically during the course of a three-hour flight, there was no way to warn the pilot.

This Achilles' heel led to one of aviation's greatest safety developments: two-way radio communications, ground-to-air and vice versa. Early in 1929, Western hired as its communication chief a young graduate of Stanford University with a master's degree from Harvard. He was, in a way, inherited from the Guggenheim Fund, which had granted him a fellowship to study airline economics. His greatest love, however, was not economics but radio—he had been tinkering with radio sets since he was fourteen years old. Western hired him for his knowledge, not his name, which happened to be Herbert Clark Hoover, Jr. If WAE officials expected him to toss weight around because his father was President of the United States, they were way off base. Young Hoover was quiet, intense, and effusive only about the job to which he had been assigned.

Eventually he was to set up a Western Air Express communications system starting with three small stations over the CAM-4 route and expanding this to twenty-seven stations spread over fifteen thousand miles of airways. His first task, however, was to refine work already accomplished jointly by Western engineers and an electronics wizard from Boeing Air Transport named Thorp Hiscock, who was to become a close friend and associate of Hoover. In November of 1928, the government granted both Western and Boeing experimental wavelengths for two-way communications, and Western had eleven of its aircraft so equipped A good many bugs had to be worked out before radios became standard equipment on the entire fleet, but the Western/Boeing collaboration went down in history as the first example of a safety problem relegating competition to the rear of the room.

By the end of 1928, Western's image had changed from that of a pioneering little airline of infant status to a fast-growing adolescent threatening to become a giant. In midyear, only a month after the Fokkers began flying the Los Angeles–San Francisco route, Hanshue had made his second expansion move: He bought Pacific Marine Airways and dovetailed this acquisition with the purchase of a nine-passenger Sikorsky S-38 amphibian for the Los Angeles–Catalina excursion market.

From expansion, Hanshue then turned to consolidation. For some time he had been watching developments throughout the airline industry that he considered dangerous to Western's very existence. There were storm clouds on the horizon, and most of them were coming from the East, where the mushrooming airline industry had begun attracting immense capital from nonaviation sources. Giant conglomerates were in their formative stages, and these included interlocking relationships between airlines and the airframe/engine manufacturers who supplied the former with their equipment—such as Boeing Air Transport, already married to the Boeing Airplane Company, which, just before 1928 passed into limbo, acquired Gorst's Pacific Air Transport.

Hanshue's acuity was as sharp as his tongue. He talked over the situation with Jim Talbot of Richfield Oil, one of the original WAE backers and by now Pop's major adviser in matters of high finance. Quietly they moved on two fronts aimed at (1) assuring Western of its aircraft needs and (2) increasing its financial strength.

Talbot and a few of the larger Western stockholders took the first step by acquiring control of the Fokker Aircraft Corporation of America.

Hanshue emphasized that a group of Western stockholders, not the airline itself, had bought into and taken over Fokker. Pop had adamantly rejected several offers to merge Western with aircraft companies, feeling—as he phrased it in the annual report— "that Western Air Express, although desiring close affiliation

with some builder, should be left free to buy its equipment anywhere without injury to its own pocketbook."

The result of the loose but effective tie-in with Fokker, he explained, was that "while Western Air Express is free to buy
equipment in the market from any aircraft builder, it can never
be rendered unable to secure satisfactory equipment by any
combination that might oppose it." The major advantage of the
Fokker acquisition by Western stockholders, Hanshue pointed
out, was to put control of the manufacturing company "into
the hands of those who by personal service and through investment have an abiding friendly interest in Western Air Express."

It was a slick and astute deal, and it was followed by another:
the original corporation, Western Air Express, Inc., of California,
became the holding company for a new corporation—Western
Air Express Corporation of Delaware, with capitalization increased to a solid $5 million. Behind what seemed at first glance
a mere financial technicality was Pop's inherent fear and suspicion of the eastern money tycoons. By incorporating in Delaware, he had gotten his foot inside the East's door in more ways
than one. Western became a stock listed on the New York Stock
Exchange, which assured wider distribution of holdings, and the
listing itself was a form of advertising. Most important—and this
was the wily Hanshue's reasoning—becoming an eastern corporation in effect was the initial stage to eventual expansion toward
the East—for Pop as much of an obsession as it was a dream.

Western Air Express, less than three years after Maury Graham
and Jimmie James kicked off service over CAM-4 in a pair of
red and silver biplanes, ended 1928 with 143 employees, including 18 pilots, and 25 airplanes flying 2,400 daily scheduled miles
—carrying nearly 6,000 passengers in the process. The third of
the three Fokkers bought with the Guggenheim loan was assigned
to the Los Angeles–Salt Lake City route, operating four trips a
week.

At the start of 1929, Hanshue called Herbert Hoover into his
office, the young engineer wondering what his blunt-speaking
boss could possibly want to discuss with a relatively lowly employee.

"What's the name of the government outfit you deal with?"

Hanshue said without preamble. "The one that gives out radio licenses."

"Federal Radio Commission, Mr. Hanshue," Hoover answered.

"Fine, I want you to apply for a license to operate an aircraft radio station at Chicago."

"Chicago? Mr. Hanshue, we don't even fly anywhere near Chicago. . . ."

"I know that," Hanshue snapped. "Apply for it anyway."

Hoover made out the necessary forms and mailed them in. He obtained the license eventually, but it never was to be used; even today, Western and National are the only major air carriers that do not serve Chicago. Yet Hanshue's order, probably stemming from sheer impulse, was just one more clue to his ambitious expansion plans. In the first month of the new year, again with Talbot's aid, he bought the majority interest in West Coast Air Transport, an all-passenger airline that had been operating between San Francisco and Seattle for about a year. By the time WAE acquired control, West Coast had become a subsidiary of Union Air Lines of Sacramento and was doing a fairly brisk business (five thousand passengers a year), using a little-known, undersized trimotor known as the Bach Air Yacht. West Coast owned eight of them, but Hanshue was interested in the route, not the planes.

Expansion was the order of the day, the battle cry, the trumpet sounding charge. It even affected the tiny Los Angeles–Catalina operations, with new excursion flights south to Tijuana and east to Palm Springs, the Colorado River, Boulder Dam, Death Valley, and the Mojave Desert. Service on CAM-4 was stepped up when the government completed installation of beacon lights over the entire route, permitting WAE to fly the mail at night. Fokker F-10s took over the daylight schedules, and Hanshue reached into the corporate coffers to buy new and more efficient mailplanes.

Practicality outweighed sentiment in this decision. The gutty little M-2s had reached the end of the line, their usefulness as planes wiped out by the Fokkers, and their efficiency deteriorating steadily as the Libertys wore out. Their replacement was the new Boeing 95—actually a modified version of a military fighter plane with tremendous speed. It was powered by a Hornet radial engine two hundred pounds lighter than the Liberty.

Hanshue, while CAM-4 still was Western's proverbial bread-and-butter route, still disliked the airline's increasing dependence on this solid but greatly restricted foundation—not when the whole airline industry was not merely growing but actually exploding. Typical was the birth of a new carrier, Transcontinental Air Transport or TAT, organized primarily by a brilliant and resourceful man who had just had one airline snatched rudely away from him. He was Clement M. Keys, described by one aviation historian as "studious, scholarly, and decisive"; he was a former financial editor of the *Wall Street Journal* who turned his journalistically acquired knowledge into formation of his own investment banking firm. During World War I, he became vice president of the Curtiss Aeroplane and Motor Company and wound up buying control of Curtiss at a bargain-basement price. Like Hanshue, he was a visionary; his creed was best expressed by the axiom for which he became famous: "Ten per cent of aviation is in the air; 90 per cent is on the ground." He was the first to apply this rule to organizational efforts, forming—in 1925—North American Aviation, which became a model for the future proliferation of interlocked aviation structures. Under the North American banner, he came close to starting an airline serving New York, Detroit, and Chicago, and he might have succeeded if Henry Ford hadn't pulled out of the project after evincing considerable interest.

Keys then raised a half-million dollars in Chicago to start National Air Transport (NAT), winning a bid for CAM-3 between Chicago and Dallas. NAT without question was the best-heeled airline in the country, boasting a total authorized capital of $10 million, and CAM-3 was a flying oil gusher—stretching as it did from the metropolis of the Midwest to oil-rich Texas via Kansas City and Oklahoma. Keys' right-hand man in NAT was an air mail specialist, Colonel Paul Henderson, who resigned as Assistant Postmaster General to become NAT's general manager.

NAT actually was owned by the Keys-created North American Aviation, which in itself was a $30 million aviation financing giant. It bought into several struggling carriers, including Mad-

dux Airlines—started by a Los Angeles car dealer named Jack
Maddux, who began by operating passenger flights between Los
Angeles and San Diego. Drawing from North America's ample
funds, Maddux was able to buy several Ford trimotors, which he
immediately pitted against Western's Fokkers over none other
than the original Model Airway. The Western-Maddux competition was fierce on that Los Angeles–San Francisco route, and
Maddux, although operating a somewhat more Spartan service,
eventually grabbed a good share of the market.

Keys had something more in common with Pop Hanshue than
business acumen—they both coveted a transcontinental route.
Where they differed markedly was in attitude. Hanshue had
quickly become an *airline* man, in the sense that he regarded the
development of passenger traffic as essential to aviation's growth.
Keys was a cold-blooded businessman who at first didn't care
what his airplanes carried so long as a flight was profitable, and
that meant a damn-the-passenger philosophy. If the mail was the
only chance to make a buck, then in Keys' eyes mail was all that
mattered. He not only regarded passengers as a general nuisance
but he actually doubled NAT's fares to discourage anyone from
flying. This was in stark contrast to Hanshue's *modus operandi* of
special promotional fares, such as a 33⅓ per cent slash in 1929
summer rates to encourage vacation air travel. Keys shunned
publicity for his airline or himself; Woolley had Hanshue's carte
blanche to send a photographer to an airport whenever anyone
remotely approaching prominence boarded or deplaned from a
WAE flight.

Keys came around to Hanshue's optimism concerning the potentiality of passenger traffic only when the Model Airway demonstrated it was operationally sound, particularly in long-haul
markets. That added up to transcontinental routes, and Keys
marched swiftly in that direction. The Canadian-born wizard
behind NAT and North American Aviation first went after Boeing Air Transport, openly coveting its Chicago–San Francisco
authority.

Unfortunately for Keys, his airline acquisition and organizational formula wasn't copyrighted. Taking a page right out of
the North American invasion manual, Boeing beat Keys to the
punch. Bill Boeing already had merged Boeing Air Transport

with the airplane division, forming the Boeing Airplane and Transport Company. He next bought a welcome suggestion from his old friend Fred Rentschler of Pratt & Whitney: Merge their two companies, the combined giant to be known as United Aircraft and Transport Corporation. They didn't stop there; under United's flag, in swift succession, went Chance Vought (a successful builder of Navy planes), the Hamilton Propeller Company, Stearman Aircraft, and Sikorsky Aviation. The result was an aviation colossus capitalized to the tune of $146 million.

Keys lost more than his fight to grab control of Boeing Air Transport. United Aircraft staged a secret raid right into NAT's backyard, acquiring one third of its stock from many of the Chicago backers who had helped Keys start the airline. The infighting was brutal, Keys finally meeting defeat on the battleground of a court case. Just prior to a showdown meeting of NAT shareholders, Keys had changed the bylaws to reduce the quorum limitation by a whopping one third, and also issued three hundred thousand new shares to North American Aviation, the conglomerate which he himself controlled. By winning the shareholders battle, he lost the war; a court ruled his last-ditch maneuvers illegal, and United Aircraft took over NAT, making it part of the great system that was to become United Airlines.

Undaunted, Keys did what comes naturally to an entrepreneur of his caliber: He started a new airline, namely TAT. And this was to bring him in direct conflict with Hanshue and Western Air Express, inasmuch as both carriers were avidly seeking a new transcontinental route. To Hanshue, the issue was crucial. As he explained to Talbot, Garland, and other top associates, there had to be another transcontinental route soon and possibly two—one running through Kansas City and the other via the as-yet virtually untouched Southwest. Western, he argued, had to get at least one of these or its very life was threatened.

"Come on, Pop," Talbot challenged, "is it really that serious?"

"It's a matter of Western's survival," Hanshue said firmly. "Look, sooner or later you're going to have a second transcontinental route to the East via Kansas City. Its western section would be flown over the terrain lying south of the Rockies. The guy who operates that route is going to divert every bit of traffic from our Los Angeles–Salt Lake City route he can possibly grab.

Anyone who wants to fly farther east than Salt Lake City sure as hell isn't going to fly Western. He'll go from Los Angeles to Kansas City, or if he lives in northern California he'll take Boeing from San Francisco to Chicago. And where the hell does that leave us? I'll tell you where: we'll end up as a half-assed spur line starting in LA and stopping in Salt Lake City, which is exactly where we started!"

With fight talks such as this, Pop won an immediate green light to commence planning for expansion eastward. Survey flights began over the proposed Los Angeles–Kansas City route, radio and weather stations were installed, and 10 new Fokker F-10s were ordered. When Hanshue found out that the government hadn't gotten around to installing beacons over a 245-mile stretch, he advanced $35,000 to finish the job and accepted a Post Office Department promise to repay the money.

Inevitably, Western's ambitious plans reached the radarlike ears of Mr. Clement M. Keys, who was busy making his own preparations. It was indicative of the respect held for Hanshue throughout aviation that Keys at first tried to steer away from direct competition. In setting up TAT, he had sold the Pennsylvania Railroad on a proposal to operate a plane-train transcontinental service between New York and Los Angeles via Columbus; Kansas City; Waynoka, Oklahoma; and Clovis, New Mexico. At the time he came up with the idea, there were no lighted airways along most of the route, so Keys suggested that passengers fly during the day and shift to trains at night. The combination would make possible a forty-eight-hour schedule instead of the more than three or four days an all-train trip required.

Aware of Hanshue's own plans and equally aware of his reputation for moving fast and capably, Keys wrote him and asked that he attend a meeting at Keys' home in New York City. The subject: a TAT-Western merger, to establish a new single transportation system between New York and Los Angeles via Kansas City, starting with the train/plane combination but eventually becoming an all-air operation. Hanshue discussed the offer with the WAE directors and got their permission to decline not only an immediate merger but even the meeting to discuss the possibilities. His letter, quoted in part, outlined the reasons for his refusal on both counts:

> We believe the future problems of a transcontinental air and train, or all-air service, should await further development before attempting to join these forces into a one-company operation.
>
> As an alternative, we suggest joining with you in a transcontinental service, each company providing equipment and operating independently in its particular territory to meet the necessities of a continuous through service.
>
> We are substantially influenced by the fact that we are a western group of men for the primary purpose of serving a populous center of the western territory. We are experienced in and equipped for flying in the high western altitude and over western terrain. If we permit ourselves to become absorbed in a national system, we ultimately would lose our identity and control and our local interest . . .

Keys' response was surprisingly gracious. He wrote that he accepted the rejection "in the spirit in which you made it," but expressed the hope that in some way or another, Western Air Express would yet be merged into the transcontinental picture "even though it seems very remote at this time." But the cold water Hanshue had thrown on the merger offer was promptly tossed back at him boiled in a government kettle. Colonel Henderson, who had joined Keys in organizing TAT, informed the Post Office Department of Western's refusal to merge. Warren Irving Glover, Second Assistant Postmaster General and in charge of air mail contracts, wrote Hanshue that he was making a mistake.

"Things are moving pretty fast in the passenger game," he warned, "and I hope Western Air Express will not be squeezed out of the picture."

It was a warning that Hanshue rejected as firmly as he had turned down Keys. Hanshue was too busy making plans to beat TAT while simultaneously protecting his flank in the Southwest.

Glover had informed him that the Post Office Department was under "persistent pressure" to establish an air mail route stretching from Los Angeles to either Birmingham or New Orleans via San Diego, Yuma, Phoenix, Tucson, Douglas, El Paso, and either Fort Worth or San Antonio. Hanshue's answer was that such a route to the extreme south would involve communities so sparsely populated as to make the route permanently dependent on mail revenue. He again called Glover's attention to the far more desirable central route to Kansas City via Albuquerque and Amarillo.

Yet with his uncanny intuition, Hanshue sensed that the unwanted southern route could not be ignored totally—not when the government itself seemed to be nettled over his refusal to merge with TAT. Glover had made no outright threat, but Pop was taking no chances. In the spring of 1929, he and Talbot bought into Standard Airlines, which had begun by operating single-engine Fokkers between Los Angeles and Tucson via Phoenix and later extended service to El Paso. Standard had been formed by two skilled and enterprising pilots, Jack Frye and Paul Richter, both to play leading roles in the eventual growth of TWA.

Hanshue and Talbot, who were after Frye and Richter as well as Standard's route system, didn't actually buy into the airline, but the company that owned it as a subsidiary—Aero Corporation of California—and their stock purchase was of sufficient proportions to get them named as Aero directors. In another year, Western was to purchase Aero outright and thus acquire Standard and the services of its two founders.

On May 15, 1929, Hanshue began firing his broadsides: Western's Fokkers started flying between Los Angeles and Albuquerque, and seventeen days later the red trimotors were serving Kansas City. This was slightly more than a month before TAT opened its well-publicized and historic central transcontinental route via train and plane. TAT's accomplishment was hailed as a milestone in aviation progress, and there was no doubt it was a brilliantly conceived, well-executed operation—the route itself was planned by Charles Lindbergh, whom TAT wisely hired as chairman of its technical committee. Keys got more than merely the Lindbergh name; the Lone Eagle was an

[1] April 17, 1926. Part of the crowd that watched the birth of America's senior airline.

[2] Vail Field, circa 1927. The hangar was once a movie studio.

[3] The Four Horsemen and their boss. Left to right: Fred Kelly I, Jimmie James, Al DeGarmo, Maury Graham, and C. C. Moseley.

[4] The mail comes first — as this shot of a couple of early passengers demonstrates. They were boarded only if the mail load wasn't too heavy.

[5] Maude Campbell, Western's first woman passenger. The flowers were a gift from President Hanshue.

[6] Queen of the "Model Airway." A Fokker F-10 — the last word in 1929 air transportation.

[7] The giant F-32, the 747 of its day. Note the unusual mounting of the four engines.

aeronautical genius who advised TAT on everything from choice of equipment to laying out the final route.

That route called for train service from New York to Port Columbus, Ohio, where TAT's Ford trimotors took over. Passengers flew by day as far as Waynoka, Oklahoma, where they entrained again for Clovis. Fords carried them the rest of the way into Los Angeles. Lindbergh himself flew the first eastbound trip out of the Grand Central Air Terminal at Glendale, California.

Refueling stops were at Kingman, Winslow, Albuquerque, Wichita, Kansas City, St. Louis, and Indianapolis—these and the slower pace of the trains added up to a forty-eight-hour schedule. The fare ranged from $337 to $403, depending on the rail accommodations chosen, and passengers could go on to San Francisco from Los Angeles on Maddux Air Lines—which TAT partially owned through Keys' North American Aviation. TAT was to buy out Maddux later that year, acquiring in the process the nation's biggest fleet of Ford trimotors; Maddux was operating fifteen Fords at the time TAT took it over, plus four single-engine planes.

On the day TAT launched its New York–Los Angeles route, however, Western had been operating its own version of transcontinental service for more than a month. Hanshue had on his payroll a soft-spoken, personable young man who had previously worked for Pop as a car salesman. His name was Henry A. Burgess, originally hired as manager of air express traffic. Hanshue promoted him, assigning him the imposing title of "assistant to the president," and he was just that: a kind of alter ego who became an extension of Hanshue's mind and methods.

Some time before Western started flying to Kansas City, Hanshue dispatched Burgess east to negotiate with various railroads. Burgess returned carrying contracts with thirty-five lines, enabling Hanshue to offer coast-to-coast air-train service in forty hours—eight less than TAT's advertised schedule. Western's boast of crossing the country in only forty hours was slightly suspect, because to make that kind of time, a passenger had to make connections with certain trains. Yet while TAT's schedule was a bit more realistic and consistent, there is no doubt that Western, not TAT, provided the first train/air transcontinental service—a fact that most aviation histories have ignored, although certainly there was glory enough for both carriers. Western had one great advantage over TAT in the early stages, thanks again to the farsighted Hanshue. By advancing the funds for completion of a lighted Los Angeles–Kansas City airway, he was able to schedule some WAE flights at night; TAT, operating for the most part over unlighted airways east of Kansas City, had to fly solely by day, and its Fords required more refueling stops than Western's Fokkers.

Burgess' successful railroad mission raised him even higher in Hanshue's esteem, and he became Pop's closest confidant and most trusted employee. A close second in personal relationship to Western's president was Jimmie James, who was Hanshue's favorite among all the pilots. When Moseley resigned early in 1929, climaxing months of angry confrontations with his irascible boss, James was promoted to part-time duty as an assistant operations manager. Moseley wound up as head of the big Glendale airport (where Western's bitter rival, TAT, was operating) and went on to achieve considerable wealth as a Los Angeles businessman and real-estate investor.

Hanshue, by this time, was ready to move out of Vail, which WAE had outgrown hopelessly. Glendale would have been a good and obvious choice for new quarters, but Pop evidently didn't want to move where TAT already was ensconced. With the directors' permission, he purchased a 188-acre tract on Valley Boulevard in Alhambra, California, and spent $1 million building one of the world's finest terminals. He took William Garland, James, and Kelly out to the site before construction started.

"What do you think of the location?" Pop inquired in the tone of a man expectingly asking his wife what she thinks of the new mink coat he has just bought her.

"It's too small," Jimmie decreed.

Hanshue laughed, but James was to prove right. It was an ill-spent $1 million, for Western was to abandon Alhambra only two years after the terminal was completed. At first, however, it was a literal showplace—the Pacific Coast's first modern air passenger terminal, with a waiting room of sheer luxury. Also built was a new hangar revolutionary in its architectural concept: It was hexagonal, and nothing like it had ever been seen before.

Eventual failure though it was, the Alhambra facility was one more demonstration of Western's increased efforts in passenger solicitation. Air travel still was very new to very many, and even a single, uneventful flight made something of a news story. Al Stensvold, aviation editor of the San Francisco *Bulletin* in 1929, wrote a daily column, and his main source of news was flight arrivals and departures, which he ran much like the New York *Times* shipping news.

"Western Air Express trimotor Fokker monoplane hopped off for Los Angeles at 5:10 P.M. with 10 passengers; Laas-Drury pilots," was a typical entry.

"The flights were so few that it was easy to mention every one coming into or leaving the Bay Area," he recalls.

Hanshue's chief weapon for attracting recalcitrant customers was his combination of safety and service. He worked hard at both, but the former became a joint industrywide effort, whereas service involved stiff competition. The standard provided on the Model Airway was tough to live up to as Western expanded; the very cost of all those innovative amenities—relatively expensive food, reading material, and free airport transportation—had contributed to the deficit operation. Yet butting heads against TAT and Maddux, Hanshue became convinced that Western couldn't compete successfully on any penny-wise-pound-foolish policy. Borrowing from retail business the idea of hiring professional shoppers to scout the opposition, he sent Burgess on a forty-day, seven-thousand-mile tour over three airlines—WAE, TAT, and Maddux. The report Burgess handed Hanshue upon his return offers an interesting and nostalgic look at air travel as it was in 1929. It consisted of two parts: some general observations and suggestions, plus an extensive description of a flight on TAT.

Excerpts from the over-all summary:

> TAT courier service [*TAT called its stewards "couriers"*] is good, but in my opinion their method of serving the lunch is all wrong. I believe if we could arrange to use their idea of detachable tables for each passenger, it would be an improvement although not a necessity.
>
> Would suggest that our stewards arrange the lunch on the tray in an appetizing way, removing all wrappers from the sandwiches etc. and arrange them on a plate,

not paper, and supply a cloth napkin, a knife and a spoon. The knife should be comparatively small, so as to be used to pare fruit or to cut sandwiches into smaller portions if desired. Plate should be distinctive WAE design and for sale as souvenirs. . . .

Have found occasions when stewards had no matches for smokers, would suggest paper matches with WAE advertising be available and possibly cigarettes for sale . . . suggest that consistent smokers be asked to sit forward as by opening the forward windows slightly, an out-draft is created and the rear windows (when) opened create an in-draft.

I believe stewards should be provided with footstools, similar to those used by railroads but of course much lighter, to be used in loading and unloading passengers—ladies are very apt to catch their heels in the present hook-like step. There should be padding or something on the back of the seats to cover rough edges, screws etc. which have frequently torn ladies' stockings. Footrests of some sort would be an added comfort on long trips . . .

Lunches should be given careful thought so there would be a minimum of duplication, especially when two lunches are served in one day as on Division 5. Also it is very disconcerting to a passenger to bite into a sandwich and drag out the entire insides because the meat was tough . . . meats should be tender. If beef is used, it should be potroasted and if ham is used it should be baked. . . .

I believe the steward should have one of the rear seats and not go forward and sit on the arm of one of the seats as I have seen done at times. There are times when the pilot wishes to attract the attention of the steward for some reason. Now he has to wave his hand or cap; a push button and buzzer would be more in keeping. Stewards should have clean jackets at the start of every trip and possibly an extra one for an emergency. I have seen some at the start of a trip that were very untidy. He should be careful his hands and nails are clean . . . stewards should have a bulletin giving full instructions . . . when to serve lunch, etc., in fact it should cover all their duties so that their service will be uniform on all divisions.

Burgess was frank in praising TAT for doing things Western wasn't doing. He recommended adoption of TAT's practice of giving passengers small gifts, such as sending desk pen sets to their homes. He suggested that free pens be handed out on the aircraft instead. He praised TAT's baggage checking system: "a tag is fastened to your grip; this tag has your name and address on one side and on the opposite side is printed in large red letters the initials of your designation, such as ALB for Albuquerque." Finally, Burgess said Western's pilots should wear uniforms, and while they should be permitted to take off their coats in the cockpit during hot weather, they should wear them while walking through the cabin (a present-day rule on all U.S. airlines).

Excerpts from Burgess' account of a TAT flight:

. . . Just before taking off, traffic man checks my baggage which is weighed. I am then requested to get on the scales, my weight and the baggage weight are noted on a sheet. The courier introduces himself, hands me a log and a map and explains them—I am the only passenger. The courier takes up my ticket after the plane takes off.

After we are off the courier offers me cotton for my ears, also chewing gum and a collection of TAT literature. Copies of the *Times* and *Examiner* and several magazines also are offered, all free. He also had playing cards for sale at 75 cents per pack. After we were out about an hour the courier offers lemonade and cakes and points out interesting scenes. As we neared Kingman, I noticed the pilot signaling through the window to attract the attention of the courier who was sound asleep opposite me. I aroused him. The pilot wanted a rag to wipe his windows. . . .

Landed at Kingman at 12:35 P.M. . . . as we were

taking off, the courier asked me if I was ready for lunch. I replied as soon as we were up. I didn't get it until about 1:30. He fastened a small table to the wall of the plane with a supporting leg to the floor, lavender table linen, a metal plate that looked like gold with a fork and spoon to match, also a metal saucer with porcelain and metal cup for hot drink. He then brought a traylike affair with assorted meats, salad, olives and buttered bread, a pair of tongs to help myself. The meats were sliced turkey, corned beef and prime roast beef . . . for drinks I had the choice of tea, coffee or milk. . . . I saw no ashtrays and asked the courier if smoking was permitted. He said it was not allowed but "I don't know what you are doing when you go to the rear."

Many of the Burgess suggestions were adopted, not all at once, but gradually as Western continued to mature in every area—service, operating efficiency, and air travel promotion. Hanshue wasn't through with his 1929 expansion activities, either; before the year ended, he formed a subsidiary—Mid-Continent Air Express—which inaugurated passenger and express flights on a Denver–Pueblo–Albuquerque–El Paso route. This linked CAM-12 to the two new southern routes: Los Angeles–Kansas City via Albuquerque, and Los Angeles–El Paso, the latter flown by Standard, which by this time had become, in effect, a Western subsidiary.

By now, WAE was flying a 4,700-mile route system embracing nine states. The 1929 passenger total was just short of 22,000—three times the number carried in the airline's first three years combined. True, everything wasn't coming up roses; the record $1.87 million profit stemmed entirely from mail pay on CAM-4, which grossed more than $2.2 million, with all other divisions operating at a deficit. And there were rumbles from Washington in the form of an amendment to the Kelly Act that threatened to close off about half of the air mail trough at which the airlines had been feeding.

Passage of the amendment threw a scare into virtually every air carrier, Western included. Signed by President Hoover in mid-1929, it gave the airlines the option of exchanging their current four-year mail contracts for new ten-year pacts. This was a sugar coating over a bitter pill, for the amendment also gave the Postmaster General authority to adjust mail rates—and no airline operator expected any upward adjustment. For Western, literally subsidizing its money-losing passenger routes with mail pay profits, it was a huge red danger signal. Smartly, Hanshue hired himself an able lobbyist with excellent Capitol Hill contacts—William MacCracken, former Assistant Secretary of Commerce for Aeronautics. MacCracken, who knew his way around the Washington jungles, worked with other airline lobbyists and succeeded in winning a six-month extension of the amendment's effective date. They figured this brief breathing spell was all they needed, for a major reorganization of all mail contracts was in the works.

Given this reprieve from a drastic cut in mail revenues, Hanshue had every reason to view the future with unbridled optimism. Western Air Express bid 1929 farewell with $1 million in bank deposits, and its major opponent—TAT—was losing money faster than a novice crap shooter in Las Vegas. TAT had gone all-out to build a professional operation, spending $1.5 million on ground facilities, including runway and terminal improvements at many airports on its system. Some of the lighting installations it provided exceeded Department of Commerce requirements and were correspondingly more expensive. Its pilot-training program was the most extensive in the industry—and the most costly. What TAT achieved was praiseworthy technical competence as good as Western's and in some ways better, reflecting Lindbergh's influence, but the price was high. In its first eighteen months of operation, TAT lost more than $2.7 million. It had built an imposing edifice which too few customers were entering, and it had been structured, unlike WAE, without the life-saving transfusions of mail revenue.

Keys was not the type of commander who would let his ship sink without sending an SOS. His airline may have lacked Western's lucrative mail pacts and its all-lighted airways, but Keys possessed what Hanshue didn't and even resisted: influence with huge eastern financial circles and the government itself. Nor was the figurative father of Western Air Express really aware of what was brewing in the mind of the man Hoover had named Post-master General—Walter Folger Brown.

If Hanshue had been, he would not have been so sanguine about Western's own future, one that looked so promising as to prompt a public statement by Jim Talbot that WAE was considering purchase of Guatemala Air Service, a never-to-be achievement that would have spread the wings of the red Fokkers all the way to Chile in South America.

As 1930 dawned, Western, by most over-all standards of measurement—route mileage, fleet size, and passengers carried—was the nation's largest airline. But behind all the euphoria-inducing pink clouds loomed the twin specters of political calamity and human tragedy.

CHAPTER FIVE

Shotgun Marriage

Of all the Four Horsemen, Maury Graham was the most unpredictable and paradoxical.

Nowhere was it more marked than in his attitude toward flying: He was a paragon of caution who occasionally took unexplainable risks.

Al DeGarmo remembers that Graham was the only Western Air Express pilot who insisted on carrying three altimeters in every plane he flew—the regular one in the instrument panel and two additional altimeters mounted on a small board that he carried in his flight bag. It was just one more means of boosting the odds in his favor. He possessed the wary, intuitive alertness to danger of a deer; when he was descending in a thick overcast through one of the numerous mountain passes on CAM-4, if he didn't see the clouds begin to darken by the time he was down to a certain altitude, he would climb immediately.

His skill at sensing, weighing, and combating danger led to his taking apparent chances that appalled the other Horsemen—who had more than the average supply of intestinal fortitude.

"Maury was the toughest bastard I ever flew against," DeGarmo recalls with a kind of grudging admiration mixed with equally grudging censure. "I used to come down in really lousy weather, put my mail on a train, and then call in to ask where Maury happened to be marooned like me. They'd tell me, 'Oh, he's still flying.'"

Few of the young copilots joining WAE in ever-increasing numbers got to know Graham very well, because Maury flew more mail runs in the biplanes than passenger flights in the Fokkers, but those who did work with him had nothing but unqualified respect. These included a newly hired rookie whose chief claim to fame at that point was his name—Fred Kelly. He instantly became Fred Kelly II, his predecessor was Fred Kelly I, and both bore the numerical tags forever after. To such newcomers as Kelly II, Maury gave advice only when it was asked. He obviously preferred the one-man responsibilities and solitude of the open-air planes, being something of a lone wolf.

It was in a biplane that Maury Graham took his last flight. On January 10, 1930, he left Los Angeles in a Boeing 95 carrying a full load of mail—including a reported $1 million worth of negotiable securities. The last time he was seen alive was at Las Vegas, where he landed to refuel. The weather was foul, and Graham was impatient to take off again. East of Vegas, a snowstorm was building up in massive and deadly proportions.

"I think there's a break in the weather ahead," he told the mechanic. "Hurry it up so I can get through."

It was a long time before investigators pieced together, as best they could, what probably happened after he left Vegas. He apparently first ran into trouble over St. George, the same area where only a few months before he had successfully landed a storm-tossed Fokker flight. This time he made it past St. George, but snow conditions worsened as he neared Zion National Park. He began a letdown toward the pass near Cedar City, Utah, but with visibility now almost zero, he decided to turn back. Witnesses reported later that he had dropped flares as if to try an emergency landing, but they never saw him come down.

When Salt Lake City notified Los Angeles operations that Graham was overdue, both ground and search parties were organized quickly. Search headquarters were centered in Vegas, in the belief that Maury had tried to return there, with the airway into Salt Lake City totally impassable. Jimmie James and Fred Kelly I were among the first to arrive in Vegas, taking off in search planes even before the weather had entirely cleared. DeGarmo was not far behind them; although he was working for another airline, he asked for and obtained leave to help look for the missing Horseman.

The hunt centered in the region around Cedar City where the

plane had last been seen, groping through the white death that
was one of the West's worst recorded blizzards. The search
planes probably flew right over Graham's plane several times,
but the heavy snow must have covered it up almost immediately.
Kelly I took a mechanic, Evan Lewis, with him on one search
flight—Evan volunteering to parachute out if they located
Graham or his plane. Neither saw a thing, nor did anyone else—
the mailplane and its pilot had been swallowed up by some of
the wildest terrain in the country. The search flights themselves
were hazardous, the planes usually dropping below the tops of
the jagged mountains as they skimmed over the snow-covered
forests of cedar trees and squeezed down into gorges just wide
enough for wings. The search continued for more than a month
before the weary crews gave up, knowing now that if Graham
was ever found, it wouldn't be until after the snows melted.

Inevitably, the vicious rumors began spreading; Graham, it
was whispered, hadn't crashed at all but had flown to Mexico
with the $1 million in securities. That particular bit of slime still
was in the air on June 24, when some young ranchers stumbled on
the wreckage of Maury's Boeing. They had been prowling on
horseback in the Kanarra Mountains, about twenty miles from
Cedar City, looking for some wood strips with which to fix a
fence. A flash of red caught their eyes and they rode toward it,
thinking it must be an old barn; it was Graham's battered plane,
in fairly good shape although unflyable. But there was no trace of
the pilot—obviously he had survived the crash, or perhaps a
crash landing, and had wandered away to find help or shelter.
The cowling was found about seventy-five yards from the fuselage; Maury, it was presumed, had removed it to use either as a
cover from the snow or as a sled. The mailbags were unopened
and the contents intact—including the securities that had
spawned the slanderous gossip.

Western was notified of the discovery as soon as the youths
raced back to Cedar City with the news. Kelly I and James, accompanied by a pilot who had been hired after DeGarmo left
WAE—Jimmy Carson—flew an F-10 to Cedar City and immediately went to the crash site. Souvenir hunters had preceded
them; despite terrain that would have given pause to a mountain
goat, a number of Cedar City citizens had raided the wreckage,

stripping it virtually to a skeleton. The heartsick James did manage to salvage a canvas side panel from the fuselage; it bore the words "Western Air Express" and the Indian head with the thin arrow running through it.

"Maury's wife will want this," Jimmie muttered to Kelly, who nodded in sorrowful agreement. James did send it to Alice Graham, who later presented it to Western, which now displays it in its museum—a sad, three-foot-long memento from a distant past when the Four Horsemen flew their frail craft with that improvised logo on the side of the fuselage.

Not for another three weeks was Graham's body found—by a cousin of his wife, James F. Allen, who had joined the search party. Allen was walking alongside a stream when he noticed a few stalks of wheat growing behind a large log. He knew wheat wasn't supposed to be found in this region, so he decided to investigate—and stumbled on what remained of Captain Maury Graham, Western Air Express. His body was six miles from the plane.

Some months before, Maury had determined to quit smoking and, in a typical demonstration of his willpower, he began carrying on his flights a coffee can filled with raw wheat. If the urge to smoke hit him, he'd merely grab a handful of wheat and munch away. When his body was found, he was wearing his old red sweater, and his revolver and gun belt were strapped to his waist. He apparently had succumbed to exposure while trying to open a can of tomatoes. There was evidence of a head injury, and he may have been wandering around dazed. When Allen found him, the wheat had grown out of his pockets.

Long before the uncertainties of Graham's disappearance became the facts of his death, his last flight seemed to portend the disasters that would overtake Western in the coming year. Only a little more than a month after Maury's plane went down, on February 23, WAE suffered the ignominy of becoming the first U.S. airline to report three accidents in the same day—and narrowly missed a fourth. The latter involved Jimmie James, who was flying to pick up mail stranded when a new Fokker F-14 (a single-engine job with the same type of parasol wing Al DeGarmo had hated on the Lockheed Will Rogers bought) crashed on takeoff at Cedar City. Heavy snow forced Jimmie into an emergency landing too far away for him to reach a phone, and for a few long hours, it was feared he had met Graham's fate.

While James still was unreported, Kelly I joined the ranks of the missing. The numerous search flights plus 150 hours of flying regular monthly schedules had taken their toll of the seemingly tireless Kelly; he was piloting a Boeing 95, staying close to the ground under a low cloud cover, when carelessness generated by fatigue caught up with him. A wing sliced into a small hill Fred didn't see, and he went in. Ironically, both he and James disappeared in the same area where Graham was lost.

Now there were two pilots and planes unreported, plus the F-14 known to have crashed. On the same night, Jim Doles was flying an F-10 from Albuquerque to Los Angeles and ran into blinding snow. His was one of the handful of Fokkers equipped with new radios, and he informed operations he was turning back to Albuquerque. That was the last contact with his flight. At first there was a noticeable lack of concern, because Dole had been the hero of a near disaster only four months before, when he landed an F-10 on a snow-covered field in New Mexico to sit out a snowstorm. On board were the copilot (Allan Barrie, who was to become one of Western's crack captains and, briefly, an executive), a steward, and two passengers, who spent the night in a nearby trapper's cabin. Dole took off the next morning after the storm cleared and arrived in Los Angeles to be warmly greeted as having returned from the dead.

This time, however, he wasn't so lucky. The Fokker's wreckage was located twelve days later in the San Bernardino Mountains near Lake Arrowhead. Both pilots and the steward, the only occupants, were dead.

James had made it into Cedar City the morning of February 24, and so did Kelly—he walked away from the wreckage, hiked his way painfully to a road, and thumbed down a passing car. His neck hurt to an excruciating degree, and by the time he was flown back to Los Angeles, he was unable to turn his head or move his right arm. He had to be carried out of the plane, and subsequent hospital X rays disclosed he had a broken neck. Being Kelly I, he refused to be taken off flying status, and for six weeks he flew mailplanes while wearing a brace, taking it off when he was assigned a passenger flight because "it wouldn't have looked good for passengers to see the brace."

Even if Kelly hadn't been able to return to duty almost immediately, broken neck notwithstanding, nobody could have kept him off a mission flown at the request of Alice Graham. Kelly and James had flown to Cedar City after Maury's body was found, and talked briefly with his widow. The remains had been cremated, and they were supposed to fly them back to Los Angeles for burial.

"Would you drop his ashes along the way instead?" she asked. "I think Maury would like that."

Kelly and James not only agreed but also got in touch with DeGarmo, who flew into Cedar City as soon as he could. Together, the trio complied with Alice Graham's wishes, scattering their comrade's ashes along the route he had helped them pioneer. They used a rented Boeing 40-B-4, Kelly flying the single-engine plane while DeGarmo and James sat in the tiny cabin. Approaching Las Vegas, the engine sputtered and quit. DeGarmo yelled from the cabin, "Switch it over to the other tank, Fred!"

Kelly did and the engine roared back into life.

"I guess it was Maury's way of saying good-bye," Kelly commented after they landed.

The last flight the Four Horsemen made together was a poignant interlude in a far greater drama beginning to unfold on the stage of U.S. commercial aviation, one that cast the pudgy figure of Pop Hanshue in the role of the defending commander at a corporate Thermopylae. Admittedly, the metaphor may not be entirely appropriate, because when the battle really started, Western Air Express wasn't exactly a small army pitted against overwhelming forces: By mid-1930 it had become the largest air transportation system in the world.

Adding WAE's own routes to those of affiliates, the system comprised nearly sixteen thousand miles flown by a fleet of more than forty aircraft—including the biggest land transport plane ever built. This was the giant Fokker F-32—the "32" standing for the number of passengers it could carry. It also was aviation's first four-engine airliner and was so far ahead of its time that it went down in history as a failure instead of a success.

Western was not the first airline to operate the huge F-32. Universal Air Lines System ordered four, including the prototype, which crashed taking off on its inaugural flight—a mishap followed immediately by Universal's canceling its order for the remaining three. That didn't deter Hanshue, who bought two F-32s for Western Air Express for delivery in the summer of 1930, assigning them immediately to the Los Angeles–San Francisco market, where Maddux was giving WAE fits.

The cost was $110,000 per aircraft—making the F-32 the most expensive as well as the biggest land-based airliner flying. The plane had to be seen to be believed; not until the Boeing 747 came along some four decades later would a commercial transport invoke such incredulous gasps. The only aircraft of its day to match the F-32 in sheer luxury were Pan Am's giant flying boats, but their swankiness was almost taken for granted in what amounted to a ship's hull with wings and engines attached. The land-based F-32 was something else.

The first one delivered to Western had a cabin divided into eight compartments, each with four chairs facing one another. The seats themselves had three reclining positions—a first for the industry—and their cushions were stuffed with rubber balls to give the passenger "the feeling that he is riding on air." Walnut paneling went from the floor to the windowsill, and above the window was a wall fabric symbolizing the colors of California's varied landscape—the sandy browns of deserts and mountains, and the greens of palm trees and cactus leaves.

Compartment 2, used exclusively for smoking, was furnished in black paneling, with wall fabrics done in a black, silver, and red brocade of tobacco-leaf motif. Some 240 pounds of balsa wood were installed for insulation and sound-deadening purposes. Seats in the regular compartments were covered in gray alligator skin with black piping; those in the smoking compartment had blue piping.

There were call buttons to summon the two white-jacketed stewards assigned to every F-32 flight, indirect lighting, a folding table for each compartment, two chemical lavatories, interior baggage racks, two galleys (one with running water and a dry-ice refrigerator), plus china cups and plates for meal service, a coat closet, and individual reading lights above every seat: This was air travel at its finest. Even the exterior featured a special paint job: The fuselage was red with black and gold edges, and the wings were silver.

Safety also was stressed, starting with what was supposed to be the great reserve power of four engines. In truth, the F-10 had more usable muscle than its huge younger brother whose airframe design was a few years ahead of its power plants. Although the F-32 was advertised as a 32-passenger aircraft, the Department of Commerce limited it to 22 passengers when a full fuel load was carried. But the pilots enjoyed some of the F-32's technical innovations even as they bemoaned the inadequacies and idiosyncrasies of the engines. An extra light was installed in the nose, adjustable for taxiing. The instrument panel had both indirect and rheostat-controlled lighting. Unlike the F-10, whose gas tank was located in the center-wing section directly above the passengers, the F-32 had outboard wing tanks. Perhaps the outstanding safety feature was a fire-extinguishing system for each engine, believed to be the first ever installed on a commercial transport.

The engines themselves were unique. Air-cooled, they were mounted in tandem, two under each wing. The front engines were equipped with two-bladed steel propellers, but the rear ones had three-bladed props. Front and rear props counterrotated to eliminate torque pull. It was an interesting concept but one that proved impractical; the rear engines never got enough air and were constantly overheating. Although all four engines developed the then-impressive total of 2,300 horsepower, they really weren't efficient enough to carry the F-32's gross weight of more than 24,000 pounds.

Even so, the great Fokker could cruise at 123 mph with a top speed of nearly 150, could climb 850 feet a minute or almost as fast as the Ford trimotor, and the "useful load" (as they termed payload in those days) was upward of 9,000 pounds. The plane's massive weight limited the maximum ceiling to 13,000 feet, however, and over-all the F-32—while it was a passenger's dream— was more of a nightmare to pilots and Western executives. One of its few virtues as far as pilots were concerned was surprisingly good cockpit vision; like their future 747 brethren, they sat high above the cabin, connected to the cockpit by a three-foot ladder.

If they wanted to avoid going through the cabin, they could enter or leave the cockpit via a trap door leading into the spacious baggage compartment.

The cabin itself was 35 feet long, and 8 feet high and wide, roughly half the dimensions of Western's "little" Boeing 737s but providing enormous space for its time. It must be noted that only the first F-32 delivered to Alhambra Field was furnished so luxuriously; the second ship wasn't quite as fancy, although it still was light-years ahead of any other land transport flying. Hanshue had a crack at a new American-built transport before he ordered the big Fokkers, and that was the twin-engine Curtiss Condor biplane, which proved to be a far more successful aircraft with both American and Eastern. Pop, however, considered it underpowered, and when Curtiss representatives approached him to ask if he'd be interested in the Condor for Western's routes, his answer was pure Hanshue.

"Not before they build a tunnel through the goddamned Rockies," he snorted.

Hanshue's new-equipment plans usually contained a clue as to his future expansion plans, and the F-32 was no exception. Fokker designers told him the plane easily could be converted into a sixteen-passenger sleeper plane, and while it wasn't known at the time, even then he had visions of going all the way to the East Coast. WAE's F-32s were never used as sleepers, but they had the capability; so, for that matter, did the Condor, which eventually did become the first sleeper plane used on domestic routes, Pop's low opinion of the Curtiss product notwithstanding.

Not that Hanshue couldn't be budged when it was proved he had been wrong; he gave up on the F-32 after only two years of service. The power plant difficulties were just one nail in the giant's coffin, making it too unreliable and expensive to operate. The government's refusal to let a fully fueled F-32 carry more than twenty-two passengers was another handicap, albeit a minor one, inasmuch as there seldom were thirty-two passengers available for a flight in those Depression days. And Western badly needed high load factors on F-32 trips because of the excessive operating costs—the big plane, despite all its technical advancements and great passenger appeal, was simply impossible to fly profitably. All that Western Air Express really got out of its F-32 investment was a lot of publicity and prestige.

The $1 million facility at Alhambra also wound up in the white-elephant category. It was dedicated on April 17, 1930, on Western's fourth anniversary, with California Governor Clement C. Young delivering the main address and large crowds of the curious wandering through the beautifully furnished terminal and inspecting the famed "Hex Hangar." The latter attracted almost as much attention as the terminal building; Woolley's prededication publicity had emphasized not only its unusual shape, permitting six planes to be worked on simultaneously, but also the fact that its floor was slightly inclined—this was to make it possible to evacuate the entire building in less than two minutes if a serious fire broke out.

Beauty and uniqueness failed to compensate for the deficiency James had pointed out right from the start—the field was, indeed, too small for safe operations. Hanshue finally was convinced of this when a pilot cracked up an F-10 while attempting a go-around; even as Woolley was adding the airport dedication clippings to his swelling scrapbooks, Pop was scouting around for larger facilities. Alhambra was to be phased out about the same time the F-32s were taken out of service and sent to an inglorious end; one eventually would be scrapped and the other became a corner gas station in downtown Los Angeles, a sightseer's delight but a monument to overoptimism.

Hanshue was listening to James more and more in the one area of the airline business Pop never really understood—operations. Shortly after Graham's death and the plethora of accidents in February, Hanshue named Jimmie operations manager. Si Morehouse, the man with the most Fokker experience, was appointed chief pilot, and there were two newcomers who showed promise. One was a lanky, quiet youngster whose field was accounting. He lived near Vail and on weekends would go out to the field and watch Western's operations. Airplanes themselves didn't fascinate him as much as the challenge of this new, exciting young industry; he lived in a world of figures, balance sheets, and ledgers, but he developed a desire to inject the cold, clean logic and symmetry of accounting into the hectic, frequently undisciplined world of aviation.

He finally decided to knock on Western's door, going down to the general offices at Ninth and Grand and asking for a job in the accounting department. Hugh Wright, the WAE treasurer whose outward grouchiness hid a heart bigger than a dinosaur's, interviewed him and was impressed by the applicant's background and sincerity. The young man was a graduate of Marquette University's School of Business Administration and had worked in Los Angeles banks both as an accountant and a teller.

"Okay," Wright growled, "we'll give you a job. But I don't know what the hell we're gonna call you with that funny name of yours—I can't even pronounce the damned thing, let alone spell it."

"Dwerlkotte," the twenty-six-year-old prospect said eagerly. "Leo H. Dwerlkotte—it's German and Dutch. Just make believe there's a 'y' at the end."

"Dwerlkotty," Wright repeated phonetically. "All right, Leo, you can start Monday with a couple of weeks' indoctrination out at Vail, and then we'll put you in the payroll department."

The young accountant left with both feet in the air. Like anyone stepping across a career threshold, he had confidence without clairvoyance; he had no way of knowing that in the not too far distant future, he would be running Western as its chief executive officer and its president in all but actual title.

Another airline "rookie" who joined WAE even before Dwerlkotte was Arthur Beggs, assigned to the traffic department in San Francisco because his brother Bob already was employed by the airline in Los Angeles; it was Western's policy not to let relatives work in the same city. Beggs, now retired but still alert, precise, and possessing the memory of a computer, is one of the few persons around with vivid recollections of Western Air Express in the late twenties and early thirties.

The traffic salesmen like Beggs had a set routine. They'd start at the top floor of a big office building and work their way down, stopping at each office to deliver a sales pitch and leave an air mail packet and WAE literature. Other sales targets visited frequently were travel agents, hotel transportation desks, department stores, and motion-picture studios. The traffic department also kept track of sporting events, professional wrestling (a major attraction then) in particular; wrestlers used air transportation frequently in those days because they could double or even triple their earnings by staging a match in a different town each night. Ed "Strangler" Lewis and Jim Londos were two of Western's best customers for a long time.

A small but welcome source of revenue was the practice of running weekend sightseeing flights, at five dollars a head. Beggs and others in the traffic department also frequently visited schools and service clubs, to show WAE films and talk briefly about air travel.

Close liaison was maintained with the film industry, not only because performers, producers, and studio officials liked the prestige and time-saving element of air transportation, but also for Western's own publicity advantages; to this day, Beggs occasionally sees old movies in which the Western Air Express logo appears in the background of an airport scene. In later years, TWA was used most frequently by film makers needing airline shots, with American and United also supplying considerable footage. But in the thirties Western was something of "Hollywood's own airline," the famed Indian head symbol gaining nationwide recognition.

The logo, incidentally, by now was being displayed on more than just WAE aircraft, thanks to the enterprise of a new employee hired in 1929 as a self-described "flunky." His name was Willard Wright, who served in Western's maintenance department for years.

"The Indian head was on the sides of our airplanes," he says, "but not on any other equipment. I decided they should be everywhere, so in my spare time I painted it on our trucks and everything else in sight."

Wright was something of an artist, although he had no formal training. His logos looked as if they had been carved out of stone; he trimmed them in twenty-four-karat gold leaf with a black outline, and all by hand. He would sketch the head in chalk first, then paint it with a camel's or squirrel's hair brush. Hanshue was so enamored of Wright's masterpieces that he had him paint new logos on all the planes; the last ones to bear his handiwork were three new Boeing 95s.

Such above-and-beyond-the-call-of-duty performances were

not unusual as Western scrambled for business. Stewards occasionally doubled as limousine drivers, picking up passengers downtown, driving them to the airport, and then working their flight. There was something about that Indian head symbol commanding loyalty and affection; even as Western grew, it remained a kind of closely knit family whose pride transcended adversity. Hanshue's own intense, driving ambition was oriented to the airline's welfare, not himself—and much of this washed off on every official and employee. In a way, Pop was as much of a symbol as the logo itself, and this may have been more literal than figurative. When Western strove to establish some identity on the East Coast, even though its routes ended in Kansas City, it was decided to put some Western Air Express signs around various New York City vantage points. Beggs and another WAE salesman were watching one of the signs being posted in a Manhattan hotel lobby.

"Art," his colleague remarked seriously, "you want to know something? That head looks more like Hanshue than an Indian."

In the interests of a broader reputation, it was decided that Western should have a song. The genius behind this inspiration has never been identified, but Mr. James Woolley was a natural and logical suspect; at least he enthusiastically supported the idea, going so far as to con Hanshue out of five thousand dollars, which was paid to George Whiting, a well-known New York songwriter, for composing a suitable WAE ballad. Whiting was picked not only for his reported musical skills but because he also owned a music publishing firm.

It is entirely possible that the only way Woolley talked Pop out of that five grand was to present the scheme not only as a publicity gimmick but also as a means of making considerable money. The agreement signed between Whiting on the one hand, and Woolley/Hanshue acting for WAE on the other, called for the airline to take all the proceeds from the first fifty thousand copies of the sheet music. All sales above fifty thousand were to be divided equally between Whiting and Western.

Woolley, having committed Western Air Express to its first diversification project, was taking no chances on this Tin Pan Alley venture. He paid Whiting three thousand dollars down, the other two thousand dollars to come when the song was finished and accepted. Then Woolley conceived the idea of dredging up some publicity *before* any music was written—he got newspapers in nine cities (New York, Buffalo, Cincinnati, Cleveland, San Francisco, Oakland, Indianapolis, Boston, and Kansas City) to sponsor contests for a song title. Whiting was to write the lyrics to the winning title. Nine finalists were to be chosen, their award being a twelve-day trip around Western's system.

Note that Western served only two of the areas where the contest was run—San Francisco/Oakland and Kansas City; with Machiavellian skill, Woolley deliberately had concentrated on non-Western points—using the contest as a means of getting people aware of the airline from the West. How many entries actually were received was never recorded, but at least Woolley managed to get his nine finalists. From their talented ranks came the winning title, submitted by Frank Keenan, a paint manufacturer of New York City:

"Big Boy Jess of the Western Air Express"

Whiting wrote the lyrics, and two of his employees, Charles Abbott and Edwin Weber, supplied the music—and it is feared that not even Irving Berlin or Cole Porter could have done much with that title. For the sake of Messrs. Abbott's and Weber's professional reputations, not to mention the fact that both were undoubtedly good to their respective mothers, no attempt will be made herein to reproduce their music. For the sake of historical detail, however, it is necessary to quote a few lines from Mr. Whiting's contribution to the James G. Woolley I'd-Do-Anything-to-Get-Western-Air-Express-Mentioned Foundation:

Steamboat Bill! Casey Jones! And others I could mention.
I used to think that they were fast,
Back in the dim and distant past!
There's a new someone who has won the world's attention.
He's of the modern school, and he's a flying fool!
    (Chorus)
"There he is!" you'll hear somebody cry.
And then out from the sky, drops BIG BOY JESS

Of the Western Air Express!
How those air-cooled mammas gather around,
Yes sir, they certainly hound that BIG BOY JESS
Of the Western Air Express!

The second verse was as bad as the first—or as good, depending on one's taste in music. Western's own employee publication, a mimeographed little newspaper called *The Dashboard Record,* hailed "Big Boy Jess" as *the* song-writing achievement of the decade—"orchestra directors have pronounced it a pip and it is expected to be a real hit," the *Record* proclaimed, calling it a "snappy fox trot."

A collector's item, maybe, but never a hit. "Big Boy Jess" laid down and died a merciful and early death, despite a full-page plug in *Variety.* Whiting got his five thousand dollars, Woolley more clippings for his scrapbook, the nine finalists a wonderful trip of nearly two weeks, and Western lost money—the sheet music sales were insufficient to cover the sum paid to Whiting. It's easy to joke about the project today, of course, but "Big Boy Jess" had the overtones of a swan song. While it was being distributed around the country—most of the slim sales were in Texas—Pop Hanshue finally found an enemy he couldn't lick.

This was a presidential Cabinet officer, namely the Postmaster General of the United States.

Walter Folger Brown was an attorney from Ohio who became chairman of the Republican National Committee and was a close friend of Herbert Hoover. When Hoover was Secretary of Commerce, Brown served under him as Assistant Secretary, and it was a natural step for Brown to assume the role of Hoover's campaign manager in the 1928 presidential campaign. After the California Quaker's election and subsequent inauguration, Brown received the usual reward for a successful candidate's chief political brain—nomination as Postmaster General.

Brown was an imposing figure, both in personality and physical appearance. Tall and thin, always immaculately clothed, he wore steel-rimmed glasses that seemed to reflect the glint from his hard eyes.

He was not the cold-blooded, ruthless villain portrayed in so many aviation histories; cold-blooded and ruthless, yes, but to call him a villain was to question his motives—and Brown if nothing else was a totally sincere, well-meaning man with intense convictions. His chief conviction, in fact, was identical to that of Hanshue: the necessity for developing passenger traffic, and reducing the overreliance on mail pay. Where they bitterly differed was in how to achieve it, and it was this difference that led two men totally devoted to aviation progress into a bloody war.

Immediately after his nomination was confirmed by the Senate, Brown began studying the contents of the traditional black-leather portfolio then presented to new Cabinet officers as a means of outlining their duties. He was the kind of lawyer who did his homework on every case, and the "case" in which he evidenced the most interest was that of the sprawling airline industry.

It was the task of the Postmaster General, the portfolio instructed, "to encourage commercial aviation . . ." and to this Brown applied an interpretation of startling broadness. For almost two years, Brown conducted an intensive study of the air carrier industry—then composed of no less than forty-four companies whose health resembled the economic status of a typical Latin or South American country: either wealth or poverty. There were the well-run, financially secure giants like Western Air Express and the big United conglomerate. At the other end of the scale were the small, undercapitalized operators clinging to mail contracts as a shipwrecked sailor clutches a life preserver. The plan gestating in the unquestionably astute mind of Walter Folger Brown basically was designed to get rid of the latter, consolidating most of the former, and in doing so, redrawing the air map of the United States.

He found legal authority for this drastic surgery in the form of the third amendment to the Kelly Act, legislation introduced by Representative Lawrence H. Watres of Pennsylvania and Senator Charles D. McNary of Oregon, both Republicans; it became known as the McNary-Watres Act and later was shortened to the Watres Act. Its real purposes were twofold: to squeeze small airlines out of the picture and to foster passenger traffic among the survivors. It achieved these through two principal provisions:

1. An air mail contractor with two years' operating experience could exchange his present authorization for a ten-year route certificate, and pioneer rights would be recognized—which sounded perfectly fair, except that the Watres Act defined an airline with "pioneer rights" as the "lowest responsible bidder who has owned and operated an air transportation service on a fixed daily schedule over a distance of not less than two hundred and fifty miles and for a period of not less than six months prior to the advertisement for bids." That definition disqualified a number of small pioneer airlines flying minuscule routes, many less than one hundred miles.

2. The practice of paying the airlines by the weight of mail carried was scrapped in favor of a new system based on payments by the space offered. The maximum rate would be $1.25 a mile regardless of whether the space was filled. While outwardly reasonable, there was no doubt the provision was a death blow to the smaller airlines with relatively little mail capacity, and it meant considerably reduced mail revenues for the larger ones. Brown justified it on the grounds that it would encourage the airlines to expand their passenger business.

Brown tried hard to insert a clause that would have eliminated all competitive bidding for mail contracts, giving the Postmaster General sole authority over choosing which airlines would fly the mail. Congress was ready to go along with this awarding of total dictatorial power, but the U. S. Controller General, John McCarl, raised the roof, and the provision was taken out of the bill.

The Watres Act became law in April 1930, but Brown wasn't satisfied yet. When mail bids were advertised, the notice included an eligibility requirement that operators had to have at least six months' experience flying at night over routes of 250 miles or more—another jolt for the small carriers, yet one that also technically affected big TAT, which was still operating only in the daytime. The requirement actually was about as legal as selling liquor, but Brown argued that it was purely a safety measure.

The Watres provision that armed the Postmaster General with

a club the size of a redwood trunk was authority to extend or consolidate routes "when in his judgment the public interest will be promoted thereby." To Brown, this rather vague statement was a blank check to revamp the whole air transportation route structure—and he was to cash it quickly.

Early in May, less than a month after the Watres Act was passed and signed, the hard-nosed Postmaster General summoned various airlines to Washington for a series of meetings. The "guest list" itself was only too indicative of Brown's ambitious plans—he invited only the biggest carriers, completely ignoring the smaller operators. He was later to explain, "there was no sense in taking the government's money and dishing it out to every little fellow that was flying around the map and was not going to do anything." The meetings were not secret, as was later charged; they merely weren't very well publicized.

Between May 19 and 30, Brown discussed his blueprint for the nation's future air transportation with Western Air Express, TAT, United Aircraft, the Aviation Corporation (better known as AVCO, the holding company for what eventually became American Airlines), Eastern Air Transport, and the Stout Line (which already had been absorbed by United). The twelve days of heated discussion and debate went down in history as the infamous "Spoils Conference," and the harsh sobriquet was not entirely unwarranted—to those participants who liked Brown's scheme literally went the spoils.

Among them was *not* Harris M. Hanshue, who came to Washington accompanied by his male secretary, Gilbert Givvens, and about a dozen pieces of luggage. Pop always invaded the capital with the apparent expectation of staying at least a month, and he carried an appropriate number of suitcases. One of Gil's chief tasks was to count the luggage items when they arrived.

Hanshue knew he was in for a rough time—how rough, though, he wouldn't find out until Brown lowered the boom on an airline whose prime weakness was the very fact that it was a *western* carrier. Passage of the Watres Act already had given WAE a sad indication of where the winds of politics were blowing. The new law was cutting Western's air mail revenues nearly 65 per cent, and upon mail pay rested the future of Hanshue's plans to continue development of passenger traffic. Hanshue himself had informed his directors that the airline's $1 million in cash reserves on hand at the end of 1929 were being depleted at the rate of $175,000 a month. If the mail profits weren't enough to support passenger service, and the latter had to be subsidized out of the reserves, the airline would be faced with virtual collapse in less than seven months.

That was the gloomy prospect Hanshue took with him to the "Spoils Conference." He had one more worry on his mind other than Western's crumbling fortunes: The pressure for a TAT-WAE merger had resumed even before he went to Washington to confront Brown. Early in 1930, Hanshue got a call from Brooks Parker of Philadelphia, whose company handled Western's insurance.

"I'd like you to meet with D. M. Sheaffer of the Pennsylvania Railroad," Parker said, "preferably at my home here."

"Why?" Hanshue asked with his usual bluntness.

"Well, as you know, Sheaffer's chief of passenger transportation for the Pennsylvania, and he's also chairman of TAT's Executive Committee. Now, just hold on a minute, Pop"—Hanshue was sputtering into the phone—"you know damned well that Western and TAT are competing against each other destructively. I think it's time you consider working out some kind of consolidation."

Hanshue bellowed and cursed, but the upshot was his reluctant agreement to talk to Sheaffer in Philadelphia. Nothing came of the meeting; the discussion, in fact, was so vague that Hanshue didn't even bother to inform his associates that it had taken place—"because I knew they were so definitely opposed to it [a merger]," he was to explain later.

But he also had a strong suspicion that a WAE-TAT merger would be brought up when the airline chieftains met with Brown—and he was right. The Postmaster General lit the fireworks without preamble, informing them that under the authority granted him by the Watres Act, he wanted the industry's route systems realigned. He said he would grant new air mail franchises for the central and southern transcontinental routes and, looking squarely at the glowering Hanshue, he added that under no circumstances would a company be allowed to operate more than one transcontinental mail route.

Pop exploded with rage, loudly pointing out that Western already was operating large segments of both the proposed central and southern routes.

"The solution is simple," Brown said calmly. "I suggest that Western merge with TAT, and we'll give the combined carrier the central route."

"But this will prevent us from bidding on the southern route," Hanshue protested. "We're flying as far east as Dallas now."

"Of course it will," the Postmaster General agreed, "so I advise you to sell your Los Angeles–Dallas operation to Southwest Air Fast Express [a subsidiary of American Airways]."

Hanshue, as lacking in diplomacy as he was in political maneuvering, told Brown he could go to hell. The first session broke up with Hanshue refusing to budge—even though the tough, gutty little man from Michigan probably knew right then and there that he was beaten. That same night, Sheaffer phoned and asked if he could see him. Almost wearily, Pop consented, and the railroad official, representing TAT at the conference, flatly proposed that TAT take over Western Air Express through an exchange of stock.

"I don't think our people would be interested in any such proposal," Hanshue responded with—for him—rare civility. "They don't want to lose control of their operations."

But Sheaffer persisted, pleading that Hanshue should at least contact Western's major stockholders and sound them out. Hanshue put through several calls and got 100 per cent rejection of any merger—particularly one in which Western Air Express would lose not only control but all identity. Throughout the remainder of the meetings with Brown and his fellow airline executives, Hanshue maintained a position set in solid concrete. He managed to alienate not only the austere but equally tough Postmaster General of the United States but some of Pop's colleagues as well. After one particularly volatile session, someone asked Pop—brooding sourly at one end of the long conference table—how he felt about whatever matter was under discussion.

Hanshue looked around at this distinguished assemblage in the manner of a machine gunner about to spray a helpless target.

"I think you're all crazy as hell!" he rasped. And this was reported to have been one of his few printable comments.

He finally left Washington in what one observer termed "a black rage." He also left Washington, for all intents and purposes, without his airline. He scarcely had time to unpack his bags when Brown phoned to request another meeting—this time just between the two of them. Pop had just written him his reasons for not wanting to merge with TAT nor selling Western's Los Angeles–Dallas route to American—a letter expounding his views in somewhat calmer language than he had used orally. Brown said he had read the letter carefully and had another idea he wanted to talk over with the embattled WAE president.

Pop went back to Washington and found the Postmaster General pleasant and even conciliatory. Obviously, Brown knew of the most recent Sheaffer proposal—a complete takeover by TAT —and he wisely deduced that this approach was not only futile but wrong. What TAT wanted was not merger but an acquisition—and not even Walter Folger Brown could ask Hanshue to swallow that size pill.

What Brown now suggested, hoping it would be more palatable to the fiery leader of Western sitting gloomily in front of his desk, was the formation of a new company.

"It would take over the assets of both TAT and Western on a fifty-fifty basis," Brown said, "along the routes where you're now competing."

"Including Los Angeles–San Francisco?" Hanshue asked—his strained expression reflecting those bittersweet memories of the Model Airway's glory days, and the sweat-stained efforts that had gone into the pioneering adventure; for by 1930, TAT had bought out Maddux.

"Including Los Angeles–San Francisco," Brown said firmly.

Brown added that the new corporation should take in a third "partner"—namely the Pittsburgh Aviation Industries Corporation (PAIC), which had been formed by a group of Pittsburgh industrialists. In actuality, it wasn't even an airline—it had built an airport near Pittsburgh, where it ran a flying school and air taxi service. But the latter operations had been conducted over the rugged terrain east of Pittsburgh, and when Brown put the central transcontinental route up for mail bids, PAIC claimed it held pioneering rights on this small but vital segment. This, in PAIC's view, gave it priority over TAT, which had never flown east of Columbus, Ohio—an argument that Brown bought, despite the fact that PAIC itself had never operated the "fixed daily schedule" required under the Watres Act. This deficiency, in Brown's mind, seems to have been outweighed by PAIC's financial and political status—among its backers was the Mellon family, with strong influences in the Republican party.

To keep intact his master plan of an air transportation system made up of a few large airlines, Brown had convinced TAT that it should let PAIC into the central route by making it part of a merger deal with Western, PAIC holding 10 per cent of the stock. Hanshue didn't like it and said so to Brown, who couldn't have cared less; he had Hanshue over a barrel, and both men knew it even as they sparred, Pop reiterating his arguments against any merger.

"Our people have never been interested in going in with the Pennsylvania Railroad or the TAT group," he repeated, "and they're not interested now. They refuse to give up control, and what you're suggesting now would be very difficult to work out."

"I don't see any great difficulties," Brown said blandly.

"You're proposing consolidation on a fifty-fifty basis. Hell, from the point of view of operating value, our assets are worth more than theirs—we've always been conservative in accounting for capital expenditures, and our equipment depreciation rates are comparatively high. You're demanding a fifty-fifty deal, and damnit, TAT doesn't deserve it. I repeat, Mr. Postmaster General, our directors and stockholders will never approve any merger in which we can't retain control!"

Brown's eyes narrowed. "Then, Mr. Hanshue, I must inform you that if Western wants to get in on any transcontinental route —*any* transcontinental route, mind you—the merger I've suggested is the only way you're going to do it."

"All we wanted was the Kansas City–Los Angeles portion, but under your plan that's impossible," Pop muttered, almost as if he were talking to himself.

"That's correct—impossible," Brown agreed.

"If you insist, I can talk to my associates," Hanshue said resignedly, in partial surrender. "All I can do is try."

"And that's just what I insist you do, Mr. Hanshue—try."

Hanshue returned to Los Angeles, despondent and discouraged.

"We have no money with which to fight," he confided to Woolley. "In fact, the way things are going, we have only enough money to live a few months longer. There was nothing else for me to do but say I'd try."

Try he did—but only so far as bringing up the merger for discussion with Western's directors. Hanshue himself still refused to raise the white flag, going to the extent of recommending rejection of the merger and then making the meaningless, empty gesture of bidding formally on both the central and southern transcontinental routes. His final, gallantly futile attempt to block the merger was staged at New York's Savoy Hotel, where he met with his directors and a full hour pleaded with them not to let it go through. He asked the impossible—not only to fight Brown but also to go all the way to the White House if necessary. But he might as well have been rehearsing the plea in front of a mirror, alone; Western's board was 100 per cent Republican, and not one man at that meeting was willing to take on the Administration.

Postmaster General Brown held all the aces, plus a few kings and queens as well. By July 1, Hanshue had entered into actual merger negotiations, which stumbled along briefly until Mr. Brown put his well-polished shoes down on the bickering. Hanshue was objecting to giving PAIC 5 per cent of Western's holdings in the newly formed carrier, with TAT giving up an equal percentage of its own shares. He insisted that the PAIC share come out of TAT's half interest, arguing that the minority partner was on the eastern leg of the central route.

Sheaffer likewise was vehement in demanding that PAIC's share should be deducted equally from both TAT and WAE. When they informed Brown that they had reached a stalemate, the Postmaster General suggested a compromise that leaned toward TAT's side—reduce PAIC's share to 5 per cent, Western giving up 2.5 per cent of its stock, and TAT doing the same. He presented this formula on a take-it-or-else basis.

"If you don't agree this time," Brown warned, "I'll delay awarding any mail contract until the issue is settled."

Faced with this ultimatum, Hanshue caved in. TAT and WAE

were to hold 47.5 per cent each, and PAIC 5 per cent. A tentative merger agreement was reached July 16. Western's stockholders approved it with two conditions: Western had to retain management control of the new airline for one year, in exchange for giving TAT voting control, and Western would not have to contribute any cash to the new corporation, whose president would be Hanshue.

The presidency was not the most important item Hanshue salvaged from the whole shotgun marriage. The major concession he had wrung from his determined opponents was to allow Western Air Express to survive as an independent airline, operating CAM-4, the original Los Angeles–Salt Lake City route, along with a San Diego–Los Angeles extension added just before Brown fired his fatal torpedo during the airline conference. Also to be operated by Western Air Express was the Cheyenne–Pueblo route, the Catalina operation, and the Mid-Continent system. Having already disposed of the San Francisco–Seattle route as too costly to run without a mail contract, Hanshue had little left of the air empire he had built—but it was enough to keep his pioneering airline in existence by a slim but sturdy thread even as the huge carrier created by the unwanted merger began operations.

On October 1, 1930, Brown awarded the southern transcontinental route to American Airways.

On the same day, he completed Western's dissection by awarding the central route to Transcontinental and Western Air, Inc.

Otherwise known as TWA.

CHAPTER SIX

Airline Within an Airline

If the first four years of Western Air Express represented a steady climb, the next four could be classed an out-of-control dive.

WAE, just before formation of TWA, had a fleet of some 40 airplanes—including 21 Fokker trimotors and the two giant F-32s—plus 100 pilots and 500 other employees. By 1934, the airline that once had been the nation's biggest carrier was down to 6 pilots flying 4 aircraft, and less than 150 employees. It had gone from zenith to nadir in just 48 months crammed with such corporate and political convulsions that its survival bordered on the miraculous. It even lost the F-32s, which TWA operated briefly as back-up planes before retiring them permanently.

That it did keep from sinking into oblivion was due to the doggedness of Pop Hanshue, who refused to give up on an airline that on more than one occasion was pronounced dead. To any reasonable observer, Western was a bankruptcy flying someplace to happen—its chances of surviving as a separate entity were roughly the same as Custer's odds at Little Big Horn. Hanshue had his faults—temper, rudeness, and all the diplomatic finesse of a bull being among them—but above all he was a fighter with a cause. And the cause was the airline he started and stubbornly refused to desert. Even as president of TWA, he paid as much (and perhaps more) attention to the fortunes of struggling Western Air Express and its emasculated system. The stories told about him are myriad. Art Beggs, one of the few Hanshue contemporaries still around, has fond memories of Pop's dynamic and vitriolic personality. According to Beggs, Hanshue never spoke two words when one could get his point across.

"He was a powerfully built guy," Art remembers, "with a bull neck and a rasping, husky voice. He had a way of commanding loyalty and generating enthusiasm, and an equally impressive capacity for choosing the right men for certain jobs. But he could crack down!"

Hanshue's closely cropped hair gave him the appearance of a Prussian general, and his sharp tongue did nothing to offset that physical impression. Beggs, who was one of the many WAE people transferred to TWA, was later enticed back to Western with an extremely generous salary offer. Publicity Director Clancy Dayhoff took Art's picture and wrote a story extolling Beggs as a fast-rising executive of the new-blood type who at WAE would be the youngest general traffic manager in the industry. One of the Los Angeles newspapers printed Clancy's fulsome release as well as the photograph. Hanshue called Beggs to his office. Art showed up more than half expecting to be complimented on the great publicity, but he discarded this notion instantly when he glimpsed Hanshue's sour countenance.

"I saw your advertisement in the paper," Pop snarled sarcastically.

While Hanshue held his PR types like Woolley and Dayhoff in high regard and dined well on the fruits of their usually ingenious efforts, he seemed to care little for personal glory; it was Western he wanted publicized, not himself. In fact, Beggs believes Pop actually was rather shy, hiding introvertism under a façade of invective.

Beggs, like a number of his fellow Westerners, was not overjoyed at the transfer to TWA. Friction inevitably developed between TAT and WAE personnel, who suddenly found themselves like enemy soldiers exchanging reluctant salutes during an armed truce. The tiny cadre left behind to man the forts of CAM-4 and CAM-12 (133 employees) showed outright hostility toward TWA, and not all the ex-Western Air Express people were exactly paragons of undying co-operation. Beggs was one of the latter, freely admitting now that he and others used to route eastbound transcontinental traffic through Salt Lake City, connecting with United there, instead of ticketing passengers via

TWA's Kansas City route. It was a surreptitious way of boosting their "alma mater's" revenues, even though it obviously cut into TWA's—to such an extent that Beggs one day was called into a meeting of top TWA executives and told to cease and desist.

The atmosphere became heated, and when one TWA official accused Beggs of transgressions beyond traffic diversion, Beggs blew up.

"If you tell one more lie," Beggs shouted, "I'll toss you out that window!"

Fisticuffs were averted and tempers cooled, but the incident reached the ears of Pop Hanshue. He called Beggs the next day.

"I hear you made a damned fool of yourself," Hanshue remarked.

"Yes, sir."

A slight, almost inaudible chuckle from the president of TWA.

"Don't worry about it, Art," Hanshue said—"but don't do it again."

Neither Beggs nor anyone else saw much of Hanshue in those days; he was usually in Washington, battling on behalf of TWA but also of the still-breathing but decidedly sick airline he had fathered. The real tragedy of Western Air Express was that it was forced into the TWA dissection at a time when its professional expertise had reached a peak. One of the last steps taken prior to the merger was organization of an engineering department under Herbert Hoover, Jr., who co-ordinated the activities of four technical divisions—communications, weather, airports, and airways.

Hoover's earlier efforts in the field of communications had matured into a far-flung radio telegraph system involving more than thirty stations—TWA inherited most of them in the merger. With Thorp Hiscock of Boeing concentrating on ground-air communications (the two were soon to form Aeronautical Radio, Inc., a nonprofit organization that acted as an industry research clearinghouse), Hoover's once-tiny operation had blossomed into a full-scale technical effort.

The President's son had started with Western by setting up shop in a small room at one end of a hangar. By 1930, he had a well-equipped laboratory with seventy-five engineers, researchers, radio operators, and maintenance men under his direct supervision. His influence within Western in general and on Hanshue specifically was immense; it was on his recommendation alone that WAE, only a few months before the shotgun marriage, shelled out $200,000 for new airplane radio equipment.

Hoover was quick to give credit to his subordinates—including a couple of foreign-born electronics specialists whom Western had hired to work with Hoover, Geoffrey Kreusi of Switzerland and Gerhardt Fischer of Germany. From the fertile minds of these two engineers came the first directional radio compass, at the time the most important single safety advancement in the field of navigation. They were installed on several WAE planes, including both F-32s, and the device sometime later was sold to Bendix, which further developed it into an instrument that became standard equipment on all airliners.

But the brilliance of the Hoover-supervised technical department was the flareup of a light bulb just before it goes out. Western Air Express didn't expire, of course, but coinciding with the "merger" was the virtual disappearance of its prestige, industry leadership—and its profits. WAE ended 1930 with its first deficit since its inception. Mail pay on its bread-and-butter route, CAM-4, had been cut under the Watres Act from $2.50 to $1.14 a mile—a slash sufficient to propel the battered airline to a net loss of more than $200,000 for the year. (CAM-4 actually showed a profit of almost $900,000 but this was drowned under the losses pouring from the all-passenger routes, such as Los Angeles–San Francisco, Los Angeles–Kansas City, and Los Angeles–Fort Worth. TWA took over these markets too late in the year to keep them out of Western's deficit column.) In one short year, WAE had gone from a healthy, thriving company with $1 million in cash reserves to an emaciated midget struggling to stay alive.

As bad as the depletion of assets, routes, and credit was the loss of so much skilled manpower. The initial general reaction to the merger was resentment and, in some cases, panic; it meant job changes not only affecting position but also location. Yet once the shock was over, employees and officials adjusted easily to working for a new company and, in a majority of cases, the old ties with Western disintegrated quickly. The two remaining Horsemen—James and Kelly—stayed with WAE, the former as vice president of operations, but the majority of the crews went over to TWA and never left. George Rice, Si Morehouse, and Dutch Holloway were among them; Jack Frye and Paul Richter were to rise high in TWA's hierarchy, Frye becoming its president in 1934. Woolley also was one of those attracted to TWA's apparently greener pastures.

One of the few who refused to go with TWA was Leo Dwerlkotte. The merger decimated Western's financial department, treasurer Hugh Wright and chief accountant Harold Finnegan being among those transferred to the Transcontinental and Western Air payroll. Dwerlkotte won promotion to chief accountant via this attrition, and thus began his own ascent to prominence. Much of Hanshue's own resilience and determination had been injected into the veins of the handful trying to keep WAE alive as a separate airline. Pop's optimism occasionally was in the whistling-by-the-graveyard category; only a few weeks before the merger negotiations began, he had summoned Beggs, then running the New York sales office, to meet with him at the Carlton Hotel in Washington, where Hanshue always stayed.

"We'll be flying into New York in a week and I want you to get ready," he announced confidently. Even at that late stage, he seemed unwilling to admit publicly, anyway, that merger was inevitable. And when Western fell on hard times in 1930, he spent more time trying to solve its problems than those of the airline he had just begun to run. WAE's troubles were of such magnitude that its once gilt-edged credit rating evaporated. With debts mounting and western banks refusing for the first time to help an airline whose blood, bones, and flesh had come out of the West, Hanshue was forced into seeking aid from the one source he intensely hated: eastern financiers. In this he relied on Talbot, the director he was closest to, who had a friend make the necessary contacts.

General Motors was the samaritan in this hour of need—naturally not for any altruistic motives. GM had been trying to get a major foothold in the aviation industry for a long time, and the unfamiliar sight of Harris M. Hanshue holding a supplicating hat in hand was a welcome one. The automobile firm had organized a subsidiary, General Aviation, which ended the dominance of western investors over WAE by acquiring 60,000 shares for

$900,000—enough to give GM control of the airline, and Fokker Aircraft as well.

Hanshue's own tenure at TWA was not only shaky but also short-lived; he had trod on too many toes, insulted too many persons, and made too many enemies. In the spring of 1931, he was hospitalized with a serious case of pneumonia, and during his absence, Richard W. Robbins, former top official at PAIC, took over as TWA's managing director. When Hanshue recovered, he went immediately to Washington, where he successfully bid on a new mail contract for WAE, extending CAM-12 southward from Pueblo via two spur routes—one to Albuquerque and the other to Amarillo. Both already were part of the system flown by Mid-Continental Air Express, Western's subsidiary, and with mail revenues secured, WAE was able to absorb Mid-Continental into the corporate structure by the fall of 1931.

Hanshue soon found he had more than adequate time to deal with Western Air Express; in fact, he learned he could devote himself exclusively to WAE. It was four months short of the full year in which he was supposed to serve as TWA's president when Hanshue was "relieved" of that title. "Relieved" is the word he used himself, but while there seems to be little doubt he was fired, there also is little doubt he didn't shed any tears. All the loyalty, affection, and emotion he packed into his compact, energetic frame was directed toward Western, and while he resumed full-time control over a veritable shambles, he felt he was back home where he belonged.

It was not the easiest homecoming, considering the shattered state of Western's route system. Yet Hanshue engineered an almost incredible if modest comeback; WAE closed 1931 with a net profit of nearly $200,000, although part of this was achieved by the process of deliberate contraction. The money-losing Wilmington–Catalina operation was sold to the Wrigley family, which owned Catalina, along with several amphibians and an old Boeing flying boat, and Hanshue had found a financial "angel" in GM's General Aviation Corporation, which gradually increased its WAE holdings from 30 per cent to 51 per cent.

Hanshue and his hard-working subordinates rated medals for making any money whatsoever—Western was one of the few airlines showing a profit in the midst of the Depression. And it was the nation's steadily worsening economy that presented Pop with a crisis of major proportions. Early in 1932, the Post Office Department announced it would cease all mail pay for night flights between Los Angeles and Salt Lake City—the order coming right from Walter F. Brown in what appeared to be, although there was no proof, a personal vendetta against Hanshue and WAE.

The Postmaster General rationalized his action on the grounds of economy. Congress had passed a Treasury-Post Office Department Appropriations bill, cutting the requested sum by 10 per cent and also failing to designate funds specifically for night mail service on CAM-4. Brown, a master at interpreting any piece of legislation in accordance with his own frequently biased views, seized on this omission to give Hanshue the well-known shaft. Brown claimed that when the Department of Commerce completed the lighting for the eastern half of TWA's new transcontinental system, it spent so much money that funds were insufficient to support the Los Angeles–Salt Lake City night mail payments. When Hanshue protested, Brown calmly pointed out that the appropriations measure didn't even mention CAM-4, and thus he had no authority to pay for the night service.

WAE had been operating two daily flights over the route, connecting with United's transcontinental service at Salt Lake City. The schedules, geared to efficient mail delivery, demanded that one of the eastbound trips had to be flown at night—and it was this flight which Brown's order wiped out. It also happened to be the most heavily used and lucrative trip Western operated, a salient point that Brown ignored when it was brought up. He seemed bent on destroying the one man who had tried, albeit unsuccessfully, to alter his blueprint for reshaping U.S. commercial aviation. This is not to belittle the plan itself, which in many respects was what the airline industry needed, but to spotlight Brown's ruthlessness. When the first wave of protests against his CAM-4 action reached Brown, his only comment was, "Let 'em squawk!"

But not even Brown could stay aloof from the heat that boiled out of the outraged western communities affected by the unexpected cut in mail service. More than just Los Angeles and Salt Lake City were involved; cancellation of that single flight, for example, caused an eighteen-hour delay in delivery of air mail to Denver from the West Coast. Brown underestimated Hanshue's ability to stir up support on an issue that touched people on a personal basis.

Hanshue worked closely with four Western colleagues in his campaign to put pressure on his old enemy. Beggs, back with WAE by now after his unhappy stint at TWA, helped line up allies along with Clancy Dayhoff in the areas Western served; in Washington, Pop's other chief cohorts were Burgess, and later a young firebrand named Sigmund Janas, who would someday become president of Colonial Airlines; Janas served briefly as WAE's Washington representative, one of the several men receiving their first training in the Harris M. Hanshue School for Tough Airline Executives.

Beggs enlisted the aid of MGM's Louis B. Mayer, not only Hollywood's most influential studio boss but also a personal friend of President Hoover. Another influential figure joining what amounted to a "to hell with Walter F. Brown" movement was F. G. Bonfils, colorful Denver newspaper publisher. Burgess and Janas went to work on California, Utah, and Colorado congressmen, concentrating on Utah's two senators—Reed Smoot and Peter Norbeck.

Valuable help in generating pressure from Capitol Hill came from Harold Fabian, a promiment Salt Lake City businessman and president of the city's Chamber of Commerce. Fabian, who would be elected to Western's board of directors in 1935 and serve for nearly a decade, was a feisty individual with a great admiration for Hanshue and a corresponding lack of same toward Brown. When Senator Norbeck wrote him that a supplemental Post Office appropriations bill was being readied, still minus money earmarked specifically for CAM-4, Fabian wired him:

"We are fearful that Postmaster General Brown will divert the money to other parts of the country where there are more votes."

Generally, Western got the support it sought, loud and voluminous, but it was not until mid-August that night mail service was reinstated. Brown's power was such that the battle had to be taken right up to the White House, where Hoover was persuaded to endorse a $350,000 supplemental appropriation, Sena-

tor Smoot doing most of the persuading. By the time the shooting was over, WAE had spent some $50,000 pleading its case;
the importance of full service restoration on CAM-4 was underlined by the fact that in just one month the fresh mail revenue put the $50,000 back in Western's bank account. During the
seven months the cancellation was in effect, WAE was losing
$100,000 a month. It was no wonder that Western's 1932 profits
dipped to slightly more than $43,000, and this, at least, was bet-
ter than what TWA had been showing—the latter was losing
money at an alarming rate. But nobody at Western could afford
to gloat, because WAE retained its 47.5 per cent interest in TWA
and in effect was in the position of an unsatisfied major stockholder even though it no longer had any voice in the airline's
management and policies. Technically, they remained married
but separated; the divorce was to come later.

Even the equipment TWA inherited from Western had proved
to be a liability instead of an expected asset. About a year before
Brown and Hanshue clashed for the last time, an ex-WAE
Fokker F-10 now carrying TWA's insignia took off at 9:15 A.M.
from Kansas City bound for Los Angeles. The date was March
31, 1931.

Flight 5 was scheduled to reach Los Angeles at 8:00 P.M. after
stops in Wichita; Oklahoma City; Amarillo; Albuquerque; and
Winslow, Arizona; one of the boarding Los Angeles passengers
was not only a special VIP but a vociferous supporter of commercial aviation. He was a homely visaged Norwegian with a
clipped voice, a commanding personality, and the reputation of
being the finest football coach in the United States. That Knute
Rockne of Notre Dame, who loved flying, was to die in the crash
of Flight 5 would be one of aviation's greatest ironies.

The F-10 never reached Wichita, its first stop. Less than one
hour after takeoff, witnesses saw it plunging to earth with part of
the wing gone. All aboard were killed instantly; the accident was
bad enough, but Rockne's death made it a national tragedy—one
that sent reverberations throughout the industry. The obvious
structural failure of the wing cast an ominous shadow on the
wooden Fokkers, Tony Fokker himself flying to the scene of the
crash and expressing anger at TWA for letting the plane take off
in what Fokker felt was dangerous weather.

But the official finding was that the spruce wing spars and ribs cracked from wood rot. This explanation came from the Bureau of Air Commerce, the government agency charged with investigating air crashes at the time, and the Bureau followed up this verdict by requiring all Fokker operators periodically to inspect the internal components of the wings.

The inspection process was expensive and time-consuming. While Western and other airlines continued to fly their F-10s, the plane was doomed as a viable commercial transport. Not everyone bought the rot story, but the fact that the federal government put the blame there was sufficient to make all opposition moot. Western was to fly its Fokkers for another three years following the Rockne disaster, primarily because it couldn't finance new equipment, but overnight the all-metal Ford became interim queen of the airways until development of the revolutionary Boeing 247 and Douglas DC-2.

The TWA crash, however, solidified Hanshue's abiding interest in aviation meteorology. It is hardly likely, of course, that he noticed the hiring of a new WAE night cargo clerk early in 1932, a youthful graduate student at the California Institute of Technology who was destined to become the dean of private weather forecasters, and a maverick in his own field.

Irving Krick was his name. He showed up at TWA's offices one day and proclaimed that he was an expert at forecasting weather. Someone with more charity than actual foresight condescended to interview him, and Krick proceeded to rattle on nervously about studying, at Cal Tech, a new Norwegian method of predicting weather by analyzing the movements of air masses. In fact, he had written a thesis on the subject, a thick tome that he drew from a disreputable briefcase.

"You might like to glance . . ." he began.

"No, thanks," the interviewer interrupted hastily—being a man thoroughly convinced that forecasting weather was immeasurably less scientific than picking winners at a racetrack.

"But this thesis applies the Norwegian theory to airline operations," Krick said earnestly. "These maps I've drawn will show . . ."

His sincerity evidently stirred the interviewer far more than the new Norwegian method of predicting weather by analyzing the movements of air masses. Besides, the brief glimpse of the maps Krick had tried to show him looked as if the kid was smart, if a bit cracked.

"We don't have anything for you here," he said. "But why don't you go over to Western and talk to Jimmie James? He runs their operations."

The hard-bitten Jimmie wasn't impressed by the weather maps Krick proudly displayed, nor by the youngster himself. Krick was a tall, dark-complexioned, rather dandified person who talked in a nervous torrent of words, as if his mind kept getting ahead of his tongue. Nor was Jimmie influenced by Krick's modest admission that music was his chief interest; he had become a concert pianist at age thirteen.

"Your timing's pretty good," James allowed. "Joe George, our meteorologist, is going on vacation. Tell you what, young man: If you want to take a job as a clerk, handle the mail, and do some of the paperwork on cargo shipments, I'll let you draw those weather maps of yours and you can help us with meteorology on a part-time basis."

So Irving Krick's airline career began as a night cargo clerk, making out forms on mail and express poundage at the Burbank airport, where Western had moved after TWA took over Alhambra. Employees liked the area and its people, who welcomed the merger refugees with surprising friendliness. Mrs. Ed Deeter, wife of a veteran Western employee, recalls that "when we moved over to Burbank, I could go into any store and say my husband worked for Western and they'd give me all the credit I wanted."

Mr. Krick, naturally, was oblivious to the friendly Burbank surroundings, and not just because the night shift couldn't see much anyway; Mr. Krick was persisting in drawing those funny maps, and anyone peeking over his shoulder probably thought he was diagraming plays for the next Southern California football game. He was drawing one day what appeared to be an interesting off-tackle slant with a lateral pass tacked on; upon completion, he barged into Jimmie James' office, where he informed the startled operations manager that a plane leaving Los Angeles for Salt Lake City that day would run into a violent storm front just east of Milford, Utah.

"If he lands at Milford and waits it out, he can take off again in a couple of hours," Krick advised.

James looked dubious, but there was something about the boy's confidence that told him to listen—and heed. The flight was told to land at Milford as Krick had suggested, and the pilot later reported to Jimmie that the storm had hit exactly as the night cargo clerk predicted.

"Tell Joe George thanks for me," the pilot said. "He really hit it on the button."

"It wasn't George," James sighed, "it was somebody else."

Joe George took a naturally dim view of this brash young upstart. George had been trained in conventional weather forecasting methods, and to him the weather fronts Krick kept adding to George's maps were like drawing mustaches on a girl's picture. When George protested to James, however, Jimmie already had been hearing pilot reports about the accuracy of Krick's predictions.

"I think the kid's got something," James told his miffed meteorologist, "so let's keep doing it his way."

The inevitable happened—Krick gradually assumed an increasingly important role at Western, with free rein not only for forecasting but also for experimenting. Clancy Dayhoff was prowling around the airport one day and noticed a mechanic attaching some scientific instruments under the wing of a flight about to depart. Curious, he made a few inquiries, which led him to Krick—who spouted volubly, as usual, on ideas he had for predicting tailwinds. Thus was born an early Western advertising slogan: "Western Air Express—the airline with perpetual tailwinds."

Dayhoff must have had a few James G. Woolley genes wandering around in his bloodstream to come up with that boast. On too many occasions, there were no tailwinds and not even the genius that was Irving Krick could make a headwind reverse course. It is safe to say that Krick didn't think much of Dayhoff's overenthusiastic tactics; Krick was proud enough of his abilities without having them twisted into exaggerated claims. Before he became the airline's top weather expert, Western's weather forecasting sources were only 75 per cent accurate. Krick raised this to 96.1 per cent. Hanshue himself credited Krick's forecasting with saving WAE $35,000 annually and increasing scheduled flight completions by a whopping 45 per cent.

Eventually, Krick left to start teaching at Cal Tech, and in World War II he won fame as the man who called the shots on the invasion of Europe: General Eisenhower set the date for D-Day in accordance with Krick's forecasts for the English Channel area. One of his associates in that vital assignment was George, who eventually studied under him at Cal Tech and went on to become Eastern's chief meteorologist after the war.

The opportunity Western gave Krick was an example of an airline striving to maintain its progressiveness even though it had been reduced to a ragtag fleet, a shriveled route system, and a collection of frazzled hopes. In the spring of 1932, it earned a few headlines by getting involved in a Buck Rogerish gadget called television. The Don Lee Broadcasting Company had an experimental TV station, W6XAO, and wanted to see if its signals could be picked up by an airplane in flight. Western supplied an F-10, Dayhoff the publicity releases, and Hollywood the subject to be televised—a young actress. Although Dayhoff considered the event slightly less newsworthy than the Second Coming, the well-publicized flight merely demonstrated how far television still had to go.

The girl's hazy figure appeared on a screen eight inches square, mounted in a console radio cabinet just behind the cockpit. The picture came out in a blue, flickering light, and when the plane banked, the actress's hair looked as if it was streaming in the wind. The image was discernible for periods of five to six minutes, fading when the aircraft passed beyond the range of the transmitting station. History has been kinder to the young lady on the primitive screen than to the almost-forgotten experiment—she was Loretta Young.

Jimmie James became one of Hanshue's chief confidants in those postmerger days, along with Burgess and young Gil Given, who was more of an executive assistant than a mere secretary. James, who never really liked desk work, flew scheduled trips occasionally, and he always assigned himself to whatever flight Hanshue was taking. James was popular among his small group of pilots—perhaps unfortunately, because a few of them felt Jimmie was too softhearted. He was an airman first and an executive second, and the priorities should have been reversed; overidentification with one's command, it's called in the military, and it has been a booby trap for more than one airline chief pilot. Yet at the time he began running flight operations, it may have been more of a strength than a weakness; morale in once-mighty Western Air Express was shaky after the TWA earthquake, and the pilots needed a sympathetic boss like James.

To be perfectly fair, the pilots didn't have it easy—Western's nor anyone else's. Captains were flying 125 hours a month for $250, and the copilots were averaging about half that pay for 160 hours a month. They were not unionized—the Air Line Pilots' Association (ALPA) wasn't organized until 1931, and then in secret—and even if the airmen had a union, they were in no position to complain. During the Depression, there were an estimated 7,000 qualified pilots trying to get jobs in an industry employing only 1,500.

At least on Western the copilots got paid; on some airlines, the rookies flew for nothing, their training being regarded as compensation. For a long time, WAE first officers suffered the ignominy of not being allowed to wear the same style uniform as the captain. This policy was dictated solely by their cabin service duties, there not being enough stewards to work every flight. When Western's captains got their first standard uniform late in 1929—gray with what was jokingly called an "Eric Von Stroheim" military-style cap—the copilots still were wearing white duck pants, white shirt, black bow tie, black shoes, and a white cap. They resembled deck stewards fresh off some ocean liner.

While the pilots weren't trained, monitored, checked, and regulated as they are today, they still lived under some stringent rules. The Western Air Express *Handbook for Pilots & Copilots* issued in 1930 covered forty-eight mimeographed pages—it listed seventy-six general rules, twenty-eight flying rules, six ground rules, and thirty-six miscellaneous rules. The regulations ranged from "Pilots must not let their financial affairs bring discredit upon the company" (General Rule 10) to "it is better that an airplane be brought to the ground, even though damage to it may result, than flying blindly through storm conditions that may result in a tragedy by crashing out of control" (Flying Rule 28).

Pilots were admonished not to frequent "places where intoxicants are sold" under threat of instant dismissal. They were required to have telephones, keep pistols in sight while handling mail, and turn in the guns for cleaning on specified dates. Captains were told to refuse passage to drunks and remove any passenger who "becomes intoxicated, unmanageable or otherwise obnoxious to other passengers, at the first regular stop." Copilot duties included stocking the plane with all necessary passenger supplies and helping load and unload baggage. On radio-equipped aircraft, pilots were warned not to display "irritation or impatience" while handling communications—a warning frequently ignored by these rugged individualists whose tempers so often bore short fuses.

The WAE executive who got along best with the occasionally temperamental crews was the likable, breezy Dayhoff. The pilots were a good source of supply for items Clancy used in Western's employee magazine *Speed,* which he had started during the Woolley regime as a one-page sheet. The house organ grew into a widely distributed clipsheet and then into a slick magazine that cost $2,000 per issue; it was discontinued as an economy measure after the merger, much to Dayhoff's sorrow, because he really didn't have much with which to occupy his active, restless mind. About the only publicity he could peddle was the rare presence of a VIP boarding or deplaning some WAE flight—but this gimmick he parlayed into something of a blockbuster.

Clancy had been watching as Western's accumulated passenger totals compiled since 1926 began to edge toward the 100,000 mark. This milestone was reached on September 24, 1933, and it was no coincidence that the hundred thousandth passenger "happened" to be Elliott Roosevelt, son of the new President of the United States. Other than the fact that Western finished that first year of the New Deal with a surprisingly good profit of some $186,000, Roosevelt's flight from Los Angeles to Salt Lake City was about the only story Dayhoff had to report, and it got plenty of space. The President's son made the trip as official representative of the Hearst newspapers—which gave Dayhoff sufficient leeway to board him as a bona fide No. 100,000.

Jimmie James was the pilot, and Ben Redman also was invited along. Gil Givven, Western's Washington representative in this period, had obtained permission from the Federal Radio Commission for Dayhoff to stage a two-way radio broadcast during the flight, as it neared Salt Lake City, over a special frequency. Clancy wrote a script in advance, which the leading characters—James, Roosevelt, Redman, and an announcer from KSL, Salt Lake City—dutifully followed, trying hard to sound spontaneous and not quite succeeding. The outstanding performer was Redman, largely because Clancy provided him with the best lines. At one point, the KSL announcer on the ground asked him if anything exciting had happened on the flight.

"Well, I almost choked on a chicken bone that they served me in my lunch, if you call that exciting . . . that's the trouble with aviation today—it's too commonplace."

Not many could tell that the chicken bone bit had been written for Redman to read, at least a week before the meal actually was served. Young Roosevelt, introduced as "flying aviation editor" for the Hearst papers, put in the Dayhoff-composed plug for commercial aviation.

"The very fact that I am able to talk to you from this plane," he intoned, "reveals how far we have gone ahead in safety measures. Fogs and weather hazards are controlled and conquered with this plane's radio. Ships in the air are kept in close touch with the airports from which and toward which they are flying. Nothing is left to chance. Everything is considered and checked and rechecked. That's progress and there is more to come in aviation. . . ."

It sounded great, anyway, and Givven wrote Dayhoff that it was "a damn good stunt, fella."

The airline traffic salesmen had to struggle to make air travel respectable in the thirties—working hours that would have sidelined a dray horse, and with unflagging enthusiasm and willingness to make quick, on-the-spot decisions, because any delay might mean loss of a customer. They leaned heavily on the admonition "Travel by Air," on the theory that using the word "fly" might scare people. The primary sales pitch was speed; safety was seldom mentioned, and with good reason—in 1932, the fatality rate for U.S. scheduled airlines was 14.96 deaths per 100 million passenger miles flown—which was 1,200 times higher than for railroads, 900 times greater than for the interstate bus rate, and 20 times worse than the rate for private automobiles. In that one year, the airlines had more than 200 crashes, 16 of them fatal. Both the accident rate and the crash frequency would call for a half-dozen congressional investigations in today's more critical atmosphere where safety is taken for granted and a single tragedy seems to indict the entire industry.

It was not surprising that Dayhoff found so much occasion for celebration in Western's carrying its hundred thousandth passenger in 1933. But WAE's lowly status in the industry can best be emphasized by pointing out that United had carried almost that many in just the previous year—more than 97,000. Western, indeed, had been compressed into near-midget stature, and for all its admirable persistence in setting a technological pace, it still was a small frog in a big pond.

And as the reform spirit of the New Deal spread throughout the nation, Pop Hanshue's airline was about to become even smaller.

It all started with a rather innocent complaint made by a minor airline official to a young newspaperman.

The former was William Briggs of the New York, Philadelphia, and Washington Airway Corporation, more familiarly known as the Ludington Line, which had been formed by two wealthy Philadelphia brothers to offer all-passenger service among the three cities. Flying Lockheed Vegas, Stinson trimotors, and Consolidated Fleetsters, Ludington had been operating since the fall of 1930 and rather successfully, dispatching a flight every hour on the hour, much like today's Eastern shuttle.

Ludington, in fact, became the first airline in history to make money carrying nothing but passengers; net profits in the initial year amounted to slightly over $8,000. It was a well-run carrier, for although the president—C. T. Ludington—had little airline experience or background, he was smart enough to hire some underlings who did. Two of them were refugees from TAT— Eugene Vidal (father of writer Gore Vidal and later to become director of the Bureau of Air Commerce) and Paul Collins, both of whom had left TAT by mutual consent after quarreling with Clement Keys over their insistence that aviation's salvation lay in development of passenger business.

At Ludington they had found a happy niche, and it was Vidal

who suggested that the airline seek a Washington–Philadelphia air mail contract. He figured that Ludington's proven efficiency in carrying passengers made it a shoo-in for a mail bid. What he didn't count on was the famous "Spoils Conference" at which Eastern was handed the same mail route Ludington was seeking. It was at this point that Briggs was having a quiet drink with his reporter friend, Fulton Lewis of the Hearst newspapers, and mentioned casually that Ludington had failed to get the mail contract even with an extremely low bid of $.25 a mile.

Lewis sympathized but didn't think much about it until he read a Post Office Department announcement that Eastern Air Transport had been awarded a Washington–Philadelphia–New York air mail contract with a bid of $.89 a mile. Lewis put $.25 and $.89 together and came up with a distinct odor.

He got the personal approval of William Randolph Hearst to devote full time to what shaped up as a scandal. In later years, as a prominent radio commentator, Lewis's political views were described as being a few miles to the right of Calvin Coolidge, but at the dawn of the New Deal he was a crusading, idealistic newsman. For weeks, he searched through Post Office Department records and finally emerged with a devastatingly damning account of Walter Folger Brown's behind-the-scenes activities. Lewis's report was sent straight to San Simeon, where Hearst refused to approve it for publication.

Lewis was left holding a bag full of apparent scandal and no place to air the contents, until he found one in the person of Senator Hugo Black. The Alabama Democrat was chairman of a special Senate committee established to investigate ocean mail contracts—the principal means by which the federal government subsidized the U.S. merchant marine. Black was an ambitious small-town lawyer with inbred prejudice against so-called Big Business. The ocean mail probe was going along at the pace of a lame snail, attracting little attention and correspondingly few headlines, when the material Lewis had so painstakingly gathered fell into Black's eager hands—with Hearst's reluctant approval, it must be added. Now Black had a *cause célèbre*, and the result was expansion of the original investigation into the allegedly illegal awarding of the air mail contracts. It became "the Black committee," thanks to Washington's propensity for giving unwieldy committee titles the name of whoever happened to be chairman.

The smaller airline operators who had been knifed by Brown rushed to supply the receptive Black with various accusations of skullduggery and under-the-table dealings—handing him a picture that fitted in perfectly with his own preconceived image of giant corporate sharks feeding on helpless small competitors.

The Black committee hearings didn't start until March 1934, but the President didn't wait for the first witnesses to testify before he lowered the boom on the airline industry. At 4:00 P.M. on February 9, Franklin D. Roosevelt canceled all air mail contracts —thus voiding all provisions of and amendments to the Kelly Act—under authority of postal laws giving the Postmaster General punitive powers if conspiracy to obtain such contracts was apparent. As of midnight February 19, FDR ordered, the Army would start flying the mail.

Roosevelt's drastic and controversial decision apparently had its gestation seeds planted at a luncheon meeting he held at the White House late in January with Black. The senator poured into FDR's willing ears a tale of chicanery and back-alley intrigue, urging the President to cancel all mail contracts immediately because they had been obtained by fraud and conspiracy. Roosevelt, who actually knew very little about the situation, was impressed by Black's fervor and intensity—not to mention the fact that statesman though FDR undoubtedly was, he also was a consummate politician who recognized a glittering opportunity further to embarrass the already humiliated Hoover administration. All the arguments Black gave him were largely based on the Lewis material Hearst had released to the Senate committee; Black, encouraged by FDR's promise to think it over for a few days, turned his files over to U. S. Solicitor General Carl Crowley.

Crowley, in turn, condensed the data, allegations, and still-incomplete evidence and presented a one-hundred-page report to Postmaster General James A. Farley, who thumbed through the verbose copy and growled, "I can't wade through all that—just tell me about it."

The Solicitor General orally condensed the condensation, which, stripped of all the verbiage, simply recommended cancellation of the air mail contracts. Farley was shaken by the implications of what Crowley was urging; while Farley was convinced to the point of setting up a meeting the following afternoon among himself, Black, Crowley, and the President, he also had misgivings. Not for a long time was it revealed that neither Farley nor FDR read either the raw material that Black had fed to the Solicitor General, or the lengthy summary that Crowley prepared. Roosevelt took the word of both men as gospel and made his decision accordingly; Farley, while he went along, had his doubts and even urged the President not to cancel the contracts until the Post Office Department issued new bids for all air mail routes.

The Postmaster General was not only overruled but eventually became the scapegoat for the mess that followed. And the first chapter in said mess was the tragic, pitiful unpreparedness of the Army to carry out its air mail mission. Not even Franklin D. Roosevelt's strongest followers could defend his failure to give the military pilots sufficient time in which to prepare for a job they were never trained to perform. The same day the President announced cancellation, he summoned to the White House Brigadier General Benjamin Foulois, chief of the Army Air Service, and asked him pointedly if the Army could carry the mail.

Foulois must have mentally squirmed; he had been asked a question few men in his position could have answered honestly. Under constant attack by Billy Mitchell for the Air Service's admittedly sorry state of military readiness, he had to snap, "Yes, sir" to the commander-in-chief's inquiry—without realizing he was agreeing to send men to their deaths. Armed with this dubious assurance from an officer who had no other choice, FDR told Foulois to go ahead as of the specified date. The legacy of his snap answer (and any hesitation on his part might have made the President himself pause and perhaps follow Farley's go-slow advice) was catastrophe.

At 10:00 P.M. on February 18, two hours before the air mail cancellation went into effect, a brand-new silver DC-1—prototype of the DC-2—took off from Los Angeles with Jack Frye of TWA and Eddie Rickenbacker at the controls. Eighteen hours and four minutes later, they landed at Newark with the final load of privately contracted mail—setting a transcontinental speed record as they staged the airline industry's last gesture of dramatic defiance.

The next day, the Army began flying the mail—immediately running into the worst stretch of winter weather in the annals of the Weather Bureau. Two planes crashed on training flights just before the mail operations began. Within a single week, a spate of additional accidents reaped black headlines and violent editorial denunciation of Farley—who was publicly taking the rap and privately seething at the President's failure to get him off an unfair hook.

Viewing the Army's performance from the more objective vantage point of time, it didn't do as bad a job as contemporary accounts indicated. About five hundred officers and enlisted men operated sixteen thousand miles of rail routes (the commercial routes embraced twenty-seven thousand miles), carrying over eight hundred thousand pounds of mail while compiling fifteen thousand hours of flight time. The last fatal crash was March 31, the improved safety record resulting from the experience gained, a reduction in night flying, and vastly improved weather once the winter ended.

But while they flew the mail, the airlines they replaced were on the verge of extinction. TWA, for example, temporarily furloughed all of its employees the day the Army started. Hanshue decided to keep Western going—like a man told to keep moving so he won't freeze to death. He achieved this by suspending operations over the entire Rocky Mountain Division and reducing the Pacific Division to a single daily round trip between Los Angeles and Salt Lake City, carrying passengers and express.

"We're not cutting to the bone," Pop explained, "we're cutting into the bone."

While this token service was maintaining Western's feeble pulse rate, Hanshue went to Washington for the Black committee hearings—during which time he managed to become a disappointing witness, narrowly escaped going to jail, and put himself in the unique position of indirectly supporting the cancellation decision even as he denounced Brown. There was nothing dull, nor predictable, about Harris M. Hanshue.

As a witness, he generally recounted the story of the shotgun marriage, but his testimony added virtually nothing to claims that the "Spoils Conference" was an opus of deception and fraud —a lousy deal for Western Air Express, yes, but with no evidence other than that Brown acted arbitrarily rather than illegally. The only real excitement came before the hearings opened, when Hanshue got caught smack in the middle of a weird episode involving a supposed attempt to dispose of some secret correspondence.

The letters were in the files of William MacCracken, the former Assistant Secretary of Commerce for Aeronautics, who had been Western's Washington representative twice—from July 1925 to August 1926, and from January 1930 to July 1932. About a month before the Black committee hearings began, MacCracken wired Hanshue that the Senate committee had demanded all correspondence in his files relating to Western Air Express. Hanshue phoned to advise he was sending his then-Washington representative, Gilbert Givven, to MacCracken's office so he could examine what the files contained.

"It had been so long since we employed MacCracken," Hanshue was to explain later, "and so long since I had been in his office myself, I was in doubt as to what he had."

Givven was to testify that he went as instructed but didn't actually go through the files. MacCracken, he said, already had pulled out "certain letters" and handed them to him. These Givven forwarded to Hanshue in a large envelope, which Pop didn't even bother to open right away—he was expecting Gil to mail him a report on what the files contained and not the correspondence itself. Hanshue was in New York on business at the time, and when he read in the newspapers that the Black committee was raising hell about "stolen" files, he opened the envelope. The contents looked completely innocent, consisting mostly of correspondence relating to air mail matters. Hanshue gave them to a Western employee traveling with him and sent him to Washington with instructions to have Givven turn them over to the committee.

An hour after the employee left, Hanshue received a wire from Black demanding that the papers be returned immediately. An hour later, two U.S. deputy marshals appeared at Hanshue's hotel room with subpoenas for the letters. When Hanshue indignantly told him he already had sent them to Washington, they left—but in less than a week Hanshue and Givven were cited for contempt of the Senate. Also cited were MacCracken and Colonel Louis H. Brittin, executive vice president of Northwest Airways in title but in actuality the man who really ran Northwest.

All four appeared before the bar of the Senate on February 9, and five days later Hanshue and Givven were found not guilty, while MacCracken and Brittin were sentenced to ten days in jail. MacCracken had acted as recording secretary at the "Spoils Conference" and obviously was an inviting target for the dirt-digging senator from Alabama. While he had refused to hand over his files to the committee, he relented after the airlines that attended the meeting with Brown told him they had no objections. But then it developed that Brittin already had removed some of Northwest's correspondence from the MacCracken files and destroyed it. MacCracken's earlier truculence toward Black and Brittin's admission that he had burned some of the file material were enough to convict them.

The truth is that Black, as hard as he tried, failed to prove that Brown had done anything in the slightest way illegal. Some of his methods had been despicable and dictatorial, yet in his own way he had tried to be fair; for example, he insisted that smaller airlines, forced to relinquish their routes to the carriers Brown preferred, be given adequate compensation. In cases like Eastern-Ludington, where the high bidder won over the low bidder, Brown felt that Eastern offered a major North-South network covering almost the entire eastern seaboard, whereas Ludington was willing only to operate the lucrative Washington–Philadelphia–New York segment; Ludington did not offer to carry the mail all the way to Florida for $.25 a mile. And Brown made the award to Eastern contingent on its buying out Ludington—and the price Eastern paid, voluntarily, was generous.

Yet while the Black hearings fell short of proving fraud in the air mail contract awards, they did give President Roosevelt sufficient cause to break up the conglomerates that Brown either created himself or condoned on the grounds of efficiency. FDR already had been burned badly by the Army experience, even though Farley bore most of the outward singe marks. The average cost of flying the mail via Army planes was $2.21 a mile; the airlines had been doing it for an average of $.54, and the President was ready to return the job to private operators.

But he was not ready to return the air mail to status quo. When he sought legislation permitting new private mail contracts, he made no effort to oppose a move by the revengeful Senator Black, who turned FDR's request into the Air Mail Act of 1934—a bill requiring the separation of airlines from all aircraft manufacturing companies, banning all executives who had attended the "Spoils Conference" from holding office in their respective airlines, and reopening all airline routes to competitive bidding.

Boeing had to pull out of United along with United Aircraft; AVCO gave up American Airways; North American sold its TWA holdings; and General Motors put its Eastern and Western stock up for sale. In the long run, this punitive measure of Black's probably was the best course, but a new problem arose in the form of pressure from smaller airlines hungry for the routes flown by the big boys. To placate them, Farley got Congress to insert into the Air Mail Act a provision forbidding any airline who had been represented at the "Spoils Conference" to bid on a new route—well aware that if enforced, it would mean chaos and demolition of the airways.

But privately, Farley made it clear this was strictly a face-saving device. All an affected airline had to do, he suggested, was reorganize. Thus American Airways became American Airlines, Eastern Air Transport changed its name to Eastern Air Lines, United Aircraft & Transport switched to United Air Lines, and Western Air Express organized a dummy operating company called General Air Lines, in which it held all the stock.

The airline chief who suffered the most from all this reshuffling, reorganization, and forced exile was Pop Hanshue. His "crime" had been to attend an infamous meeting at which he had been mugged. He was not only blameless for what happened but had tried to stop at least some of it. Yet under the terms of the new Air Mail Act, he was one of the executives involved in the "Spoils Conference" and had to take the consequences. Western's board voted him six months' salary as a final gesture of gratitude.

So did Harris M. Hanshue depart, unwillingly, the airline he had founded and guided to greatness.

Eddie Rickenbacker gave him a job at Eastern with no official title—Pop seems to have been a general manager, but his duties were vague, and apparently he showed little interest or initiative; his heart was back in the West. High blood pressure and cardiac trouble resulted in his resignation from the last airline position he was to hold. After he left Eastern, he dabbled in various nonaviation projects—including a gold-dredging operation in northern California.

On January 7, 1937, he died in New York of a cerebral hemorrhage—at least that was what the death certificate listed as cause of death, inasmuch as there is no such official medical ailment as a broken heart.

And by then, the Western Air Express he had loved so deeply was owned by a coal mining tycoon from Pennsylvania.

CHAPTER SEVEN

"I Wonder if I Did the Right Thing"

His name was William A. Coulter, and he looked like Central Casting's choice to play somebody's kindly old grandfather.

He would have been more aptly cast as the astute businessman he really was. His white hair, easy if rather shy smile, twinkling blue eyes, and diffident manner camouflaged a man who basically was a gambler and manipulator, with a mercurial personality belying his unimposing, gentle appearance.

Coulter had made a fortune in the coal mining business and seemed to live solely on the challenge and excitement of investment risks. He never married and was something of an eccentric recluse; Western officials who knew him say his cluttered Victorian apartment in Philadelphia was only a shade cheerier than the house in *Psycho*.

He had something of a Jekyll-Hyde nature. He could be so self-effacing that it was hard to imagine he was top man of an airline and close to millionaire status. During World War II, by which time he had become president as well as Western's chief stockholder, he was bumped off a Western flight at Salt Lake City by a passenger holding a higher travel priority. Coulter stayed there three days until he could get space on another flight —and during the entire three days, no Western employee or official even knew he was in town.

Yet by the same token, he was difficult to work with or for because he had a habit of suddenly turning against subordinates.

"He'd seem to wake up in the morning and decide who he'd hate that day," a long-time Western official remembers about him.

One of his idiosyncrasies was feigned. He appeared to be surprisingly indecisive for a man of his financial experience and accomplishments—it was hard to ascertain exactly where he stood on most issues. Leo Dwerlkotte once asked Coulter, "Bill, why do you make it so hard for people to understand how you're thinking?"

"Well," Coulter said thoughtfully, "I do it deliberately."

And he actually did get a lot of mileage out of that pose of naïve, innocent gentility, for Coulter all his life was a wheeler-dealer who knew his way around the jungles of high finance. A native of Greensburg, Pennsylvania, he became a familiar figure in New York banking and investment circles—a small-town boy who made good but was always looking around for some new venture. Western was not his first dip into the rough waters of aviation; he had helped two nephews, John and Richard Coulter, finance the organization of Central Airlines (which later merged with Pennsylvania Airlines to become Pennsylvania-Central and then Capital).

His relatively cursory interest in Central whetted his appetite for further involvement in the airline business—and resulted in an introduction to the man who would succeed Hanshue. One of Coulter's best banking contacts and most trusted financial advisers was George Moore, an official at the City National Bank in New York. Coulter, bitten hard by the airline bug, had the notion he might buy out his two nephews or at least increase his holdings.

"I'd like someone to take a good, hard look at Central," he told Moore. "I want to know what my nephews should do with it, if anything, or whether I should put more money into it."

"I think I've just the man for you," Moore said. "Al Adams—he's young but he knows the airline business."

The banker briefed Coulter on Alvin P. Adams' background. He was something of a financial prodigy—after graduating from college, he had become a reporter for the *Wall Street Journal,* where he talked his bosses into letting him become the paper's first aviation editor. The job put him into personal contact with men who knew the airline business, and he absorbed their knowledge like a plant soaking up sunlight. At the decidedly tender age of twenty three, he became vice president of National

Aviation, an investment firm specializing in airline stock (on his recommendation, one of the stocks the company purchased in a fairly sizable amount was Western Air Express).

The six-thousand-dollar salary he was making with National Aviation wasn't nearly as important as the high-level friends Adams was making, including Ernest Breech, vice president of General Motors, which owned Eastern Air Transport as well as Western. Adams got a call from Breech soon after the air mail contracts were canceled.

"Alvin, my friend," Breech said, "I'm going to give your outfit an option to buy Eastern."

"How long an option?" Adams wanted to know.

"Sixty days."

"I think we'd be interested," Adams allowed cautiously.

They discussed some tentative financing details, and Adams took Breech's proposal to his bosses—President Edward McDonald and Chairman of the Board Richard Hoyt. They were intrigued, for National Aviation had been trying to get out of the investment business and into actual airline operations. In fact, it had narrowly missed buying into Western—Adams had worked out a deal with North American Aviation to sell its large WAE holdings to National Aviation, but the former reneged and sold them to General Motors instead.

The Eastern purchase would have gone through except for a small matter of ego: Both McDonald and Hoyt wanted to be president, and while they were still arguing, the sixty-day option expired, and it was Rickenbacker who raised the necessary cash to attain control of the airline he was to command for years. Adams, unhappy at the way his superiors had handled the whole affair, was about ready to quit National when Moore called him.

"I've got a very important client who wants a confidential report on Central Airlines," Moore told him. "Would you be willing to take a look at it for him?"

Adams met Coulter in Moore's office and agreed to provide an honest appraisal of Central. He came back with the opinion that it had potential but badly needed new airplanes. They talked further about the airline, and Coulter offered to let Adams in on its purchase provided that he match every dollar Coulter was willing to put up. It amounted to about $125,000, but Adams couldn't raise his share—his numerous contacts didn't think much of Central's future. Anyway, he wasn't sure about Coulter himself—the latter's style of living was an idiosyncrasy that bothered him. The first time Coulter had him to his Philadelphia apartment, Adams gazed around the dilapidated, cluttered living room and shook his head.

"You looking for something?" Coulter inquired.

"Yeah," Adams muttered. "A fishbowl with a snake in it."

But he put his misgivings about Coulter aside when Breech called him again, chiding him for missing the boat on Eastern.

"I've got another deal for you," Breech added, "but don't be a stupid ass and do it through National Aviation again."

"I won't," Al promised. "What's it all about?"

"You know GM has to get the hell out of either the airline or manufacturing side of aviation—under the Air Mail Act, we can't be involved in both. The last thing we have is Western Air Express. Interested?"

"Very."

"I'm not sure of the exact amount—we'll come to that later— but I think General Motors has around 150,000 shares. We'll give you an option on it for $2.29 a share—and you'll have yourself an airline."

"It's not much of an airline," the well-informed Adams pointed out. "I should know—I went on their board of directors two years ago, a year before you did."

"It could be, Alvin. It could be a damned fine airline."

"I'll get back to you," Adams promised.

Back he went to Coulter—who promptly offered to put up half the money for a 51 per cent interest if Adams could scrounge the rest. The young entrepreneur this time had no difficulty in finding backers, and the deal was made. Coulter had previously shown interest in acquiring control of Eastern after National Aviation let its option lapse, but the price was too high.

On December 29, 1934—which happened to be his twenty-ninth birthday—Alvin P. Adams became the second president of Western Air Express—the industry's youngest chief executive, assuming the guardianship of a carrier whose future was darker than the interior of one of Coulter's coal mines.

WAE was in sorry shape again, its cash reserves depleted and even its newly modernized fleet gone. It had managed to muster the necessary down payment for four brand-new Douglas DC-2s and thus retire what remained of its aging Fokker trimotors. But while General Motors had offered its stock at a reasonable price, it tacked on some harsh provisions before relinquishing control. Coulter was forced to turn over the DC-2s to Eastern, in which GM still held considerable holdings, although it was short of majority control.

Western also had to pay GM more than $600,000 in liquidation and regular dividends. And as Adams parked himself in Hanshue's worn leather chair, WAE was about to complete 1934 with losses of $153,000. Yet he did take command of an airline that at least had retained total independence—in accordance with the dictates of the Air Mail Act, it broke its last ties with TWA. Nearly 300,000 shares of Transcontinental & Western Air stock, which had cost Western more than $2.7 million originally, were distributed among WAE shareholders as a special dividend.

Coulter, admitting that he knew little or nothing about operating an airline (a self-appraisal he would revise eventually), gave Adams full responsibility and authority. Adams needed it—starting with two grim problems begging for immediate solution:

1. No airplanes, once the four DC-2s went to Eastern.
2. A freshly slashed route system that had deteriorated to only four cities.

To cope with Problem 1, Adams bought four used Boeing 247s from United for $25,000 each. The hand-me-down airliner didn't make much difference on a four-city system with no competition. When the Post Office Department put all mail routes up for rebidding, Western tried for two: the original CAM-4 plus the San Diego–Los Angeles leg, and the Cheyenne–Pueblo portion of the old CAM-12. The latter was the only part of the Cheyenne–El Paso mail route WAE had once operated that the government put up for bids, and was redesignated CAM-17. The Pueblo–El Paso leg later was offered as a separate route—won by Varney Speed Lines, which was to become Continental.

Western got CAM-4 back with a low bid of $.24 a mile. But its bid of $.37½ a mile for CAM-17 was undercut by a carrier destined to play a major role in Western's history—tiny Inland Air Lines, which offered to fly the mail for $.35. After eight years, Western Air Express virtually was back to where it started —and on far shakier grounds, for the new contracts were issued on a temporary, one-year basis.

In one respect, it was even worse off than in 1926—then air mail had been greeted with enthusiasm and public support, whereas this time not only Western but the whole industry had to win back confidence in the service. During the period the Army operated the mail, not a few Americans simply refused to send their letters by air. It wasn't really fair or logical, for the military pilots didn't do that poor a job, but that was the public attitude, and the decline in air mail usage was still prevalent when the airlines got their mail routes back.

It had cost the Army $2.21 a pound to carry the mail, mostly in single-engine ships with operating expenses of $255 an hour. The airlines were averaging costs of $.42 per pound, with operating expenses ranging between $75 and $125 an hour. Yet private industry's greater efficiency meant little if patronage was off; Western's first mail flight after cancellation was lifted carried only eight pounds of mail. And when it won the new CAM-4 contract, the $.24 it had bid was far too low for Adams to repeat the Hanshue formula for profits: Make enough on mail to subsidize the yet-to-be-developed passenger traffic.

Faced with this dilemma, the young president of Western Air Express did what came naturally for a man who had been weaned on the techniques of attracting the elusive passenger market. Adams had done more than merely investigate airline financial books when he was with National Aviation; he also had delved into marketing operations, scheduling, and maintenance —and one of the companies that fascinated him was the Ludington Line, with its multiple scheduling practices.

Ludington was the first U.S. airline to use increased scheduling as a means of bringing costs down. Its planes, mostly Stinson trimotors, flew at least ten trips daily between New York and Washington, and Adams was convinced that Ludington made money carrying only passengers simply because it utilized its aircraft to the fullest degree possible.

"That's what we're going to have to do at Western," Adams

told Jimmie James—who with Dwerlkotte was the only executive talent left over from the Hanshue era. Traffic Manager Beggs had left to go with United, disillusioned over Hanshue's fate.

Less than three months after he became president, Adams asked the Post Office Department (which under the Air Mail Act had authority to approve airline schedule frequency) for permission to put a second daily trip on the San Diego–Los Angeles–Salt Lake City route. There were no objections, and by June Western was operating three daily flights—with operating costs going down, as Adams had predicted. The main trouble with the route, however, was that the Los Angeles–Salt Lake City market as such was limited in potential; to put it more honestly if bluntly, not a hell of a lot of people wanted to fly just between the two cities. The only real potential lay in Salt Lake City's status as United's transcontinental gateway to Southern California—a gateway whose keys were the exclusive property of Western Air Express.

Adams began jangling those keys—and United, now headed by W. A. Patterson, was listening. Deliberately, the new president of Western launched the airline into a course of total cooperation with United. WAE's schedules were drawn up to mesh with UAL's transcontinental flights in and out of Salt Lake City. Adams moved the Los Angeles executive and sales offices from Ninth Street to United's LA domain at Sixth and Olive streets, while both carriers shared the same ticket offices in Salt Lake City. In the 247, they had identical equipment, and Western's pilots started wearing the same color and style uniforms as their UAL counterparts.

In fact, there was only one thing United had that Western didn't.

Stewardesses.

Adams remedied that discrepancy, although the day it was remedied developed into a traumatic experience. He had put a small advertisement in the Los Angeles newspapers inviting applicants for interviews. Expecting that they'd be lucky to get as many as twenty-five aspirants, he decided that he and James could conduct the interviewing themselves.

What descended on corporate headquarters was a mob scene. Adams and James put each applicant between them, one at a time, as they questioned them on age, qualifications, and the usual "Why do you want to become a stewardess?" Generally, they followed United's criteria—registered nurses, not more than 25 years of age, weight 115 pounds or less, maximum height five feet, four inches. The seating arrangement was such that when Adams asked a question, the girl would have to turn her back on James and vice versa. This enabled the two men to signal each other on what they thought of the applicant caught between the cross fire. The signal was thumbs up or thumbs down, and out of the initial interviews, they picked only two, Gladys Ruth Witt and Charlotte Lathrop. However, the honor of being Western's first stewardess went to Ursula Brown, a petite nurse from United, who had been hired earlier by James as stewardess supervisor.

In-flight service being what it was in those days, the stewardesses didn't have too many duties aboard the ten-passenger 247 other than to comfort airsick passengers (of which there were many) and serve meals (of which both the quantity and quality were on the skimpy side). The luxury of an outside caterer was beyond Western's capability, which resulted in the girls working as hard on the ground as they did in the air. A small commissary, about six feet square, was installed at Burbank, and the stewardesses would prepare the sandwiches and brew the coffee for their flights.

The advent of stewardesses (they were graduated after only a week's training) brought mixed reactions from the pilots. A few of the crustier, chauvinistic veterans would have preferred an engine fire to the presence of a woman aboard a flight. Generally, however, the girls were welcomed—particularly by the copilots, who at long last were relieved of all cabin duties.

Western got a small break in an amendment to the Air Mail Act extending contract duration from one to three years. Adams was playing things close to the vest, with strict cost controls. There was little money available for advertising, and most of it was allocated in the direction of Western's connections with United for transcontinental service. The co-operation he established between the two carriers, amounting on Western's part to almost 100 per cent collaboration, bothered some people. Adams literally attached the airline to United's coattails, to such an extent that in effect WAE appeared to be an autonomous subsidiary of the larger carrier. He was to draw some criticism for putting Western into a position of subjugation obliterating its independence, image, and identity—and this was to hurt him later, when he collided with Coulter in a head-on battle involving Western's future.

Yet working closely with United was the only course Adams could have followed if WAE was to remain a viable company. For one thing, he succeeded in turning it around—the 1935 deficit was slightly over eight thousand dollars, a vast improvement over the previous year's losses. Some of it was due to economy measures, but most of the encouraging results in his first year could be traced to his concentration on developing passenger traffic through the strong United link. And he came close, not by choice but through necessity, to making it a one-man show—he lacked capable management support throughout the airline.

Adams respected Leo Dwerlkotte's ability; one of his first internal reorganization moves was to make Leo comptroller, and he gradually kept giving the lanky, quiet accountant more responsibility and authority. But while Adams liked James personally, Jimmie's rather carefree attitude about spending company funds was a burr under the president's saddle—Dwerlkotte once wryly commented that "Jimmie was great with people but spent Western's money like it was a perishable product."

Adams began having doubts about James' executive capability in the wake of a fatal crash—a Boeing 247 on a ferry flight. There were no passengers aboard, so Western kept its record of perfect passenger safety intact, but it was a bad time for the airline to lose one fourth of its fleet. The two pilots and the stewardess were killed.

The accident occurred on September 1, 1935, shortly after 11:00 P.M. Captain George Sherwood was ferrying the plane from fogbound Burbank to Saugus, California, where he was supposed to pick up passengers and additional mail for a regularly scheduled flight to Salt Lake City; Saugus, outside the fog area, was an alternate used when Burbank was shut down by weather. The official cause of the crash was "failure of the pilot to maintain proper control of the aircraft while climbing through fog," but Alvin Adams was one of those airline presidents who looked beyond the cockpit for accident causal factors—squarely in the direction of supervisory management.

Adams, well liked by Western's pilots, was most aware of their affection for Jimmie. But the 247 crash began to nag Adams in the form of second thoughts about his vice president of operations and his disciplinary capability. His concern admittedly was vague at first, yet he began observing other pilots for signs of leadership ability—Allan Barrie in particular. Dwerlkotte could only give him an honest appraisal of both men.

"Barrie was very cost-conscious and careful," Leo recalls telling Adams. "He flew a trip like he was using his own gas. But he didn't get along with the pilots. If you could have combined the good qualities of James and Barrie, you would have wound up with the greatest operations vice president in airline history."

Adams decided to string along with James for a while, keeping Barrie in the back of his mind. The operations post was one of several personnel problems bothering the new president—the inevitable residue from a major change in command, and Adams' own rather volatile personality. He was easier to approach than Hanshue, but just as tough.

By the start of 1936, even Western's Board of Directors reflected the volcanic upheaval in its internal structure. Gone were such names as Garland, Talbot, Hanshue, and Chandler—and Ernie Breech, too, who had become a director when General Motors controlled the airline. Dwerlkotte and James were on the Board with Adams, representing management. The only link to the past was Harold Fabian, one of the heroes of the fight to restore night mail service. And strangely, Coulter remained in the background—three thousand miles away from the company he now owned, content to let Alvin Adams run the show—for the time being, anyway.

Adams was in the unique position of having himself, Dwerlkotte, and James actually outnumber the "outside" directors, Fabian and W. G. Burhenn, like Coulter a Pennsylvania coal company executive; this doesn't happen very often in major corporations, and Adams had made it with Coulter apparently ignoring everything but WAE's balance sheet. Adams' authority was total, and he used it in a major effort to strengthen Western's managerial weaknesses—particularly in the area of traffic, which on a 1976 airline would be called marketing. He found a capable man to fill Beggs' spot as traffic manager—after firing Art's immediate successor. His choice was Thomas Wolfe, who started with the airlines in 1924 after graduating from Northwestern University. Wolfe had been district traffic manager for United with thirteen states under his jurisdiction, but got into a battle with W. A. Patterson when Wolfe proposed the then revolutionary idea of issuing air travel credit cards. Patterson regarded this as he would have a proposal to serve the pilots martinis before each takeoff, and the clash between the two men resulted in Wolfe's resignation.

Adams heard about his quitting and offered Tom the job as Western's traffic manager, with a vice presidency and election to the Board of Directors as an extra inducement. Playing no small role in his proselyting this talent was Wolfe's UAL background, which to Adams represented gilt-edged credentials. Adams promoted Dwerlkotte to secretary/treasurer and finally decided to demote James—and it was quite a drop. Jimmie went back to flying the line, and Allan Barrie was named vice president of operations, also replacing James as a director.

The front-office shakeups definitely seemed justified by the results: Western closed the 1936 books with profits of some fifty thousand dollars. The year also ended, however, with a crash that destroyed not just an airplane but also WAE's proud record of not a single passenger fatality in its ten years of operation.

At 11:15 P.M. on December 15, 1936—eight months after Western received a special bronze plaque from Salt Lake City civic leaders honoring its decade of perfect passenger safety—a Boeing 247 operating as Trip 6 took off from Burbank. The destination was Salt Lake City, with an intermediate stop at Las Vegas. The captain was Samuel J. Samson, who not only was a veteran but also had logged approximately four thousand hours over the old CAM-4 route.

Trip 6 left Las Vegas at 1:27 A.M. with Samson, copilot William Bogan, stewardess Gladys Witt, and four passengers. The next-to-last contact with Trip 6 was reported by the Department of Commerce radio facility at Milford, Utah, which had seen the lights of the plane as it passed over. Samson had given

Milford a position report at 2:23 A.M. and checked in again four minutes later, advising that continuous range operation was no longer necessary because he could see the Black Rock beacon, twenty-two miles straight ahead. That placed him on course and presumably in good weather, but this 2:27 A.M. transmission was the flight's final communication—it not only disappeared, but the wreckage itself wasn't located until early in June 1937. There were no survivors.

The 247 had struck a mountain fifteen feet from its peak and disintegrated. A few small pieces of an engine, plus bits of the fuselage and wings—each no larger than the top of a desk—were found near or at the point of impact. The rest went over a thousand-foot cliff, and even at the time of discovery was still partially buried under snow. The bodies of the occupants also were finally picked up at the cliff's base. Three watches recovered at the scene fixed the moment of impact: 3:14 A.M. "Inability of the pilots to identify the south leg of the Salt Lake City Radio Range due to a local static condition which rendered both range receivers in the airplane inoperative"—that was the government's probable-cause finding.

Every fatal accident used to have a marked, immediate, depressing effect on over-all traffic throughout the industry; in the case of this accident, however, the decline was less than usual because the plane wasn't located for months, and by the time it was, the crash almost had been forgotten. This was not true of Western's second serious accident, again involving passenger fatalitics—and this time not merely names known only to the victims' families and friends, but also one of the nation's most famous personalities.

Less than a month after Trip 6 went down, another WAE 247 crashed—Trip 7, westbound over the Salt Lake City–Los Angeles route. The pilot, Captain William Lewis, had started his letdown toward the Los Angeles area when a wingtip brushed the side of a mountain near Newhall, California. The impact was slight but sufficient to impede the captain's desperate efforts to get airborne again. The Boeing skidded along the rolling side of the mountain, ground-looped, and came to rest facing in the opposite direction. Incredibly, all those on the left side of the aircraft, from the cockpit back, survived. All those on the right side were killed—including Martin Johnson, the famed jungle explorer and animal film maker. His wife Osa was sitting across from him and lived.

Pilot error, the government ruled; Lewis was accused of "descending to a dangerously low altitude without positive knowledge of his position."

There was general agreement that the verdict was fair, although there were also mitigating circumstances. Lewis had never flown before with his copilot on this particular trip, Clifford Owens, and he was performing most of the cockpit duties himself—including the radio. He made his descent through freezing rain and reported to Burbank, just before the crash, that he was picking up "quite a bit of ice"; the otherwise sturdy 247 flew like an iron bathtub in icing conditions, and Lewis testified later that he had difficulty in handling the logy plane. Finally, he might not have strayed off course if he had not experienced trouble in hearing Burbank's directional radio signals. Burbank's radio operator was using that localizer frequency to transmit voice communications to other flights in the vicinity. By the time Lewis was able to pick up the directional signals, which told him he was east of his proper course and over mountainous terrain, he already had descended too low. The impact came just as he started to bank toward the correct course.

Western at the time carried $40,000 liability insurance per passenger plus a $60,000 override with Lloyds of London. It settled out of court every claim made for death or injuries—except one. Osa Johnson sued the airline for $750,000, as compensation for the loss of her husband and for her own personal injuries, and the case went through a jury trial.

Western hired attorney Joseph Crider to represent it in the Johnson litigation, and he was an early-day combination of Melvin Belli and F. Lee Bailey. When it came time to pick jurors, he went for middle-aged women from a medium-income strata. Perry Mason couldn't have been cannier, because Osa Johnson had appeared in the courtroom prior to the jury selection wearing a smart dress, silver fox fur, and an assortment of diamond jewelry.

If she was ineffective as a witness, Captain Lewis was the opposite. Crider put him on the stand to describe that terrible night. The pilot broke down sobbing, and there were not many dry eyes on the part of the jury, either. Crider smartly rested his case right then and there; he had other witnesses but never called them. The jury returned a verdict in favor of Western, finding that the crash was "an act of God." The night before the trial opened, the airline's insurance company—Associated Aviation Underwriters—had offered Mrs. Johnson a $50,000 cash settlement, which she refused. She ended up with nothing and had to pay court costs.

Adams had no reason to blame the tough Barrie for those two fatal crashes in less than a month. But Adams had an open way of running the company, his rapport with the flight crews was excellent, and he could not help but be aware of the friction between the pilots and Barrie. A perfectionist, Barrie was as demanding toward others as he was to himself. Shortly before the Newhall accident, Adams remembered, Bill Lewis had come up to him one day, complaining about the amount of in-flight paperwork Barrie was forcing the flight crews to handle.

"He's trying to get a line on our fuel consumption, Bill," Adams said soothingly.

"I can't fly a 247 on instruments and play bookkeeper for Barrie," Lewis snapped. "One of these days somebody's gonna get distracted and he'll be in trouble."

Adams also noted that the stewardesses didn't seem overly fond of the operations boss, either. Barrie's relations with the pilots affected the small stewardess corps, basically loyal to the airmen. Esther Jo Conner, the girl working Flight 7, was seriously injured in the Newhall crash but returned to flying as soon as she recovered and became one of Western's most popular and durable flight attendants. Gladys Witt, killed in the Utah accident, also had been well liked. The crashes hurt the girls' morale, already sagging because of the Barrie situation, and Adams decided Allan was a liability as an executive. He sent Barrie back to the line. Eventually, however, Barrie was to earn nationwide recognition as an aeronautical scientist through his study of in-flight icing conditions. A penitent Charles N. James replaced Barrie. Jimmie got his vice presidency and directorship restored, stayed in everyone's good graces for a long time, and was not to feel the deadly swish of a president's ax until after World War

II. Almost as pleasing to Jimmie as his personal comeback was the promotion of his old buddy of the Horsemen days: Fred Kelly I was named system chief pilot, a move that increased James' efficiency simply by reducing his workload.

It was not easy to keep WAE in the black. No source of revenue was overlooked, including sightseeing flights and charter trips to Las Vegas for the growing "let's fly to Vegas and get married" market. The Nevada city, once primarily a refueling stop on CAM-4, was beginning to develop into a healthy source of passenger revenue. Western at the time owned the Las Vegas airport and bowed to the prevailing practice of installing slot machines in every available space. WAE's five machines were placed in the terminal building and fixed for a 65 per cent return —generous compared to the Las Vegas average of 85 per cent. The patronage was so great that in one year—Leo Dwerlkotte swears it's true, although he can't pinpoint the year—Western's profits came entirely from the two thousand dollars monthly net the five slots were making.

Adams was doing a little gambling too—but not in Las Vegas. For all his heavy collaboration with United, he had no intention of letting Western stagnate into the status of UAL's West Coast subsidiary. While James ran operations, Dwerlkotte guarded finances, and Wolfe drummed up business, Adams was pondering an interesting development. He had been approached quietly on the possibility of WAE merging with a smaller carrier.

And the latter happened to be one whose acquisition, if successfully negotiated, would resume Pop Hanshue's interrupted march to the east.

It was National Parks Airways, and the president of this tiny but colorful airline—Alfred Frank—had made the first tentative overtures to Adams. Small and losing money too rapidly for even the wealthy Frank to stomach, National Parks had three major assets in Adams' eyes:

1. It operated a route from Great Falls, Montana, to Salt Lake City via Helena, Butte, Idaho Falls, Pocatello, and Ogden, dovetailing neatly with Western's Salt Lake City terminus.

2. Most of its fleet was obsolete, but it included two Boeing 247s, which WAE needed badly.

3. Its technical personnel had an excellent reputation for safety and efficiency achieved over a route as difficult and dangerous as Western's.

National Parks was only two years younger than WAE, tracing its organization back to late 1927, actual operations starting in May of the following year. Frank was a mining engineer by profession, amassing wealth in Montana's famed copper wars. His family owned a large tea company in Ohio, but the tea business was too dull for him; his real bent was investment, and he was one of many afflicted with the virulent aviation bug of the twenties. Joined by a number of Utah, Montana, and Idaho businessmen, he launched National Parks Airways as a passenger/express line between Salt Lake City and Pocatello, and by August 1 had expanded it all the way to Great Falls—the same day his bid to carry mail over the five-hundred-mile route was accepted.

Equipmentwise, NPA got off to a better start than Western. It began with three brand-new Fokker Super Universals, a single-engine cabin monoplane carrying six passengers, and two Stearman biplanes. Thanks to the Fokkers, NPA actually carried almost as many passengers in its first month (202) as Western did in its first 8½ months (209); in many respects, the two carriers were first cousins or maybe even blood brothers, populated as they were by a collection of characters who infused life, individuality, and personality into the corporate robot for whom they worked.

Frank always was concerned about his NPA employees. At Thanksgiving and Christmas, he gave each a turkey; he loved to visit the hangars throughout the system, gabbing cheerfully with the pilots, mechanics, and station personnel. Yet no one really knew him well, nor did he get close to any subordinate. NPA almost seemed to be a hobby and the various stations just places where he could relax and talk to people, much like a man who regards the neighborhood tavern as a kind of oasis. Frank's chief interest was mining investments, a subject on which he was an export. For running an airline, he leaned entirely on the men he hired at National Parks—particularly Felix Steinle, a crusty ex-Army officer who served as general operations manager from NPA's inception to 1936. In that period, Steinle earned a reputation as the most irascible, foul-tempered despot in the airline industry. The fact that he also was one of the most beloved is the best brief description of the man everyone called "Chief."

He was a powerfully built six-footer with shoulders like a bridge girder and the most profanity-packed vocabulary west of the Mississippi and possibly east of it. Incongruously, he was the essence of sartorial splendor, a fastidious dresser in fashionable, immaculate clothes. His voice could produce the decibels of a hog caller, and did, frequently. Chief's main trouble was that his imposing figure, blood-curdling tirades, and purple rages never succeeded in hiding a heart about as rigid as a soft-boiled egg. Newcomers to National Parks quaked under his wrath; gradually —if they lasted long enough—they realized he was 90 per cent bluster and bombast.

Anton "Tony" Favero, now Western's senior vice president of operations, worked for Chief as a young NPA mechanic.

"If he liked you," Favero recalls, "you got fired twice a day."

It took a while to get used to his oral dismissal notices. He was a Barrymore at delivering them, in such apparent anger that employees sometimes fled before they heard the Chief's roar dwindle to a rumble, "and if you leave, you're *really* fired!"

He once fired Dale Nielson, an NPA pilot, with such awesome conviction that Nielson took him seriously and left town. Chief finally tracked him down three months later and rehired him.

Steinle's great love was golf; he kept his clubs at the field and used to hit golf balls in between the times he prowled around, searching for some hapless soul on whom to vent his ersatz wrath. Incoming NPA pilots quickly learned to circle when they spotted Chief swinging away in the general vicinity of a runway, landing only when he had picked up his clubs and started walking toward the hangar. He had an oversupply of inbred suspicion; if he saw a requisition slip for five gallons of distilled water, he would come charging out of his office bellowing, "Are you sonsofbitches making moonshine again?"

Steinle's pet hatred was any pilot who arrived ahead of schedule, an idiosyncrasy directly attributed to his obsession with fuel consumption. An airman who landed early faced an immediate session on Chief's carpet. The dialogue was identical in every instance:

Chief: "Okay, tell me why you got in ten minutes early."

Pilot: "I had a pretty good tailwind, Chief."

Chief: "THEN WHY THE HELL DIDN'T YOU THROTTLE DOWN, SAVE FUEL, AND ARRIVE ON TIME INSTEAD OF BURNING UP FUEL AND ARRIVING AHEAD OF SCHEDULE, YOU STUPID ⚡*⚡@(%⚡*⚡⚡?! YOU'RE FIRED!"

Nobody ever came up with an answer for the curmudgeon of National Parks Airways. And he had some sharpsters flying for him, too. One was Ralph Fry, who for some mysterious reason could talk Steinle out of anything. Art Stephenson, NPA's chief pilot, was totally unafraid of Chief, and the verbal battles he waged with Steinle in behalf of the pilots were close to sonic booms in intensity; he was the only pilot Steinle never fired. Chief's favorite was Hank Hollenbeck, possibly because he burned less fuel than anyone else (the mechanics suspected, but never dared tell Steinle, that Hollenbeck also caused an epidemic of burned valves from running too lean) and maybe because Hollenbeck also was something of a grouch.

Compared to Hank, a miser was a big-time spender. He was a tall, good-looking Annapolis graduate of military bearing except that he had a cigarette or pipe in his mouth constantly, and his blue uniform was always untidily speckled with ashes. "Horrible Hank," the copilots called him—he never said more than ten words to the first officer all the way from Salt Lake City to Great Falls, which meant about five hundred miles of virtual silence. He seemed to consider copilots excess baggage; Favero remembers that if Hollenbeck found there was an NPA mechanic he liked on one of his trips, he'd invite him to sit in the cockpit and would send the copilot back to the cabin. Hollenbeck's eyesight was poor enough to require glasses, but his vanity and pride made him recoil from letting anyone but his cockpit colleague watch him don them; he would grope his way to the cockpit before putting them on.

Bert Mooney was another pilot personality. He ran a fixed base operation at Butte and flew as an NPA reserve pilot. Favero worked for him at the time and went over to National Parks when Mooney did. Joe Fogarty, an ex-NPA mechanic who is now a Western maintenance official, swears that although Mooney was an excellent airman, "he had more trouble landing than anyone else I knew."

"He'd get disinterested when he was ten feet from the ground," Fogarty explains.

Mooney's weakness was poker; if you gave him five minutes' leisure time at an airport, he'd start up a game. Favero tells a story about Mooney when he became chief pilot at Salt Lake City after NPA merged with WAE. Bert was having trouble with one of his underlings and summoned him to his office. A poker game was in progress.

"You wanna see me, Bert?" the pilot asked.

Mooney looked up just long enough to impale the pilot with a frown.

"Wally, I don't know what the hell you're doing wrong, but quit it. Okay, whose deal?"

The copilots' favorite was Ray Elsmore, who hated to fly in bad weather—the result being additional logged time, not to mention experience, for the right-seat occupants. Earl Vance, Montana's best-known barnstormer, was another NPA pilot about whom countless stories are told, but not all the interesting people were airmen. There was one unsung hero working for National Parks whose sole job was to mail a registered letter to each station daily. This was to make sure NPA had at least one mail bag per trip; the letters were sent registered because registered mail required a special brass padlock—which weighed enough to give NPA an extra $.85 in mail pay per trip.

National Parks originally had its main operations office in Salt Lake City, but it moved to Butte largely because the Montana city lay approximately in the center of CAM-26. Not everyone agreed with the decision, for Butte winter weather could be miserable, with temperatures going down to thirty degrees below zero. It was an expensive move, too, necessitating the construction of a new hangar and the transfer of all Salt Lake City maintenance facilities. Nobody complained, not publicly anyway, inasmuch as questioning an Al Frank order was like spitting at the flag. NPA's president was so popular that when he went to California—his favorite winter vacation area—employees would have his car at the airport waiting for him on return, washed and polished, with the motor running so he wouldn't have to step into a cold automobile.

It was a relatively small but prosperous airline Frank headed. His greatest if unofficial asset was employee loyalty to himself and to NPA—like early Western, it enjoyed the intense, family-like closeness that somehow managed to overcome all the disadvantages, difficulties, and dangers of a limited route largely over hazardous terrain. In small cities like Pocatello, Idaho Falls, and Butte, it had the status of a community airline—local pride and interest generating more business than the market appeared capable of developing. By 1936, it was carrying more than sixteen thousand passengers annually, only four thousand fewer than WAE. There was no doubt it was well run. NPA had only one fatal crash in the nine years it was in existence—and that occurred only a month after operations began.

National Parks Airways became involved in Postmaster General Brown's previously mentioned "Spoils Conference"—Frank's was the smallest carrier represented. It must be added, however, that Frank wasn't invited; another airline president had wired him suggesting that he come to Washington, because under Brown's new route proposals, NPA seemed about to gain an extension from Great Falls to Lethbridge, Canada, for which it had recently applied.

Frank came to the nation's capital, attended not more than three sessions, and left town four days later in something of a disappointed huff. The Great Falls–Lethbridge route was never discussed, and when Frank attempted to bring it up, even informally, nobody paid any attention. Adding insult to injury was Brown's cavalier treatment of NPA when Frank applied for extension of CAM-26 to Missoula and Billings, Montana. The Postmaster General merely sat on the application without acting on it, and when his new route structure came out, Northwest Airways had been given access to Billings and Missoula from the east. Brown's defenders argued it was far more logical to connect the Montana area with an airline based in Minneapolis than with one originating in Salt Lake City—which may have been true, except that Brown ignored NPA's pioneering rights in Montana and would have not hurt his master plan by being fair to Frank.

Cancellation of all air mail contracts in 1934 stunned National Parks, just like everyone else. Frank tried to operate for a brief spell with an all-passenger/express service, but he bowed to the inevitable and shut the airline down—whether temporarily or permanently, no one could tell at the time. Both Favero and Fogarty still have vivid memories of the day the cancellations were announced; Chief came out of his office, his foghorn voice reverberating through the hangar:

"All you sonsofbitches are fired!"

If Al Frank had been a vindictive man, he could have gained sweet revenge on Brown. When Senator Black was getting ready for his committee hearings, he was told about Frank's treatment at the "Spoils Conference." With senatorial mouth figuratively watering, he interviewed NPA's president and got—or thought so, anyway—the idea that Frank was only too willing to crucify the former Postmaster General of the United States before the Black committee.

Willing to testify, yes. Crucify Brown? He might have, except that—to paraphrase that ancient vaudeville wheeze—a funny thing happened to Alfred Frank on the way to testifying. He showed up at the first day of the hearings ready to be sworn in. It was seven weeks later when he finally was called to the stand. Black greeted him like a long-lost brother, which he certainly was—long-lost, that is. Unfortunately for Chairman Black, he mistook the glowering, unhappy look in Frank's eyes as the hot lava of indignation about to inundate Brown. But while the president of National Parks Airways indeed was angry, his target was not Walter Brown but Hugo Black. Alfred Frank wasn't used to being kept waiting—not for seven weeks.

It was a replay of Black-vs.-Hanshue. Frank absolutely refused to confirm allegations that Brown called the "Spoils Conference" to parcel out new route awards to the airlines present at the meeting. There was no collusion or fraud, Frank kept insisting—and he refused to alter that view in the face of Black's grueling questions. Frank told, simply and effectively, the story of how he had gotten involved in the "Spoils Conference"—showing up uninvited to protect NPA's interests. The closest he came to sink-

ing the apparently unsinkable Walter Brown was when he
testified about trying to get the Lethbridge extension. He said
Brown kept telling him NPA's application couldn't be granted
for lack of funds—and gave him the same reason for not approving Frank's attempt to serve Billings and Missoula. As a matter
of fact, Frank had as much to say about the Senate committee
listening to him as he did the "Spoils Conference." He made it
clear he didn't like the way the committee made him wait from
January 12 to March 1 before allowing him to testify. When
Black asked him rather sarcastically why he had stayed, Frank
snapped he would have gone home early in February if the
Roosevelt administration hadn't canceled the air mail contracts—
leaving him without an airline to run.

Black may have gotten his revenge on Hanshue through his
Air Mail Act, deposing every airline president who had attended
Brown's conference. But he never could reach Frank, who not
only remained as NPA's president but also won his air mail contract back again. In accordance with Farley's dictate, he bid for
the old CAM-26 route, now redesignated CAM-19, under the
name "Alfred Frank, air mail contractor, lessee, National Parks
Airways, Inc.," thus meeting the meaningless technicality that
Farley had imposed. He was the only executive whose airline
was represented at the "Spoils Conference" who didn't have to
resign.

Yet even with his airline operating once more, some of the
challenge, the excitement, and the pioneering spirit that had motivated Al Frank to start NPA seemed to have been weakened.
Certainly, his Washington experiences were major sources of dis-
illusionment. Perhaps, too, Frank saw no real future for National
Parks—it was a midget surrounded by giants, lacking their resources and manpower. To the sturdy, loyal, hard-working crew
that ran NPA for their quiet boss, acquisition of two Boeing
247s—first leased from United and later purchased—was an occasion for rejoicing, an indication that the airline was growing
up. To Alfred Frank, the same acquisition symbolized the company's lowly status—like a sandlot football team receiving a do-
nation of discarded uniforms, pads, and helmets. He must have
begun thinking about merging NPA with a larger carrier fairly
soon after he won back CAM-26; Al Adams says Frank first

approached him early in 1936, before he had much chance to warm Western's presidential seat. Adams sent Jimmie James and Tom Wolfe on a tour to inspect National Parks' system, warning both not to say a word about the reason behind their trip. They completed their task without raising suspicion, gossip, or rumors, and reported to Adams that NPA was "one damned fine little airline with good people," as James phrased it.

Adams kept Coulter informed of Frank's interest in selling out, and the absentee owner told him to keep negotiating. There is no evidence that Frank considered merging with anyone but Western Air Express, and it would have been surprising if he had tried. The NPA-WAE systems linked up at Salt Lake City, and both were small airlines struggling to compete in what essentially remained Walter Brown's "let the big boys play with the football"atmosphere—Hugo Black and Franklin Roosevelt notwithstanding. And there were emotional ties between the two carriers—their western roots, their mutual shafting by big government and big industry alike, their history of operating successfully over some of the worst terrain in the nation and with generally obsolete equipment.

By the time Adams and Frank began talking seriously, NPA's fleet was something of a hodgepodge. Gone were the Stearmans and Fokkers. The pair of 247s carried the bulk of traffic, with a Waco biplane and a Boeing 40-B used for pilot training. For a short time, National Parks operated an ancient Boeing Model 80-A, a trimotor biplane that had once been the queen of United's fleet. NPA assigned it to summertime vacation or sightseeing flights into Yellowstone National Park and the Grand Tetons; on a few occasions, the 80-A subbed for a 247 down for maintenance. It had metal inserts above the windows along the cabin wall, much like those carried on streetcars and buses for selling advertising space. And that's precisely how NPA utilized the space— the inserts carried advertising cards, a throwback to the days when many airlines resorted to this practice as a means of digging up extra revenue. The 80-A was an anachronism in more ways than one, however; it was so slow that Joe Fogarty says "When you saw it on the horizon coming into Great Falls from Butte, you still had time to drive to the downtown post office, pick up the mail, and get back to the field before it landed."

The 80-A finally was scrapped in favor of a Ford trimotor for the seasonal trips. Hank Hollenbeck bought the fuselage for thirty-five dollars; one of the few things Horrible Hank could get sentimental about was that Boeing 80-A—he really loved the ancient pelican. There's a story about the plane, perhaps apocryphal, that began making the rumor rounds while Hollenbeck was converting what used to be the cabin into a car trailer. While they were dismantling it, Hank reportedly discovered they had been flying it for two years with most of the wing bolts missing.

Hollenbeck had just about completed the conversion when Frank decided to dismantle National Parks itself. With a green light from Coulter, Adams and the NPA president agreed on an exchange of stock. A last-minute hitch developed when Frank suddenly upped his price—he refused to sign the merger agreement unless Coulter personally bought ten thousand shares of his own NPA stock at about double its market value. Coulter was furious but Frank remained adamant, and Adams finally convinced the Pennsylvanian that the purchase still was a bargain. He may have been planting the seeds of his own destruction, however, for once the merger was consummated, Coulter seemed to turn on Adams as if the youthful president was the one who forced the extra stock deal. There seems to be little doubt that Adams was riding high with this major step in Western's comeback—maybe too high, for Coulter was used to making his own deals, and the little green god of jealousy appears to have invaded Bill Coulter's bloodstream for the first time.

On August 1, 1937, nine years to the day after National Parks Airways inaugurated Salt Lake City–Great Falls service, it became part of Western Air Express. Frank and the other NPA stockholders received nearly forty thousand shares of WAE stock, turning over to Western the air mail contract for CAM-19 and all physical assets, valued at just under $390,000. There was no way to estimate the value of NPA's personnel involved in the merger; in cockpit talent alone, it was considerable, for many of National Parks' pilots—Stephenson, Mooney, Hollenbeck, and Elsmore, to name a few of several—went on to become senior captains on Western. Such men as Favero and Fogarty had given NPA an industrywide reputation for good maintenance.

To the very end, Frank kept the merger negotiations secret. The first Fogarty heard about the impending death of his airline —and his case was typical—came when a Western employee walked into the NPA hangar at Salt Lake City.

"All you guys are gonna be fired," he announced. "We're taking over your airline."

It was natural that morale in the tightly knit National Parks family promptly nosedived; few airlines had NPA's *esprit de corps*. It was a carrier run by the employees who cared little about labor contracts because they were too busy; the first mechanics' union contract, in fact, was written on a single 8½-inch-by-11-inch sheet of paper. The company's most popular fringe benefit was purchase of a cabin in the mountains of West Yellowstone where employees could go on their days off for fishing and relaxation.

Absorption by Western, which itself wasn't the most stiffly run airline in the United States, brought to an end NPA's rather informal, convivial, and unorganized way of life. Gradually the resentment and bitterness diminished, as it usually does in any airline merger.

"For a while," Tony Favero philosophizes, "you got the feeling that people with the surviving carrier looked at you like a bastard calf. But we got over it—hell, in a lot of instances, National Parks people became bosses at Western before very long."

The merger was Western's outstanding and most promising event for the otherwise unsatisfactory year of 1937. WAE's books showed a net loss of thirty-five thousand dollars for the period, but the potential for future growth gained from the NPA acquisition was far more important than the deficit. Overnight, Western had doubled its route length to more than thirteen hundred miles, and in the rugged airway that was CAM-19, Adams saw the key to further expansion. Regrettably, this had to be achieved by dissolving a brave little airline that was cast in Western's own mold. Even today, former NPA employees still speak of their old company with nostalgic pride, and all vestiges of animosity toward Frank have long since disappeared. In fairness to Al Frank, he had to merge, and he chose the airline that most closely resembled his own in background, character, and style. Those who persist in believing that NPA could have made it on its own forget that it had lost money steadily from 1934 up to the Western takeover.

Yet necessary though the merger was, it had to be a difficult time for any NPA officer or employee possessing a speck of sentimentality. Gone forever was their proud insignia—a red, white, and blue triangle with the names UTAH, MONTANA, and IDAHO on each point to show the states served. In the center of the triangle was a painting of a park area.

Alfred Frank came out to the Salt Lake City airport after the final papers were signed. Silently he watched the last NPA flight being loaded for departure to Great Falls. The 247 thundered down the runway and clawed its way up toward the northeast. Frank sighed and shook his head. Favero was standing close enough to hear him utter the airline's epitaph.

"I wonder if I did the right thing," murmured the first and the last president of National Parks Airways.

CHAPTER EIGHT

Lost: One Merger—and One President

Al Adams always took umbrage at claims that he changed Western Air Express into a virtual United subsidiary.

As he was to prove later—at the cost of losing his job—he had no intention of submerging Western's identity on a permanent basis. The then-youngest airline president in the United States was too much of an individualist himself to accept total dominance by another company, or to rely forever on United's transcontinental feedback as Western's prime reason for existence. Acquisition of National Parks was the first step taken toward an independent future.

Adams' relatively obscure rank in aviation circles merely reflected Western's own diminutive stature in the late thirties. To most of his contemporaries, he was a smart, brash young man who kept his airline alive by trotting worshipfully along in United's path like an obedient puppy. Yet a few, including United's Patterson, knew him for what he really was—a man with maturity and judgment far beyond his years, an executive of considerable ability and strength, and an instinctive leader with much of Hanshue's vision and tenacity.

Short but muscular, Adams had been an Army bantamweight boxing champ during a short military stint in Hawaii, and he loved sports—hunting and fishing in particular. His chief forte as an executive was his willingness to delegate authority, without relinquishing an iota of his own; nobody at Western was allowed to forget who was really running the show regardless of the immediate source of an order or decision. There were times when other Western officials served as a buffer zone between erring employees and the president's wrath. James, for example, bore the brunt of complaints from pilots when he began posting the monthly speed and fuel consumption of every pilot—"You're running this airline like a goddamned railroad," one of them protested, unaware that the order was Adams' idea.

Only once did he get embroiled in a labor hassle, and that involved the company's first union, the infant Air Line Pilots' Association. A pilot who had organized a Western ALPA chapter was fired; other pilots felt strongly that he had lost his job because of his union activities. Adams denied this with equal vehemence, claiming that the airman in question habitually violated required instrument approach procedures—and James backed up the president.

ALPA president Dave Behncke, the militant airman who started the pilots' union in 1931, came out to Los Angeles at the discharged pilot's request and confronted Adams on the dismissal.

"Reinstate him or you may have your first strike," Behncke warned.

"Listen," Adams snorted, "the day we're required to take back a pilot we've fired for good reasons, I'm leaving this company, and don't think I'm fooling!"

Behncke apparently believed what Adams told him concerning the alleged transgressions, for he returned to Chicago with no further threats. The pilots never did accept the story, however, although the man stayed fired. Adams could be tough, and his crews respected him for it, even when they protested what they considered a raw deal. For one thing, they admired his efforts to restore the airline's health. Among the pilots, there was little resentment toward the love affair with UAL; they seemed to understand better than many other employees that Adams' strategy was a temporary crutch while Western got strength back in its withered legs.

"I'm gonna put that Indian head right into Newark Airport," he used to boast in boyish, contagious enthusiasm. If the Indian had to ride partway on United's wings, it was nothing to be ashamed of. Adams had confidence in Pat Patterson's well-run airline.

Adams had none of Pop Hanshue's almost grim solemnity, and his hearty, booming laugh was a cathartic for gloom. His great passion was hunting, the bigger the game the better, although he went about it rather unconventionally. He hunted both upwind and downwind, in blissful defiance of normal operating procedures, and usually wore tennis shoes rather than boots. On one occasion he was seeking deer in the wilds of Montana and shot a fine, huge buck, which he loaded on a car, driving to Helena just in time to catch a WAE flight to Los Angeles.

"I've got a lot of friends in Pasadena [his California residence] who love fresh venison," he happily informed Western's Helena station manager. "I'm taking this flight home, but you put that deer on our next flight and I'll meet the plane."

The station manager wasn't very enthusiastic; the carcass was so large that there was little room left for mail or express. But station managers seldom argue with airline presidents, and he promised to follow Adams' orders. The deceased buck forthwith departed—on a flight involving stops at every Western-served city between Helena and Los Angeles. At each airport, cargo handlers would remove a few choice cuts. When the plane landed in Burbank, Adams rushed out to the ramp area.

All he found was the head and a few large bones.

"What the hell happened to my deer?" he bellowed. "I'll have the FBI in on this! You can't rob important interstate commerce . . . !"

Adams could be as brutally brusque as Hanshue on one of his worst days. Yet he was far more approachable and usually enjoyed an affable relationship with most employees. Behind the occasional banter, joking, and casual conversation, however, was a probing, never-ending search for employees who showed initiative and talent. One man in particular intrigued Adams even before he was hired—a handsome Irishman with an engaging personality, a smile that could have thawed an iceberg from fifty yards away, and the heart of a born salesman. His name was Arthur F. Kelly, who joined Western after the National Parks merger—and thirty-six years later became its sixth president.

Kelly was a native of Clifton, Arizona, and with classic Irish stubbornness marched in a direction opposite to where his father was trying to steer him. The senior Kelly started out in Tomb-

stone, Arizona, as a bank examiner and became a top officer in a
Salt Lake City bank. He always wanted his two sons to go into
the banking business, but neither was interested. Art was accepted by the Harvard School of Law—not a minor achievement
in itself—having become mildly interested in the legal profession. Said interest, however, was more directed toward politics
than actual law practice, which cost Harvard a new student and
led Kelly into the airline business almost by chance.

Kelly was serving as executive assistant to the Salt Lake City
commissioner of airports, and one of his tasks was to handle airport leases and contracts. It was in this capacity that he became
acquainted with Alvin Adams, who had just begun negotiating
with Frank of National Parks.

"He mentioned some of the long-range plans he might have in
expanding Western," Kelly says, "and we discussed the possibility of my joining Western."

He talked further with Adams who, while he had no opening
at WAE, urged Kelly to go with United at least temporarily and
get some airline experience. In effect, Adams laid out a blueprint
for young Kelly's future—almost a formal training program, with
the end goal of someday going with Western. In working with
UAL, Adams had become a good friend of R. E. "Dick" Pfennig,
one of those many underrated, unsung pioneers contributing so
much to aviation. Pfennig, for example, had set up United's first
flight dispatch system, ending the days when pilots served as
their own dispatchers and too frequently took unnecessary risks.

"You go see Dick Pfennig," Adams advised Kelly. "I've already
talked to him about you, and I think he'll give you a job. It won't
be much, but by the time things loosen up around Western,
you'll have a better idea of what it's all about."

"But when do you think you'll have a place for me?" Kelly
wanted to know—instinctively sensing that his paycheck was
heading for a sharp decline.

"If we buy National Parks, you're in," Adams promised.

Kelly saw Pfennig and was sent to Chicago for a brief training
program, which Pfennig himself had established. The curriculum
included reservations, the general basics of airline operations,
and UAL procedures. After training, the ten "graduates" were
assigned to various divisions throughout United's system—Kelly

drawing San Francisco, which he considered a great break until he met his immediate boss, station manager Robbie Robinson, who had the disposition of a crocodile with ulcers.

Robbie couldn't have cared less that Kelly might be his boss someday; to him, the young Irishman was just another raw rookie to be badgered, browbeaten, and barked at. Robinson's finest attribute was total loyalty to United, and nothing ever got in the way of that self-imposed code—including Arthur F. Kelly, who found himself performing such glamorous airline chores as cleaning out the "honey buckets" (emptying aircraft toilets), loading meals, unloading baggage, checking weight and balance, and other duties invariably accompanied by Robinson's outraged tantrums, biting sarcasm, and unbridled criticism.

The training and abuse brought Kelly a monthly paycheck of $72.50; he had been making $350 a month when he quit his Salt Lake City post. He had to buy his own uniform, and he needed a car to get to and from the airport—financial drains necessitating his rooming with four fellow sufferers enrolled in the Robbie Robinson School of Airline Discipline. There were no unions offering shoulders to cry on, so Kelly decided to establish his own system of collective bargaining. Loquacious and articulate, he became a natural spokesman for those with grievances to be laid before Mr. Robinson's fearsome scowl and questionable mercy. Kelly was nothing if not brave—although foolhardy might be a better adjective. As the unofficial representative of United's Unhappy Minions, his brilliantly composed orations in their behalf, touching enough to draw tears from a Gestapo agent, usually resulted in his getting fired. Robinson then would rehire him, solely because Kelly was one of the few people around who was good at weight and balance—the technique of loading an aircraft so the center of gravity would avoid nose-heavy or tail-heavy extremes.

Robbie canned him officially at least three times. On one occasion, Art became justifiably perturbed over the lack of support he was getting from his colleagues. The next time he was asked to present a series of grievances, he laid down the law.

"Okay, I'll speak to Robbie," he decreed. "But this time I want you guys to go in with me."

This pronouncement was greeted with courageous snarls, mut-

terings of grim determination, and loud assurances of willingness
to run through a brick wall if necessary. Thus fortified, Kelly
marched into Robinson's office, his small but gallant army following in formation, like Spads diving on a German zeppelin.

"Now, what, Kelly?" Robbie growled, chewing on the pipe
that always jutted belligerently from his mouth.

Kelly launched into a forensic masterpiece that would have
done credit to Clarence Darrow.

"And furthermore," he concluded firmly, "I want you to know
that my four associates who are running this airport agree with
me. Don't you, fellows?"

He turned around. The four compatriots had long since departed; while Kelly was talking, he had failed to notice that
Robinson had stared them right out of the room.

Kelly worked seven days a week, sometimes twenty-four hours
a day. Every two weeks or so he would call Adams frantically.

"This guy's chopping me into little pieces," he would report.
"When can I go to work for you?"

"Someday soon, I hope," Adams would reply patiently. "Just
hang in there."

Kelly's "hanging in there" usually was by his fingernails. He
had just about given up hope on Western when Adams phoned
him.

"We finally made the deal," he reported. "Get your ass down
to LA."

Adams greeted the refugee from San Francisco warmly, introduced him to Tom Wolfe, and Kelly began working in Western's
Los Angeles sales office, where he found he still wasn't entirely
free from United's influence—not with Western's interlocking
sales efforts, and Wolfe's own UAL background. His immediate
supervisor was a veteran airline salesman named Homer Merchant, who gave Wolfe and Adams good reports on their new
hiree. Then came the day when Adams told Kelly he was going
to transfer him.

"Where?" Art asked suspiciously.

"It's time you moved into the National Parks area," Adams
said. "You're going to Butte, Montana."

To Kelly, a good-looking bachelor who had become quite well
adjusted to Los Angeles life, this was the equivalent of exile to a

monastery deep in the Himalayas. Kelly wasn't even sure where Butte was, and suspected strongly it still was subject to Indian raids. In this crisis, he turned to a beloved airline character named George Cousins, who had once worked for WAE and TWA and who eventually headed Flying Tiger's marketing department. He was a father confessor to more than one youthful airline employee, and Kelly sought him out—in his "office" at the Biltmore Hotel bar, where Cousins had the third stool staked out on a daily basis.

Art approached him utilizing the usual *modus operandi* for obtaining his advice: He found him sitting Buddha-like on that third stool and offered to buy him a scotch and water. Kelly unburdened himself of his considerable woes.

"I've got a choice of staying here in Los Angeles where I'm very happy," he confided, "or taking a job in Butte."

"I've got to think about this for a while," Cousins said solemnly—also following a set ritual.

He sat meditating while Kelly ordered him several more drinks. Finally, Cousins cleared his throat—an oracle at Delphi about to hand down the wisdom of the ages.

"Well, Art," he began pontifically, "I've finally made my decision as to what you should do. I've decided you will go to Butte."

"I think I'll take your advice," Kelly said. "But why do you want me to go to Butte?"

"Because I want you to get your name on the carbon copies of letters."

"You've got to be kidding. What the hell do you mean?"

Kelly never forgot the oracle's reply.

"Well, you could stay here and be a salesman and a hack and probably you'd be happy. But that's all you'd be. If you go to this Butte, you become a personality, an individual. When the boss writes things about the system and reports go in, your name starts to appear on carbon copies because they've got to keep you advised, whether you're important or not."

Kelly took the sage's advice and shortly thereafter drove to Butte in the wheezing, secondhand Plymouth he had purchased during his days of bondage under Robinson.

His initial duties were rather vaguely defined. Officially he was regional traffic manager, his chief responsibility being a general marketing transition from National Parks to Western Air Express. He reported directly to Tom Wolfe, who in his own way could be just as demanding as Robbie Robinson. On one of Wolfe's earliest visits to Kelly's new territory, they were in Helena and were walking by a large Catholic church with twin steeples.

"You're a pretty devout Catholic, aren't you?" Wolfe inquired.

"Very," Kelly allowed.

"Okay. Hang a Western sign between those two steeples or get the hell out of here."

Fortunately, Kelly didn't take him seriously. But he did manage to get a banner strung across one of Helena's principal streets: "WELCOME WESTERN—GOODBYE NATIONAL PARKS." It stayed there nearly two years, becoming part of the scenery.

Hanging rather ostentatious signs was only too typical of an airline trying to develop its own image while simultaneously pouring virtually all its resources into increasing co-operation with (and reliance on) United. Wolfe even came up with an idea for swapping free tickets in exchange for advertising or promotion help—Western's already modest advertising budget was almost entirely committed to that Salt Lake City tieup with United, and even its publicity and reservations offices were part of UAL's operations.

And when it came to modernizing WAE's rather obsolete fleet, Adams also went the United route. He ordered two new DC-3s in sleeper configuration, and leased one of UAL's "Sky Lounges" for use on the Los Angeles–Salt Lake City run pending delivery of Western's own DC-3s. The "Sky Lounge" was a DC-3 with a unique interior—instead of the usual twenty-one capacity, it had fourteen oversized swivel seats that were more like plush lounge chairs. United introduced them on its New York–Chicago route, charging a $2.05 premium for the extra luxury and room, but the innovation was a financial flop; UAL lost seven full passenger fares for every $28.70 collected in surcharges per each fully booked flight. Adams leased one of them only because United was hastily converting them to twenty-one-passenger ships and had a "Sky Lounge" available.

He also bought two small twin-engine Lockheed transports, as replacements for Boeing 247s over National Parks' old system. Trying to strain maximum promotion out of what was *not* the last word in passenger equipment, someone composed "teaser" publicity giving the impression that Western was about to introduce a revolutionary transport plane. A release was issued with this introductory paragraph:

> Rumors of the construction of a new mystery transport plane from the plant of the Lockheed Aircraft Corporation were cleared up today when Alvin P. Adams, president of Western Air Express, announced that performance tests were satisfactorily completed for a new type transport airplane which Western Air Express and Lockheed engineers have been working on in secrecy for many months.

The "new mystery transport plane" actually was nothing but the far-from-mysterious L-12, a smaller version of Lockheed's L-10 (the first all-metal, twin-engine airliner Lockheed had built —called, incidentally, the Electra). Nor was it any secret project; the WAE announcement was released in November 1937, but the L-12 had made its first test flights seventeen months before that and already had been ordered by at least one airline— namely Varney Air Transport, which was to be renamed Continental.

This is not to disparage Adams' efforts to milk the L-12 purchase for promotional reasons; he was trying to give it big-league aura and, perhaps, erase part of that Western's-just-a-finger-at-the-end-of-United's-arm stigma.

For that matter, he made a mistake when he ordered the tiny but fast Lockheed "Baby Electra" for the National Parks route. The WAE-Lockheed contract included an item called Provisional Gross—which meant the L-12 could take off at a certain weight but couldn't land until the load had been reduced substantially. Western discovered, much to its chagrin, that the L-12 had to fly about four hundred miles before it burned off enough fuel to reach the allowable landing weight. The stations along the NPA system were too close together for this fuel reduction, the result being that the two planes WAE bought had to take off with reduced loads. Western operated them for only a few months before Lockheed agreed to take them back.

The L-12s were replaced by 247s whose versatility and reliability more than compensated for their relative antiquity; the tough little Boeings could land on top of a phone booth, and pilots loved their stability even though they were not the easiest plane to fly. It was the first transport for which Western set up comprehensive transitional training, largely because it was the first truly sophisticated airliner the airline operated—much more so than the mammoth but primitively equipped F-32. And with the advent of the DC-3, Western—for all its diminutive size— was growing up again. Alvin P. Adams had plans, and many of them did not involve United. The one that did would someday become commercial aviation's first interchange—an agreement under which one airline operates another's equipment to eliminate the necessity of changing planes.

Few of his associates realized it, but a possible WAE-UAL interchange at Salt Lake City was one of the major reasons Adams deliberately worked so closely with United. It made sense to W. A. Patterson, too; American and TWA were clobbering United in transcontinental traffic to and from Los Angeles, because they operated through flights while UAL's passengers had to change planes at Salt Lake City. An interchange, in which Western's crews would fly the Salt Lake City–Los Angeles leg while UAL crews operated the same plane east of the Utah capital, would eliminate a major United handicap. That was why Adams, when he ordered Western's first DC-3s, insisted that they be sleeper planes—equipment that would fit into overnight transcontinental schedules.

Adams had another dream, too: a Los Angeles–Denver route, which he considered a far more logical leg in transcontinental operations than Los Angeles–Salt Lake City. He talked this over with Patterson, who was more than interested, for a UAL-WAE interchange at Denver would slash several hundred miles off United's transcontinental access to Los Angeles. Adams did more than dream—he dispatched Kelly and a team of experts on a number of survey flights aimed at establishing an airway between Los Angeles and Denver; it seems hard to believe, but no such airway existed in 1937 when Adams ordered the surveys.

Adams even had George Taylor, Western's meteorologist at the time, organize people all along the intended route to keep careful records of weather conditions. For almost an entire year, a half-dozen times daily, they would record data on wind conditions, temperatures, precipitation frequency, and visibility, sending it on to Taylor in Los Angeles. Years would pass before this information would prove valuable, but it illustrates how serious Adams was about a Denver–Los Angeles route and how far-sighted he could be.

Also in his constantly boiling pot was an application for an increase in mail pay and another—filed with the newly established Civil Aeronautics Authority—for extension of Western's system from Great Falls to Lethbridge, in Alberta, Canada. History would repeat itself in this route bid, for WAE's opposition was a carrier it would someday absorb just as it did National Parks–Inland Air Lines.

The new CAA was the child of the Civil Aeronautics Act of 1938, an aviation milestone that ended the quarrelsome, clumsy system of dividing regulatory authority over the airlines among three federal agencies—the Post Office Department (mail contracts and routes), the Interstate Commerce Commission (mail rates and fares) and the Bureau of Air Commerce (safety, airways, and pilot/aircraft licensing). The Act created a five-member Civil Aeronautics Authority, the name being changed later to Civil Aeronautics Board. Set up within CAA was a three-man Safety Board charged with the responsibility of investigating air accidents and armed with complete independence. The once all-powerful Post Office Department retained only its authority to approve air mail schedules, losing its right to award contracts. The Act, more familiarly known as the McCarran-Lea Bill, after its congressional sponsors (Senator Pat McCarran of Nevada and Representative Clarence Lea of California), also broke the thread of the Damoclean sword hanging so long over the airline industry's head—specified duration of mail contracts, which in effect had made all route awards temporary. Route certifications became permanent but not exclusive, with the CAA given power to order competition in markets where the traffic justified such competition.

Over-all, the Civil Aeronautics Act of 1938 brought stability and reasonable regulation to an industry that had been walking a tightrope between czarlike controls and government permissiveness. Preceding its passage was a $7 million allocation for airway modernization, an exchange for which the airlines gladly welcomed stricter safety rules and a far more realistic and independent accident investigation system.

Western may have been small, but it became the first airline to hand the new CAA an extremely hot potato—namely, the Authority's initial merger case. While Al Adams was pursuing various means to strengthen Western, a small but influential group of directors had approached a very receptive United Air Lines with a proposal to merge. Adams knew nothing of the negotiations until he received a phone call from Coulter on a warm June day in 1939.

"I'd like you to come down to the Town House Hotel," Coulter said. "Something's come up you should know about. Bring Dwerlkotte, James, and Wolfe with you."

"What's it all about?" Adams asked, puzzled—and, sensing trouble, also worried.

"I don't want to discuss it on the phone," Coulter answered brusquely. "Just get down here with the others as soon as you can." He hung up after giving Adams the room number where he wanted to see him.

Adams knew that this would be no casual conference—Coulter's presence itself indicated a major crisis was brewing, for Western's largest stockholder seldom visited Los Angeles, and had slipped into town unannounced. Adams notified his three fellow officers, all as mystified as he, and they drove to the hotel on Wilshire Boulevard, where they quickly discovered that Coulter was not alone. Also present were James "Quig" Newton, a prominent Denver attorney; Al Frank, the former head of NPA; William Nicholson, also a lawyer from Denver and a good friend of Newton's; and Charles Boettcher II, chairman of Western's Board and a wealthy Denver stockbroker. The four Western leaders were looking at men who owned a sizable chunk of the airline's stock, starting with Coulter's 51 per cent controlling interest; Adams, holding about ten thousand shares himself, was the third-largest stockholder after Frank. But while Boettcher, Nicholson, and Newton held comparatively few shares, they wielded tremendous influence among the directors—a fact of life that Adams realized the moment he walked into the room.

Newton said, "Hello, Al," and nodded to his companions. The Denver lawyer was twirling a cigar in his hand, nervously. Newton broke an uncomfortable silence.

"Al, we've decided to merge Western with United."

"You've what?" Adams blurted incredulously.

"The deal's already made," Coulter said. Adams thought he seemed embarrassed.

"Oh, really?" Adams asked sarcastically. "And why the hell should we merge at this particular time? You all know the plans we have for Western. The increased mail rate. The interchange with United. The foothold we'll get in Canada with that extension to Lethbridge. For Christ's sake, Mr. Coulter, I'd have no objections to merging with United or anyone else under the right set of circumstances, but this is a lousy time to be even considering it."

"It's a very good deal for all concerned," Newton said softly. "Including you fellows."

"And what price is United talking about?"

"Roughly, we'll get one share of United for three shares of Western."

"And you call that a good deal?" Adams said angrily. "You're screwing the hell out of our own stockholders."

"I don't see how you can say that," Newton argued. "This would give us control of United."

"It gives a few guys in this room control of United. It doesn't do a damned thing for the rest of our stockholders. It's nothing but a giveaway."

"One share of United for three of Western is no giveaway, Al."

"The hell it isn't. What value per share are you putting on our stock?"

"Three dollars and thirty-five cents a share," Newton replied.

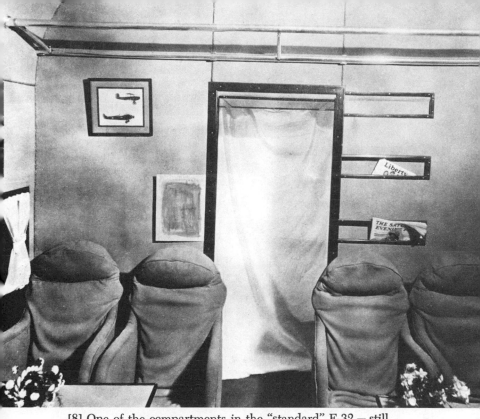

[8] One of the compartments in the "standard" F-32 — still luxurious by 1930 yardsticks, anyway. Note the touch of the freshly cut flowers.

[9] For 1930, this was the last word in terminal facilities. The picture shows the interior of Western's ticket office at the Alhambra airport.

[10] Boeing 247.

[11] DC-3.

[12] DC-4.

[13] DC-6B.

This gallery of WAL aircraft shows
the evolution of the airline's insignia scheme.

[14] Lockheed Electra.

[15] Boeing 720-B.

[16] Boeing 727.

[17] Boeing 737.

[18] DC-10.

[19] Another F-32 compartment, emphasizing the unusual cabin height and tapestry effect on the wall and bulkhead.

"United's stock is selling, roughly, at ten dollars a share. That three-to-one ratio seems very fair."

"In a pig's eye it's fair! Our stock is sure to go up to around eleven or twelve bucks a share if we get the mail rate boost and the interchange. You still don't call *that* a giveaway?"

"The deal's been made," Newton said in a stiffening tone.

"Well, you're gonna have to forget about me," Adams bristled. "And I don't have to rely on a bunch of goddamned lawyers to tell me how to fight this thing."

The silence in the small room was coated with a thick layer of hostility. Dwerlkotte, James, and Wolfe looked stunned.

"Look," Adams pleaded, "this is wrong. I've got to put myself in the position of fighting for our stockholders as a whole—not for you, Mr. Coulter, or Al Frank and any of you fellows. This is just not a good deal for Western's shareholders, and I won't stand for it."

"I told you, Al," Newton repeated, "we've already made the deal with Patterson. I'm sorry you're not going to stand for it, but exactly what do you propose to do?"

"I'll take a six-month leave of absence," Adams retorted, "and I'll spend those six months fighting this merger."

"Without pay?" Coulter asked.

"Without pay!"

"I think that can be arranged," Coulter said quietly. "I just hope you know what you're doing."

"I know damned well what I'm doing. I wonder if you guys do. You pull this on us when everything's going our way . . . when everything's shaping up to make us a really damned good airline."

There was an uncomfortable silence. Except for Coulter, the directors present wore expressions of defiance bordering on belligerence. Coulter seemed on the verge of trying to placate the infuriated president but remained silent. Adams made one last effort to change minds.

"You can't sell out this company now, not when we have these things going for us," he implored.

"Yes," Newton said, "but the same things will happen to United when we get control through their stock."

Adams uttered an obscenity and strode from the room, his

three bewildered colleagues close on his heels. No one spoke until they were on the sidewalk outside the hotel.

"I guess you fellas feel the same way I do," Adams said— although it was more of a question than a statement. They nodded. "I think we have to fight this. We've got time. The CAA has to approve it, and I can line up a helluva lot of support before there's a final decision. What we need first is some dough."

"What about the airline while you're gone?" Dwerlkotte asked.

"Hell, you three guys have been running it anyway. My being away for six months won't make much difference. Coulter probably will ask you to take charge temporarily, Leo. You've been around longer than Tom, and Jimmie's field is strictly operations."

They went back to the general offices, Adams vastly encouraged by their promises of support. His first task was to raise money, and he talked over the situation with Norman Chandler, who had replaced his father as head of the Los Angeles *Times*. The young newspaper executive wasn't on Western's Board, but Adams respected both his ability and his influence. When Chandler pledged to back the antimerger fight, Adams turned next to United's competitors, who would be sure to oppose a merger so beneficial to UAL. Jack Frye of TWA kicked in a thousand dollars to the "war chest," and Croil Hunter of Northwest added another thousand. From these and a few other sources, Adams raised an initial kitty of some five thousand dollars, which he knew would fall far short of paying for an expensive, prolonged legal battle. Not that he lacked legal advice; on Western's Board was a reputable Los Angeles attorney named Stanley Guthrie, whose firm represented WAE. Adams had placed the airline's legal affairs in his hands on the recommendation of Hugh Darling, a tall, distinguished-looking attorney who was a member of Guthrie's firm. Both Darling, a close friend of Western's president, and Guthrie himself had to warn Adams that while they opposed the merger, their firm's status as Western's legal representative made involvement impossible. They also advised against an expensive proxy fight, although Adams did send letters to some fifteen thousand stockholders explaining his position.

In this dilemma, Adams turned to his father-in-law, who was head of a large New York City law firm.

"We need a good lawyer," Adams said, "but you can't charge us anything because we don't have enough money. All we can pay is expenses."

His father-in-law offered him the free services of Leslie Craven, a brilliant if somewhat eccentric and colorful attorney, and Adams accepted gratefully. From that day on, he worked closely with Craven in deciding strategy and action. Craven, for example, urged him to follow up on Adams' own suspicion that Coulter might not be as hell-bent for merger as his associates. Adams to this day is convinced that the brain behind the merger plan was not in that hotel room nor even on Western's Board, but was Quig Newton's father, James Q. Newton, Sr.

Acting on this hunch, and knowing that without Coulter's backing there would be no merger, Adams phoned him at his home in Philadelphia.

"Mr. Coulter," Adams said earnestly, "I just have an idea you don't want this deal with United any more than I do."

"I feel badly about it, Al," Coulter replied, "but these fellows . . ." He hesitated momentarily. "Let me think it over again. I know it's a terrible thing from your point of view. I appreciate it, Alvin—you've been very loyal."

Adams had a sudden inspiration.

"Suppose someone other than United had the money to buy you out, Mr. Coulter. Would you sell?"

"Well," Coulter said hesitantly, "that might be all right."

"I'd like to come East and see you before this thing is signed."

"It's pretty well along," Coulter hedged, "but I'll be glad to talk to you—and good luck."

Adams began looking into various possibilities of raising some $670,000 in cash—the amount needed to acquire Coulter's stock. He had further encouragement only a few days later, when he again asked Coulter if he would dispose of his shares to anyone except United.

"Would you sell them to me, for example?" was his blunt query.

"Well . . ."

"You're against the merger, too," Adams pressed. "If you want to sell your stock, why not sell it to me?"

"Newton pressured me into the deal," Coulter said without directly answering. "I'll talk to you about it in a few days, Al."

The next time they met, Coulter said he had changed his mind about the merger.

"Come back East to see me, and if you can meet the same proposition United's offered, you have it," he said. "You don't think I'd sell you fellas down the river, do you?"

At that particular moment, Adams thought the merger was dead. By now he had every confidence he could raise sufficient cash to buy Coulter's 51 per cent interest—some 200,000 shares —for the same $3.35 per share United was willing to pay. He was so confident that he confided to James, Dwerlkotte, and Wolfe that there was "a damned good chance" of buying out Coulter and getting in some new stockholders inexorably opposed to merger. He flew immediately to Chicago, arriving early on a Sunday, where he met with the top brass of the Chicago Corporation, a prestigious investment company. They promised him an answer by the time he returned to Los Angeles that same night, so he phoned Coulter again to make sure he would be available for a call Monday morning.

"I'll be right here in my apartment all morning," Coulter promised.

The next morning Adams received a telegram from the Chicago Corporation, confirming that they'd underwrite purchase of Coulter's majority interest. Overjoyed, Adams put in a call to Philadelphia, and Coulter's secretary answered.

"Alvin Adams in Los Angeles, I'd like to speak to Mr. Coulter."

"Just a minute, Mr. Adams, he's just hanging up on the other line." Adams waited, his heart pounding both for impatience and sheer exuberance. It was only four seconds later, but it seemed like five minutes before the secretary returned.

"I'm sorry, Mr. Adams, but I guess Mr. Coulter has gone out."

Adams detected a nonkosher aroma in the air. "Do you know where I can reach him?"

"No, sir. He didn't say where he was going."

Adams hung up. Then he remembered that Coulter frequently used a private club in New Jersey as a kind of sanctuary from business worries and contacts. He waited about two hours and called the club. He asked for Coulter, and the man who answered said pleasantly, "Yes, sir, he just walked in—I'll get him for you."

Not more than a minute later, the same man was back on the phone. "I'm sorry, but I guess I was mistaken. He's not here."

"I'll bet," Adams muttered. For several more days he tried to reach the man who held Western's fate in his hands—along with those precious 200,000 shares representing majority control. Coulter ducked every call with the agility of a skilled boxer avoiding roundhouse punches. Adams finally gave up after George Moore, the New York banker who had introduced him to Coulter, phoned.

"Al," he said not without sympathy, "I know you've been trying to contact Coulter, so I thought I'd better tell you—it won't do you any good. He has decided to make that deal with United, and you might as well save yourself time and worry. That's the way it is."

Adams thanked him and plunged into his next move—in the tricky, uncertain area of political influence. He flew to Washington, accompanied by Tom Wolfe, and obtained an early appointment with Senator Joseph P. O'Mahoney of Wyoming, who was more than merely one of the most powerful men on Capitol Hill; he also happened to be chairman of the Temporary National Economy Committee, with a well-anchored pipeline right into the White House. Even more important, he was mad at United.

The latter point was the main reason Adams figured he could enlist O'Mahoney's support. United had moved its maintenance and headquarters base from Cheyenne to Denver, and hell hath no fury like a senator whose home state has lost an important industrial facility. As Adams expected, O'Mahoney's resentment toward United brimmed over into alacritive opposition to the merger. He asked Adams and Wolfe to write up a statement denouncing the deal—"You know," the senator added, "stuff about it being a well-conceived scheme by Wall Street bankers to gain control of this tiny airline and so on."

The two Westerners couldn't get back to their hotel fast enough In less than an hour, they composed an antimerger statement and took it to O'Mahoney, who loved it.

The statement, which appeared on page one of the New York *Times*, included this Adams-created paragraph:

> One report current here [*in Washington*] was to the effect that the operating officials of Western Air offered their principal stockholders more for the controlling stock than did the New York bankers of United Airlines, but that the Western Air stockholders turned them down because they preferred to receive the block of United stock which the financiers offered them.

Conforming to O'Mahoney's suggestion for mentioning a "scheme of Wall Street bankers," Adams and Wolfe wrote in such phrases as:

"This transaction is being promoted by New York banking interests which are not primarily concerned in the development of air traffic in the West.

"There has been a great disposition on the part of financial interests which have controlled aviation to neglect services to intermediate communities."

All of which, of course, was hitting somewhere south of United's beltline. United didn't instigate the merger talks; they were originated by a few Western stockholders and directors, and United couldn't be blamed for getting interested in what obviously was an advantageous merger. The prime reason behind the merger proposal in the first place was the desire of Newton and his compatriots to win control of United by acquiring a huge block of United stock.

Having fired the first broadside, Adams loaded up for another. He and Wolfe conferred with Senator Burton Wheeler of Montana, who told them they were staging a losing battle but agreed to help anyway. A statement by Wheeler, again written by Adams and Wolfe, also made page one of the *Times*. The same morning the statement appeared, Adams ran into big Cy Thompson, United's Washington representative, who obviously wasn't aware that Western's president was fighting the merger.

"Alvin," he moaned, waving a copy of the *Times*, "look at this story on Wheeler! What's happening to this thing? Who's doing all this to us?"

Adams, trying not to laugh, muttered something about it being a shame.

Between the two of them, Adams and Wolfe wheedled antimerger statements from a half-dozen lawmakers, all of which got good newspaper space. But mergers aren't decided on the basis of press clippings, and Adams had every reason to worry about the real battleground: the CAA hearing room. Because the case was so controversial, not to mention it being the new agency's initial merger consideration, the CAA appointed a special hearing examiner in the person of Dean Roscoe Pound of the Harvard Law School, one of the nation's most distinguished barristers. He was over eighty years old when he agreed to hear the case, and his eventual decision—approving the merger—was so loaded with factual errors that it actually hurt the merger's case when the five-man CAA reviewed it.

Errors or no errors, his decision stunned Adams and his tiny army, which began deserting him. Dwerlkotte virtually was forced into it; Coulter had asked him to take over in Adams' absence, naming him first vice president in addition to secretary/treasurer; Western's 1939 annual report, in fact, was signed by Dwerlkotte, although the list of officers still included Adams as president. Leo hated the very thought of merger, but as more or less the acting president, he was in no position to display any open disloyalty toward Coulter and the directors.

Wolfe's support also wavered after the examiner's initial decision: He informed Adams he had decided to be "neutral." Other officers, hearing of Wolfe's retreat, also decided to stay on the fence—for which Adams couldn't blame them. It looked as if the merger was going through, and their own jobs were at stake. One prominent exception was Art Kelly, who sided with Adams from the start and refused to budge—even after he was warned that if he didn't start behaving himself and the merger was consummated, he was through. This admonition came from several United officials, but Kelly had his Irish temper up and continued doing everything Adams asked. This included an interview over a Butte radio station, in which Kelly asked the questions (in a disguised voice) and Adams supplied the antimerger answers.

It is a strong possibility that Coulter could have smashed the whole deal and actually was leaning in that direction, before

Dean Pound's decision was announced. Coulter confessed to Adams, just prior to a meeting of Western's Board of Directors, that he regretted going along with Newton and the others.

"If you feel that way, why don't you go before the Board and tell them you don't favor the merger?" Adams said. "I'll go with you, even though I'm not supposed to be there."

Coulter muttered something along the lines of "I'll think about it," but what he said to the directors—if anything—will never be known. Says Hugh Darling:

"I don't know because Guthrie never told me, and I don't think Al knows. But you have to remember that Coulter was a very changeable man; the fact that he took a position one day was no assurance that he'd take the same position the next."

Dwerlkotte, who knew the mercurial Coulter probably better than anyone else, also got the impression that he became resentful toward the Newton-Boettcher clique, which he believed was forcing him out of the picture, his 51 per cent interest notwithstanding. He badly wanted to assume a major role at United, probably the chief motivation behind his early propensity toward merger, but it was apparent that Newton and Boettcher had no such plans for him.

Adams continued fighting a presumably hopeless rear-guard action. United already was holding most of Western's stock in escrow for the day the CAA would issue its final decision. All Adams could do was to make speeches around Western's system, seeking community support for his cause; on one occasion, he engaged in a public debate in Salt Lake City with Patterson himself. The newspapers thought Adams was the winner, but it was a meaningless success; the five men meeting in Washington to decide the merger presumably didn't read Salt Lake City papers.

Adams saw one truly bright ray of hope when the CAA held open hearings. Pound, aged and feeble, was hacked to pieces by Craven in the latter's rebuttal to the initial decision. The myriad weaknesses in Pound's own brief proved to be a major factor in what followed: The CAA rejected the merger as "undesirable at this stage in the development of properly balanced system of air transportation."

W. A. Patterson was bitter, not only at the decision but also at the fact that it was widely known before it was announced officially.

"Long before the Authority's announcement was published," Patterson told the Los Angeles *Times* in an interview, "at least a half-dozen people knew what its ruling would be. You lose confidence when an agency posing as a judicial body peddles 'information' as if it were a political group."

His reaction was understandable, but in truth United came out of the brawl surprisingly healthy. The CAA already had approved the proposed Salt Lake City interchange before rejecting the merger, and the former in many ways made the latter unnecessary. The man who had the right to be far more embittered than Patterson was Alvin P. Adams. For him, the CAA's ruling was a Pyrrhic victory; it came after Western's Board of Directors already had voted to fire him, at Coulter's request. And this, not the controversial merger, was the real story behind the ordeal of a man who might have become one of the industry's giants if he could have stayed with WAE.

Dwerlkotte, who had run the airline in Adams' absence—officially as first vice president and unofficially as acting president— once talked to Coulter about the merger.

"I never really wanted it to take place," Coulter confided.

"Bill, if you felt that way, why did you ever sign an agreement with United?"

"Because," Coulter said in his soft voice, "I wanted to get Al Adams out of the company."

If that was Alvin Adams' epitaph with Western, it was someone else's coronation proclamation.

On March 11, 1940, William Coulter—who suffered so badly from gout that a trip to Los Angeles was torture to be avoided at all costs—became the third president of Western Air Express.

CHAPTER NINE

Western Goes to War

Al Adams' departure created no major earthquake at Western; as far as running the airline was concerned, he had voluntarily abdicated that leadership the day he decided to fight the merger, and his dismissal was more in the nature of an anticlimax.

There were those who regretted his removal—Art Kelly and Jimmie James in particular—and a few who resented it, but airline people have remarkable corporate discipline. When the top command is changed, theirs is a kind of "the king is dead, long live the king" philosophy. It certainly was the case when Adams was forced out of power. Not many Westerners knew Coulter either personally or indirectly, but they did know the quiet, solid Leo Dwerlkotte, who had great ability if not Adams' drive and flamboyance. And after the latter's departure, there was no doubt Dwerlkotte had been president of Western Air Express in everything but title.

He scrupulously consulted Coulter on major issues of policy and deferred to the older man's judgment on more than one occasion. Most of the day-to-day decisions were Dwerlkotte's, however, and he was a more positive and forceful executive than his retiring, rather shy nature led people to believe. Some employees thought him dour, cold, and unfeeling, but in his own way, he was a warm and considerate person. Ed Deeter, a Western stock clerk, remembers the time he was making $125 a month and asked Dwerlkotte for a raise.

Leo's thin, professional face bore the expression of one who has just been told his mother-in-law was moving in permanently. "Ed, I can get anybody for your job at $80 a month."

Deeter decided not to pursue the matter, but when he opened his next pay envelope, he found Dwerlkotte had given him an increase.

Dwerlkotte's executive team stayed largely intact from the Adams regime—James in charge of operations and Wolfe as vice president of traffic, with likable Paul "Pat" Sullivan moved into Leo's old post as secretary/treasurer. Sullivan had joined Western when it acquired Standard, and he possessed considerable legal and financial background. It was typical of the pedantic Dwerlkotte that he did more than merely admire Pat's legal training; he went to Loyola University law school at night and obtained his own law degree.

It was while attending law school that he met a fellow student who impressed him to such an extent that Dwerlkotte offered him an accounting job at Western. Nine months later, the reluctant object of his wooing caved in—and without knowing it, Leo had hired a young man who would someday become the airline's fifth president under highly dramatic circumstances: J. Judson Taylor, employed initially as an assistant accountant.

Taylor's doubts about the wisdom of going into the hectic airline business were more or less confirmed the first day he reported, on a February morning. He asked his superior in the accounting department if he wanted him to start working on current bills and tax records.

"Hell no," was the answer. "We're still doing stuff from last October."

A surprise survivor of the merger fight was Art Kelly, largely for two reasons: First, Dwerlkotte had backbone and was determined to resist any Coulter vendetta, especially when it might cost the services of able young executives; and second, because Coulter, happy with the idea of being an airline president, made no serious purge attempts—apparently, he was satisfied with Adams' ouster.

After World War II, Western commissioned Jack and Peggy Hereford, a husband-wife writing team, to do a history of the airline; Peggy had been Western's director of news from 1939 to 1942. After months of extensive research, they turned in a manuscript that eventually reached Coulter's desk for final approval. When the authors saw the results of Coulter's editing job, they were stunned—most of the favorable references to Al Adams had been eliminated, and Coulter came out looking like a combination of C. R. Smith and W. A. Patterson; there was no reference, for example, to the fact that Coulter was an absentee president who seldom came to Los Angeles. Major credit was given to "the Coulter-Dwerlkotte team which led Western gradually into the sanest, surest expansion of its history," but Coulter's own role in a merger fight that almost ended the airline's existence had been not just glossed over but ignored.

When the book, *Flying Years,* reached the hands of Alvin Adams, he wrote Coulter a blistering letter in which he charged that "you have considerably changed the manuscript." Adams' letter ran nearly two thousand words and was a point-by-point refutation of statements resulting largely from Coulter's alterations. Most damaging from the standpoint of pure objectivity was the virtual omission of Adams' own previous achievements and plans for the future.

Adams was in no small way responsible for much of Western's success in the immediate prewar years. WAE closed 1939 with a modest profit of nearly $75,000, and it netted more than $135,000 in 1940. The interchange with United began in August of the latter year, the teamwork between the two companies again being so close that Western painted the UAL trademark "Mainliner" above the cabin windows of its DC-3s. And as the interchange proved successful, WAE recorded another triumph late in 1940 when the Civil Aeronautics Board, formerly the CAA, awarded Western its coveted route from Great Falls to Lethbridge, providing the long-sought gateway to Canada.

The interchange led to an incident that became an airline classic. It involved the president of a company who was flying from Los Angeles to Omaha via Salt Lake City on one of the interchange sleeper planes. The Western flight he boarded late at night had, naturally, a WAE crew, and he asked the stewardess to be sure and wake him up when they reached Omaha.

"I'm making an important speech there," he added.

"A United crew takes over at Salt Lake City," she said, "but I'll pass the word to their stewardess."

She did, but the United flight attendant failed to wake him at Omaha as ordered. When he opened his eyes, the DC-3 definitely was not on final approach into Omaha—a fact only too apparent to the passenger as he looked down and saw a large body of water passing under the wings. He rang for the stewardess.

"Where the hell are we?" he demanded.

"Over Lake Michigan, sir. We'll be landing in Chicago shortly."

"You've got to go back to Omaha!" he shouted. "I'll miss my meeting!"

He raised so much fuss that the copilot came back to placate him, explaining that they didn't have enough fuel to make it all the way back to Omaha. After they landed, and the irate passenger deplaned in a cloud of smoking profanity, the copilot remarked, "I've never seen such an angry guy."

"I have," the crestfallen stewardess sighed. "You should have seen the man I put off in Omaha."

While this was a story Westerners loved to tell about United, UAL personnel had a few items to talk about concerning Western—usually uncomplimentary, for the bigger airline was not enamored of WAE's over-all performance. Dwerlkotte was kept busy investigating and then answering incessant United complaints about dirty interchange planes, soiled equipment, poor maintenance, inferior cabin service, and woeful on-time performance. When WAE became Western Air Lines, UAL employees referred to the new initials as standing for "Western's Always Late." Significantly, Dwerlkotte and not Coulter had to bear the brunt of such interline criticism.

While Coulter relied heavily on Dwerlkotte, he wasn't staying entirely aloof. Financially speaking, his hold on the airline was tightening like a vise. He bought out the disappointed Boettcher and Newton, adding their 23,000 shares to the block of stock he already held, and while he never admitted it to anyone, the merger defeat turned out to be extremely profitable to him personally. If he had sold his stock to United for cash, which he really preferred to a stock exchange deal, he would have received $670,000. By the end of 1945, his original 200,000 shares of WAE stock were worth, according to then-current market value, $7.8 million.

The UAL interchange lasted longer than the other ties that were severed early in 1941 as Dwerlkotte fought to regain Western's own identity. He ended the joint traffic, reservations, and ticketing operations, established Western's own traffic offices, and even ordered "Mainliner" scrubbed from WAE aircraft. Stewardesses got new uniforms and pilots switched from United gray to spiffy brown outfits, which were to remain the trademark of Western airmen for the next thirty-five years. Also changed was the name of the airline itself. On March 11, 1941, the first anniversary of Coulter's presidency, Western Air Express became Western Air Lines with the approval of its Board of Directors.

From all the available facts, the change appears to have been mostly the idea of Ted Cate, the energetic advertising manager who had joined Western in 1939 and promptly launched a campaign against the name "Western Air Express." Cate objected to the use of the word "Express" on the grounds that it connotated an airline that carried nothing but priority packages. He ran into heavy opposition from the traditionalists, but his chief ally was Tom Wolfe, who had been recommending a name change even before Cate but hadn't been able to muster much support among the diehards. Cate had the persuasive personality of an evangelist and quickly reduced the hard-core objectors to an ineffective minority. The initials went from WAE to WAL in time for celebration of the airline's fifteenth anniversary on April 17, 1941.

As of that date, Western had 417 employees, 42 of them pilots and no less than 100 people assigned to maintenance. The fleet consisted of seven DC-3s and five Boeing 247s, which flew a 1,400-mile route system stretching from San Diego to Lethbridge.

Not on WAL's payroll but still a member of the family was Susie, a lady of doubtful morals but an irresistible personality. She was a nondescript mutt abandoned at the Burbank airport one day and instantly adopted by the mechanics.

She rode around on company trucks like a queen, and occasionally a softhearted pilot would seek her on his airplane for a trip. She ate better than a pampered Pomeranian, mostly the leftovers from aircraft buffets, and one day showed her gratitude to Western by depositing a litter of four pups on the hangar floor. The father's identity was as unknown as Susie's own ancestry (she seemed to be part Scotty), but this made no difference; her love affairs provided a regular source of pets for Western households throughout the system.

When Susie died in the late forties, she was buried under the front lawn of what was then the general offices—some of the old-timers still walk by the spot and tell their younger colleagues, "That's where Susie's buried."

"Who the hell was Susie?"

"Oh . . . just a dog that used to run around here. Kind of a mascot, I guess."

Western still was a small airline but one with big dreams. Air traffic was expanding fast, spurred partially by the popularity of the DC-3 and also by the prewar prosperity. Dwerlkotte was inherently more cautious than Adams but wise enough to recognize the merit in the growth plans his predecessor had begun to develop before the merger bloodletting. He applied not only for Los Angeles–Denver authority, via Las Vegas and Grand Junction, Colorado, but also nonstop rights between Los Angeles and San Francisco—the old route of the Model Airway. With these major applications went a spate of minor ones: Los Angeles–El Centro via Palm Springs, San Diego–Phoenix via El Centro and Yuma; and Los Angeles–San Francisco and Los Angeles–Sacramento via Bakersfield, Visalia, Merced, and Stockton.

To aid him in the fast-growing traffic department, Wolfe hired an experienced assistant in Richard Dick, formerly with Northwest and United. With admirable foresight, they began experimenting in the then-embryonic field of air cargo. Technical surveys to determine what types of cargo shippers would send by air were followed by trial runs with flowers, deer, dressed trout, baby chicks, and eggs.

As 1941 drew to a close, the future indeed looked bright, although profits would amount to less than $6,000 because of heavy equipment expenditures. Western took delivery that year on three new DC-3s costing almost $400,000, and paid a large chunk of that sum in cash. The most promising aspect was the growth in passenger volume; it was up 40 per cent over 1940 and generated 52 per cent of total revenue—Pop Hanshue's vision of an airline that didn't have to depend primarily on mail pay had finally become a reality.

What turned out to be Western's most significant route application in the war years to come was filed with the Civil Aeronautics Board late in the year. Dwerlkotte asked authority to fly between Lethbridge and Nome, Alaska, via Calgary, Edmonton, and Grand Prairie, Canada, and a second route from Lethbridge to Juneau, Anchorage, and McGrath, with an Anchorage–Fairbanks shuttle spur. Once again, this came out of the Alvin P. Adams expansion book. He had envisioned Lethbridge as merely the first step in spreading Western's wings northward, moving next to Calgary and then up to Yukon Territory and Fairbanks. A Seattle–Alaska route intrigued him, but the weather was considered too much of an obstacle on such a coastal route, and Adams was more interested in an "inland passage."

The Great Falls–Lethbridge extension via Cut Bank and Shelby was only 170 miles long, but that tiny segment was the final link in an 11,250-mile intercontinental airway stretching from Santiago, Chile, to Nome, Alaska. At Lethbridge, Western connected with a number of small Canadian carriers, opening all of western Canada to air transportation to and from the United States. The rich oil fields of Alberta province became accessible by air from the United States, and so did the burgeoning Alaskan defense program.

Wolfe saw possibilities in a vacation travel market, for the new route put the magnificent Banff and Lake Louise areas within easy reach of Western's planes. Any plans for developing a pleasure market, however, were shoved into a save-for-future-use file on December 7, 1941. Along with all other carriers, WAL already had experienced the pressures of the spreading global conflict. Even before Pearl Harbor, it was forced to lease two of its five 247s to the Army for use as military cargo planes. Employees were being called into the service, some via the draft, and a flood of others volunteering after Japanese bombs and torpedoes plunged the nation into war.

On May 15, 1942, a momentous meeting was held in Washington, with representatives of the entire airline industry attending. The presiding officer was the Military Director of Civil Aviation, and the edict he laid down was simple but blunt: no more business-as-usual. The airlines would have to turn over the major portion of their aircraft to the military, presumably for the duration of the war.

Western received its fleet-slashing orders shortly after that meeting. It was to sell its 247s to the War Department, including the two already under lease. Also to be sold were four DC-3s, two each to the Army and United, whose own fleet had been decimated. This left Western with three DC-3s with which to operate its 1,400-mile system. For a brief spell, Dwerlkotte feared he would have to suspend service over the new Great Falls–Lethbridge leg, but Continental agreed to sell WAL a Lockheed Lodestar, the fourteen-passenger civilian version of Lockheed's Hudson bomber. Western used the Lodestar for a daily round trip between Salt Lake City and Lethbridge, the three DC-3s flying reduced schedules over the San Diego–Los Angeles–Salt Lake City route.

WAL officials could only grimace as, one by one, aircraft representing two thirds of the fleet were turned over to the Army. All they could salvage from this painful if necessary experience was a wry chuckle the day a rather smug, officious young Army lieutenant arrived to inspect one of the 247s the military had commandeered. The pompous shavetail had never been inside a 247 in his life and had no idea that the massive center wing spar ran right through the cabin, hidden by a small, carpet-covered metal step. He strode briskly through the passenger compartment en route to the cockpit and tripped over the spar.

"The first thing we do," he ordered, "is get rid of this damned step."

The fleet and schedule cuts actually were drastic only in the sense that they slowed regular passenger traffic to a trickle—which made little difference anyway, because commercial operations were limited to priority travel, and flights were almost always full. What the airlines lost in the way of reduced schedules was made up by military contracts for hauling cargo and personnel. And for the latter assignments, the carriers got back some of the aircraft they had surrendered to the government—usually not the same ones, of course. Western, for example, received a contract for operating an Army freight service from Los Angeles to Sacramento and from Los Angeles to Edmonton, Canada; it utilized a pair of converted DC-3s acquired from United, and these were followed by a number of cargo-configured DC-3s assigned to WAL by the Army.

WAL's chief World War II mission stemmed from that tiny spur into southwestern Canada at Lethbridge and the obvious interest WAL had shown in Canadian and Alaskan service with its prewar applications to serve Nome, Juneau, and Fairbanks via Al Adams' old dream of an inland passage route. Thus was born Operation Sourdough, a 2,451-mile aerial lifeline from Great Falls to Nome via Edmonton and White Horse, Canada, and Fairbanks. Added to this then-dangerous and difficult route were branches to Anchorage and Nome—all of which exposed Western's flight and ground crews to a combination of weather/terrain conditions they had never encountered before.

Dwerlkotte and James picked a veteran pilot, well liked and respected, to head Sourdough—the airline's major contribution to the war effort. Pat Carlson had come over to Western from Standard in 1930, and there wasn't a better pilot nor a more natural leader flying the line. Carlson had been the first Western pilot to make an instrument landing; he was a stickler for following regulations without being a martinet, and he skillfully blended strong discipline with a deft touch of tolerance. Pat had never flown to Alaska before, but James recommended him for Sourdough as the kind of man even the most hell-raising airman would follow.

They all did, without question. It was a horrendous operation out of which sprang countless stories of bravery, hardship, and humor.

Carlson set up Sourdough's headquarters at Edmonton in the summer of 1942. The winter of that year turned out to be Alaska's worst since 1898. Temperatures sank to sixty-five below zero for weeks at a time. Rubber fittings crystallized to the point where the slightest touch would shatter them like fragile glass. Oil took on the consistency of thick mud, and grease simply froze in wheel bearings. Fuel hoses became so brittle they would snap in a modest wind. Altimeters, their air intakes often blocked by ice and heavy snow, could be a thousand feet off in either direction. Airports, at least in the early stages of the war, were nothing but dirt strips, and radio navigation aids were virtually nonexistent.

Compounding all these difficulties was the inadequacy of the navigation charts, most of them the product of pure guesswork. A WAL pilot once described to a new Sourdough crew his scientific technique for flying from Fairbanks to Anchorage.

"You just put your ship into a steep climb as soon as you take off," he advised his rapt audience. "Don't level off until your props are churning stardust. Then you hope you're at the spot in the Alaskan mountain range where Mount McKinley ain't."

Officially, Sourdough was operated as the Alaskan Division of Western Air Lines. Unofficially, it was operated by a collection of rugged individualists to whom improvision came as naturally as breathing, calculated risks were a daily occurrence to be taken for granted, and off-duty hours provided a time in which to play as hard as they had worked. Nearly a hundred employees were assigned to Sourdough, which started out on a modest scale, carrying ferry pilots from Fairbanks—where their aircraft had been flown for eventual delivery to the Soviet Union—back to Great Falls. Later, Western's planes, mostly C-47s or DC-3s converted to all-cargo aircraft, flew every conceivable item, from lumber to heavy diesel machinery.

The military weight manifests were even less accurate than Alaskan aeronautical charts. Carlson once questioned the weight of a diesel engine being loaded on a C-47. The manifest listed it at less than six thousand pounds.

"It must be made of aluminum," Pat snorted. "I want it weighed again before that plane takes off."

It weighed some ten thousand pounds.

The best that could be said for Sourdough's various runways was their length—and the pilots, taking off or landing with abnormally heavy loads, needed every foot offered. In the winter, ice was the biggest problem; runways turned into skating rinks, and a landing roll on glare ice seemed to last into the following day. Captain Ed Schuster, one of the Sourdough pilots now retired, recalls one landing only too vividly:

"I was flying with Jerry Miller as my copilot, and we came out of the overcast, hitting the deck a little hot. I tried to brake, but it was like riding on a sled. There was a big bank of snow at the end of the runway, and I knew we were going to hit it. I yelled to Jerry to unlock the tailwheel and brace himself.

"Just as we reached the snowbank, I hit the rudder hard and went full throttle on one engine. All I saw was a cloud of snow, and when things cleared, we were pointing 180 degrees in the other direction. I looked outside, and there was all the emergency equipment roaring up. I slid open the cockpit window and some guy yells, 'Are you in trouble?'

"I shouted, 'Hell no—we always land this way!' "

Engine oil had to be diluted with gas if a plane sat on the ground in the freezing cold any length of time, to keep the oil cooler from rupturing. Snow and ice would accumulate on airfields all winter, successfully defying all efforts to scrape it off. The supposedly welcome spring thaws made matters even worse; the ice would turn into heavy slush during the day and freeze all over again at night. Warmer weather brought no respite, because instead of ice or slush, the crews had to battle ankle-deep mud. Nor was it always possible to build new runways in line with prevailing winds. Western's pilots became highly efficient in crosswind landings that in civilian operations would have been illegal.

One of Carlson's most frequent chores was to stave off, as diplomatically as possible, complaints from Alaskan hotel operators concerning pilot decorum—or lack of it. The crews at various times stayed in three different Fairbanks hotels, shifting because they had become *personae non gratae* at one or the other. The main food staple was steak—beef steak, bear steak, and moose steak; the latter was coarse, and some pilots thought it tasted like veal. Fresh vegetables were virtually unattainable, and the crews began yearning for greens in the same way an alcoholic craves a drink. Carlson once paid $1.75 for a lettuce sandwich, and Schuster recalls landing in Great Falls after a flight from Edmonton. He walked into a restaurant featuring the finest steaks in Montana and proceeded to order every salad on the menu.

New transferees to Sourdough would bring cases of fresh eggs to the North country, expecting to be welcomed with open arms. All they got were a few ungrateful grunts and such comments as, "What the hell do we need those for?" The pilots and mechanics had gotten so used to powdered eggs that they spurned the fresh.

"The hotel I remember best," says Carlson, "was the old Nordale. They never made the beds. When you'd sign in, they'd hand you your sheets, and they were always wet. They had phones in each room, but none of them had a bell—the bell box was on the wall. If it rang, you'd stumble out of bed half asleep and tear the damned box off the wall trying to find a receiver that wasn't there. At all the hotels, the plumbing was frozen half the time."

A few pilots latched onto a small cabin near Edmonton and somehow made friends with a black bear that came around to wheedle food. One visiting pilot hadn't been briefed on the bear's status and shot it. He was promptly evicted from the premises in utter disgrace, the anguished cry of an unhappy fellow airman ringing in his ears:

"You lousy sonofabitch—you killed the only friend we have up here!"

All the vicissitudes, of necessity softened by occasional she-nanigans, never obscured the fact that Sourdough was efficiently, even brilliantly, executed. Western never lost a plane nor a man, and this perfect safety record could be classed as incredible, considering the technical handicaps under which it was achieved. The average flight between any two points was five hundred miles, and most of it had to be flown on instruments. Typical was one trip flown by Captain Jack Orwig; it took twenty-three hours, and he was on instruments for seventeen of those hours.

Things did get somewhat easier as the war progressed. Navigational aids improved immeasurably, and huge new airfields were built. Even emergency landing strips were modernized to the point where they surpassed the facilities of the original main airports Sourdough served. The pilots eventually began flying brand-new airplanes, too, and some were comfortably configured for passenger volume that by the war's final year matched what was being carried in cargo. The latter, of course, was Western's primary mission. By 1945, when Sourdough ended, WAL planes flying under the Air Transport Command flag had hauled more than twenty-two million tons, ranging from mattresses to Soviet gold being flown to the Denver mint.

A large proportion of the Sourdough fleet consisted of ex-airline DC-3s, many of them former United planes—even World War II, it seemed, couldn't sever the UAL-WAL bond that Al Adams had once forged as a means of economic survival. But Western also operated a few C-46s, the famed Curtiss "Commando" which most pilots cordially hated despite its impressive cargo capacity—about double that of a C-47. Western not only operated a training school for C-46 pilots but also winterized the fat twin-engine transports at Burbank.

By the end of the second year, Sourdough was a fully scheduled operation over two routes: Edmonton–Nome and Great Falls–Fairbanks, each with a minimum of two daily round trips. Although the flight crews maintained their civilian status, they wore the uniforms of the Air Transport Command—with special wings, insignia, and shoulder epaulets. They looked enough like officers to draw salutes from green G.I.s, with one exception: Jack Orwig. He invariably wore a double-peaked English hunting cap and smoked a curved Meerschaum pipe, giving him a resemblance to an overweight Sherlock Holmes. Orwig was a rarity—a United copilot who switched to Western because he'd be a captain flying for Sourdough.

In terms of tonnage and personnel carried, Sourdough was rather small stuff compared to what the giants like Pan American, TWA, American, and United accomplished in World War II. But Western, while it ran a minor-league operation, did it in big-league style. Coupled with its astounding safety record was the highest aircraft utilization rate in the ATC—15.9 hours a day was the top figure reached, and average utilization was almost 12 hours, 2 hours higher than the runner-up achieved.

The airline operated two schools for the Air Transport Command, one in Fairfield, California, and the other in Salt Lake City. The latter school was set up to train C-46 crews for the dangerous job of flying the Hump in the China-Burma-India Theater. Western took the pilots after they completed preliminary instruction at Air Corps schools and gave them ninety days of concentrated training in transport operations.

Approximately half of the airline's more than three hundred employees went into military service. The war, of course, furnished a preview of the 1970s Women's Lib movement. His traffic department depleted of salesmen called to the colors, Tom Wolfe hired saleswomen—dubbing them "counselaires" and giving them special training in selling techniques, public relations, and even some technical background. They took a basic course in aeronautics that included some time in the Link trainer and the maintenance department. Hollywood makeup specialist Max

Factor taught them grooming and hairdo, and they wore special brown uniforms topped with a perky overseas cap. The first 7 counselaires were chosen from 136 applicants; Wolfe's prerequisites for hiring specified that counselaires "must be between the ages of 22 and 30, well-educated, and charming . . . they must possess well-modulated voices, good radio technique, and experience in public speaking."

The standards actually were higher than those Wolfe applied to male applicants, and he acquired some capable personnel. Three counselaires became Western's first female station managers: Lois Lake in Salt Lake City, Peggy Cox in Long Beach, and Clarice Tripp in Pocatello. Like the other counselaires, they had been hired originally to promote air travel, but their duties and responsibilities expanded as the giant magnet of wartime demands drew off the airline's manpower.

That Sourdough avoided serious accidents was a miracle; the operation was an invitation to disaster, yet the lone damage to any WAL aircraft was the fault of inexperienced Army ground personnel driving their loading vehicles too close to the planes. The WAL pilots had frequent reminders of their good fortune: reports of missing planes and actual crashes in that untamed wilderness. Often they flew search or rescue missions, for whenever a plane was reported down, whatever flight was coming into a Sourdough facility was unloaded immediately and sent off to search. And one had to be lucky to find anything, especially in the winter. A Northwest plane crashed near a Sourdough airport, but the wreckage wasn't found for almost a day—the plane had come down in a snow-covered clump of trees so thick that the wreckage was almost impossible to spot.

No Western pilot patted himself on the back for the safety record. They all recognized it as the product of at least some luck, although skill and Pat Carlson's tough operating rules were large factors; Pat may have winked at certain recreational activities, but he could crack down on an errant airman before the sinner became an accident statistic.

When tragedy did strike, it was on a supposedly far safer commercial flight from Salt Lake City to Burbank via Las Vegas, on December 15, 1942 exactly six years from the day of Western's first crash involving passenger fatalities. This time it was Flight

1, commanded by Ed Loeffler. The stewardess was Cleo Booth of Los Angeles, who had been with Western only since the previous April; the copilot was James Lee, and also in the cockpit was a pilot/trainee, Doug Soule, whom Western had hired a month before the accident. All four crew members were killed, and only two of the fifteen passengers aboard survived.

The accident occurred only a few minutes after takeoff. CAB investigators later deduced that Loeffler wasn't in the left seat; it was occupied by copilot Lee, and the young trainee, Soule, was in the right seat, where Lee normally would have been sitting. Whether Lee or Soule was flying the DC-3 was never learned, but Loeffler's body was found *behind* the two cockpit seats—he either had been standing or was on the jump seat apparently monitoring the younger pilots.

Examination of the wreckage disclosed that at least one and possibly both wingtips had failed in flight, along with the horizontal tail surfaces, the failure being caused by an unexplained sharp pullup.

"No definite conclusion can be drawn from the evidence as to whether the pullup was caused by operation of the controls by the crew, or by some other forces beyond their control," the CAB report stated. "Due to the lack of any plausible theory for the latter, it seems more probable that the maneuver was initiated by the crew, possibly in an attempt to avoid collision with a bird, another aircraft, or some object which they saw or thought they saw."

The investigators got valuable help from one of the two survivors, Marine Lieutenant Arthur Gardner, who not only had logged several hundred hours of flight time but also had gone through a month of advanced DC-3 training with American Airlines and had flown for American as a copilot on DC-3 cargo planes over a two-month period. Seldom has there been a more qualified surviving witness to a crash; the CAB quoted his testimony at the accident hearing in considerable length, an occasion on which Gardner impressed not only the Board but also Western officials present.

Jimmie James was present when Gardner testified. After Gardner finished, James walked over to him and shook his hand.

"Lieutenant," he said, "when the war's over and you want a job with an airline, come see me. You've got one with Western."

Gardner did just that. Nearly three decades later, he was to be named Western's senior vice president of operations after a long and honorable career as a line pilot.

The CAB had frozen all route applications at the start of the war, but partially thawed out that order long before the fighting ended. There was plenty of room for expansion, and Western got its share. Approved was its application to add San Bernardino, Palm Springs, and El Centro to the Los Angeles–Salt Lake City route, and a bigger wartime plum was the rewarding of Los Angeles–San Francisco nonstop authority in August 1943. As the Axis began to crumble, the airlines started receiving some of their planes back—Western being allocated several DC-3s, sufficient not only to increase its regular schedules but also to resume Los Angeles–San Francisco service by May 1, 1944.

Five months before V-J Day, Western was awarded a Los Angeles–Denver route, culminating a bitter court battle. The CAB granted the application in late 1944, rejecting similar bids by TWA, Continental, and United, but United took the decision to the U. S. Circuit Court of Appeals, only to lose. Tipping the scales in Western's favor was the foresight shown by Al Adams before he was ousted; the CAB was impressed by the fact that WAL as far back as 1937 had spent fifty thousand dollars surveying a Los Angeles–Denver route, even to the extent of gathering weather data and mapping possible emergency landing sites.

Western inaugurated Los Angeles–Denver service on April 1, 1946, using DC-4s equipped with oxygen outlets for every passenger and crew member. The minimum instrument altitude over the most mountainous segment of Route 68—between Grand Junction and Denver—was sixteen thousand feet, and many flights cruised as high as twenty thousand feet in the unpressurized plane. The pilots went on oxygen a lot sooner than the passengers, who for the most part donned the small masks dutifully as needed. Occasionally a rebellious soul trying to get away without oxygen would pass out, the stewardess rushing over with a walk-around bottle and reviving him.

Despite the inconvenience of flying a high-altitude route in unpressurized aircraft, traffic was heavy almost from the start of service. The prime route was to supply a fateful chapter in Western's turbulent history, but its award was not the most significant, potentially important event to occur during the war years insofar as Western's future was concerned.

On October 7, 1943, Bill Coulter and Leo Dwerlkotte had signed an agreement to acquire the routes and equipment of Inland Air Lines—and with the scratching of pens on legal documents went the addition of twelve hundred new route miles in Montana, Wyoming, Nebraska, and South Dakota.

Now, at long last, the wings of Western were truly spreading.

CHAPTER TEN

Growing Pains

If Western at times had been operated on a shoestring, Inland often resorted to sewing thread.

Its founder, inspiration, leader, and greatest asset also was, on occasion, its biggest liability. That is the best description one can give of the president of Inland Air Lines—hard-drinking, hot-tempered Richard Leferink. Compared to this stubborn Dutchman, a pilot by profession and a businessman by instinct, "colorful" airline executives appeared as mild pastels.

Dick Leferink was born in Holland but grew up in Grand Rapids, Michigan, and this Wolverine state background wasn't the only thing he had in common with Pop Hanshue. He had Hanshue's qualities of fiery leadership, love of the West (and corresponding distrust of the East), and undaunted willingness to buck the odds.

Leferink dreamed about becoming a flier from boyhood, and World War I gave him his chance. He enlisted in the Army at the age of seventeen as a flying cadet, won his wings as a second lieutenant, and was good enough to be assigned instructor duties. After the war, he did what came naturally to so many ex-military pilots—he barnstormed, eventually settling in Casper, Wyoming, where he married and began raising two children. It was a chicken-scratching-for-corn kind of existence, but Leferink knew nothing except aviation, and he tried to make a living out of it with a succession of rented or borrowed planes; at one point he started a makeshift airline but went broke swiftly. The turning point came the day after Christmas 1929, when Leferink and his wife arranged to meet in Denver with an old friend who had just been married and was taking his bride to Colorado for a honeymoon.

Dick Leferink had known George Gerald Brooder since 1922; Jerry Brooder, although born in a small Pennsylvania town, had lived much of his life in Wyoming. He saw wartime service in the Navy. After the war, he went to work for Adams Express Company in Sheridan, Wyoming, and eventually got a job in the oil fields near Lander, Wyoming.

For a brief time, Jerry flirted with flying as a career, taking pilot lessons at the Ryan School of Aeronautics in San Diego, where Lindbergh's *Spirit of St. Louis* was built, but returned to the oil fields, where he was working when his marriage found him in Denver celebrating with the Leferinks.

The two couples flew back to Casper on New Year's Eve, in a Fokker Universal that Leferink had borrowed. En route, Leferink talked about the area's need for air transportation, and by the time they landed, they had agreed to start an airline. Between them, they managed to raise five thousand dollars in capital, which they spent on two airplanes—a three-passenger Stinson monoplane and a Hisso-powered Eaglerock. Neither was much of an aircraft; the Stinson looked as if it had been through the Battle of the Marne, and the Eaglerock, it was said, acquired its name because "it went up like an eagle and came down like a rock." But Leferink had his airline, which he called Wyoming Air Service, and Brooder became vice president. A third backer, Dr. Allan MacLellan of Casper, was named secretary/treasurer.

Wyoming Air Service began operations in May 1930, although calling it an airline was stretching the truth considerably. WAS engaged in charter and sightseeing flights, student training, and plain barnstorming for almost a year before it began what might pass for scheduled passenger service. By that time, Leferink had been discussing the possibility of obtaining a tristate air mail contract with Earl Vance, a Montana aviation pioneer who also nurtured dreams of starting an airline. With financial support from a number of Casper, Sheridan, and Great Falls businessmen, they formed a loose coalition that actually was two carriers—Leferink's Wyoming Air Service and Vance's Border Airlines.

WAS, they decided, would fly from Denver to Sheridan and

connect with Border's Sheridan–Great Falls route. The joint operations began on March 16, 1931, fueled by additional stock investments from residents of Casper and Sheridan. Even with this capitalization, however, resources were so limited that the first flights went only from Casper to Denver; Leferink flew the inaugural trip with his brother Joe, hired as a WAS pilot. Border began operating at about the same time, but folded in less than four months when it became apparent that no mail contract would be forthcoming.

For that matter, Wyoming Air Service might as well have been bidding to fly mail to the moon. Leferink figured if he could stay in business for six months with a reasonably efficient passenger service, he stood a good chance of wangling a mail contract. The Post Office Department ignored him, and Leferink stayed alive by scrounging whatever passenger traffic he could. His chief aide and promoter in this endeavor was an ex-railroad engineer named Marvin Landes, who quit a part-time job piloting locomotives for the Chicago and Northwestern Railroad to join Leferink when Wyoming Air Service still was primarily a barnstorming operation.

He was quite a salesman, Marv Landes—so much so that he almost cost Leferink his pilot's license. They were in some small Wyoming town with the Stinson, and Landes was hawking tickets for sightseeing rides. Marv already had boarded four passengers in a plane built to carry three and was fervently seeking a fifth.

"Come on, folks," he exhorted. "Room for one more. The thrill of a lifetime, believe me! Find out what air travel's about! One more, and we'll take off on a flight you won't forget. . . ."

On the fringe of the entranced but nervous crowd he spotted one man who looked like he might be wavering. Landes, with the zeal of a hungry shark zeroing in on a hapless prey, moved to the attack.

"You're the kind of MAN we want!" he pressed. "Plenty of room, sir. The minute you board, we'll leave."

"Is there really room for one more?" the prospect asked.

"Easily," Landes assured him glibly.

"That's all I wanted to know," the man said. "I'm an inspector for the Bureau of Air Commerce."

It took all of Leferink's persuasiveness to talk the inspector out of lifting his license right on the spot—the president of Wyoming Air Service attributing the whole "misunderstanding" to Marv's lack of aeronautical knowledge.

"He really didn't know how many people the damned plane could carry," he explained to the inspector with a straight face, "and I didn't look around to see how many he was putting aboard."

Leferink was a crack pilot with that common failing of many airmen in the twenties: He mistrusted instrument flying, almost as if the practice were a sign of weakness. His forte was instruction; he taught Landes how to fly, and Marv soloed after twenty-five minutes of dual time—although he remembers that solo as consisting of "one takeoff and five landings."

Leferink was a likable extrovert, yet with a dark streak of suspicion toward everyone—except such close friends as Brooder and Landes—and usually with no logical reason for distrust. In the airline industry, he became known as "the Ted Baker of the West"—Baker being the hotheaded wheeler-dealer who founded National Airlines. Both would have made great pirates; they had colorful pasts allegedly involving illegal liquor flights, identical prejudices toward anything smacking of government regulations, and, politically speaking, they were about five miles to the right of such archconservatives as Eddie Rickenbacker.

Brooder and Landes still regard him with genuine affection, even as they concede he could be difficult and intractable. Landes ran afoul of him constantly, such as the time they were on a barnstorming trip and heard about a carnival playing a small Wyoming town about a hundred miles west of Casper. Leferink flew there while Landes drove up with a friend, and Marv sold quite a few flight tickets in advance—about $125 worth. He proceeded to lose all of it shooting dice, and Leferink, without knowing it, was flying the sightseeing trips for free. The next morning, he decided it was time to go back to Casper.

"Better buy some gas, Marv," he advised. "I don't think I've got enough for the trip."

"I don't have any dough," Landes confessed. "I lost it in a crap game."

Leferink's glare would have fried a ten-inch-thick slab of asbestos. "I'll tell you what, Landes, you ride back to Casper with me in the airplane. If we run outa fuel, you're gonna be with me."

They did—landing in the sagebrush at Powder River, Wyoming, thirty-five miles from Casper. It took them several hours to thumb their way back to Casper, and it took Landes two years to pay back the $125.

The Air Mail Act of 1934, the same legislation that took Western away from Hanshue, was a bonanza for Dick Leferink. He first submitted a bid for Route 17, Cheyenne–Pueblo via Denver and Colorado Springs, and only a month later applied for a mail contract on Route 28 from Cheyenne to Billings, Montana, via Casper and Sheridan. He won both—beating out Western and Northwest for the latter—and Wyoming Air Service suddenly became a bona fide scheduled airline. Leferink promptly bought three new Stinson Reliants, leased a United 247 for the Cheyenne–Denver leg, and kept adding more equipment as WAS prospered—United being the principal source. Two single-engine Boeing Monomails—the only ones built, incidentally—were purchased from United along with three additional UAL 247s. From Northwest, Leferink acquired a pair of Lockheed Orions, and with this hodgepodge fleet Wyoming Air Service started to make some modest profits.

Wyoming never hired stewardesses, but on the new Denver–Cheyenne route, Leferink discovered that quite a few United flight attendants based in Cheyenne were always asking for passes to Denver. He mentioned this to Landes one day, along with an excellent if hardhearted suggestion: Give them the passes provided that they work the trip in uniform.

Wyoming's service always was on the impromptu side; if a passenger was bold enough to ask for cigarettes, they were requisitioned from whatever pack the copilot was carrying that day.

Even with the new routes, it was tough going, and just as Western relied heavily on its connections with United at Salt Lake City, so did Wyoming at Cheyenne. The Stinson Reliants Leferink bought were too small for the Cheyenne–Denver schedule, and this led to the initial leasing of a UAL 247. In truth, Leferink had taken too big an expansion bite—he didn't have the funds for the equipment needed to serve a twelve-hundred-mile system efficiently, and W. A. Patterson finally suggested that Wyoming sell the Denver–Cheyenne leg of Route 17 to United. Leferink, with Brooder and Landes approving, agreed, and the papers were drawn up. With the sale of Route 17's Denver–Cheyenne segment consummated, Leferink was left with a rather useless spur—the Denver–Pueblo portion. Varney Air Lines, like United panting for access into Denver, had offered to buy it, but Leferink held off until the deal with United went through. Now he was ready to talk to Bob Six, the fire-eating youngster who had bought into Varney and who would soon become its president, just before Varney's name was changed to Continental. Leferink not only was ready to talk, but also he had to—the Post Office Department had ordered him to sell the leg as a condition of its approval of the UAL transfer.

Putting the volatile Six and the unpredictable Leferink into joint business negotiations was mixing fire with gasoline. Their first serious discussion was conducted with the uneasiness of two tigers circling warily. Six came alone, while Brooder accompanied Leferink.

"Okay, Dick," Six finally announced, "how much do you want?"

"Fifty grand," Leferink snapped.

"Okay," Six said with unexpected swiftness.

"Wait a minute," Leferink said suspiciously. "Do you have enough authority to agree to something like this without your Board of Directors okaying it? You aren't the president of Varney, damnit."

"Anything I recommend, they'll agree to," Six assured him.

"Well," Leferink said with a trace of uncertainty, "I guess you've got yourself a deal. I'll have the papers drawn up, so give me a call in a couple of weeks and we'll get together again."

Two weeks later, Six phoned to suggest a meeting at the Brown Palace Hotel in Denver. Leferink showed up with Brooder.

"I'm ready to sign," Leferink informed Six. "Is our deal still on?"

Six hesitated. "Yes, but I've got to tell you that our Board wouldn't go for the fifty thousand dollars. They won't approve anything higher than thirty-five thousand dollars."

"You sonofabitch!" Leferink roared. "You've got us over a barrel and we've got to sell."

"I'm sorry, Dick," Six apologized.

"How much did you *really* recommend?" Leferink asked angrily.

"The whole fifty grand," Six insisted.

"Okay, Six," Leferink snarled, "but I'm gonna take that other fifteen thousand out of your goddamned hide, and right now!"

Leferink proceeded to pull off his coat, shirt, and necktie, and he removed his wristwatch. Six, tall, burly, and with a reputation of his own for handling his fists, did likewise. The two squared off, but Brooder stepped between them before either could throw a punch.

"You're both acting like a couple of kids," Jerry scolded. "This won't get you anything but a pair of bloody noses."

Six began laughing and so did Leferink.

"Okay, Bob," he chuckled, "but you had better buy me a drink, you bastard."

Given Leferink's suspicious nature, it is probable that he never believed Six asked Varney's board for the agreed-upon fifty thousand dollars and was turned down. But even thirty-five thousand dollars was not an unfair price to pay for a route that Wyoming couldn't operate profitably, any more than it could have made much money on the Denver–Cheyenne leg. Leferink knew that United was going into Denver sooner or later, and in retrospect, he not only made the best out of an untenable position but also strengthened his airline over-all. Shortly after disposing of his Route 17 segments, Leferink applied for and obtained authority to serve Route 35. This newly established airway ran from Cheyenne to Huron, South Dakota, via Scottsbluff, Nebraska; Rapid City; and Pierre. By the summer of 1937, Leferink also had extended Wyoming's Cheyenne–Billings route to Great Falls. To serve the mushrooming system, he had six Boeing 247s—all ex-United planes.

His next expansion effort pitted him against Western, both carriers seeking the Great Falls–Lethbridge route. Even when he lost his bid, he still retained hopes of making his airline a money-maker. Before applying for Lethbridge authority, he had changed Wyoming's name to Inland Air Lines, reflecting the carrier's larger system that by 1938 embraced four states: Wyoming, Montana, South Dakota, and Nebraska. But when the United States entered World War II, Inland was doomed.

The Army's civil aircraft acquisition plan was tough on all airlines, but for Inland it was sheer disaster. Its entire six-plane 247 fleet was commandeered, and Leferink kept the airline alive only when the CAB ordered Continental to sell him a Lodestar, which he used to operate Inland's butchered schedules. The CAB suspended all service on Route 35, but Leferink revived it in August 1942 by using a handful of single-engine Beechcraft that carried only mail and express. Inland then got a fresh transfusion in the form of a contract to operate Army transport planes domestically, and a second contract to provide transitional flight training and a course in maintenance to Army personnel.

By now, however, Dick Leferink was showing signs of being fed up with the airline business. His disenchantment had preceded Inland's wartime difficulties, actually starting in the early forties, when the Civil Aeronautics Administration—predecessor of the Federal Aviation Agency—launched what Leferink considered an outright harassment campaign. The CAA suddenly began filing various pilot and maintenance violation charges against Inland, and Leferink to his dying day believed that another airline—which he never named publicly—was behind the government vendetta. One day a half-dozen CAA inspectors descended on the airline's Cheyenne headquarters for a showdown meeting held in Landes' office. Leferink had been drinking heavily and was in a black, ugly mood.

As the inspectors listed their latest complaints, Leferink lost his temper and invited any three of them outside simultaneously. Brooder and Landes calmed him down, but not for long. He broke away from his two friends and yelled, "You bastards have been after our certificate for a long time, and by God now I'm gonna give it to you—I'm gonna stick it right up your ass! Marv, where the hell IS our certificate?"

Landes and Brooder couldn't help laughing, and so did the platoon of inspectors. The tension was broken, and relations between the CAA and Inland began a slow improvement. While the feud was on, however, the atmosphere around the airline was murky. No sooner was one CAA complaint cleared up than another was filed. The agency claimed, for example, that Inland's pilots weren't properly checked out—although Leferink's airline never had a passenger fatality from the day it was founded to the day it went out of existence. Landes made a deal with United's chief pilot to work with Inland's flight crews, and the CAA appeared satisfied until it turned to maintenance, charging that Inland was using too many old parts in its engines. Leferink called in two top representatives from Pratt & Whitney, who examined all Inland's engines and informed the CAA they were in as good shape as United's.

The Pratt & Whitney report didn't seem to impress anyone in Washington, so Leferink and Landes flew there to argue Inland's case, accompanied by Pete Taylor, a CAA regional inspector who frankly agreed that somebody apparently was trying to scuttle the airline. Despite Taylor's courageous support, they got nowhere; the CAA ordered them to buy new engine parts, and Leferink, in a red rage, shelled out nearly sixty thousand dollars to meet the government edict.

Once the CAA finally got off his back, he began thinking it might be time to unload Inland; it had solid if not high-density routes, good personnel, and no huge debt backlog—virtues that would make it attractive merger bait. Tommy Ryan of Mid-Continent was interested but not to the extent of making an offer Leferink considered reasonable. After the war began, Leferink began dickering with Continental through Terrell Drinkwater, CAL's executive vice president, who proposed buying Inland's stock for four dollars a share. Leferink might have made the deal, but Bob Six, about to enter military service, thought the price was too high.

Late in 1942, Leferink actually agreed tentatively to sell Inland to Western, but it fell through when he insisted that the deal be completed by the end of the year. Dwerlkotte told him this was impossible, and Leferink backed out. But not for long.

In September 1943, Leferink, Brooder, and Landes were in New York for a meeting with Air Transport Command officials, and ran into Dwerlkotte, who also was at the ATC session. Leferink returned to Cheyenne, but Jerry and Marv stayed behind and began discussing Inland's situation with the Western executive vice president. Two weeks later, Leo called them in Cheyenne.

"If you fellows still are interested in a merger with Western," he said, "I'd like to talk to you. I'll bring Pat Sullivan with me, and you have Leferink on hand."

Brooder, who was running Inland's military contract business, and Landes, in charge of what remained of civilian traffic, promised to talk to Leferink. They were convinced the airline had no future and saw a chance to recoup what they had invested. The president's initial reaction was a sullen, "I won't have a damned thing to do with this." He finally agreed to see Dwerlkotte again, however, and a meeting was arranged in Leferink's small Cheyenne apartment. It was an evening session, and Dick, who had been drinking all day, obviously was neither in a mood nor in shape to negotiate seriously.

Dwerlkotte, recognizing the whole meeting as a charade, finally gave up. "There's no use talking about this," he said. "We might as well go back to California."

"That's fine with me," Leferink muttered.

There was no flight back to Los Angeles that night, and Brooder drove the two Western officials back to a hotel.

"Why not try it again in the morning," Jerry suggested. "We can meet before Dick has a chance to start drinking again."

Dwerlkotte agreed, and the next day's session was entirely different. Leferink, cold sober and clear-eyed, was affable and co-operative. In less than ninety minutes, they reached agreement. All but Brooder flew to Casper the same morning to examine Inland's books, and a merger pact was filed with the Civil Aeronautics Board, with CAB approval coming June 1, 1944.

Dwerlkotte offered all three Inland officials top jobs at Western, but Leferink insisted that Brooder and Landes be given contracts. Landes readily agreed. Brooder demurred.

"I don't want one," he protested mildly. "I'd like to continue working, but I'm not sure Western would want me or that I'd want them."

"You don't need a contract with us, Jerry," Dwerlkotte smiled. "I'd like you with me right in Los Angeles."

"That's exactly where I don't want to go," Brooder protested.

"I'd like to stay in the Rocky Mountain area. My roots here are too deep and so are Wanda's [his wife]."

"How about taking charge of Inland's operations and staying where you are?" Leo proposed.

"No, you should move a Western man in—one who's familiar with your policies and procedures."

"We'll figure out something," Dwerlkotte promised. "Would you be willing to move to Denver?"

"That's as far as I'd go, Leo."

The upshot was that Brooder was named regional traffic manager in Denver, reporting to Tom Wolfe and Dwerlkotte himself. Landes became assistant to Jimmie James, and Leferink accepted a thirty-month contract as a consultant—at a rather generous salary he admittedly didn't earn. He did virtually no work for Western, and once his last ties with Inland were severed, he drank even more heavily. A Sheridan barber asked him after the merger what he was doing to keep busy.

"I'm a consultant with Western Air Lines," Leferink replied.

"Really? What capacity?"

"Oh, about a fifth a day," Dick drawled.

Frank Eastman, an ex-racing driver who had started with Western as a mechanic in 1929, was put in charge of the Inland division, with headquarters in Cheyenne; a legal technicality had forced Dwerlkotte to operate Inland as a subsidiary rather than an integral part of WAL. The merger agreement gave Leferink, Brooder, Landes, and MacLellan approximately $363,000 cash for the 83.57 per cent of Inland stock the quartet owned. But Inland was incorporated in Wyoming, where state law required 100 per cent stockholder approval of any merger. Western offered the remainder of the shareholders $2.53 a share, the same price paid to Inland's officers, but a few held out, and Western was unable to dissolve the Inland corporation for another eight years. It took Jerry Brooder until 1952 before his lobbying efforts got the state legislature to amend the Wyoming Corporation law, a change requiring only 75 per cent stockholder approval instead of 100 per cent. Until then, Inland was run as a separate airline —in the early years by Eastman, who had gained a reputation as a troubleshooting station manager.

Its subsidiary and semiautonomous status notwithstanding, Inland quickly disappeared as an airline entity. Its pilots, several of whom were in the million-mile category, gradually were worked into Western's system. And Leferink himself, his job as consultant a mere sop to both his pride and his pocketbook, faded into obscurity. Liquor inevitably affected his health; his once strong, rather handsome face turned puffy. Brooder and Landes visited him a couple of years before he died in 1963 and were shocked at his physical deterioration. He suffered a fatal heart attack in Sheridan, and Jerry served as one of the pallbearers at the funeral.

Leferink was a true aviation pioneer, albeit on a small scale, but one who brought commercial aviation to a part of the nation that the bigger airlines had passed by. As such, he was respected by all who knew him and beloved by many. The stories told about him would fill a book—such as his habit of canceling Wyoming Air Service flights because, as he confided to a subordinate, "I gotta pick up a load of booze in Canada so we can meet the payroll this week."

The airline Dick Leferink turned Inland over to was healthy, relatively prosperous (it netted more than $1.2 million from 1942 through 1945), and its expansion plans were staggering. By the end of the war, Western's *new* route applications totaled more than 24,000 miles; between 1941 and V-J Day, the CAB already had granted WAL an additional 2,617 route miles, a two-thirds increase in the system. Within six months after the war ended, Western had no less than nineteen additional route applications pending before the Civil Aeronautics Board. They included service from Los Angeles to Brazil, Argentina, Mexico, Costa Rica, Guatemala, Panama, Colombia, Bolivia, Paraguay, and Uruguay. They called for putting the Indian head into such cities as Seattle, Portland, Spokane, Minneapolis/St. Paul, and Dallas. They sought authority for a West Coast–Hawaii route from both Los Angeles and San Francisco. They also were aimed at giving Western prime long-haul routes between these other major city pairs:

Las Vegas and San Francisco
San Francisco and Seattle
Lethbridge and Nome

Seattle and Nome
Denver and Minneapolis/St. Paul
Salt Lake City and Dallas
Reno and El Paso

The postwar dreams indeed were rose-hued; no one expected the CAB to grant all of WAL's requests, inasmuch as the entire airline industry was equally sanguine about a postwar commercial aviation Utopia. But Coulter, more than the cautious Dwerlkotte, was so sure of Western getting its share when the route floodgates opened that he kept contributing to the water building up behind those floodgates. Not that Coulter could be blamed; he wasn't the only airline president who figured civil aviation was in for a postwar boom of immense proportions. The major mistake he made, dragging a not entirely willing Dwerlkotte behind him, was to expand Western's physical and manpower assets before assuring that the route system itself, not to mention traffic on the existing routes, would mushroom as expected.

Western came out of the war with an aircraft fleet more than four times larger than it had at the start of hostilities—sixteen DC-3s, a Lodestar, a Stinson mailplane, and a DC-4 that was its first four-engine transport since the F-32. A payroll with only 330 names on it in 1941 had swelled to 1,641 by 1945—and was to keep climbing. To Coulter, gambler and promoter, the already expanded and projected route system and the influx of manpower all added up to a need for a bigger aircraft fleet. In 1946, Western's optimism-infected Board of Directors approved Coulter's plans to buy some $12 million worth of new airplanes. The orders called for:

• Thirteen DC-4s and converted C-54s (military version of the DC-4), costing $425,000 apiece.
• Ten pressurized DC-6s, Douglas's bid for postwar transport supremacy, costing $630,000 each.
• Twenty Convair 240s, a twin-engine pressurized airliner that promised to be the long-awaited successor to the DC-3, costing $225,000 per plane.

To come with the new planes were orders for millions of dollars' worth of supporting equipment, some of which was not really needed. Cost of the ground equipment, the new aircraft, and the DC-3/DC-4 fleet delivered mainly in 1945, added up to some $23 million.

Originally Dwerlkotte and Taylor had mapped out a plan to buy only ten Convair 240s and five DC-6s, but Coulter told them they were being foolish.

"When this war is over," he argued, "planes are going to be so hard to get that some airlines will be waiting two years for delivery. If we have surplus equipment, they'll pay us double for what we don't need."

So Western doubled its new plane orders in anticipation of a postwar demand that never developed.

There were two things wrong with this multimillion-dollar commitment. First, it was far too big for a carrier of Western's size and resources; true, the Convairs were intended as replacements for the DC-3s, but the four-engine equipment was supposed to serve a number of long-haul routes WAL didn't have yet and wasn't even sure of winning. Second, the contracts were signed before adequate financing was arranged.

Dwerlkotte might have been able to blow at least a muted whistle at this overextension, but by this time Bill Coulter was beginning to turn on the man who had run the airline for him while the absentee president took most of the bows. Any chance Coulter had of averting a debacle evaporated in the first six months of 1946 when Western lost almost $1 million, with no prospects of recouping in the second half of the year. The red ink was accompanied by mounting debts that seriously damaged the airline's credit standing.

It was not all Coulter's fault; many factors leading to WAL's sudden decline were beyond his control, and Western was not the only airline having difficulties. In many ways, Coulter was a kindly old gentleman, well liked by many employees who never saw his greatest weakness: his penchant for turning suddenly on men who had given him loyalty, devotion to duty, and skill in performing that duty. Dwerlkotte was one; so was Tom Wolfe and many others in Western's executive ranks. With rank-and-file employees, he usually was reasonable, at times shy, and more often than not rather mild-mannered.

He loved cigars, a Mexican brand in particular that smelled

like burning engine oil. One day he lit up the Mexican stogie on a WAL plane, causing stewardess Mary Grace Jafferty to assume immediately that they were on fire. It took only seconds to determine the source of both the smoke and the stench, and she marched up to where Coulter was puffing away.

"No cigars, sir," she said politely. "Just cigarettes."

Coulter frowned. "What's your name, young lady?"

"Mary Grace Jafferty."

"Well, Mary Grace, do you know who I am?"

"No, sir."

"I'm the president of this airline, and if I want to smoke a cigar, I will!"

Miss Jafferty happened to come from a wealthy family; she was, in fact, the only Western stewardess (and possibly the only stewardess in the United States) who drove to work in a new Cadillac. While she tried not to flaunt her affluence, it gave her a sense of security and independence that few flight attendants possessed.

"Oh, no you won't," she said quietly—and pulled the cigar right out of his mouth.

Coulter thought it was funny and frequently told the story on himself. In truth, he loved being president of an airline. It gave him dignity, and a prestige not usually accorded a man who basically was retiring and far from imposing. It must be conceded that for some time he and Dwerlkotte formed a highly effective team; Coulter had the wealth and Leo had the knowledge. The roof began to cave in when Coulter decided he had learned enough about the airline business to assert more authority and make more decisions on his own.

He was not only ill equipped for this role but he also became the victim of hard luck and circumstances that would have challenged far more experienced airline executives. First there was the impact of terminating the lucrative wartime military contracts; peacetime traffic in the supposed postwar boom, counted on to take up the slack, never materialized in the proportions expected. The statistics looked great on paper—the thirteen million passengers who flew the scheduled airlines in 1946 represented an increase of 2,500 per cent in only twenty years. But thirteen million still fell far short of what the industry hoped for; 90 per cent of the nation's adult population still hadn't stepped foot on a commercial transport, and the impressive total of those who had, failed to compensate for skyrocketing labor costs, enormous investments in new equipment, and war-bloated payrolls that continued to swell in anticipation of the predicted postwar boom.

Western was not only no exception to these adverse conditions but was even worse off than most carriers in many respects. In mid-1946, alarmed over WAL's mounting losses, Dwerlkotte called in three efficiency experts from Consolidated Vultee, builders of the Convair 240, who spent ninety days investigating Western's labor expenditures. The trio didn't charge the airline a dime, incidentally; Convair, it seemed, had inadvertently goofed in quoting Western a price on the 240 by listing as standard equipment items that should have been optional at extra cost. The result was that Consolidated was losing nearly $100,000 per aircraft under the WAL contract. The manufacturer got Dwerlkotte to pay the full price, but agreed to finance Western's 240 advertising program and toss in such additional services as the labor survey.

That survey provided Leo with some unpleasant reading material. It disclosed that Western's direct labor costs were among the highest in the industry—14 per cent above the average, and in some areas more than 200 per cent higher. And while the three experts were gathering their damning data, WAL was hiring more employees, boosting the payroll by October 1946 to almost 2,600. Some, of course, were veterans returning to their prewar jobs—like Lieutenant Colonel Art Kelly, who came back from the Air Force with new maturity and confidence and was named director of general sales. A few were to become key figures in the airline's future, such as a young former lieutenant commander in the Navy named Dominic P. Renda, who was assigned the initial task of negotiating new airport lease agreements; that formerly had been Marv Landes' job, but Dwerlkotte, in a mid-1946 front-office reorganization, gave him the newly created post of vice president of customer and station service.

By and large, the company's bloated payroll stemmed from its reluctance to fire anyone while it was taking back returning veterans and hiring new executive blood. There seemed to be a top-level rationalization that with all of Coulter's grandiose expansion plans, it would be best to hang onto personnel.

And at least some of the overoptimism was only too natural when veteran officers and employees alike remembered how past adversities had been overcome. There were even occasional reminders of those days—like the time a Los Angeles businessman, J. A. Richmond, bought an air travel credit card from Lois Lake, traffic manager in Salt Lake City, where Richmond was opening a branch. His name didn't mean much to her until she learned that Richmond had been the sixteen-year-old boy who stowed away on the wing of Moseley's M-2 in 1925, losing all his clothes by the time they landed. Such mementos of Western's past tended to blind many to the troubles of the present and future.

Adding to the growing financial problems was the necessity of moving out of Burbank. Western had outgrown Burbank to the point of hapless inefficiency and was forced into the heavy expense of moving to the new Los Angeles International Airport; it was a WAL plane, as a matter of fact, that made the first scheduled flight out of "LAX," on December 9, 1946. The physical move was completed early the following year. The latter brought fresh headaches; construction costs for a new hangar plus a new general offices building at Los Angeles Airport ran 100 per cent over contractors' estimates. Delivery dates for the new planes were uncertain, turning new schedule plans into hash, and the cost of converting wartime DC-3s and DC-4s into civilian transports soared far beyond budgeted figures.

The whole industry was suffering from growing pains, but the most crippling blow came in the vital field of air safety. The airlines suffered a wave of fatal crashes in the immediate postwar years; two vaunted new airliners, the DC-6 and Constellation, had to be grounded because of fatal design mistakes, and Western itself contributed to the public's sinking confidence in air travel. It was bad enough that service itself deteriorated throughout the industry, in the form of delayed and canceled flights, sloppy reservations, dirty terminal facilities, and poor in-flight performance—mostly the result of abnormally heavy personnel turnover. It became far more serious when safety, the cornerstone on which the industry had so proudly built, turned into a virtual crisis condition.

In 1946 the airlines suffered nine fatal crashes—and Western was involved in three of them. The first was on an engineering test flight; while no passengers were aboard the DC-3, all three crew members were killed. On November 13, Flight 23—a DC-3— en route from Las Vegas to Burbank, crashed into White Mountain fourteen miles south of Lebec, California, with all eleven occupants perishing. The CAB pinned the blame largely on the pilot, Captain Garrel J. Miller, for making an instrument letdown without establishing a positive radio fix, although the Board also cited severe static conditions, unusually high winds, and an inoperative radio range as contributing factors.

Only a little more than a month later, on the day before Christmas, another WAL DC-3 hit a mountain while en route from El Centro to San Diego. All twelve occupants were killed in the accident, which the CAB again attributed to pilot error, accusing Captain George B. Sprado of erroneously determining his position in relation to the mountains. Western's once-proud reputation for safety leadership was in shreds.

There were a few bright spots. Los Angeles–San Francisco service resumed, and the CAB approved WAL's application to operate between Los Angeles and Mexico City. Yet the latter was a somewhat empty triumph, because the Mexican Government balked at letting an American carrier into its capital; years would pass before service actually started. Both Western's return to San Francisco and the Mexico City route award were mere slivers of light in the blackness of looming financial disaster. Coulter was unable to raise financing for the new aircraft he had ordered, Western was in default of several large bank loans, and over-all debts by the end of 1946 totaled some $9 million.

Front-office feuding didn't help matters. Brooder and Wolfe didn't get along, Dwerlkotte settling the issue by moving Jerry out from under Tom's jurisdiction and making him assistant to the president, reporting directly to Leo. At Brooder's insistence, however, he was allowed to remain in Denver, where his forte for lobbying and his wide circle of friendships in the old Inland area could be better utilized.

Wolfe was unhappy, too, Coulter's increasing hostility making his position almost unbearable. He finally decided to leave—against Hugh Darling's advice—accepting a top post at Pan American. Wolfe, at the time holding more stock than anyone else except Coulter, sold some shares to the president at what Tom figured would be a healthy profit. According to Wolfe, however, Coulter never paid him the price they had agreed on—not from any desire to cheat him, Wolfe believes, but because Coulter himself was starting to run short of cash. The old man wasn't often smiling benignly those days as he ran from one financial source to another, trying to raise funds to meet the huge equipment orders and pay off debts.

Early in that grim year of 1946, Fred Kelly I began experiencing chest pains, particularly while exercising. He was hospitalized for a month, and while doctors could find no solid evidence of heart disease, the pains continued. Kelly, asked to be relieved of his duties as chief pilot, flew the line briefly and then grounded himself voluntarily and, it turned out, permanently—after logging more than seventeen thousand hours in the air.

His personal misfortune seemed to parallel Western's own decline. Dwerlkotte assigned him to public-relations duties for a while, mostly making speeches at schools, service clubs, and other groups; the highlight was an appearance on "The Ed Sullivan Show" in New York, where he wore his old WAL captain's uniform. Outwardly, he remained his usual, cheerful, happy-go-lucky self, but those who were close to him knew he was restless and frustrated. With Jimmie James no longer doing any flying, the last of the Four Horsemen had taken off his Western wings.

And it was the end of an era in more ways than one. Coulter, still president and majority stockholder, began quarreling bitterly with Dwerlkotte even as his own grip on the airline weakened in the crumbling financial situation. He finally turned to eastern banking sources for help; Western's standing by this time was so badly tarnished that he couldn't have borrowed five dollars from any institution or individual west of the Rockies. Only now it was Coulter's own reputation and record he was forced to lay on the line—and they did not qualify as secure collateral.

The only company willing to listen to him, one that had sufficient financial rescue equipment capable of pulling WAL out of its morass, was the big New York investment banking concern of Dillon, Read & Co. Its officials turned over Coulter's plea for help to Charles Rheinstrom, a former American Airlines official who had quit American after a row with C. R. Smith. Hired by Dillon, Read as a consultant on airline matters, he was thoroughly competent to judge the Western situation—and furthermore he knew where to go for unbiased, factual information and background that Coulter couldn't have supplied. Rheinstrom's prime source was Hugh Darling, the attorney who had been representing WAL in most of its route cases for some time and had won several major victories—Los Angeles–Denver and Los Angeles–Mexico City authority in particular. In those days, CAB officials referred to him as "Snarling Darling"—a backhanded tribute to the way he manhandled witnesses in cross-examination.

Darling was especially qualified to give Rheinstrom the judgments and advice he needed to decide whether to aid Coulter. The lawyer was not an official member of Western's hierarchy; his law firm merely represented the airline. But Darling knew WAL's executive personnel as well as anyone, and Rheinstrom approached him when the two men were at a CAB hearing involving Pan Am's application for domestic routes.

"Hugh, first I want to know if Coulter really can handle that airline, and if not, who can," he told Darling. "You've been with Western almost from the start. I need your views."

"Charlie," Darling replied, "let me toss this around and see what my position is. I'll talk to you tomorrow morning."

That night, Darling thought it out. He decided he was working for Western Air Lines and not Coulter or any other individual—and that it would be perfectly proper for him to tell Dillon, Read what he considered would be in the best interests of the airline. As promised, he met with Rheinstrom the next morning, and he delivered his view with frankness.

"No. 1," he began, "Bill Coulter doesn't know a thing about the airline business. Furthermore, he isn't really Western's president —Leo Dwerlkotte is—because Coulter isn't qualified to be president."

"Okay," Rheinstrom sighed, "then who is?"

"Several people. Al Adams for one, but Coulter won't accept

him. Remember, Charlie, Coulter still owns the majority of stock in the company; you might be able to get him out of the presidency, but he has one hell of a lot of muscle in deciding who succeeds him. The same goes for Tom Wolfe. Coulter wouldn't buy him, either. For that matter, Tom wouldn't take the job. I've already talked to him about the possibility. He told me he'd be tempted, but that when he went with Pan Am, he promised Juan Trippe he'd stay there for a certain length of time. My third candidate would be Terry Drinkwater at American. He's competent, he has tremendous ability, and I think Coulter would accept him."

Rheinstrom nodded, and the machinery was set in motion to hire Western's fourth president. Rheinstrom informed his superiors of Darling's recommendation and his concurrence. Drinkwater had all the credentials: experience in virtually every phase of the airline business, ambition, courage, and leadership qualities. He was a Denver attorney who had made aviation law his specialty, acquiring a reputation in handling route cases that attracted the attention of Bob Six. The Continental president made Drinkwater a director and later named him executive vice president. At the outbreak of war, just before Six went into the Army, he put Drinkwater in charge of CAL for the duration.

Drinkwater was ambitious, and he attempted a move that would have had the effect of taking the airline away from Six. It failed because Six was tipped off to a special directors' meeting called for the express purpose of ousting Six. Six showed up at the meeting with sufficient support to retain his presidency.

Drinkwater stayed with Continental after the war but only for a brief time. C. R. Smith of American, who had long admired him, offered him a job, and Drinkwater accepted—without realizing that American would be only a prelude to a far more challenging task. He became solidly entrenched at American, and there is good evidence that Smith was grooming him as his replacement. At American, he was not only a vice president but also held the same rank in American Overseas Airlines, the subsidiary that operated the parent company's transatlantic routes that were later sold to Pan Am.

His first reaction to the Western overtures was, in effect, a fence-straddling "maybe—I'm interested but not very much."

But by this time, Coulter was completely sold on him as his successor; Coulter had been given the blunt word by Dillon, Read—no aid unless he resigned as president.

Coulter was backed against the proverbial wall. Late in 1946, he had met with regional officials of the Reconstruction Finance Corporation in Los Angeles, seeking a loan, but he received no encouragement. Dwerlkotte already had talked him into tentative cancellation of five DC-6s and 10 Convair 240s, halving the original orders. When the RFC refused to loan WAL any money, it was then that Coulter went to Dillon, Read and met his personal Waterloo.

The investment firm attached its resignation demand to a financing program that called for a new stock issue—enough to net Western $6.5 million, with Dillon, Read underwriting the issue. If the stock could be sold, the Chase National Bank of New York and a half dozen other banks promised to loan the airline another $7.5 million during 1947, to be repaid in five years. Coulter had no choice but to agree, and he began abetting the pressure being applied to the still reluctant Drinkwater.

Western's dubious financial status was just one reason for Drinkwater's hesitancy. His strong ties to American in general and to C. R. Smith in particular were another, along with the promising future he definitely had with what was then America's biggest airline. On the other hand, Drinkwater disliked the East intensely. Further, if Smith really had him tagged as his eventual successor, there still were no indications that C.R. was ready to give up American's reins in the immediate future. Western's geographical location was a strong selling point, and so was the prospect of fulfilling a burning ambition: to be president of a major carrier.

Smith was no help. He told Drinkwater, "I think you're nuts, and I just don't understand why you're even considering it." But when Terry confessed he had just about made up his mind, Smith did what was so characteristic of him: He called Sam Gates of America's legal department.

"If the damned fool wants to make a mistake," he told Gates, "let's write up a good contract for the silly bastard and protect him all we can."

Gates did—without charge, incidentally—and Drinkwater entered into negotiations with both Coulter and Hugh Darling, mostly the latter, although Darling was hesitant. He had recommended Drinkwater, and yet he really was representing Western; there was something of a conflict of interest here, he thought. But Coulter at this point was desperate to land Drinkwater, and Darling conducted most of the tough bargaining. The contract he originally drew up differed considerably from the one Gates was suggesting, but an agreement finally was reached at a meeting in New York's Ambassador Hotel. Just before the last items of dispute were resolved, Coulter phoned Darling.

"How you doing?" he asked.

"Well, all right."

"Give in," Coulter urged.

The five-year contract was signed at Dillon, Read, and the three participants—Drinkwater, Gates, and Darling—went out to celebrate over a few drinks. They got to discussing Western's plethora of problems, and Drinkwater said he realized he had a mountain-sized task ahead of him.

Darling sipped his drink thoughtfully. "Terry, when you get to Los Angeles, don't try to be a ninety-day wonder. Don't try to do things too fast. Feel your way for a while."

"Terry," Gates agreed, "you'll never get better advice in your life."

On December 21, 1946, William Coulter resigned as president of Western Air Lines.

The following day, the WAL Board of Directors elected as its fourth president a tall, husky man with a pixielike smile, a brilliant mind, an iron will, and a proclivity for bow ties, pipes, and good whiskey.

Thus did thirty-nine-year-old Terrell Croft Drinkwater take command of a proud but beleaguered air carrier—and thus began what is known in the annals of American's senior airline as the Drinkwater Era.

CHAPTER ELEVEN

"Constructive Contraction"

Terry Drinkwater literally, not figuratively, put the handwriting on the wall almost as soon as Coulter departed and he took over his predecessor's rather tiny office.

Several Western executives who had walked into one of his first staff meetings blinked at two pictures he had hung on the wall. One depicted a sloppily fat Indian, the other a lean, hard warrior. Drinkwater pointed first to the obese brave.

"This is what too many of you guys are today," he growled.

Then he gestured toward the thin Indian. "And this is what you're gonna be if you want to stay with this airline!"

They got the point.

Actually, he did take Hugh Darling's advice—for a while, anyway. He did not start swinging an executive ax or wielding his new broom from the moment he took office. His initial move was to enlist the loyalty and aid of the one man who had a perfect right to feel embittered: Leo Dwerlkotte. He called Leo from New York even before accepting the WAL presidency.

"I've been having some discussions about the job," Drinkwater told him, "but I'm not going to accept it unless you agree to stay on."

Dwerlkotte, who already had been informed by Coulter that Drinkwater had been chosen, readily assented. He was disappointed, being only human and having given his best in WAL's behalf, and he honestly could not help but wonder why Coulter hadn't supported him for the presidency. Curiously, the enmity between Coulter and Dwerlkotte was one-sided; Coulter made

increasingly nasty remarks about Leo but not to his face, and
Dwerlkotte says, "In all the years I knew him, there was never a
harsh word between us."

Now, however, he realized he had been put in the same category as the others on whom Coulter had turned—not merely
WAL officials but also men like Harold Fabian, one of the better
directors, and able attorney Les Craven, who had helped Adams
kill the United merger. Drinkwater, he thought, was implying he
could stay on in his post as executive vice president and general
manager, and that was fine with him.

For a time, Drinkwater and Dwerlkotte worked well together.
Western's king-sized financial difficulties required Drinkwater's
presence in the East for long periods, and during such times
Dwerlkotte continued to run the airline as he had in the Coulter
regime.

Drinkwater had to devote considerable time to organizing a
new executive team, one molded by himself and not by tradition,
seniority, or sentiment. He seems to have fought hard to retain
Dwerlkotte as his chief lieutenant, at least in the early stages.
While Drinkwater still was negotiating for a Western job, he had
talked to Hugh Darling about Leo; Drinkwater knew most of
WAL's brass, Dwerlkotte, Taylor, and Art Kelly in particular,
and was anxious for them to stay aboard.

"I know Coulter's gunning for Dwerlkotte," he told Darling,
"and if I take on Western I'm going to insist that Leo be given a
contract."

"Terry, keep out of that fight," Darling advised. "You'll have
enough to do running the company without getting involved in
Coulter's feuds."

One of Drinkwater's first acts was to strip Dwerlkotte of his
combined title, making him executive vice president without the
additional designation of general manager—but not because of
any antipathy toward him. Terry simply hated the whole idea of
having a general manager; he thought it weakened a president's
authority and diluted his responsibility for making the majority
of executive decisions. For Leo, however, it was a small cloud on
his personal horizon; he interpreted it as lack of faith in him, and
apparently it sewed the first seeds of dissension between the two
men.

Drinkwater brought to Western, along with his five-year contract at thirty-five thousand dollars a year, a hard-nosed attitude best expressed by the slogan he coined for his over-all policy: "constructive contraction." He knew the airline had overexpanded to dangerous proportions, and he intended to make it healthy again even if he had to resort to major surgery. This meant that some executive heads were going on the guillotine, but Drinkwater wisely delayed any executions before he decided who was worth saving. Most of Western's executives met him for the first time at a dinner he gave the day he arrived in Los Angeles to assume the presidency. There were approximately thirty men there, and Terry called each by his first name. There were four lower-echelon officers present who, although they didn't know it, Drinkwater already had tagged as exceptionally able and promising: Art Kelly, Jud Taylor, Jerry Brooder, and Dom Renda.

He thought highly of the effervescent Kelly, whom he had met previously and liked at first sight. While Darling was briefing Drinkwater on various WAL executive personnel, Kelly's name came up, and Darling disclosed that Art wasn't happy. There was considerable turmoil and poor morale in the sales department, and some of the older hands seemed to resent Kelly's youthful enthusiasm. Art had received a good offer from Delta and was seriously considering leaving Western. When Darling told this to Drinkwater, Terry frowned.

"Tell Art to hang on," Drinkwater said. "I've got plans for him."

After Drinkwater became president, Kelly got a call from Al Adams offering him a job at Pan American, where Adams had been named a vice president. Following protocol faithfully, Art told Drinkwater about it, went to New York to discuss the job with Adams, and then decided to stay with Western. Drinkwater's gratitude was expressed in a practical way: He named Kelly his personal assistant.

There was not a doubt in the world that in Terry Drinkwater, Western got a man for the times. He was not afraid to make decisions, nor was he hesitant to consult, probe, and investigate before a decision was forged into direct action. It is undoubtedly true that Dwerlkotte, a steady plodder, put at least some of Terry's "constructive contraction" into operation before TCD, as Drinkwater was referred to, began really to assert his authority; between October 1946 and October 1947, Western's payroll was slashed from almost 2,600 employees to less than 1,600. But it was Drinkwater alone who took the most drastic action of all: He sold the recently won Route 68, Los Angeles–Denver, to United Air Lines in a desperate move he considered necessary to save WAL from bankruptcy.

It came as a shock to the entire airline. He already had instilled a kind of comeback spirit among officials and employees alike. The first day he walked into the general offices, a big bear of a man oozing confidence, he climbed on top of a table, introduced himself in a voice that could be heard five blocks away, and announced that Western was going to survive come hell or high water. He shook hands with everyone in the building. Even the cynics were infected by his enthusiasm and they, as much as anyone else, were stunned when only three months later he proposed to sell one of WAL's two long-haul routes to United. What no one knew, however, was that Western had reached the end of its rope.

The clincher was the failure of the stock issue Dillon, Read had floated; Western had sunk so low that there were only a handful of takers. And on the sale of $6.5 million worth of stock hinged the conditional $7.5 million loan of Chase National, a bank already holding $3 million in overdue Western notes. The airline's over-all debts amounted to more than $9 million, with almost $2 million owed to a single fuel supplier. The cash supply was so slim that WAL sold a load of surplus DC-3 tires left over from the war in order to meet a payroll.

Drinkwater got the grim tidings about the stock issue when he was in New York, accompanied by Taylor and Dwerlkotte. They were called into the office of Fred Brandy, a Dillon, Read partner who was handling Western's account, one rainy January day —Taylor still remembers the vivid contrast of the cheerful fire blazing in Brandy's office and the gloomy announcement he was about to make. It was the day the stock was supposed to have been snatched up by eager investors.

"I've got bad news for you guys: We pulled the plug and it wouldn't go," he said, not without sympathy.

Drinkwater paled.

"Let's get out of here," he muttered. "I badly need a drink."

The doors to the big banking and investment firms seemed to be closed, and Drinkwater turned next to a source of help he viewed not only with reluctance but also with outright distrust—the United States Government, in the form of the Reconstruction Finance Corporation. Almost the only anti-Depression weapon of the Hoover administration that Roosevelt's New Deal had retained, RFC had been established to keep ailing industries from going bankrupt, and apparently there wasn't much question but that Western qualified for the about-to-go-under category. The RFC regional office already had turned down Coulter, but the persistent Drinkwater managed to become friendly with regional director Hector Haight, who was impressed with Terry's retrenchment plans and unwillingness to expand further without some financial stability.

Haight frankly identified for Drinkwater Western's biggest liability: Coulter. He told TCD that the airline would always have financing problems because of Coulter's influence via his massive stock holdings. Obviously, Drinkwater was in no position to do anything about this, although he agreed with Haight's analysis; Drinkwater confided to Dwerlkotte, for example, that he thought it was best to get Coulter out of the company and distribute his stock more widely. This coincided with Leo's beliefs, too, and for personal as well as financial reasons—Drinkwater told him Coulter was pressuring him constantly to fire Dwerlkotte.

TCD did manage to achieve a few small steps toward recovery. Four overdue temporary notes were extended a few months, giving him a little breathing room, and a revised application was made to the RFC for a $4.5 million loan. What Western needed desperately was some pressurized aircraft—already ordered but without a penny of solid financing. But what WAL did have was something for which another airline was panting: Route 68 between Denver and Los Angeles.

Drinkwater entered into negotiations with W. A. Patterson, with almost immediate agreement, inasmuch as each airline had an asset the other wanted: United the money, and Western the route. Hugh Darling met with Ed Leasure of United and quickly worked out the details. Western would sell UAL its Denver–Los Angeles authority for $3.75 million, throwing in four DC-4s and related ground facilities. United also agreed to loan WAL $1 million to meet some of its current obligations and payrolls, in return for a mortgage on Western's planes. In addition, United assumed Western's contract for the five DC-6s still on order.

The sale of Route 68 gave Darling some embarrassing moments. He had pleaded Western's case in the original CAB proceeding when WAL was pitted against United, Continental, and TWA; Drinkwater, as a matter of fact, had been one of Continental's principal witnesses.

"I had argued before the Board with tears in my eyes," Darling recalls with a grin. "If the CAB hadn't approved, we couldn't possibly have survived. Now I had to go right back to the CAB and tell them if they didn't let us give up the route, we were finished."

Drinkwater ran into some internal opposition over the United deal. Dwerlkotte, for one, was against it, and so was Brooder. Leo thought it was not only unwise and unnecessary for survival, but also points out that eventually it cost Western a lot of money. When it came time to give WAL a retroactive mail pay adjustment not too long after the Route 68 sale was consummated, the CAB figured that Western had made almost a $2 million profit from the transaction and reduced the adjustment by that amount.

Brooder felt that if Western could have held out a little longer, it could have fought its way back to more solid financial footing. There is no way to judge whether this could have been accomplished, but in favor of Drinkwater's decision is the fact that Western's surprisingly fast recovery was due largely to the United deal. Western finished 1947 with operating losses of more than $945,000 but still netted nearly $1 million from the sale of Route 68 and the adjusted mail pay.

Drinkwater had a few uneasy moments before the agreement was consummated and approved by the CAB. While the hearings were still in progress, the Board suddenly extended United's transcontinental route to Los Angeles via nonstop authority from Chicago. Both Terry and Darling held their breaths—the award seemed to negate any UAL need for Route 68, and Patterson was about to testify in the latter case.

"That Chicago–Los Angeles nonstop authority was all Pat really wanted," Darling says in recalling the near miss. "But he was a gentleman, make no mistake about it. He could have sunk us if he had given a lukewarm defense of the Route 68 transfer, yet he testified as strongly as if it was United's only way to get into Los Angeles."

Patterson wasn't being entirely altruistic, however. He once told Jerry Brooder that by taking over Western's DC-6 contract, he saved much of what Route 68 cost him in cash. Western, one of the first carriers to order the DC-6, had been quoted a rather low price, and United obtained the five WAL DC-6s for about $350,000 per aircraft, less than what it was paying for the same plane under its own contract with Douglas.

The sale of Route 68 was filed in March 1947 and approved by the CAB in August of that year. Drinkwater occupied the interim period between signing and government sanction with a flurry of cost-cutting activities under his avowed "constructive contraction" plan. Payroll trimming continued—the reductions begun by Dwerlkotte, with Taylor's help, plus TCD's relentless economies, cut the employee ranks to only 1,300 by the end of 1947—and it was to stay at that level for another three years. Advertising and public relations were merged into a single department. All offices were consolidated under one roof—the company's new maintenance facility at Los Angeles International Airport. As of August 31 that year, WAL's operating budget had been pruned by $150,000 a month. The rolls of fat that Western had acquired can be typified by one story. When the Convair efficiency experts were surveying ramp employees, a supervisor told them he needed twenty-five additional persons. The report they handed Dwerlkotte commented that the supervisor not only didn't need more help, but actually should fire thirty people.

With the cost cutting went the sad but inevitable head chopping. Drinkwater considered Western an airline still being run with a kind of seat-of-the-pants philosophy, particularly in the operations department. That meant Jimmie James, who became the first major victim of the Drinkwater purge, and later Dwerlkotte himself. Terry bided his time, waiting to pick new blood before lowering any booms, but everyone was bracing nervously. While the rank and file welcomed TCD like an Indian-surrounded wagon train glimpsing the U. S. Cavalry, Western's executives for the most part were scared to death. A change in command in the airline business must by its very nature involve an element of ruthlessness; seldom does an outgoing president leave behind him no additional scapegoats for past mistakes.

A replacement for James was the first item on Drinkwater's priority list. Drinkwater was in New York with his new assistant, Art Kelly, and decided to drive back to the West Coast, for several reasons: He figured the long trip would give him a good chance to know Kelly, and he wanted to stop off in Tulsa to interview a prospect for James' position.

They did get better acquainted, to the point of achieving mutual respect. Accompanying them part way was Wayne Parrish, who had founded American Aviation Publications and was something of the airline industry's Boswell; Wayne wanted to see his parents in Decatur, Illinois, so Drinkwater dropped him off there before deciding where to head next.

"I'd like to visit my own family in Denver," he told Kelly, "but maybe we should head southwest, toward Tulsa. American has a very fine operations man there, a guy I worked with at American. Name is Bill Hooten. I was thinking he might be interested in going with Western."

They started out toward Tulsa but encountered a violent electrical storm, with the rain so heavy that they had to pull off the road, parking behind a billboard. A lightning bolt hit a sign directly across the road; the storm was coming from the southwest, and both were so shaken that they changed course and headed northwest instead, winding up in Denver, where Drinkwater was reunited with his wife and two children, Terry, Jr., and Darcy. They spent a few days there, during which Drinkwater decided to pay a visit to an old crony and colleague—Continental's head of maintenance, with whom Terry had worked closely in wartime when he was running Six's airline. Somewhat to Kelly's surprise, Drinkwater offered his friend the equivalent of his Continental job; Art had figured TCD wanted Hooten of American.

"We're broke," Drinkwater told the Continental official. "I don't know where we're going, but maybe we can have some fun."

"Terry, I'm perfectly happy with Bob Six. I know how you feel about him, but he's been fair to me. I've got a good job at Continental, and you're asking me to leave security for insecurity."

"What the hell," Drinkwater laughed, "if we can't make a go at it, we're both young and we can try something else."

When Kelly and Drinkwater left Denver for Los Angeles, they had hired a new vice president of operations. Thus, as much by the chance occurrence of a thunderstorm as anything else, did Stanley R. Shatto become a part of Western Air Lines—one of the most controversial airline executives in aviation history. He was to be Drinkwater's closest friend and most trusted adviser, he was to stamp his own philosophies and methods on Western as a rancher brands a steer, and he was to gain a good measure of unpopularity mixed with fear, yet grudging respect. He was to wield incredible power and authority second only to Drinkwater, and in some cases even surpassing TCD in influence.

Stan Shatto was a man of humble origin; much of his fierce independence, excruciating bluntness, and dislike of social trappings stemmed from the crusty façade a self-made man erects around himself. His father was an Internal Revenue Service agent whose limited income kept his son from going to college. After graduating from high school in the small Missouri town of Reger, Stan learned the watchmaking trade, but he caught the aviation bug from Lindbergh's flight. When his family moved to St. Louis, he confided to his father that he wanted to get into the airplane business, in any way. The elder Shatto had a friend working for Universal Air Lines in St. Louis, called him, and arranged for his son to meet him.

"What can you do around an airport?" Stan was asked.

"Nothing," he admitted. "All I know is how to fix watches."

But he got a job anyway—building a metal shed to house OX-5 engines. When the shed was finished, Shatto graduated to various cleaning chores around the Universal hangar. It was menial work, but the youngster was bright and observant; he picked up enough knowledge on his own to qualify as an apprentice mechanic, and from Universal he went to a succession of airlines—Pennsylvania, Hanford (which became Mid-Continent), and then to Braniff, where he was named superintendent of maintenance. Bob Six offered him the head maintenance job at Continental in 1941, three years after Drinkwater became CAL's legal counsel. It was a tribute to Shatto's ability that Six kept him on the job after Terry's abortive attempt to take over Continental; Shatto, who ran CAL's Bomber Modification Center in Denver during the war while Drinkwater was in charge of the airline, was extremely close to TCD and reportedly had sided with him during the internal feud. Throughout Shatto's entire career, even those who disliked him also conceded that he was one of the best airline maintenance men in the industry, and possibly *the* best.

His coming to Western as vice president of operations meant only one thing: Jimmie James was out—not fired, technically, but demoted so far down the executive ladder that Jimmie's self-respect rebelled. Exactly what job he was offered was never quite clear; Art Kelly remembers that Drinkwater suggested a position as director of safety, which would have given him continuity and an eventual pension if he had stayed long enough to come under a pension plan that even then was in the formulative stage. Yet another story is that James was given the choice of accepting a position as a station manager or quitting. It made little difference, anyway—a bitter James resigned and took a job with Bendix at a salary lower than what Western had been paying him.

Leo Dwerlkotte was bitter, too—his time also was coming, and in some ways, his demise at Western was far more torturous than James'—Jimmie was axed suddenly and swiftly, while Dwerlkotte's description of his own fate is one of slow humiliation in a kind of bloodless execution.

There are two accounts of Leo's leaving Western, and they are at variance—which is natural, inasmuch as one comes from Dwerlkotte and the other from Drinkwater. Leo believes Drinkwater gave him the well-known shaft, and Terry insists he was treated humanely and fairly. Dwerlkotte's story:

"Things began to go sour in the latter part of 1947 and early part of 1948. Terry began doing some things that made it apparent he was trying to scuttle me. I heard, for example, that he tried to undermine me with the CAB. One day he walked into my office and informed me he wanted to reduce my salary and change my title. This didn't surprise me—I knew I was bound to get some kind of demotion when he took over completely. Then he gave orders to have my mail sent to him. I'd sit in my office for days without even mail to examine. Sometimes I'd sit there for three days just looking out the window.

"Finally he walked in and told me Coulter wanted me out of the company. I asked him why. He said there were three reasons. First, because I had fought the Route 68 sale. Sure I was against it—it was a bad idea and I still think so to this day, but I never did or said anything to stop it. Second, he said he couldn't trust me. Third, because I was a Catholic.

"The next day he came back again and asked me once more to resign. I told him I had been working on an employee pension plan. 'I've been here twenty years,' I said, 'and if I get out now I'm going to be deprived of a pension. So there should be some reimbursement for me.'

"He said he'd think about it. The following day he came in and offered me ten thousand dollars in severance pay. I went home and talked it over with my wife. A couple of days later, I told him I wanted twenty thousand dollars to get out of the company and give up my stock options. He balked at this, but agreed to give me a job as a consultant for one year at twenty thousand.

"Sure I was bitter. Drinkwater tried to take credit for cost reductions and employee reductions in the latter part of 1946 and early 1947. It was Jud Taylor and myself who started the cost-reduction program even before Drinkwater joined the company. We knew the payroll had gotten excessively high. Western had a very rapid expansion after 1943 and we hired a number of inexperienced, inefficient people with the cream of the crop going into the service. I'll admit the Route 68 sale probably was inevitable. I didn't oppose it because there was no alternative. The airline climate was bad—crashes, overconfidence, postwar recession. But maybe . . . just maybe . . . we could have hung on."

Drinkwater's side:

"Yes, I finally fired Leo. But I made him a rich man. I got him a very liberal stock option deal and liberal severance pay. Leo was always a loner. He never could communicate. I saved his job for I don't know how long, and then saved his stock. Coulter for some reason got a wild hair about Dwerlkotte. He had an idea that Leo was stealing from the company, that he was dishonest. He kept after me to fire him and I kept resisting him. Coulter was senile, almost paranoid, I think. As for firing Leo because he was Catholic, that's ridiculous."

After his dismissal, Dwerlkotte opened a law office in San Diego, where he practiced several years before moving to Phoenix because of his wife's failing health, and becoming treasurer of the Salt River Project utility. His wife was his whole life, and when she died in Phoenix, he took up residence in Las Vegas—still a loner, as Drinkwater said. He kept only a cursory contact with his old airline until two decades after his firing, when he was to come back into the Western story—as an instrument of revenge against an embattled Terrell Drinkwater trying to save his own job.

As Dwerlkotte disappeared from Western's stage, younger men were rising fast in the airline's hierarchy. One was Art Kelly. Drinkwater really didn't need an "assistant" any more than a football team needs two quarterbacks calling signals. But he did need a troubleshooter, a confidant, a kind of alter ego who wasn't afraid to say no and who wasn't adverse to tackling any kind of a job.

Kelly once booked Tom Wolfe for a promotional visit to Calgary when Western was trying to expand its system into Canada. Unhappily, he neglected to investigate whether Wolfe's trip involved conflict with other events—and on this occasion, the conflict was a lulu: Wolfe showed up to meet the city fathers the same day that the Queen of England was making her first visit to Calgary.

"How the hell are we gonna get any attention?" Wolfe demanded, with devastating logic.

The Irishman, as resourceful as he was impetuous, assured Wolfe that everything was going to be fine. He went down to the hotel lobby and tipped two bellboys ten dollars each.

"I want you to page Senator Wolfe of Wyoming," Kelly ordered. "Remember that: *Senator* Wolfe. Say that the local news-

244 THE ONLY WAY TO FLY

papers are trying to reach him. If anyone asks about him, tell him he's in Room 360 at the hotel."

"Suppose Senator Wolfe answers the page?" one bellhop asked. "What are we supposed to tell him?"

"He won't answer," Kelly allowed, and thereupon went to Room 360, where he briefed Wolfe.

The script went as planned. The lobby was jammed with reporters waiting for the Queen's procession to arrive; they heard the page, and inasmuch as curiosity is a journalistic disease, they inquired of the bellboys where they could find Senator Wolfe. Room 360 was soon filled with the gentlemen of the press.

"Senator, what are you doing in Calgary?" was the first question, the newsman obviously unaware that Wyoming had no senator named Wolfe.

"Boys," Wolfe intoned, "I've selected this time when Her Majesty is here to give you the greatest story in many years. I can now reveal to you from absolutely unimpeachable sources that Western Air Lines has plans to expand its service into the great province of Alberta. I am told by officials of this fine airline that Western considers Calgary a key city in its future plans to . . ."

The next day, the Calgary newspaper carried right next to the lead story on the Queen's arrival a headline reading:

SENATOR WOLFE SAYS CALGARY HAS
GREAT FUTURE IN AIR TRANSPORTATION

In the first year of the Drinkwater regime, Kelly found himself embroiled in events dwarfing senatorial masquerades of the carefree old days. The airlines were Big Business by the postwar years, and Drinkwater was giving him a front-row seat. They were in Washington on one occasion, working on the RFC loan and sharing—for economy reasons—the same room at the Carlton Hotel. The phone rang at 3:30 A.M. and Kelly answered, figuring it had to be important because nobody called Terry Drinkwater after 11:00 P.M.—he never tolerated early-morning telephone calls except for a dire emergency.

"It's Noah Dietrich," Kelly said in a matter-of-fact tone that didn't quite hide his excitement and curiosity. Dietrich was Howard Hughes' right-hand man and chief adviser.

Drinkwater stumbled out of bed, muttered a few terse words on the phone, and hung up.

"The next time he calls, tell him I'm not available," Terry growled.

Drinkwater went back to bed but the next morning disclosed that even before he had accepted the Western presidency, "I had a chance to become president of a large airline and turned it down to come to Western." He didn't identify the carrier then, but the middle-of-the-night call from Dietrich and subsequent contacts between Hughes' top aide and Drinkwater left little doubt that Hughes-owned TWA was the airline involved.

Kelly's constant proximity to the Western president made him privy to Dietrich's incessant wooing. One day, in Art's presence, Terry told Dietrich, "Why the hell should I go to Kansas City or New York? I love the West and I hate the East."

For some reason, Dietrich seemed to think Drinkwater was about to swallow the baited hook; at any rate, he gave Hughes that impression, because Drinkwater informed Kelly one night that they were going over to meet the Mystery Man himself. It was the first time Kelly had even seen the famed, eccentric billionaire, who greeted them at his home in back of the Beverly Hills Hotel. Kelly remembers that Hughes was wearing a white turtleneck sweater and was hard of hearing.

"Well, did you and Noah work this thing out—you ready to go with TWA?" Hughes asked without preamble.

"No, I've made no commitment."

Hughes looked as if Drinkwater had just told him he was penniless. "You mean you didn't make a commitment with Noah?"

"No, I didn't, Howard. I'll tell you what I told him—I want to build a transportation system serving the West; that's the only thing I'm committed to, and that's what I'm going to do."

Hughes was visibly annoyed, and the discussion went on this way for another ten minutes before Hughes abruptly stood up, snapped "Thank you very much," and strode angrily out of the room.

He was to make one more futile effort to put Terry in charge of TWA in the midfifties, after they became good friends. But that remark Drinkwater made to Hughes about building "a transportation system serving the West" was, in effect, the credo behind Drinkwater's "constructive contraction" program. He envisioned primarily a north-to-south airline that would not fly east of the Rockies, and this was to be his seldom-violated policy for many years. Financial aid might have been the principal motive behind the Route 68 deal, but another factor was that disposal of the route fitted in with his creed. After the CAB approved the sale, Drinkwater sent this teletype message throughout Western's system:

> To all stations WAL and Inland
> To all employees

> It gives us extreme pleasure to announce to you that the Civil Aeronautics Board today approved the sale of Route 68 to United Air Lines. We cannot emphasize too strongly to you the significance of this transaction, for it means the CAB has approved our philosophy and our function as a regional carrier in the West. While we will now be able to utilize our resources and our talents to the building of a strong regional system of air transportation, we will at the same time be in a stronger position to co-operate closely on interline arrangements for both passengers and freight to and from the East with the transcontinental carriers. . . . It means that Western Air Lines has returned to the West to perform a definite mission in the over-all pattern of transportation both regional and nationally. . . . It means that we no longer are interested in further extending our operations east of the Rocky Mountains and that now we can provide equipment, service, and schedules tailored specifically to the transportation needs of the West.

The teletype message ended with this sentence: "We will continue to operate Inland Air Lines as a subsidiary of Western Air Lines." That came as welcome news to Jerry Brooder and a number of others, for right after he signed the Route 68 agreement with United, Drinkwater had informed Brooder:

"The next thing we have to do is get rid of the Inland division. I'm going to make you general manager of Inland and you can go right to work packaging a deal to dispose of it."

Brooder had guts; he already had openly opposed the Route 68 sale, and he proceeded to fight Drinkwater's plans to dispose of Inland.

"We need Inland for some expansion east of the Rockies," he told Terry.

"That's exactly what I don't want," TCD snorted. "Get with it before anybody else gets some crazy ideas about expanding."

He was virtually alone in his eagerness to dump Inland. And it would have been a major mistake; subsequent developments were to turn part of the old Inland system into WAL's most profitable route. Several factors intervened to prevent his making a serious immediate issue of it, beginning with RFC approval of the $4.5 million loan. Terry had canceled virtually every route application Western had filed with the Civil Aeronautics Board, but not in time to prevent the CAB from awarding WAL two new routes—one of which delighted Drinkwater and the other toward which he was totally indifferent. The first was authority to compete with United between Los Angeles and Seattle via Portland, Oregon. The second was, on the surface, an award with the same profit potential as selling ham sandwiches at a synagogue supper: Rapid City, South Dakota, to Minneapolis/St. Paul.

All the latter achieved was access into the growing Twin Cities market, but via a circuitous routing that on paper looked ridiculous. Western had been operating to Rapid City over the original Inland system—via an airway that wandered first in one direction and then another. This inherent deficiency didn't seem to bother Drinkwater, but it was something Brooder and several others kept pondering.

Of far more interest to Drinkwater was the RFC's financial transfusion, the loan being followed by Coulter's unexpected attempt to regain Western's presidency. He suddenly went into his patented about-face, this time turning against Drinkwater and warning the RFC that it would never get its money back as long as Drinkwater ran the airline.

Coulter made so much noise that RFC regional director Hector Haight agreed to hear him out in an open session attended by the former president and his lawyers, and also Drinkwater plus WAL's top officers. Coulter's attorneys did most of his talking, but when Haight at one point asked for more elaboration of charges against individual executives, Coulter selected Shatto.

"He's a pinhead," the old man explained. "He laughs at me."

After Drinkwater and his fellow officers defended their management of the airline, Haight turned to Coulter.

"If there's any change in Western's management," he said quietly, "I'll recommend to Washington that the RFC withdraw its financial support."

Coulter left the room steaming. Drinkwater was so impressed by Haight's firm fairness that two years later he talked him into joining Western's board, but Drinkwater's immediate concern was Coulter. The ex-president still was the majority stockholder, and TCD knew he had been added to Coulter's list of enemies. The only question was the direction in which Coulter would move, and it wasn't long before Terry found out.

The RFC loan, together with United's aid, allowed Western to proceed with its reduced order for the ten new Convair 240s. The new airliners, each needing eighty-six modifications before they could fly Western's mountainous routes, started coming off the assembly line early in 1948. Kelly, with his background of sales and marketing, was given the task of promoting the latest queen of the WAL fleet, and Art was the first one to admit that his aeronautical knowledge at the time consisted of a vague belief in the law of gravity.

Drinkwater had no qualms about introducing the Convair on Western's prime noncompetitive routes such as Los Angeles–Salt Lake City, but to gain any kind of a foothold in the recently acquired Los Angeles–Seattle market he figured Western needed a top sales effort. United was firmly entrenched on this route, using new four-engine DC-6s, and the minute that Western received Seattle authority, UAL increased its Los Angeles–Seattle schedules 200 per cent—Pat Patterson may have been honorable and decent in the Route 68 case, but he wasn't about to let Western beat him in a competitive situation.

Kelly finally came up with a successful Convair campaign, and Drinkwater began to realize he had to keep him in sales and marketing full time. TCD gradually was organizing the nucleus of an executive team as good as there was in the industry. Dom Renda appeared especially promising; the two men had rapport

right from the start, partly because there were certain similarities
between them. Both were brilliant lawyers. Both loved to read—
their talents were intellectual as well as legal. Both were tough
yet with streaks of sentimentality. Both had academic backgrounds, although Drinkwater came from a relatively affluent
family, while Renda's parents could not afford to send him to college completely on their own.

Born in Steubenville, Ohio, Renda in his youth was an outstanding athlete, track being his specialty. He ran both the mile
and half mile, once setting the Ohio State record for the mile in
a time that withstood all challenges for years. He graduated
from high school six months before his sixteenth birthday and
went to work in a steel mill for three years, to earn money for college. With some help from his family, he worked his way through
undergraduate school at Ohio State and then earned a law degree
from the OSU College of Law.

Renda's earliest interest was in politics. After a brief stint in
general practice in Steubenville, he worked also briefly as an assistant to a district attorney and then managed to land a job as
an administrative assistant to a congressman before Pearl Harbor. He was discharged from the Navy in Los Angeles after the
war, intending to return to Ohio and go into politics as a career,
but funds were low, and he decided to take a stopgap job. A
friend had suggested that Western might need a young lawyer,
with all its expansion plans, and Renda walked into the WAL
employment office, where he announced his availability as an attorney. Dwerlkotte interviewed him and hired him, Renda going
to work while studying at night for the California bar examination. He became Leo's assistant, fell in love with the airline business, and soon forgot all political ambitions. He frankly didn't
expect to survive the payroll cuts Drinkwater ordered, but TCD
had done some checking and found unanimous opinion that
Renda was not expendable. Renda had then and still does possess a kind of executive character that marks so many successful
top airline officials—a respect for the past without ever using it
as an anodyne for present failure; an intense hatred for vacilla-
tion and red tape, tempered by an equally strong dislike
for headstrong impulsiveness; an ability to lead, strong convictions, positive actions and personal integrity. That was Dominic

P. Renda in the early days of the Drinkwater era. He never changed.

Terry called him in one day and announced that the time had come for Western to stop relying entirely on outside legal advice.

"We need our own legal department," he declared, "and you're the man to be it."

It was a hunch typical of TCD. At the time, Renda knew little about aviation law, but it also was typical of Dom that he accepted the new assignment without hesitation; the story of his life had been one of learning while working, and this would be no exception. He was promoted immediately to assistant corporate secretary, with the bulk of his duties in the field of route cases, which he was to handle for many years. In the latter, he worked closely with Jerry Brooder, who became a kind of "ambassador without portfolio" for Western—packing a great deal of influence and fielding important assignments without a title befitting his work. Not for five years would Jerry's name appear on the first page of the Annual Report listing the company's top officers along with the directors—as assistant to the president. By that time, Art Kelly had been vice president of sales for four years, succeeding Richard Dick in 1949.

Brooder's old sidekick at Inland, Marv Landes, became a vice president the same year Drinkwater took over, heading a new department with the catch-all designation of "Service." Basically, it embraced all employees and activities involving direct contact with the public—stewardesses, ticketing, in-flight service, reservations, baggage, passenger complaints, etc. Jud Taylor, another officer of whom Drinkwater thought highly, served as corporate treasurer until 1952, when he was named a vice president. The rest of the 1948-vintage command consisted of Pat Sullivan, vice president and secretary, and the man whose advice, counsel, and technical acumen Drinkwater relied on more than anyone else in the airline: Stan Shatto.

Shatto became TCD's second-in-command from the day he joined Western. His official title, changed shortly to vice president of engineering and maintenance, in no way reflected his growing influence on Drinkwater and his immense authority within the company. Significantly, he became a director at the same time he was named a vice president—the only officer at the time whom TCD honored with that distinction. No one ever doubted that Terry Drinkwater ran Western, but no one ever forgot that an order from Shatto might as well have come from the president. Terry gave Shatto almost total authority; Stan gave him in return 100 per cent loyalty.

Theirs was an odd friendship, for in many ways they were totally unalike. Drinkwater was worldly, erudite, articulate, and—when he wanted to be—totally charming. Shatto was rough-hewn, curt, and disdainful of anything resembling small talk. Drinkwater, who could be moody at times, wanted everybody to love him; being popular and well liked was essential to his peace of mind. Shatto—outwardly, anyway—couldn't have cared less what people thought of him; his singleminded purpose in life was to serve Western and Terry Drinkwater, and anything or anybody not directly connected with that goal didn't interest him. He lived in a technically oriented world and seemed to hold far more respect for machines than for the men who built and operated them. He hated executive staff meetings, for example, considering them a waste of not only his time but also everybody else's.

"Thirty guys at a two-hour meeting adds up to sixty man-hours," he once grumbled to an associate.

He brooked no interference with his own department. When Brooder reported to Shatto that he had noticed a DC-4 in an exceptionally dirty condition, Stan's response was a curt note to stay out of affairs that didn't concern him.

Initially, Shatto's influence within Western generally and on Drinkwater specifically was confined to his own areas of expertise: airplanes, engines, safety, maintenance, and operations. Gradually, however, his authority broadened to the point where his position resembled that of a crack executive officer on a ship—Shatto was to run Western, leaving Drinkwater free to concentrate on long-range policy matters, such as routes and financing.

The main reason for Drinkwater's growing reliance on Shatto was the fact that he not only admired him in a professional sense, but also had implicit trust in him as a friend and colleague. There evidently was never any boss-underling relationship between them; rather, Drinkwater regarded him as a virtual equal, a status that could only have come from total trust.

In a society where almost every chief looks over his shoulder not just to see who's following him, but also to see which one of the Indians wants to be the next chief, TCD never had to look back. Terry at first wasn't sure of the loyalty of many WAL officers, but he always knew he could count on Shatto.

Next to Drinkwater in those trying days of the late forties and the more promising fifties, Shatto probably was closest to Dom Renda. The three of them, in fact, became social friends as well as business associates, often traveling together. Renda began molding a group that he still considers "the best route-development team in the industry at that time." It consisted of Brooder and Tom Murphy on state, federal, and community affairs; Jim Mitchell on regulatory and economic matters; John Simpson, who was a young lawyer Renda hired away from the CAB, and Renda himself, arguing all the cases. The team was to stay intact for almost two decades, winning for Western new route awards totaling more than six thousand miles, exclusive of Hawaii and what was acquired via merger.

With a young, crack executive unit established, Western began its slow turn back toward solvency. The economy measures continued; a number of ticket offices and other facilities were consolidated with those of other airlines, unneeded space in the new $2.5 million general offices building at Los Angeles International Airport was leased out (years later, WAL not only occupied the entire building but also had to erect a new general offices building twice the size of the old one), and operational costs were cut more than 20 per cent. The payroll for a time hovered at around the 1,300 level—much to Shatto's displeasure. When he agreed to come with Western, the airline had some 2,500 employees.

"When you get it down to 1,200," he told Terry, "we'll start cutting."

The second year of the Drinkwater era, 1948, ended with only a modest improvement—a $339,000 net loss, but with optimism permeating the entire airline; the red ink wasn't nearly as scarlet as the nearly $1 million dropped in 1946. Part of the '48 deficit was due to interest payments and the delivery of the ten new Convair 240s, which started scheduled service that September. And the effects of the various economy moves weren't really felt until the second half of the year. WAL lost more than $680,000 in the first quarter and nearly the same amount during the second quarter; to finish the year with only a $339,000 loss had to involve a second-half comeback of impressive proportions. There also was one major area of cost-cutting where the "penny wise, pound foolish" adage applied.

This involved the controversial, widely publicized decision to abolish all in-flight meal service. The new policy, which went into effect on February 1, 1949, reportedly was the brainchild of Marv Landes, but it had Drinkwater's wholehearted support. It definitely was a courageous experiment aimed not merely at cutting expenses but also at reducing fares. What Western offered along with mealless flights was a 5 per cent fare reduction, Drinkwater confidently expecting general rejoicing on the part of the public. His application to the Civil Aeronautics Board late in 1948, seeking permission to drop food service, said Western was "acting on the theory that the serving of meals is an illogical and uneconomical function for an organization engaged solely in air transportation."

Unfortunately, Drinkwater was too far ahead of his time. Passengers deserted Western's flights on the hotly competitive Pacific Coast routes in droves, particularly in the Los Angeles–Seattle market, where United's already superb DC-6 service made Western's economy flights look shabby. Les Warden, a retired WAL captain, recalls that he flew only four passengers to Seattle the final day of the no-meals experiment and had a full load coming back the next day. In a few weeks, Western was back to the 63 per cent load factor it had achieved when it first butted heads against UAL.

The noble effort was abandoned after a six-month trial period, but Drinkwater came up with a substitute that had far wider appeal. In the fall of 1949, Western inaugurated the first scheduled economy coach service on the Pacific Coast—using high-density DC-4s, which gave passengers a choice between lower fares and the regular first-class Convair flights. Drinkwater had conjured up a scheme to combat the increasing inroads being made on the West Coast traffic by nonscheduled airlines, which began proliferating after the war and were starting to offer some embarrassing competition. It was impossible to cut fares down to the nonskeds' level—the CAB would never approve slashes of that

magnitude—so Drinkwater set up a separate corporation, Western Air of California, leased it WAL's own DC-4s, and matched
the opposition's $9.95 fare between Los Angeles and San
Francisco.

When the CAB protested, Terry inquired innocently, "Where
in the law does it say we're doing anything wrong?" He had
made sure everything was kosher; Western Air of California had
separate officers, sold tickets through Western Union offices, and
Drinkwater piously informed the Board that the two airlines had
no interlocking directorates. It was all perfectly legal, and the
offspring airline lasted about a year before Terry decided the
small profits weren't worth all the trouble; but Western Air of
California marked the start of WAL's coach service.

WAL turned the corner in that year of 1949. Net profits
amounted to $432,000, and Drinkwater felt confident enough to
order another five Convairs. Shatto began investigating four-engine equipment along with plans to dispose of the now-obsolete
DC-3s and DC-4s—remembering the day he and Drinkwater
had walked into the Douglas executive offices, shortly after
Shatto came to Western, to discuss with one of their top officers
the question of a $150,000 debt WAL still owed on some
previously purchased airplanes.

"I'll tell you what," Terry had said, "I'll match you for what we
owe—double or nothing."

"You're on," agreed the Douglas official.

Drinkwater called out "heads"—and it came up heads. They
walked out with the debt wiped off the books, and Terry still has
that coin. Donald Douglas, Sr., raised cain when he heard about
the incident.

"What the hell," his subordinate pointed out, "they couldn't
have paid us anyway."

He probably was right. When Drinkwater first became president, he was stunned to learn that the slot-machine concession at
McCarran Field in Las Vegas was producing more revenue than
the passenger traffic in and out of the city. How far WAL had
progressed in two years is best underlined by the fact that by the
end of 1949, Western had repaid the bulk of the RFC and
United loans and still was able to report a small profit. The carrier's financial standing had improved so immeasurably that the

RFC unhesitantly loaned it another $2 million to help finance the additional Convairs.

The only cloud on Drinkwater's horizon was cast by the persistent shadow of William Coulter, determined to make one final attempt at unseating the man who not only had succeeded him but who also had done what Coulter had failed to do—turn Western around.

His weapon was his huge holdings in WAL stock. Coulter's original investment was $300,000, and at one time the value of his shares soared to $10 million. Now, with the memories of his glory days as an airline president and the achievements of his successor burning inside him like acid, he still possessed 250,000 shares of the airline's 500,000 outstanding shares—and he decided to get rid of TCD by selling the whole shebang to a man he considered anti-Drinkwater: I. W. "Tubby" Burnham of I. W. Burnham and Company, a large New York investment firm.

Hugh Darling was the first to hear of Coulter's scheme, when a Los Angeles broker phoned him. "Hugh, what the hell's going on at Western? Tubby Burnham called me to ask how many shares I'd take on what amounted to a second offering, but that Burnham wanted to hold the proxy."

Darling knew this could mean only one thing: Coulter was dumping his stock, apparently to Burnham, who was, in turn, offering part of it to other brokers but only on the condition that Burnham would have the power to vote their shares. Darling immediately notified Drinkwater.

"What should we do, Hugh?" Terry asked. "We've got an annual stockholders' meeting coming up soon. We could be handing Western right back to Coulter if they vote in their own directors."

"Terry, this is a one-shot deal for Coulter or Burnham," Darling advised. "If they don't take control at this meeting, they'll never get it. They're only retaining the proxies for this one meeting, and if we can get by it, I don't think we have anything to worry about."

Drinkwater told Darling to handle the whole affair, and the latter got confirmation of his fears when an attorney representing Burnham called to request the list of Western's stockholders. Darling informed Drinkwater of this development, and Terry simply said, "You're calling the shots—I'll do anything you recommend."

"Fine," Darling snapped. "As a starter, I'm going to tell them they can go to hell."

When the Burnham lawyer phoned again, Darling refused to turn over the list.

"Hugh, you know damned well I can go to court and get those stockholder names," the lawyer protested.

"Sure," Darling agreed affably, "but not in time for that meeting."

Stymied in this strategy, Burnham came around with a compromise offer: If Drinkwater agreed to let him designate two of the five directors on the Western Board, there would be no attempt made to overthrow TCD.

"Who would be your choices?" Drinkwater wanted to know.

"Myself and L. Welch Pogue. He's a former chairman of the CAB."

Terry went back to Darling, who thought the compromise was something of a victory for Drinkwater.

"That still leaves you with a three-to-two majority on the Board," he pointed out, "and Welch Pogue is nobody's patsy. He's not going to be twisted around Tubby's little finger, and furthermore he'd be an asset to the company. My advice is to tell Burnham we agree."

Drinkwater took the advice, although he had some qualms about putting Pogue on the Board—later admitting, however, that his concern was unjustified because Pogue turned out to be not only an excellent director but also a good friend of Terry's. The crisis also shouldn't have left Coulter unhappy, for he received approximately $1 million for his stock. He sold it for $5.50 a share, with Burnham getting $.50 a share as a commission for handling the secondary offering. The latter benefited the airline, too, for it now had more than 4,000 shareholders, most of them in western states, instead of the majority of stock being held by one man.

Any fears Drinkwater had about Burnham trying to oust him were eradicated after Tubby became a director. Burnham actually had given Coulter an oral promise to fire Terry after acquiring the stock, but changed his mind when he got a firsthand look at how TCD was running Western. It still was a close call. Drinkwater actually received a telegram from Coulter after Burnham bought the stock, reading:

"How do you like your new boss? Ha, ha."

With the 1949 crisis over, Terry won the directors' approval to double the size of the Board, to gain wider representation from the areas Western served. His dreams had been solidified into tangible gains and future plans.

His Indian, indeed, was now hard and lean as the airline of the West prepared to enter the next decade.

CHAPTER TWELVE

Dawn of the Golden Decade

Someone once asked Jerry Brooder what he thought of Terry Drinkwater.

Jerry pondered the question a few minutes before replying.

"Well, I'll tell you," he finally said, "nobody ever treated me better—and nobody ever treated me worse."

That's about as objective an appraisal as ever made of the complex man of many contrasts who guided Western to greatness. Terrell Croft Drinkwater always seemed to have a tug-of-war going on inside of him, one facet of his personality constantly struggling with some conflicting or diametrically opposed element. This was true even in physical appearance—his cherubic smile, twinkling eyes, and an affectionate nature that was almost puppylike, this was Drinkwater at his warmest, ingratiating best; but he also could be petulant and ruthless, a man who manifested displeasure and anger in some terrifying modes.

He often went out of his way to be kind and considerate. When Art Kelly's mother died, Drinkwater called him in. Terry had known Art's parents well, and was particularly fond of the elder Kelly. Drinkwater sensed what his wife's death meant to Kelly's father; they had been totally devoted to each other.

Drinkwater expressed some conventional condolences, then handed Kelly a small plastic card. Art looked at it in disbelief.

"Ask your dad if he could use it," Drinkwater said gruffly.

It was a gold pass, with positive space authority on all Western flights—given only to directors and top officers.

"That pass was a lifeline to my father," Kelly admits. "That's the kind of guy Terry was—90 per cent of the time he could be the kindest, most generous man in the world."

This unquestionably was true. When Western set up its first retirement and pension plan, it was generally expected that some big insurance company would get the business. Under California law, WAL would have to pay a brokers' commission to the insurance company, and the obvious choice was Prudential; its West Coast operations were being handled by Harry Volk, who later became a director and was a good friend of TCD's. Volk himself explains why Prudential was cut out of the traffic pattern:

"Western had a young guy named Jack Emmerich who worked in the research department, making up CAB exhibits and so forth. He began to go blind and decided that selling insurance would be easier for a blind person than working at an airline. Drinkwater heard about it and insisted that Emmerich handle Western's pension plan—the commission set him up in business."

That was pure Drinkwater. But also pure Drinkwater was the day he walked into Western's office in Washington, D.C., some years ago and started taking the pictures off the walls.

"I'm closing down this office," he announced—which was the first knowledge the stunned then-Washington representative had of the decision.

Outwardly, anyway, TCD was the personification of the hail-fellow-well-met guy who loves to be the life of the party—at times he could be loud, rather boisterous, and embarrassingly gregarious. Yet some of his closest friends insist that this side of him was mostly sham.

"He'd rather be alone and read than go to dinner parties, make speeches, and spend his time socializing," one of them says. "Terry, when you come right down to it, always was an intellectual, almost an egghead."

Much of his social extrovertism might be traced to what so many saw in him—that subconscious desire to be loved by everyone. He tried to dominate any gathering he was in, and sometimes he seemed to try too hard. He had a propensity for telling off-color jokes that weren't too bad, except that he often picked the wrong time to tell them. There was nothing wrong with his

sense of humor; it was merely clumsy at times, giving him a reputation for flippancy that was not always deserved.

Some employees liked him, some feared him, and almost all respected him. For a man of such positive convictions, virtually
total authority, and domineering personality, he was, in the
earlier years, surprisingly free from dictatorial tendencies; he
could be, in fact, tougher on officers than on the rank and file.
No one was ever able to find Terry in his office about an hour
before he was scheduled to leave on some out-of-town trip, and
the reason was simple: he'd leave the building early so he could
spend time talking to skycaps, ramp agents, and ship cleaners.
Yet on a plane he often was curt and demanding.

He cared little about personal publicity—he preferred seeing
Western's name in print to his own, although TCD himself was
delightfully quotable, frank, and straight-talking. He would
rather be personally popular than personally well known; there
was little egotism in Terry Drinkwater, in marked contrast to
some of his contemporary airline colleagues.

Drinkwater loved to give nicknames to his fellow UAL brass,
and once he settled on an informal monicker, he never used the
man's real name. Phil Peirce, a WAL veteran who became senior
vice president of marketing, was "Coach," because he once
coached at a South Dakota high school. Shatto was "Buck"—no
one, including Stan himself, knows why. Landes was "Casey,"
from his background as a railroad engineer. Pat Sullivan, almost
bald, naturally was "Curly." And Jerry Brooder, whose rapport
with politicians was one of the airline's greatest assets, was always "Senator."

Western, rightly or wrongly, became known as an airline
whose pilots hated management, and vice versa. But this was not
the case in the first years of Drinkwater's regime. Not too long
after TCD became president, Ted Homan asked to see him
about some extra instrumentation Ted thought should go on the
new Convairs. Homan was chairman of Western's ALPA chapter, and understandably was a bit nervous when Drinkwater consented to see him. Past Western presidents had been known for
their anti-union feelings; Hanshue was violently against unions,
for example, and Adams wasn't exactly enamored of them. Pop,

in fact, fired a pilot who tried to organize Western's airmen before ALPA became respectable.

Drinkwater was cordial but blunt. "Ted, you're always welcome in my office—any of you fellas. You can put your feet on my desk and we'll talk about whatever problem you want to talk about. But that doesn't mean I'll always agree with you."

For a long time, that brief speech mirrored TCD's policy toward his pilots. Terry was never anti-ALPA, nor was he ever really anti-union—on several occasions he proved to be more reasonable and yielding than either Landes or Shatto. When the Teamsters during the 1960s demanded a closed shop for a large number of WAL employees under their jurisdiction, Shatto balked like a stubborn mule; it was Drinkwater who broke the apparent impasse.

"You guys know how I feel about the closed shop," Terry said quietly. "Hell, we once took a strike over that damned issue. But things change. People change. Buck, let's give in, but make sure they give something in return."

The pilots were the first WAL union to propose a pension plan, Pat Carlson and Milt Shirk going in to see Drinkwater to discuss the proposal. TCD's reaction was on the tepid side.

"We came out and I thought, 'What the hell, we'll never hear any more about this,'" Pat recalls. But the second time the pilots approached Drinkwater, his attitude toward pensions was not just a show of interest, but also wholehearted support—not only as a pilots' retirement plan but also as one applying to all employees and officers.

"We suspected he had figured out where *he'd* fit into a pension deal," Pat chuckles. "He didn't agree with us very often, but I believe he tried to be fair. It was Shatto, not Drinkwater, who gave us the most trouble."

The WAL veterans who lived through the Drinkwater era back up that last statement.

"The pilots never hated Drinkwater," one captain remarks. "Most of us liked the old man—it was Shatto who gave us fits. Our goal at negotiations was to make Shatto crawl in on his hands and knees and surrender. But he never did. Usually he stayed out of actual negotiations, but it was his attitude that always seemed to prevail: 'Don't give the bastards a goddamned thing!' Yet I'll say one thing about Shatto: He wasn't two-faced. If he didn't like you, he'd say so. You always knew where you stood with Stan. In that sense, I had to respect the guy."

Before Shatto's influence began to be felt in the critical field of labor relations—and this development took a number of years—Drinkwater got along fairly well with the unions, including ALPA. Captain Les Warden, active in the Scouting movement, once asked him for permission to hold a weekend Air Scout Jamboree on the grounds next to the general offices.

"How many kids?" TCD growled.

"About four hundred."

"How long are they gonna be parked here?"

"Friday night to Monday morning, Mr. Drinkwater. They'll just need overnight space for their sleeping tents—we'll have them off the premises every morning, and we won't bring them back until after the general offices close."

Drinkwater thought it over. "Okay, Les, I'll let you do it on one condition: They have to leave the grounds by 7:00 A.M."

"That's a deal," Warden said happily.

"What about chow?" Terry asked as Warden was leaving.

"Well, I was hoping we could get 'em through our cafeteria before the morning breakfast rush. We won't bring them back until after supper."

"I guess we can feed them breakfast," Drinkwater allowed in a tone suggesting he was agreeing to feed all California's unemployed.

The four hundred or so Air Scouts descended on Western that Friday evening. At 6:00 A.M. Saturday morning, Warden and other pilots escorted the youngsters to the company cafeteria. There, behind the counter, was Terry Drinkwater, helping to serve the food. On both Saturday and Sunday, he also arranged to make an airplane available for sightseeing rides, the pilots volunteering the flight time. The Scouts paid $2.50 per trip to defray operating expenses; Drinkwater insisted that only $1.50 go to Western, with the Air Scouts keeping a dollar for their own treasury.

TCD always was a sucker for kids. He once gave the Girl Scouts permission to sell cookies throughout the general offices. For some reason or other, he was mad at passenger service at the

time and ordered every man in the department to buy two cases
—not boxes, but *cases*. Nobody rebelled, either; one did not
argue with a Terrell C. Drinkwater command. He was never a
martinet, but he was tough—like the time he began fining top
executives five dollars per minute for being late to a staff meeting.

Drinkwater's memory was incredible, and it was never displayed more impressively than at those staff meetings. He would
go around the room telling each officer to do this or that, and
they knew it had better be accomplished by the next meeting.
Terry never took a note, but he remembered every order and
every problem on which he wanted some action. His frequent
acts of kindness were punctuated by even more frequent acts of
stern discipline; officers and employees, however, heard about
the latter with the swift efficiency of a prison grapevine, whereas
the former often went unnoticed except by the individual recipi-
ent.

In many ways, Drinkwater was a rather paternalistic president, although not in the completely natural manner of W. A.
Patterson at United, who seemed to have invented paternalism
in the airline industry. Terry tried hard to emulate Patterson and
at times succeeded, but Drinkwater could also be a bit awkward.
He established a ritual, for example, of giving the officers gifts
on their birthdays—items he would buy at the beginning of each
year. The presentation ceremony was supposed to come as a
complete surprise but seldom did, the executives feigning as-
tonishment at both the advent and nature of the gift.

Another Drinkwater-inspired company custom followed the
annual shareholders' meetings: a gathering in Palm Springs,
where all executives would take their annual physicals at a small
clinic. It was run by a doctor who had successfully treated Terry
for an allergy—a feat which TCD placed in the same category as
the discovery of anesthesia. After the physicals, everyone relaxed
for a few days.

Few dared skip the annual executive Christmas party. This
was Terry at his best—or worst, depending on whether you were
a worshiper like Shatto or a cynic. Everyone would get a little
bombed, and TCD would make a speech, often with tears in his
eyes, about how much he loved his Western family—which he

really did. He was sincerely solicitous toward the executive corps; if a late-afternoon fog gripped the Los Angeles area, Terry would make the rounds of the executive offices, telling each man, "Now be sure to drive carefully."

His efforts to make his officers feel that they were part of a family extended even to socializing. He liked them to eat together and play together, inviting several or even the entire corps of vice presidents to his home on weekends to play gin rummy and watch football games.

Ken Smith, a veteran newspaperman who became Western's public-relations director in 1950, agrees that the Western of the fifties was a closely knit family.

"Drinkwater was the godfather," Smith relates. "He rewarded you, he gave things to you. But the reason we got them was because he knew we didn't give a damn. If we had asked for something or demanded it, he would have told us to go to hell. That's why we had such fringe benefits as paid-up life insurance and stock options—it was the way he handed out his largess."

The Golden Fifties was a period in which Drinkwater was considered one of the most able airline chiefs in the industry. The way he ran a directors' meeting, for example, was a lesson in corporate finesse and skill. One extremely effective Drinkwater technique at Board meetings was to go around the table and ask each director to give his views on Western's operations, current economic problems, and any other subject deemed pertinent to the airline industry in general and WAL in particular. Terry allotted a full forty-five minutes to such discussion. He also came up with the idea of holding the directors' meetings in various cities on Western's system; from the 1950s on, Western's Boards were always well balanced geographically, yet thanks to Terry's diversified meeting locations each director understood the needs, problems, and wishes of other areas.

He was an astute judge of executive talent and a brilliant organizer, the latter a quality in which he had few if any peers. The team he began molding in the late forties reached fruition and maturity in the fifties, and much of its strength lay in middle management—a vastly underrated factor in airline efficiency and prosperity. The best vice president in the industry can have his efforts diluted and even sabotaged by the management echelons just below him—the latter are the top sergeants of an airline army. Drinkwater had the brains to recognize ability at this level, and few carriers could surpass or even match Western's middle management. It was, like WAL itself, lean and hard—daring, innovative, hard-working. The bulk of this imaginative young corps was hired in the forties or early fifties, some before the Drinkwater era began, others shortly thereafter, but all of them sharing Terry's faith in Western's destiny not as one of the industry's giants but as one of its best. They were WAL's young Turks, courageous enough to challenge Drinkwater's almost instinctive negative reaction to anything approaching the unconventional, and talented enough to get away with it occasionally. Kelly, the oldest in seniority, and the only one with vice presidential status, was something of their ringleader, but he had some able allies, and by the midfifties their abilities had carried them to that management level where their ideas were at least being listened to if not always adopted.

There was Dick Ensign, who started out as a microbiologist and went to work for Western in 1941 for what he thought would be a year, during which time he intended to save up enough money to go back to medical school. What the medical profession lost, the airline industry gained; Ensign rose from a passenger-service supply man to director of in-flight services in 1955, the year when middle management seemed to reach a peak of effectiveness.

There was Phil Peirce, director of stations that same year. He had not only coached football, track, baseball, and basketball in that small South Dakota high school and also taught history, math, and economics—"If you couldn't also handle the band," he recalls, "you weren't very well qualified to teach." After his discharge from the Navy in World War II, he didn't want to go back to South Dakota, and through a friend he knew at the CAA he got a job at Western in the Reservations Department.

One of Peirce's sidekicks was Bert Lynn, who was running a small advertising agency when Art Kelly hired him. Like the others Lynn was an idea man, unafraid to try new schemes. Ironically, both he and Peirce were rather scholarly and pedantic in appearance, yet Kelly, Peirce, Lynn, and Ensign comprised a quartet of boldness, originality, and ingenuity in sales, service,

and advertising—their youthful enthusiasm occasionally collid-
ing with the more conventional Marv Landes. Kelly as a vice
president had to do most of the battling with Landes and/or
Drinkwater.

Jerry Brooder was another young Turk, qualifying in spirit if
not in age. But the middle-management strength went beyond
the departments entrusted with selling Western and air travel to
the public; it embraced flight operations, legal, finance, reservations, maintenance, and accounting. Shatto, for example, thought
highly of Tony Favero; Stan was not one to take advice easily,
but he was listening when Art Kelly—at their very first meeting
in Denver, when Drinkwater offered Shatto a job—told him of
his high regard for Favero's abilities. Twenty years later, Favero
would be holding down Shatto's job as senior vice president of
operations.

Charles Fisher was in charge of flight schedules in 1955—he
still is, as a vice president, the industry's most experienced
scheduling executive. Soft-spoken, coolly efficient Norm Rose
was head of flight control—and still is, as an assistant vice president. Jack Slichter was director of passenger services—and is
now vice president of field management. Charles J. J. Cox was in
charge of accounting and taxation—and is now senior vice president of finance; he joined Western in 1951 after nearly twenty
years of accounting experience.

Peirce and Lynn, too, reached the vice presidential level. The
names on that crack middle-management team of the midfifties
are too numerous to list in full—names like Frank Vosepka, one
of the better nuts-and-bolts experts who was in charge of maintenance inspection; and Peter Wolf, director of communications,
who still runs communications as a vice president. These were
just some of the men who helped Terry Drinkwater transform
Western from an airline looking nostalgically back on a glorious
past into an aggressive present-day competitor.

No man, of course, could be president of an airline for some
twenty years and not make mistakes. Terry made his share, and
often they were beauts, yet there is an only too human tendency
to remember him more for the things he did wrong than for
what he did right. And sometimes he was criticized from the
vantage point of hindsight—for example, his ill-fated attempt to

eliminate all meal service while reducing fares laid an egg of which a mother dinosaur would have been proud. He and Jud Taylor had been the only ones who voted for it, TCD overruling the majority. At the time, however, the experiment made sense. Western was serving fifteen thousand meals a month at a cost of thirty-four thousand dollars—which was more than 5 per cent of total revenue. Drinkwater abolished in-flight meals after a survey showed that fewer than half the passengers were eating food for which all the passengers had paid. Today, "no frills" service is part of the airline industry.

Terry was supposed to be penurious, stingy, and overly cost-conscious to the extent of blocking progress under the guise of essential economy. Yet there was one area in which he refused to cut corners: safety. He was riding the jump seat in a DC-3 in 1947, flying out of Yellowstone Park from a short, grass-covered field with a large clump of trees at the end.

"What would happen if we lost an engine on takeoff?" he asked the captain.

"Mr. Drinkwater, we'd go right into those trees."

The next day, a teletype message went out: "Discontinue all service to Yellowstone Park until further notice." Service was not resumed until a new airport was constructed eighteen years later.

He was often accused of being dictatorial, but for many years he actually governed Western rather democratically. He seldom talked separately with his officers, preferring to call them together and thrash out problems as a group instead of unilaterally —the one exception being labor relations, in which he shared responsibility with Shatto. Until his corporate menopause of the sixties, Drinkwater usually was open not only to discussion but also to compromise, many times giving in partially or even wholly to proposals he himself opposed. The management team he forged was exceptionally well balanced, the firebrands and progressives like Kelly and Renda pitted against the conservatives such as Shatto and Landes—the result being decisions and policies that had taken into account divergent views.

Terry himself ran the gamut between reactionalism and radicalism, depending on what mood he was in, the status of WAL's current bank balance, and other factors that might or might not be apropos of the situation under discussion—in a sense, he was a kind of balance wheel between the liberal and conservative factions, usually siding with the latter but on occasion agreeing with the former. He was fiercely competitive, yet cautious when it came to battling the big boys. At least one WAL official still believes the real reason behind TCD's "We won't fly east of the Rockies" edict was his reluctance to butt heads against United, American, and TWA on east–west routes.

Renda, to some extent, shared that philosophy. He was one of the first WAL executives who talked to Drinkwater about expanding to the west—across the still-undeveloped North Pacific from Pacific Northwest cities. It was for this reason that Renda, early in 1950, urged that Western take over then-ailing Northwest Airlines.

"It just doesn't make sense to put a sick horse into a barn with a healthy stallion," Drinkwater argued, and the opportunity to merge with NWA went down the drain after Donald Nyrop became its president.

There were a lot of things right about Drinkwater's restrictive route policies, but there also were two chief weaknesses, and both stemmed from lack of foresight. First, Terry never anticipated the rapid growth of the local-service airlines that were steadily becoming regional carriers much like Western; they were turning into real competitors instead of harmless supplements in the air transportation industry. True, they were mere infants in the early fifties, looked upon by the trunk lines with amused tolerance, but they were expanding fast and beginning to seek longer-haul routes. Second was Drinkwater's failure to perceive soon enough the impact of the jets on distance, operating efficiency, economics, and ability to generate new traffic; neither, it must be admitted, did a number of other airline presidents, but Western was later than most in getting into the jet age. He persisted in scoffing at the jet long after it was apparent it represented a commercial aviation revolution, not just another airplane.

He was, in other words, a leader whose vision wore bifocals; he could be incredibly farsighted one day and dangerously nearsighted the next, qualities that were only too natural in a man of paradox, contrast, and unpredictability.

"In no other business," former CAB chairman Secor Brown once wrote, "does the character of the chief executive officer sift through to the customer in less diluted form than an airline president."

That certainly was true of Terrell Drinkwater; his image was Western's image for as long as he stayed in power. And in the midcentury years, it was a happy one—almost a period of euphoria, as Terry kept WAL small, content not to make the waves that come from reaching out for new territory, new marketing schemes, and new equipment. Once TCD had been talked out of ditching the Inland division, his period of contraction was over, but there was not much expansion, either. In 1950, only three cities were added to Western's system: a leg from Lethbridge to Edmonton in Canada, plus service to Brookings, South Dakota, and Mankato, Minnesota; WAL's routes at the time embraced forty-five cities in thirteen western states and Canada, with a total of just over five thousand route miles. The airline was small enough to require only four vice presidents: Shatto and Landes (who also were directors), Kelly and Sullivan; two decades later, Western was to have an executive vice president (Renda), five senior vice presidents, twenty-one vice presidents, five assistant vice presidents, and ten regional vice presidents—a total of forty-two.

The airline was carrying nearly seventeen hundred passengers daily—more than double the number Western carried in its first two years. It was small stuff compared to the Uniteds and Americans, but nobody was complaining; what with a 50 per cent increase in revenue passenger miles over 1949 and Western's participation in the Korean War airlift (using DC-4s), 1950's net profits reached $750,000. And Drinkwater relented in his opposition to expansion by permitting two new-route applications. One was minor, extending WAL's Imperial Valley route from Yuma to Phoenix—although entry into Phoenix itself was to prove vital in the future, when the fast-growing city became one of the nation's most lucrative airline markets.

The second seemed unimportant on paper, but it turned out to be a route case of enormous significance to Western—far more than Drinkwater himself realized when it was first proposed. It was to change WAL from a virtually exclusive north–south carrier to an east–west airline as well. It was to give Western a long-haul route that for years was the backbone and mainstay of the entire system—a skyway that turned out to be a gold mine. It linked the Inland division directly with the rest of the airline, ending forever Inland's status as an almost forgotten spur. It became known as the Casper cutoff case—and to a large extent, it was Jerry Brooder's baby.

The case had its origins in that previous Civil Aeronautics Board decision granting WAL a route between Rapid City and the Twin Cities. In simplest terms, the Casper cutoff was a 532-mile leg that closed the gap between Salt Lake City and Rapid City, providing an east–west route from California to Minnesota instead of the north–south routing via Great Falls. Casper was the focal point; it lay on a direct line between Salt Lake City and Rapid City running east–west, and it also was the center of Inland's old north–south route between Great Falls and Denver. The proposed cutoff linked Casper with Salt Lake City on the one hand and with Rapid City on the other.

Western already had been operating a Denver–Twin Cities route, but when it sold Route 68 to United, it also abolished a more direct California–Minnesota airway and hence skyrocketed the importance of the Casper cutoff. The latter's true value to Western was not to be established until the CAB granted the application nearly two years after Dom Renda filed it, but it did not take another two years for Drinkwater to realize why Renda and Brooder had considered the case absolutely vital to the airline's future. In the first year of operation, the direct Los Angeles–Twin Cities route brought in an additional $3 million in revenue, and this was long before WAL received nonstop authority between the two points. As of mid-1975, Western had grossed no less than $250 million from the route—in some years, it was virtually the only moneymaker on the entire system.

Drinkwater was later to call the Casper cutoff Western's salvation and perhaps the most important single route case in its history. But he didn't feel that way when it was first proposed by Brooder after the sale of Route 68. It was something Brooder had thought about long before he ever came to Western; he had discussed with Leferink and Landes the possibility of Inland filing for a Salt Lake City–Casper–Rapid City route when the war was over. After WAL absorbed Inland, Brooder continued to gnaw mentally on the idea of closing the Salt Lake City–Rapid City gap with a route running through Casper.

He began hammering away at Drinkwater and kept striking out—until the Route 68 sale opened the floodgates. His unexpected ally was Welch Pogue, who by chance had been talking to Mason Mallory, regional sales manager in the Twin Cities. Mallory, along with many other employees, was stunned when Drinkwater peddled Route 68—accepting Terry's "We had to amputate a leg to save the patient" explanation but still not liking the decision. He had a personal interest in the sale, because it wrecked the only major east–west route Western had.

Unaware that Brooder already had been trying to sell a Casper cutoff proposal to Drinkwater, Mallory had drawn up a rough sketch of the same plan. He showed his crude map to Welch Pogue, who was in Minnesota visiting an ailing brother. Pogue expressed interest and followed up by asking some questions of TCD. This resulted in Brooder's getting a call from TCD.

"Jerry, Welch Pogue and Tubby Burnham are in my office. Come on down—we'd like to talk to you."

Mystified, Brooder walked into the president's office. Drinkwater wasted no time. "Jerry, these fellas want to ask you something, and I hope you have the answer."

"Shoot," Brooder said.

"Jerry," Burnham said, "if you were in complete authority here, what would you do to improve Western Air Lines?"

Brooder didn't hesitate a second. "The first thing I'd do is file an application to link up Salt Lake City with Rapid City and give us a direct Los Angeles Twin Cities route."

"Why?" Burnham pressed.

"Because we're predominantly a north–south carrier, and very few airlines have been able to cut it without east–west routes."

"That sounds very interesting," Pogue smiled. "It's something the directors should decide, but I'd like to get together with you later today."

"I've got some maps to show you," Brooder said—not daring to risk a glance in Drinkwater's direction. He met Pogue in Renda's office that same day, and the three of them went over Brooder's proposed route maps. By this time, Drinkwater had been sold—he might have been able to turn down Brooder, but he couldn't fight at least two fifths of the Board of Directors.

"It's all yours, Jerry," Terry told him, "and you've got to see it through."

That order was easier given than carried out, for Brooder and Renda ran into heavy flak—from United, Northwest, and Frontier, all of them grasping the import of the Casper cutoff faster than Drinkwater had. It was Jerry's first major involvement with a major route case, and he worked closely with Renda's legal eagles. Jerry and Dom got along beautifully, each respecting the other's forte and jurisdiction. Brooder was a consummate lobbyist mostly because he never acted like one. With his snow-white hair, easy smile, informal manner, and disarming friendliness, he gave the impression that he had just climbed off a bus from Kansas and was ready to be sold the Washington Monument. His appearance, however, was about as misleading as a used-car salesman's promise. On one occasion, a Western official was standing near two lawyers outside a CAB hearing. Brooder was off to one side, conversing with a representative of a city seeking new service, and one of the lawyers glanced over in Jerry's direction.

"Who's the old goat with the white hair?" he inquired.

"That's Jerry Brooder of Western," the other lawyer told him.

"Looks harmless," the first attorney observed.

"Harmless? Listen, chum, by the time he gets through with that guy, he'll have his watch, wallet, and proxy."

It would be hard to find any Westerner, past or present, who would not assign the word "beloved" to Brooder. He seemed to get along with everybody, inside the airline and out, from Drinkwater to ship cleaners, senators to skycaps. Tony Favero got to know him very well when Jerry was cultivating new friends for Western around the Inland system; Tony learned that going to dinner with him was an obstacle course.

"If you visited Brooder in the winter at any place in Wyoming and the Dakotas," Favero reminisces, "you learned to wear heavy clothing when you walked with him from the hotel to the restaurant. He couldn't go ten feet without stopping to talk to somebody. Once we were going to eat in a place only two blocks away, and it took us 2½ hours to get there. I damned near froze to death."

Articulate and personable though he was, Brooder hated making speeches. A friend asked him why.

"Did you ever hear of anyone listening himself out of a job?" Jerry replied.

But he did a lot more talking than listening in the difficult Casper cutoff case. Drinkwater himself had inadvertently erected a serious obstacle, of which the Civil Aeronautics Board took due notice: In convincing the CAB that it should approve the Route 68 sale, he had assured the Board that Western had no aspirations east of the Rockies. Now Renda and his legal crew were faced with explaining the change in policy. In that task, he had plenty of help from Brooder and his plethora of contacts throughout the area involved.

Two such contacts were particularly helpful. President Truman had just named former Senator Chan Gurney of South Dakota to the CAB, and Gurney was an old friend of Jerry's. The other was Senator Joseph O'Mahoney of Wyoming, the same lawmaker who had given Al Adams such valuable support in the UAL-WAL merger battle. O'Mahoney, it seems, was still mad at United for pulling major facilities out of Cheyenne.

Brooder concentrated heavily on garnering Pentagon support; the Korean War was in full swing and the cutoff would mean faster, more efficient movement of supplies and personnel from the network of military bases scattered throughout many of the states Western served.

"I wore out a pair of shoes in the Pentagon making sure nobody dropped the ball," Brooder recounts. "The first thing we had to do is get the Pentagon to become a party in the proceeding—it would be the first time any government department had intervened in a CAB case. We lined up endorsements from the Air Force Base in Rapid City, from the Eighth Air Force in Omaha, and from Hill Air Force Base at Ogden, Utah, among others. Hill was the main support base for the Strategic Air Command base at Rapid City."

The initial victory came when the Department of Defense officially intervened as a party to the proceeding, and named the Air Force as its representative. But this didn't happen without some rugged behind-the-scenes maneuvering. Brooder at one point got a call from a Pentagon official who told him the Pentagon would stay neutral.

"We've been ordered to discontinue any further efforts to intervene in the case, Jerry," he said unhappily. "We're not going to file any brief supporting Western."

Brooder shot over to O'Mahoney's office to report this dire development.

O'Mahoney promptly picked up a phone and put in a call to Thomas Finletter, Secretary of the Air Force. O'Mahoney mentioned that his appropriations subcommittee had just voted the funds Finletter had sought; the rest of the conversation went something like this:

O'Mahoney: "By the way, I've just heard something that disturbs me deeply. I understand the Defense Department has decided not to intervene in that Western application. The route they want goes right through my state, and it means a great deal to me."

Finletter: "I'll call you back in five minutes."

He did.

"Senator, everything has been straightened out. DOD will file a brief and participate in oral argument supporting Western."

Brooder's *modus operandi* was not only effective but also completely above board. "Not a single penny ever changed hands," Jerry points out, "and that's the way Drinkwater wanted it in all our dealings with Washington."

"If you had to single out one man largely responsible for winning," Renda says, "it would have to be Brooder."

And with this victory came new maturity for WAL—along with new challenges and new responsibilities. Like a ballplayer suddenly promoted from the minors to the majors, Western had to grow up in a relative hurry. It is to Drinkwater's lasting credit that he recognized this fact of life even though it meant the collapse of his "constructive contraction" policy and made somewhat obsolete the slogan he loved so much: "The Best in the West." Now it had to be more than that.

Drinkwater wasn't the only one who knew Western's world was changing as its borders expanded. Employees did, too. Gone were the days of incredible penny-pinching—TCD never wavered from his cost-conscious creed, but expansion meant expenditures, too. Some—not all, but some—of the old informality of the flight crews had to be relegated to certain items one talked about with fond memories but that were not to be repeated. Like the day Captain Penny Penrose, a diminutive pilot built like Mickey Rooney but who flew like Lindbergh, surreptitiously attached a sanitary napkin to the back of stewardess Jessie Bathgates' uniform skirt; she served lunch that way. It was almost symbolic that Jessie assumed a far more dignified role in the "new Western"—she was named chief stewardess, and proved to be a tough supervisor. With increased discipline went the byproduct of better service. It might be fun to recall, as that 1946 Convair report on Western's labor situation had pointed out, the proclivity of some girls to serve the pilots their meals ahead of the passengers (or, when insufficient meals were boarded, serve the crew at the expense of some passengers), but now such favors were to be frowned upon.

The pilots themselves had to tone down a bit, although Western's flight crews included enough characters to occasionally strain the airline's forthcoming mantle of respectability. Penrose, as usual, was a prime offender. He was flying a DC-4 trip and was suffering the pangs of thirst of prospectors crossing Death Valley on foot. On the DC-4, the only source of drinking water was by the galley in the rear of the plane; Penrose made four round trips between the flight deck and the galley, each time carrying a water-filled paper cup back with him. After the fourth time, a passenger stopped him.

"Captain," he asked politely, "would you mind telling me why you're bringing all those Dixie cups up front?"

"The cockpit's on fire," Penny explained.

Arlie Gillespie, who is still flying as a Western captain, became a devoted television fan in the days when television was something of a novelty. He was overjoyed to find that one of the hotels housing Western crews on layovers had installed TV sets in its rooms. As is the custom, the hotel had blocked out certain rooms for WAL pilots, and Gillespie drew Room 903 on every layover. On his first stop, the TV set wasn't working, so he reported the malfunction to the desk clerk. The next time he was assigned Room 903, the same set—also not working. He reported it again. Ditto the third time. Also the fourth time. On his last trip of the month, Gillespie walked into Room 903, turned on the set, and once more couldn't get a picture. He unplugged it, opened a window, and threw the set out, into an empty courtyard nine stories below. Then he picked up the phone and rang the desk clerk.

"This is Captain Gillespie in 903," he said pleasantly. "There's no TV set in my room."

Gillespie's ordeal brings to mind another pilot complaint that went down in whatever historical repository pilot complaints are filed in. It concerned the DC-4, a sturdy and reliable airplane but cursed with the fact that no two DC-4s ever built flew exactly alike. One would handle like a baby carriage and another would have the aerodynamic qualities of a cast-iron bathtub. A Western captain drew one of the latter breed, and upon landing at Salt Lake City, in the section of the aircraft log normally devoted to precise technical descriptions of aircraft irregularities, he wrote:

"Airplane flies funny."

Off he went to his layover and reported to the airport the next morning for the return flight in the same plane. One of the first things he did was check the mechanical writeup log to see if his beef had been corrected. Next to his "Airplane flies funny," a mechanic had written:

"You mean funny ha-ha or funny peculiar?"

Drinkwater, with his penchant for assigning nicknames to his officers, had a counterpart in the pilot ranks. That was Jimmy Dunn, still flying for WAL, who tagged a goodly proportion of his fellow airmen with sobriquets they never could get rid of. There was "Shaky Jake," for example, pinned on a captain who was good at his job but somehow managed to give the impression (fortunately not to the passengers) that every flight was a suicide mission. A pilot who had a terminal case of dandruff was henceforth known to his comrades as "Flaky." George Ryan acquired the name "Knuckles" after he decked another captain whom he had overheard criticizing one of Ryan's landings.

Ryan quite possibly might have been the inspiration for Disney's "Grumpy" in *Snow White*. He insisted that every cockpit was too warm, announcing this verdict by yelling the single word: "Hot!" The copilot or, later, the flight engineer would have to turn up the cooling system. Ryan would sit there in his shirt sleeves while everyone else froze. A stewardess once entered the cockpit and found the copilot wearing his jacket, overcoat, and a blanket.

Air traffic controllers knew Ryan as well as did his fellow Western pilots. George became known for frequently rejecting clearances or vectors—"I refuse to assept [his own pronunciation of accept] that clearance," he'd tell ATC. George never bid anything but Los Angeles–San Francisco–Seattle, resisting any new route. Hence his voice became so familiar to controllers that the tower would routinely advise the en route center, "Here comes George." The center, in turn, would pass the word to the next center along the route, "George is leaving."

One of Ryan's idiosyncrasies was a habit of never really listening to a checklist; so long as he heard *some* answer, that was all he wanted. Ryan would call out an item like "temp valves," and the copilot would respond, "full cold." But when pilots began to suspect that George wasn't paying much attention to the responses, one first officer decided to prove this growing suspicion. Ryan reached the line "temp valves" and called it out.

"They've fallen off," the copilot said.

Ryan went right on with the rest of the checklist.

At least he wasn't actually deaf—it was the firm tone of the voice he heard, not the actual words. Western had another colorful pilot who really was hard of hearing—Ken Turner, a former Inland captain, who always wore a beret in the cockpit.

"A real iron ass when he was flying," Captain Jack Keyes recalls. "He was so opinionated that if you told him it was a nice day, he'd argue that it was raining. But he had a heart the size of a DC-10 engine. We had a stewardess named Bonnie Bueller who lost an arm and a leg in a boating accident. It took us a long time to find out that Turner had helped pay a lot of her medical bills."

Like all airlines, Western's pilot roster included a handful of captains to whom the cockpit was a stage and the cabin PA an instrument for the amusement and edification of passengers. The DC-3 was the first airliner to have cockpit-cabin communications, but WAL didn't go in for this gadget until the Convair 240 came along. Few pilots really enjoy using the PA, Western's included, but there are noticeable exceptions—among them Jim Andrews, a sharp, exceptionally skilled WAL veteran who loves making a PA announcement almost as much as he loves flying.

Andrews, who was awarded the Dunn-composed nickname of "Jimmy Jet" early in the jet age, became hooked on the PA back in his piston-engine days. Jimmy, it must be admitted, is widely admired by passengers for his in-flight messages and equally admired by his fellow airmen—but *not* for his in-flight messages. Some of his PA's were so syrupy that his copilots would wince—like the time he confided to a planeload of passengers, "In seat 4B is my wife, and we're going to have a baby." This was delivered in a tone of voice that would have made Liberace sound like a Marine drill instructor. The copilots sometimes would sabotage him; when he'd ask for the PA, the copilot would hand him the mike with one hand and pull out the plug with the other. Andrews would talk earnestly for several minutes into the dead mike. He didn't find out what his first officers were doing to him until one day a stewardess came up to the cockpit with coffee, and Jimmy asked her, "How did you like my announcement?"

"What announcement?" she asked.

In 1951, the airline celebrated its twenty-fifth anniversary, and with the formal observance came the realization of how far Western had come—and how far it still was to go. On April 17, 1951, the fleet included 10 Convairs, 10 DC-3s, and 5 DC-4s—manned, maintained, promoted, and supported by nearly 1,500 employees. Profits for calendar '51 were to hit $1.2 million, while the company used $2.5 million from a newly granted $8 million bank credit to pay off the RFC loan in full. The number of stockholders was up to 5,000 and would shortly soar to more than 6,500 as Western sold an additional 169,000 shares of capital stock, netting almost $1.8 million. By the fall of 1951, WAL went off federal subsidy for the first time in its history, and stockholders were informed at the close of the year that they would be receiving their first dividend in 15 years.

The only cloud in that Silver Anniversary year was a 15-day walkout by the Air Carrier Mechanics' Union, which subsequently was ousted by the employees, who voted for the Teamsters in the collective bargaining representation election. The strike, Western's first, was not much of a success, for the airline had to cancel only 5 per cent of its flights over the two weeks it lasted. One reason for its ineffectiveness was Drinkwater's reportedly passing the word that if it continued, he would sell all ten Convairs and slash the mechanics' force correspondingly. Whether he was serious will never be known, but even before the strike was over, TCD had taken off in the opposite direction.

He ordered, at a cost of $6 million, five brand-new Douglas DC-6Bs—four-engine giants that more than anything else symbolized the rebirth of America's senior airline.

CHAPTER THIRTEEN

"The Only Way to Fly"

The DC-6B was the personal and carefully considered selection of Stan Shatto—the first of many aircraft-equipment decisions he would make for Western.

In this area, along with maintenance, he had few equals. Drinkwater trusted his judgment implicitly and with good reason; Shatto's technical competence was unquestioned and his engineering instincts unerring. It was even more remarkable considering the fact that he virtually was self-taught in the field of aeronautical engineering—a bottomless well of knowledge he had dug himself without the books, lectures, and theories that are the inherent tools of formal education.

He was strictly a nuts-and-bolts man who cared little about either the internal or external aesthetics of an airliner—to Stan, choosing a transport plane because it looked pretty was like selecting a wife for solely the same reason.

WAL had only three choices in the way of four-engine pressurized equipment: the DC-6, the Constellation, and the DC-6B. The first already had acquired a black eye when it had to be grounded for several months to correct a flaw in its fuel transfer system, and the Connie also had gone through a grounding ordeal after two fatal crashes disclosed major electrical troubles. This left the DC-6B, Shatto's choice even before he looked at another airplane. Basically it was a modernized, modified DC-6 with a stronger structure and vastly improved engines.

"It was an honest, straightforward, basically sound piece of machinery," Shatto says. "We talked to Lockheed because they were a Southern California company, but my mind was made up beforehand. Our relations with Douglas were so good that we could have ordered the DC-6B with a phone call. For example, some airlines keep fifteen or twenty inspectors around an aircraft manufacturer's plant, looking over shoulders—for some reason they think they have to have people standing around telling 'em how to build airplanes. I never kept a guy at Douglas, nor later at Lockheed or Boeing. I figured it was their responsibility, and the only time I'd butt in was to check on some specific problem."

This *laissez-faire* philosophy Shatto extended to interior design. Shatto believed the airframe companies had perfectly capable designers and decorators or could call on consultant help if necessary; he refused to hire any outsider to design the interior of a WAL aircraft, relying almost entirely on the manufacturer. Shatto had veto power but seldom exercised it—he was more concerned with the number of seats than with how the seats looked. In that respect, he was very much like another rugged individualist of the industry—Eddie Rickenbacker. Mike Simpson, a now-retired WAL station manager, remembers visiting the Douglas plant one day to see Western's DC-6Bs on the assembly line and also to inspect the cabin mockup. Also present was Rickenbacker, who was trying to decide whether to buy the DC-6B for Eastern.

Douglas had an interior designer, a woman, who was showing Simpson and the Eastern president various seat upholstering colors and fabrics.

"Western's considering this very attractive cowhide, to provide a western motif," she said. "What color and fabric do you think you'd like for Eastern, Mr. Rickenbacker?"

Rickenbacker frowned. "Miss, I really don't give a damn what you put on airplane seats except fannies."

Shatto wasn't quite that Spartan-minded, but he came close. Yet if he cared little about aircraft decor, officers like Art Kelly did—not only as it applied to interior appearance but also in the far more personal realm of service and passenger satisfaction. Both Kelly and Landes regarded the DC-6B as a competitive challenge, aimed squarely at United's dominance in the Los Angeles-Seattle market. Operating the sturdy, reliable, but rather prosaic twin-engine Convairs against UAL's DC-6s, Western

had less than 25 per cent of that market. The DC-6B would be a
superior airplane, but not one passenger out of a thousand could
have told a DC-6 from a DC-6B. Besides, United also was ordering DC-6Bs, and if they were assigned to the Seattle route,
WAL's minor competitive advantage in aircraft would dissipate.
Although Shatto had indeed chosen a superb airplane, one that
would serve Western faithfully and efficiently for more than a
decade, it was not revolutionary in concept and performance—as
the jets would be. Comfort and service are the key factors in the
airline industry, with equipment diminishing in importance even
as each carrier usually is forced to match the competition's new
aircraft. Thus, while Western's service, sales, and advertising
officials welcomed the DC-6B, they did not regard it as a "Beat
United" millennium. They wanted something different, something daring, something unique in the form of in-flight luxury.

They got it.

Champagne flights.

The concept was the product of several men, and it evolved
from a handful of tentative ideas, suggestions, and schemes that
materialized into a concrete program. It seems hard to believe in
these days, when complimentary champagne is almost as much
of an airline staple as coffee, but in the fifties serving champagne
was not only unconventional but practically unheard of. TWA
carried champagne on transcontinental flights but served it only
on request—it was bulky, hard to store, and difficult to chill. Several European airlines had been serving it for years and, as a
matter of historical fact, this practice was one of the factors involved in its adoption by Western.

In 1953, around the time WAL was preparing to put the DC-
6B into service, Bert Lynn and his wife were returning from
Europe on SAS, and WAL's director of advertising and public
relations (the two functions were then a single department) was
duly impressed with the SAS meal service. While the Lynns were
enjoying dinner, a stewardess brought them a split of champagne
with a note from the captain, welcoming them aboard. Bert—
who never before had been offered champagne on a flight—
thought about it all the way back to the United States. He
brought up his experience at a staff meeting at which various
ideas for improving meal and beverage service were discussed,

and Dick Ensign—then director of in-flight service under Marv Landes—sent Landes a memo proposing not only champagne but also a good steak dinner and perhaps special favors for women passengers. Kelly provided enthusiastic support but also a warning that the plan faced two major obstacles: one named Landes and the other named Drinkwater. Landes was as cost-conscious in his own field as Shatto was in his; Drinkwater, although definitely no teetotaler, was opposed to serving alcohol in any form on an airpane—a view that he shared, interestingly enough, with W. A. Patterson. The Three Musketeers of market-ing, advertising, and in-flight service got by Landes without too much trouble, but Drinkwater was unyielding—up to a point. In the end, it was Landes whose influence with Terry as far as this one issue was concerned probably exceeded Kelly's; TCD ap-parently took the attitude that if someone as conservative as Landes liked the idea, it couldn't be all bad.

Another factor in Drinkwater's change of heart was an inci-dent that occurred during a directors' meeting in Seattle. A char-tered bus was taking officers and directors sightseeing, and Landes, at the suggestion of Kelly, had loaded the bus with chilled champagne. Wearing an improvised badge around his neck like a sommelier, Marv broke out the bubbled beverage and started popping corks. If Western's stewardesses had been assigned Landes as an instructor in gracious cabin service, cham-pagne flights never would have gotten off the ground; when he opened the first bottle, the contents sprayed all over a couple of directors.

But the experiment was a success. Director Harry Volk said in a voice loud enough for Drinkwater to hear, "This is a great idea—it's too bad you can get champagne on a bus and not on an air-plane."

From that time on, Terry began wavering in his opposition—at least he did not stay as adamant on the subject as Patterson, who refused to serve alcoholic drinks on United flights until a year after everyone else was doing it. Pat always denounced the practice as one that turned stewardesses into "glorified cocktail waitresses," but eventually pressure from the public forced him into adopting the practice. Drinkwater himself had been con-cerned about adverse reaction from a certain portion of the public—namely the Mormon Church. He was horrified when *Time* ran a story on Western's champagne flights; normally he loved all favorable publicity about his airline, but this article— largely pegged to Dick Ensign's role in planning the new service —started out: "A young Mormon boy is the biggest purchaser of California champagne in the world."

TCD really did have a lot of respect for Mormonism. Mormon elder George Albert Smith was on Western's Board until he died, and as long as he served, Drinkwater treated him with deference and affection. At one Board meeting, Terry anounced that in re- spect to Elder Smith, the directors would have to refrain from smoking and swearing. It was not only quite a bit to ask of the Board but somewhat of a burden on Drinkwater himself, whose profanity was uninhibited and who smoked a pipe or cigar at about the same frequency with which he breathed. At the end of the meeting, Smith came up to Terry and put his arm around him.

"Brother Drinkwater," he said softly to the Scotch-Presby- terian president of Western, "let us not cut more than we can harvest."

Drinkwater did insist that if Western was to serve champagne as wine, it would be only with meals and never as a predinner or postdinner cocktail. His early rather halfhearted approval caused some concern, and it was decided that free champagne wasn't enough—what was needed was a total package embodying several new service gimmicks. This larger concept was turned over to Ensign, who already had proposed serving steak with the champagne. Ensign, at Landes' request, also had been the one who came up with the idea of improving meal service on forty-four-passenger Convairs which had only one stewardess per trip. Ensign had accomplished this by putting everything on a prepackaged tray except the hot entrée—salad, butter, bread, wrapped silverware, and beverage cup were boarded on trays ready to serve as soon as the entrée was added.

Dick adopted this galley organization for the DC-6B. To this eminently practical arrangement he added such items as cigars for the men, orchids for the ladies, and, eventually, free perfume. The latter was the result of a visit Ensign got from Hercules Els- bach, president of an importing firm. Elsbach was a character in his own right—Ensign describes him as "a kind of lovable guy, the type that the first time you see him you want to take him by the hand and lead him across the street." But he was sharp, a savvy businessman with ideas, and one of the ideas he had was to popularize a new brand of perfume called Carnet de Bal by handing out small samples to airline passengers.

He had flown champagne flights and knew they were a huge hit. Now he came to Ensign with a proposition.

"If you'll put our perfume on your champagne flights," he suggested, "we'll give you the perfume for just the tax on each bottle—ten cents."

Ensign took him right down to Landes.

"Is the perfume any good?" Marv asked in the tone of a Prohibition era customer inquiring of a bootlegger whether his whiskey was right off the boat.

"Smell it yourself," Elsbach said. He laid a bottle down on Landes' desk—but with such a proud flourish that the bottle broke. Landes could only watch as the scented liquid ate the varnish right off the beautiful wood finish.

"Well," said the unperturbed Elsbach, flicking cigarette ashes over his well-tailored suit, "they're not gonna drink the stuff."

Despite the miniature crater on his mahogany desk, Landes agreed that while Carnet de Bal might not make it as a furniture polish, the scent was intriguing and Elsbach's offer tempting. The perfume was added to the package—a tenth of an ounce wrapped in a tiny green and gold box with a tag reading, "Created in France especially for Champagne Flights."

This successful promotion ran for four years, Elsbach finally calling a halt after the manufacturer advised him that Carnet de Bal sales had increased so much they either had to stop supplying Western or build a new factory.

Champagne service started out under the registered name "Californians," but passengers started asking for reservations on "those champagne flights." When this got back to Kelly, he suggested using the latter as the official name, and Drinkwater—by now an avowed convert—readily agreed. His earlier doubts as to the wisdom of serving alcoholic beverages had evaporated completely. When the service began, TCD made it a point to ask passengers what they thought of the idea.

"A lot of them were first-time fliers," he recounted later. "They liked champagne for three reasons: They thought it was stronger than it really is, they considered it mildly wicked, and it relaxed them."

His wholehearted acceptance, however, was preceded by a certain amount of procrastination. Champagne flights were inaugurated on June 1, 1954, but Drinkwater didn't give the final green light until a week before they were scheduled to begin. The delay wasn't entirely the result of TCD's lingering doubts, not by a long shot; the task of picking the brand of champagne, for example, assumed the proportions of needlepointing a rug for a football field. Drinkwater had given Landes strict orders not to spend any more than was absolutely necessary, an edict that Art Kelly viewed with great apprehension—he feared that cheap, inferior champagne would queer the whole project.

Landes contacted several wineries. One quoted him forty dollars a case, another thirty-six dollars. The lowest price was thirty-two dollars—a figure that Marv knew would launch Drinkwater into orbit. Landes finally ended up in San Francisco, where he met with Larry Solari, vice president and general manager of Italian Swiss Colony, which was a small winery at the time and wasn't doing much advertising. Landes explained the situation.

"I've got a lot of opposition to champagne," he added. "What I need is a good price for ammunition. It'll be first-class service, and we'll mention where the champagne comes from. Can you help us?"

Solari talked to his advertising manager and came back to tell Landes, "we'll let you have our champagne for twenty dollars a case."

Marv accepted the offer right on the spot and returned to Los Angeles with the good news. Drinkwater was pleased but Kelly was worried.

"We can't use that brand," he protested.

"Why not?" Landes demanded.

"We have to have a name brand—like Paul Masson."

"Art, that costs forty-eight dollars a case."

"It'll be worth it," Kelly insisted.

The debate raged for days, Drinkwater telling the contestants, "Settle the damned argument yourselves." One Friday afternoon, several officers held a taste test involving several bottles of top-name champagnes and a bottle of Italian Swiss Colony. The glasses were coded by number, with only Ensign knowing which glass contained which brand.

Italian Swiss Colony received six out of eight votes. Kelly was one of the six, and announced his temporary retirement as a connoisseur. The winning brand was chosen on the basis of having the widest appeal to the greatest number of people—it was dry, and for an inexpensive champagne very consistent.

Brand selection didn't end the various headaches of the man in charge of packaging: Ensign. But he had the resilience of youth, the uninhibited enthusiasm of a born promoter, and the deviousness of a con artist. For years he hoodwinked Marv Landes with a simple but highly effective device for circumventing Marv's tight-fisted budget controls. Landes would announce at budget-planning time that he was going to crack down on capital expenditures, Ensign nodding in pious agreement. Each year, Dick inserted into his budget an item for some two hundred beverage jugs costing seventy-three dollars apiece—not only expecting Landes to eliminate it but actually counting on it. Landes never failed him; his angry repudiation of Ensign's annual demand for fifteen thousand dollars' worth of beverage jugs came as regularly as spring follows winter. Ensign would grumble, complain, and curse publicly at Marv's heavy-handed parsimony, and privately rejoice; Landes loved slashing fifteen thousand dollars from Ensign's budget, and Ensign was left free to spend the rest of his untouched funds on items he really needed.

The biggest problem Western faced in stepping up both the quality and the quantity of in-flight meals was the time element. The steak-and-champagne service was followed quickly by other innovations—all of them involving relatively short-haul DC-6B flights. This meant overworking the stewardesses, who reacted normally and predictably—they beefed, loud and long, and with considerable justification. The original serving time between Los Angeles and San Francisco, for example, was thirteen minutes longer than the scheduled flight time. Some of the girls would come off trips in tears. Stewardess supervisors and even company officials were assigned to help them on the first champagne flights, but this was like trying to plug a breaking dam with a cork.

The principal bottleneck was the champagne itself. It took too long to open and serve, and Ensign agreed that somehow they had to save up to twenty-three minutes of serving time with a full load. One partial solution was to open two thirds of the bottles before the flight left the ramp—against the advice of the champagne supplier, who argued that the bubbles and spark would be lost. Ensign said, "The hell with that—let's try it anyway." They did, and it worked.

Corks were another problem—the stewardesses were trying to extract them too fast, and they were breaking. Ensign asked the supplier to develop a plastic cap, which some winery officials said was impossible. They were wrong—a plastic cap was perfected and quickly, inasmuch as Western was building up volume to seventy cases a day. The plastic cap not only cut seven minutes off the serving time but also reduced the price per case. The subsequent use of screw-on caps and the simple practice of returning empty bottles to Swiss Colony dropped the price to seventeen dollars—Drinkwater once remarked that "we're paying less for champagne than we do for our coffee."

Ensign had another time-saving idea: Fill twelve glasses at a time on a serving tray in the gallery, instead of pouring the champagne individually at each seat. It saved time, but the technique required depth perception as well as speed, and too much of the bubbly stuff was spilled and wasted. Ensign decided to serve the drinks after table linen had been placed down.

Problems still remained. Ensign began to make time-motion studies of the in-flight service. He describes the reasoning behind this unique (for the airline industry) experiment better than anyone else, inasmuch as he was one of those holding stopwatches on the flight attendants:

"We had a sixty-six-passenger DC-6B, so one second saved per passenger added up to more than a full minute. Our studies showed that we had to cut from twenty to twenty-five minutes off the serving time—we were thirteen minutes too long on a full plane, and we needed those thirteen minutes plus some extra time for cleaning up before landing. We also had to come up with procedures that would work for everybody, because the girls worked at different speeds—some were fast and some were slow, with most of them in between.

"After we cut seven minutes from champagne service, we went next to the trays on which we placed the meals before they were carried to the passengers. The preboarding system of preparing the trays with everything except the entrée worked as well on the DC-6B as it did on the Convair. But the time-motion studies showed us other ways we could save precious seconds—each minor in itself yet adding up not to seconds but minutes. For example, we started out having the girls place menu cards in the casserole well. It took one second for a stewardess to remove the card from the well and put it against a condiment cup so she could fill the well with the hot entrée. We saved that one second by having them hand out the menus at the same time they laid out the table linen. We finally got it down to the point where we could serve a full meal to a full plane in one hour and still have enough time to stow everything away before landing."

(Ensign's time-motion experiments won him industrywide recognition, Pan Am eventually hiring him away from WAL in 1971; he returned in 1975 as senior vice president of marketing when Phil Peirce retired.)

Several champagne flight decisions had to be made literally at the last minute, with only one week between final approval and inauguration of service. Ensign had ordered full-size champagne glasses, and then ran into a minor problem: There was only one-eighth-inch clearance between the top of the glass and the base of the galley. He sent assistants fanning throughout Los Angeles to find a hasty substitute, and they finally came back with thirty-six cases of sherbet glasses—the entire supply in the Los Angeles area.

Champagne flight service was improved and expanded as the years went on. Ensign became intrigued with something he read about people tasting with their eyes before they taste with their lips. The outcome, in Ensign's words, was "dishware designed so as you looked at a plate, it actually was tilted toward you—one side was about a quarter of an inch higher than the other."

"It was the little things," Ensign points out. "Like an idea to put a buttonhole in each napkin so male passengers could hook it to their shirts instead of stuffing it inside the shirt or putting it on their laps, where it offered almost no protection. I don't remember the source of the quote, but someone called it 'the first improvement in napkins in two thousand years.' It all stemmed from a remark Kelly had made about airplane napkins being almost useless for keeping ties clean."

For Kelly, the youngest of the vice presidents, champagne flights vindicated his belief in more aggressive marketing. He was well liked by the older officers but not always listened to.

"Twenty per cent of my time in heading the marketing division from 1949 on was spent in selling our ideas not to the public, but to the company," he recalls. "It could be a frustrating and exhausting experience."

Fighting with Landes was bad enough—and they fought frequently.

"Everything Kelly comes up with costs money," Marv kept complaining. But Landes could be a model of co-operation compared with Drinkwater, particularly in the gestation stages of a new project. Once Terry was sold, his support was all-out, but selling him was like trying to dance on quicksand. He was willing to listen to new ideas, but he was hard-nosed about cost; any project was suspect unless it could be proved it was potentially profitable enough to justify spending money on it. Once convinced, it was the breaking of a logjam—Drinkwater's backing could be as wholehearted as his opposition. From the day he suddenly walked into Landes' office and announced, "Okay—let's serve champagne," Drinkwater pushed as hard for its success as anyone else.

TCD firmly believed the airline could spend more on passenger service if they didn't waste so much in other areas—a criticism with some validity. For example, he tried hard to convince Patterson and other airline officials that all the carriers serving Los Angeles should establish a central ticketing office instead of operating individual ticket locations; he considered the duplicated facilities a "horrendous" waste of money. Long before the industry adopted "capacity agreements"—pacts under which the airlines voluntarily reduced schedules in certain markets to meet actual demand—Drinkwater proposed about the same thing between Los Angeles and San Francisco. He wanted Western and

United to stagger their flights over the route to avoid the wasteful competition of overscheduling in peak traffic hours. United wouldn't go along.

Because Western was strictly a regional carrier, lacking the profitable long-haul routes of the bigger trunks, Drinkwater had to run a close-to-the-vest operation, and this was a logical explanation for what seemed to many his hidebound reaction to new service proposals on which he had to spend money. Terry was conservative rather than reactionary; more cautious than nearsighted. He said "maybe" more than "no," and if he was not wildly receptive to new ideas, he was not averse to discussing them—and he could be talked into accepting some.

If champagne flights had flopped, Drinkwater's inherent conservatism probably would have been encased in solid concrete. Fortunately for his young Turks, it was a bell-ringing triumph. Service started with one daily Los Angeles–Seattle round trip, with stops at San Francisco and Portland. The demand was so great that a second trip was added, and then more until Western actually pulled up even with United in market penetration, even with fewer flights.

In the early stages of the fierce competition, UAL tried to introduce a champagne service of its own, but it was a matter of either going all-out to match the champagne flights or making a halfhearted attempt, which had to fail. After a couple of abortive efforts, UAL abandoned the idea. One of Ensign's friends boarded a United flight to Seattle one evening and observed to the stewardess that they had stopped serving champagne.

"Yes, sir," she replied. "It just didn't work out."

"Western's still doing it," he reminded her.

"Well, they hire younger stewardesses," she explained.

Everyone loved the new DC-6B, but it was obvious it had played virtually no role in public acceptance of the champagne flights; it was the service, not the airplane, and Terry was not blind.

He knew he lacked the inherent bent for promotion possessed by men like Kelly, Lynn, and Ensign, yet he could sense a need for innovation and experiment as acutely as anyone else. He was more instigator than innovator, and this was to serve Western well. After the champagne flights were winging their way into impressive profits, he returned from a brief visit to Las Vegas and popped into Ensign's office.

"As long as you're trying to develop service that's new and creative," he said in his high-pitched voice, "why don't you go over to Vegas and see what one of the hotels is doing? They've got a breakfast up there with a hell of a variety of foods. I was wondering if there's any way we could do that on an airplane."

Ensign, knowing that airline breakfasts stand at the foot of the totem pole in originality, flew to Vegas and went to the hotel that Drinkwater had mentioned. He saw immediately why Terry had been impressed. It was, in effect, an excellent smorgasbord, with about twenty-five different kinds of foods, including eight or nine choices of meat. Ensign went back to Los Angeles and huddled immediately with Landes—who was intrigued but added the inevitable, "Make damned sure it doesn't cost too much."

This was the origin of a service that became a Western hallmark: the "Hunt Breakfast." It is generally accepted that no airline has ever surpassed it, although a lot have tried, and the fact that WAL developed it in the DC-6B days made its status even more remarkable. Ensign started out with the major task of creating a mobile smorgasbord, a means of displaying the various culinary choices to more than sixty passengers confined to their seats. The only way was to develop some kind of cart service. The British were using something called a pram, for serving different kinds of sauces, but it wasn't really a cart, and it was too small for what Ensign had in mind.

In the end he designed his own—unique enough for him to obtain a patent on it, and safe enough to resolve the objections Ensign knew the then-new Federal Aviation Agency would raise to anything that could become an unguided missile in turbulence or a crash. Five different FAA inspectors examined Western's cart and couldn't find anything hazardous about it; the secret was the way it could be locked under a seat.

As it finally evolved, the Hunt Breakfast featured three choices of meat—steak, ham, and sausage—heated in chafing dishes aboard the cart, plus the usual eggs and three different kinds of pastries. The final touch was a tape recorder attached to the bottom of the cart. Just before the stewardesses began serving, the tape recorder would be turned on. Ensign recalls with great relish the first few times they tried the recorder before a planeload of passengers "wondering what the hell was going on."

What they heard were the strident notes of a bugle call sounding the hunting charge, followed by the thunder of hoofbeats. To top all this off, the stewardesses wore bowler hats and bright red "weskits." Unfortunately, the FAA grounded the tape recorders because of fear that they might have some detrimental effect on navigation instruments, but while they lasted, the bugle calls achieved the impossible: They put sleepy, often grouchy passengers in a happy, anticipative frame of mind and made the meal itself that much more enjoyable.

"It had a kind of spark, of pizzazz, that you don't usually find on airlines," Ensign relates with pride.

The Hunt Breakfast wasn't the only successful project Drinkwater initiated. He called Art Kelly into his office one day in 1954 and announced, "I got an idea"—the line he always used on such occasions.

"Why don't we take our stewardess graduation ceremonies into the various cities on the system?" he continued. "We could have the local businessmen, civic officials, newspaper editors—people like that—sponsor each girl. They'd graduate as individuals instead of one big, nameless group. What do you think, Art?"

"I think it's a hell of an idea," Kelly declared. "I'll talk to Dick Ensign about it."

Ensign's reaction was on the cautious side, but there was something about TCD's idea that made Kelly sense the possibilities. What normally would be a routine ceremony could be used to build community good will—something of which no airline ever has an oversupply.

"Let's try it out in San Francisco with the next graduating class," he told Ensign. "If it'll work there, it'll work anywhere."

Kelly's hunch that Drinkwater was right proved to be on target. The graduation ceremony in supposedly blasé San Francisco was a triumph, and subsequent graduations in the smaller cities were even more successful. Idaho Falls turned out the high school band to welcome the girls when they arrived, for example, and in Cheyenne, Wyoming, the governor was present. The format was informal but dignified; as each stewardess stepped forward to receive her wings, a company official described her background and interests. The sponsor then congratulated her, presented the diploma, and pinned on her wings. Each sponsor was made an honorary WAL stewardess, giving him an additional sense of participation in an event that means so much to the fledgling stewardesses themselves.

Flight attendant graduations at every airline produce enough tears to fill the cargo bins of a 747, but the lacrymose output at Western's would satisfy a dozen soap-opera producers. Mostly it is the presence of the so-call sponsors; they seem to bring a reminder of home, a touch of parental pride, an aura of individuality to what normally is an exciting but rather impersonal and stereotyped ceremony.

And, in a way, the idea typified Drinkwater. It was that paternalistic, father-image side of him, sentimentality poking its way through the layers of invective, toughness, and temper.

Champagne flights and Hunt Breakfasts were among the many developments and achievements that helped make the 1952–58 period one of the happiest and most successful in Western's history. There were some jarring notes, of course—personal as well as corporate. If these were glory days for the airline, they were sad ones for a man who loved WAL as he would a creature of flesh and blood: Fred Kelly I.

He had more than a tricky heart; his health had deteriorated farther when a slipped disc required major surgery, and Kelly became not only restless but also discouraged. He finally decided that a change in scenery might help. He took a leave of absence in mid-1950 and leased a gas station in Jackson Hole, Wyoming, which made money in the summer months but was a financial sieve in the winter. He eventually went back to work for Western—reportedly at Drinkwater's invitation—as a security guard. One account says he was put in charge of security, but some of WAL's old-timers claim that Fred was just another uniformed guard in charge of precisely nobody but himself. Whatever the case, it was a demeaning status for the man who had been Western's first pilot, one of the original Four Horsemen and at one time chief pilot of the entire system.

Art Kelly still bristles at the thought of Western's senior captain working as a guard in the employees' parking lot at the age of sixty-one, ineligible for a pension that wasn't in existence when he flew the M-2, the Fokkers, 247s, and DC-3s. Despite protestations that Western had done everything it could for him, Fred himself confirmed his unhappiness when he quit the airline and went to work for a firm overhauling Ford motors.

Just about the time the champagne flights got under way, he lost his only son in an automobile accident. This tragedy was followed by the motor overhaul firm firing him for economy reasons, and the subsequent death of his wife in a fire. Kelly sold their fire-damaged house, moved first into a small apartment and then into a trailer, and sold shoes and hosiery door-to-door. By then he was sixty-four years old. Only a handful of the older pilots kept in touch with him; as far as the airline was concerned, Kelly I was just a faded memory, a name in a mass of yellowing clippings gathering dust in the files. The Golden Years, yes—but not for Fred Kelly I.

No one could object to the way Drinkwater was running the airline. Western netted more than $1.2 million in 1952; $1.1 million in 1953; nearly $1.5 million in 1954, and just under $2 million in 1955—its thirtieth year of continuous operation. As of the thirtieth anniversary, WAL had increased the DC-6B fleet to 8, with 13 more on order for delivery in 1956 and 1957. Its six DC-4s, nine Convairs, and eight DC-3s added up to a 31-plane fleet serving a 5,525-mile system, and the payroll was well over the 2,000 mark. Route expansion still was on the small though viable side, the major award being authority to provide competitive service between San Francisco and Denver via Reno and Salt Lake City. In the CAB hopper was an application to furnish direct service from Phoenix to Los Angeles, Denver, Las Vegas, Salt Lake City, Palm Springs, and San Diego. At the same time, Drinkwater was seeking permission to turn over a number of its smaller points to the local-service airlines; he wanted to phase out the DC-3 as soon as possible, and the 1955 annual report mentioned for the first time that "under active study during the year were specifications and performance estimates of both turboprop and jet aircraft as applicable to Western's system.

"While no orders have yet been placed for future delivery of these new types of airliners," it continued, "decisions will be made soon and new equipment ultimately will be introduced into the Western fleet in line with requirements of planned growth and development."

As of the day those lines were written, Britain's Comet jetliners had been carrying passengers, Capital Airlines was operating the British-built Viscount propjet, the Lockheed Electra was off the drawing boards and in its early testing stages, the Boeing 707 prototype already was flying, and the first DC-8 was under construction.

In Drinkwater's desire to keep Western taut, compact, and basically regional in structure, he found it hard to visualize the day when he would be forced to shell out upward of $6 million for a single long-legged jetliner—the same price he had paid for the initial five-plane DC-6B order. In effect, he kept putting off the inevitable until it was coming around the corner.

Any kind of heavy capital expenditure bothers corporate chief executives under constant pressure from directors and stockholders to whom the name of the game is the regular dividend. Rare is the company president who does not feel a tremendous sense of responsibility toward stockholders; Terry not only felt that responsibility deeply, but also had the wary instincts of a nervous deer about his own position of power. An airline president has Caesar-like authority, yet it is based on some wobbly underpinnings; like the football coach who has to keep winning, he is the prime target for reprisals if major mistakes are made, dividends vanish, and heavy losses persist. Drinkwater felt especially vulnerable in this area, for Western itself seemed to attract raiders out to seize control. He had fought off Coulter and neutralized Burnham, but the threat was always there.

For this reason, Drinkwater liked to hand-pick WAL's directors. Burnham and Pogue had been rammed down his throat, figuratively, but while he always viewed Burnham suspiciously, Pogue became a trusted friend. It was Pogue to whom TCD turned for advice when a wealthy Californian named Dudley Swim openly sought election to the Board of Directors. Swim, a railroad buff all his life, had switched his affections to the airline industry and wanted badly to be a part of it. He didn't go around to any back door; he phoned Drinkwater and in his usual blunt manner got right to the point: "Coach, how the hell do I get on your Board?"

Startled, Terry mumbled something about calling him back and contacted Pogue, who was a fountain of knowledge about anyone in the airline business and also most of those on the fringes.

"Well, he's a very successful businessman, Terry," Pogue said, "but if you put him on the Board, he's going to have more ideas than Western has pilots, and you'll have to listen to them. Some will be good and some you'll have to reject."

With definite misgivings, Drinkwater decided to put Swim's name up for election; despite Pogue's warning that Dudley was his own man, Terry thought he could get along with him. He was wrong—they clashed immediately and then frequently, from the time Swim became a director in 1957 to when he left five years later. At the first directors' meeting the outspoken Swim attended, he began asking some searching and occasionally embarrassing questions, and Terry was furious.

One area of acrimony was Terry's request for a long-term contract, which Swim tried to block—the latter adhered to a philosophy generally attributed to Brigham Young: Good executives don't need such security and poor ones don't deserve it. Their feud was not only bitter but, in the end, almost fatal to Drinkwater; Swim was to sell his holdings to a group of investors trying to seize control of the airline, and if they had succeeded, Drinkwater probably would have been out.

Swim, of course, didn't become a burr under Drinkwater's saddle until that halcyon 1950–58 period was nearing an end. The era wasn't entirely devoid of unfavorable events, WAL suffering two fatal crashes, the first since the Drinkwater regime began, and also experiencing two crippling strikes—the first major labor strife in Western's history.

The first accident involved a new DC-6B, with only 826 hours of logged flight time since its delivery date. It was being operated as Flight 636, Los Angeles to Oakland, with an intermediate stop at San Francisco. There were 30 passengers aboard when the plane left Los Angeles on April 20, 1953, at 9:00 P.M. PST; commanding was Captain Robert Clark, the first officer was Robert Jacobson, the flight engineer was Robert League, and the stewardesses were Barbara Brew and Beverlee Nelson—note the curious repetition of B's, with the three flight-deck members all called Bob and both stewardesses whose names began with B. This was not the only coincidence about the flight that makes one tend to accept the validity of Ernest Gann's "fate is the hunter" philosophy. For example, everything about the flight's operation was legal—but there were borderline areas. Captain Clark had qualified on the DC-6B but had only 79 hours on the airplane and had never before flown across San Francisco Bay at night. First Officer Jacobson's qualification on the DC-6B would have expired if he had not flown this trip. Flight 636 was not a regular assignment for any of the WAL personnel aboard; Clark and the flight engineer were on reserve status and were called in to replace men who normally would have flown it. Jacobson requested the trip to stay qualified. The two stewardesses also were last-minute replacements for girls who either had reported in sick or had flown their maximum allotted hours for the month. It was, in fact, Barbara Brew's first DC-6B flight; she had just returned to work after an appendicitis operation, and she worked Flight 636 in place of a regular stewardess so she could get in some flight time. Stewardess Nelson, the only crew member aboard who couldn't swim, was the only crew member to survive after the plane crashed into the Bay midway between the San Francisco and Oakland airports.

Flight 636 took off from San Francisco at 11:05 P.M., having deplaned all but five passengers. No passenger had boarded for the flight to Oakland, less than twelve statute miles and six minutes' flying time away. Three minutes after the DC-6B left the ground, it was in thirty feet of water at the bottom of the Bay; stewardess Nelson and a passenger, Vilas Adams of Fairbanks, Alaska, were the only survivors. Clark (although it may have been Jacobson, because it was never determined positively which one was at the controls) had flown the plane right into the water while descending toward the Oakland airport.

At first it was an unexplainable accident in supposedly clear weather; tower operators at both San Francisco and Oakland said they could see the lights of the opposite airport clearly at the time of the crash. Later it became evident that Clark had been trapped by a hazard associated with overwater approaches at night. Known as "sensory illusion," it is a visual phenomenon that leads a pilot to believe he is higher than he really is. Sensory illusion occurs under light and weather conditions similar to those in which Flight 636 was operating. Clark was required to stay clear of clouds, in accordance with "Visual Trans-Bay" flight rules applying to air traffic between the San Francisco and Oakland airports. The same rules required pilots to maintain a minimum of five hundred feet altitude on the approach. The cloud cover in the immediate vicinity of Oakland turned out to be lower than Clark had been led to believe, and he apparently descended below five hundred feet in order to comply with the stay-clear-of-clouds regulation.

Bev Nelson is a peppery, friendly person who has made flying a career. She became a stewardess in 1949, when Western wasn't training its own flight attendants.

"I was one of the gals who paid $285 to attend McDonnell Aviation School in Minneapolis before Western trained its own stewardesses," she explains. "You'd get two months' training, and then airlines would send representatives to interview you. I picked Western because of a picture. The school had photographs of its graduates on a wall, and right in the center was a Western stewardess in a maroon uniform. It was the uniform that convinced me; at that point, I hadn't even heard of Western."

Bev is a refreshingly frank girl who likes to joke, "I'm a week older than our airline—I was born April 9, 1926." Nor is she reticent to talk about that night of April 20.

"I was reading a newspaper in the rear lounge when it happened. All of a sudden I heard and felt what seemed to be the nose wheel striking the runway. I was somewhat surprised because I thought it was too soon to be landing at Oakland. When the nose wheel hit, I could hear the jolting or shaking of the galley equipment—it was a clattering noise—resulting from one sharp jolt. But it didn't jar me to the point of dislodging the newspaper out of my hands.

"A second later, the lights in the cabin went out. I looked toward the front of the plane and all I could see was Barbara and a male passenger. I could see a little of the left wing and fire on the water around the area directly in front of me. There was no sign of the main cabin. The rear cabin and lounge had broken away from the rest of the plane, and all that remained of the rear cabin was the floor and the right side of the fuselage up to the window-line level. The lounge was intact, except the roof was missing.

"Barbara tossed me a foam-rubber cushion from a seat—thank God the company had ordered them as emergency life preservers in case of a water landing. I started dog-paddling around through the water, which was terribly hot from the fire. I was in the water for an hour, and it was cold once I got away from the wreckage. I thought of some crazy things, like thinking, 'Oh, my God, I've lost my uniform hat—they'll suspend me.' I could see the Oakland Bridge and the Bayshore Highway, and I said to myself, 'This is crazy—I'm not staying here any more. I'll just swim over there and look for a bar and maybe I can get a brandy or something. No, I can't—I've lost my purse, so how could I pay for a brandy? Maybe I could walk along the highway and hitch a ride—anything to warm me up.'

"When a Coast Guard boat finally picked me up, my seat cushion was so waterlogged my chin was in the water. I had lost one shoe and my wristwatch. The company bought me a new watch, and the chief stewardess brought me clothes to wear when I left the hospital—I had cracked two vertebrae in the crash. The rumor went around that Western made me buy a new uniform, but that just isn't true. I was still paying for the one I had ruined in the accident and they continued deducting for it, but they gave me a new one. They also gave me $125 to replace the few clothes I had lost. I still keep hearing that story, though. As a matter of fact, Western couldn't have been kinder or more understanding. I was in a daze and wanted to go back to flying, but the company insisted I take a couple of months off—for therapy to my back and so I'd be available for the CAB accident hearings. The only thing I wasn't reimbursed for was the cost of a locksmith. When I finally got back to Los Angeles, I couldn't get into my car at the parking lot because I had lost my car keys.

"There was another phony story people kept telling about the accident, or rather its aftermath. About five years later, I got a note to call Vilas Adams at the Ambassador Hotel in Los Angeles. He was the only other survivor, and when I called him, he said he was in town briefly and asked me to have dinner with him. I had just come in from a turnaround trip to Minneapolis and I was dead tired, but I went anyway. We had dinner at the Biltmore Hotel. I didn't even recognize him at first. He was about twenty-one at the time of the crash, and shorter than I—and I'm only five-two. In those five years, he had gained a lot of weight. He called me again a couple of times, but that one dinner was the last time I saw him. The word got out, however, that on the anniversary of the accident, we meet and have dinner together!

"I don't need an annual reunion to refresh memories. Some are only too vivid. Flying itself never made me nervous, even after the crash, but certain things kept coming back in an unpleasant way. Like the burning oil on the water. To this day, if someone lights a match suddenly, I jump."

Most of the wreckage of Flight 636 still rests in the Bay; the largest part recovered was the center wing section, with the main landing gear attached. The bodies of Captain Clark and Flight Engineer League were never found. League's widow still works for Western in San Francisco. And Bev Nelson is still a Western stewardess, with more than twenty-five years' seniority —quite an accomplishment for someone who on the day she won her wings figured she'd fly for about six months and then marry the man to whom she was engaged. When the romance didn't work out, she stayed on the job, and her own personal memories would fill a book.

"The starting salary in 1949 was $225 a month," she recalls, "and now it's $500, not including incentive pay, expenses, and fringe benefits we never heard of. A lot of things have changed. The training's far better, of course. When I got out of McDonnell, you didn't need any more training—you just rode with another stewardess on each type of airplane Western was operating, and you learned on the job—usually by trial and error, fun but not very efficient. Passengers have changed, too. When I started, they got a little white cake box with bologna sandwiches and bread that curled up at the ends. Plus a carton of milk. Everyone thought that was really living. Now they're all gourmets. They ask what *kind* of red wine it is, or what brand of scotch you are offering, or if it is a filet mignon or New York cut steak.

"Flight crews used to be a lot closer. Now I see captains I've never met. And the new stewardesses are different. When I began flying, you had to fight for your job—the airlines were hiring one girl at a time. You had to wait until somebody resigned or was terminated before you could get on. In some ways, the job was tougher. I remember bidding a trip that had thirteen stops between Los Angeles and Minneapolis.

"Galleys are better, although I suppose there will never be a galley that's completely satisfactory to a stewardess. One of the big events in my career was when Western replaced the old coffee servers, just Thermos bottles turned upside down with a little spigot attached, with new coffee jugs. We were all excited —we were like little children getting a new toy. Nora Jeroue, who's three years senior to me, got one of the new jugs on a flight, and she couldn't wait to plug it in and heat the water. Nobody wanted coffee and nobody wanted tea, either, and there was Nora dying to use the new machine and no way to do it.

"Finally, a woman with a baby came aboard on one stop, and Nora figured her chance had come. She saw her rustling around, obviously preparing for feeding, so Nora marched over and said, 'Let me warm the milk for you.'

"The woman just looked at her—and started breast feeding.

"Yes, lots of memories. Most of them wonderful, a few of them bad . . ."

Ten months later, on February 26, 1954, another Western plane went down in one of the few crashes in U.S. commercial airline history that is still carried on the books as cause unknown. It was a Convair 240, operating as Flight 34 from Los Angeles to Minneapolis, with four intermediate stops.

Between Los Angeles and Salt Lake City, the flight was routine. One hour and forty-two minutes after leaving Salt Lake City, Flight 34 disappeared in a snowstorm so heavy that the plane had been forced to overfly Casper, the next scheduled stop, and proceed toward Rapid City. The wreckage was sighted by a WAL pilot two days later, on level, open terrain near Wright, Wyoming, about a hundred miles from the Rapid City range station. There was no survivors among the three crew members and six passengers aboard.

The last radio contact was the flight's acknowledgment of the

[20] This was the famed airborne television experiment aboard a WAE Fokker. Unfortunately, the picture on the screen was too dim for the still camera to pick up.

[21] The cabin of a Western Boeing 247 — which clearly shows why early stewardesses couldn't be taller than five feet, three inches.

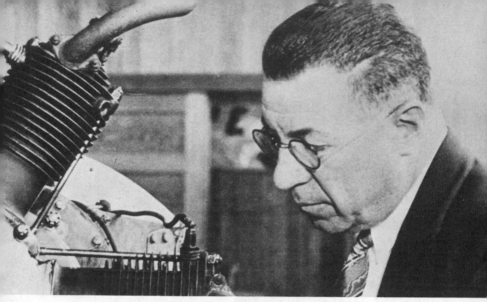

Western's first six presidents. [22] Harris Hanshue.

[23] Alvin Adams. [24] William Coulter.

[25] Terrell Drinkwater.

[26] Judson Taylor.　　[27] Arthur Kelly.

[28] Jerry Brooder and Marv Landes look at a map showing the vital Casper cutoff route that played so important a role in Western's history.

[29] Kirk Kerkorian (right), shown here with Judson Taylor, was the Las Vegas financier who unexpectedly grabbed control of Western and touched off one of the bitterest corporate fights in airline history.

Rapid City weather report, five minutes before the crash occurred. Investigators suspected that airframe and carburetor icing, combined with heavy to severe turbulence, resulted in loss of control, but while this was a possibility, it was never more than an unproven theory.

The captain was one of Western's best and most popular pilots —thirty-nine-year-old Milton R. Cawley, whom everyone called Ray because he hated his first name. He had logged more than ten thousand hours of flight time at the time of the accident, and his copilot, Bob Crowther, also was experienced, with almost four thousand hours. The stewardess was Mary Grace Creagan. Again there was the coincidence of a common initial, on which superstition feeds and from which legends are born.

Western was well into its thirtieth year of service when a controversial figure from its past died as he had mostly lived—alone. On October 12, 1955, William A. Coulter suffered a fatal heart attack in his New York City apartment at the age of seventy-eight. The New York *Times* obituary, only 144 words long, mentioned that he had graduated from Princeton in 1903 and had distinguished himself there "as a gymnast."

Coulter at one point had willed all his WAL stock to the class of '03—it was poignantly clear that his undergraduate days had been the happiest for this rather lonely, withdrawn man.

That thirtieth year, incidentally, witnessed the birth of a slogan and a symbol that were still in existence on the airline's fiftieth anniversary. They were introduced simultaneously, shortly after Western began advertising on television early in 1955. The first commercials were the usual "hard sell" used by all carriers, effective enough in their own way but lacking much originality or spark. Bert Lynn, director of advertising, wasn't really happy about them, and neither was Kelly.

Lynn was at home watching TV one night and became intrigued by a Ford commercial featuring an animated cartoon. It was clever, informal, and eye-catching. A few nights later, he caught a Bank of America commercial that was another cartoon —depicting two proud parents with a new baby who gurgled, "m-m-m-m-money."

The next morning, Lynn called the ad agency handling Western's account.

"Who does the cartoons for Ford and Bank of America?" he inquired.

The agency called back a few minutes later to report that the same company did both commercials—Storyboard, Inc., a small firm in Hollywood specializing in commercial cartoons. Lynn went to see Kelly.

"I think we should try something new," he suggested.

"I couldn't agree with you more," Kelly said. "Call this Storyboard outfit up and tell them we'd be interested in a Western Airlines cartoon. It won't hurt to let 'em try something."

About a month later, Storyboard called them. "We've got something to show you guys."

Lynn and Kelly drove over to the small studio, sat down in the screening room, and watched three sample commercial cartoons. The first was built around a fish character and the second a greyhound. The two Westerners shook their heads. "Here's the third," the Storyboard official said.

On the screen appeared a nondescript bird vaguely resembling a parrot—it looked like something James Thurber might have drawn. It was sitting atop the fuselage just ahead of the tail. From the sound track came a deep voice dripping with unctuousness: "Western—the *only* way to fly."

Kelly and Lynn exchanged glances, then whispers. "We'll talk it over and get back to you," Kelly said.

They returned to Kelly's office and discussed the bird cartoon for more than an hour. Both were impressed—and jittery. It was entertaining, but it represented a 180-degree turn from conventional airline TV advertising. Was it really the right image? Would it be persuasive? Would it make people choose Western? Sure it was cute, but would too many think it ridiculous and too farfetched?

"We'll never know unless we try it," Kelly finally decided. "Call the agency, tell 'em to contact Storyboard, and have them go ahead and finish the one with the bird."

It was a gut decision, one costing an initial fifty thousand dollars to launch the campaign, but it had far-reaching effects. The bird was to become Western's symbol for another fourteen years, and after it was shelved because Kelly and Lynn feared overexposure, public demand brought it back four years later. Along with the bird went the slogan they had first heard in the sample commercial: "Western—the *only* way to fly."

The first commercial was on the air in 1956, and in only one week, they knew they had hit the jackpot. People started calling in or writing letters praising the bird—although quite a few misidentified it. Some swore it had to be a walrus (which led to it's being named "Wally" in the first few months), others thought it was a lizard, and a number insisted that it was a turtle. Lynn decided to end the confusion by calling it VIB—"Very Important Bird."

The commercials became so popular that Western actually started advertising the times they would be aired. Part of the success stemmed from the format itself, which seemed to invite audience participation. After VIB does his little bit, the camera moves toward the plane's tail, with its "Western Airlines" lettering, and this suddenly dissolves into the name of a city the airline serves. Viewers began playing guessing games on which city would be featured; a woman in Denver wrote that she and her husband bet a dollar on what city would appear, the loser putting the money into a kitty for their son's college education. Another wrote that VIB was helping to keep her marriage happy: "When everyone in the house is mad at each other and no one's talking," she wrote, "the ice is broken when your little bird comes on TV. We all try to guess the city, and that does it!" VIB began drawing more fan mail than WAL's stewardesses.

No one seemed to tire of the pompous little parrot. The commercials were slipped into key spots and were over in ten to twenty seconds. Kelly's insistence that overexposure might ruin the whole gimmick was extended beyond the television screen: "We could promote him to death," he told Drinkwater, who was delighted at the bird's success. For that reason, Western resisted attempts to put VIB on sweatshirts, billboards, and print media ads. Much of the pressure came from WAL officials who wanted models made for ticket counters, windows, and a variety of other uses.

"TV commercials only," Lynn told all concerned. "Crazes and fads last only six months and then are finished for good—just look at hula hoops and Davy Crockett hats, for example."

Originally, VIB was shown smoking a long cigarette holder in

one hand and a glass of champagne in the other. Western got letters claiming that the bird was corrupting the morals of young
people by emphasizing drinking and smoking. One protest was
directed at shots in which VIB casually flicked away his cigarette
ashes—presumably all over the countryside. It finally was decided to eliminate the cigarette holder in favor of a swagger
stick, which worked out better, anyway; VIB twirled it expertly
just before pointing to the tail and disclosing the name of the
"mystery" city.

VIB came close to turning into a national institution. Several
military units requested permission to use the bird as the squadron insignia on shoulder patches and the airplanes themselves
(granted). Western registered VIB and also the slogan, which
achieved fame on its own. "The Only Way to Fly" became a
much-used line by such performers as Lucille Ball, Bob Hope,
Frank Sinatra, Red Skelton, and Danny Thomas. It was written
into the scripts of three feature films and was responsible for the
first commercial ever broadcast (inadvertently, but still broadcast) from outer space. This occurred during Astronaut James
Lovell's Gemini 7 mission; sitting comfortably in his underwear
while his space capsule orbited the earth at more than seventeen
thousand miles an hour, Lovell remarked, "It's the *only* way to
fly." After he landed, Western sent him a case of champagne.

VIB lasted until 1969, when it was withdrawn for what turned
out to be temporary retirement. The fan mail just never stopped.
When VIB came back, it was in a somewhat modified form,
mixed with live-action commercials—the latter selling features
like Western's legroom, while the bird continued to create the
image of an airline willing to laugh at itself and not take itself
too seriously. Imitation being the sincerest form of flattery, VIB's
proudest moment came when the Ford Motor Company ran a
TV commercial in which an animated character asks the "Ford
Dog":

"Are you the little guy on TV who rides on top of airplanes?"

Western had more than a clever symbol and a catchy slogan, it
also had public identification on virtually a nationwide scale.
The bird's fame spread beyond the geographical boundaries of
its television exposure, and so did "the only way to fly." For an
airline essentially regional, this was a major achievement and

one that appropriately enough accompanied Western into the uncertain but challenging age of jet power.

For a while, it appeared the plunge might be delayed; early in 1956, the Brotherhood of Railway and Steamship Clerks, Freight Handlers, Express and Station Employees—otherwise known as the BRC—shut the airline down with a strike lasting seventy-three days. The first-quarter losses were high enough to cause concern as to whether the thirteen additional DC-6Bs on order could be paid for, let alone whether the line could buy jet-powered aircraft. But if anyone needed proof of Drinkwater's leadership qualities during this period of carefully controlled expansion, he could find the evidence in the record for the last three quarters of 1956: WAL ended the year with profits of more than $3 million.

It also ended the year committed to the purchase of nine Lockheed Electra propjets (turbine engines hitched to propellers) costing some $2.4 million each.

But even as Western prepared to enter the jet age on a modest scale, it was facing the start of another era—one of labor and corporate strife on a massive scale.

CHAPTER FOURTEEN

Hawaii, Here We Come!

Airlines, like people, seem to run in cycles of luck—good or bad —and there wasn't much doubt that Western had been a lucky as well as a competently operated carrier during the early fifties.

Even the worst stroke of luck any airline can suffer, a fatal accident, had been tempered somewhat in Western's case by the fact that relatively few lives were lost—the Convair that went down so mysteriously in Wyoming and the DC-6B that crashed into the waters of San Francisco Bay both could have been carrying full loads instead of a handful of passengers.

And it was either luck or perhaps divine intervention that saved another WAL flight from tragedy on July 25, 1957—a day when a small, elderly, rather stockily built man approached the Western ticket counter in Las Vegas where station agent Paul O'Brien was preparing to board passengers on Flight 39, Las Vegas to Los Angeles.

It was around 12:30 A.M., and the little man was O'Brien's first passenger of the morning. He had no baggage, either to be checked or carried on—which was not unusual for Las Vegas passengers. Flight 39, which had originated in Rochester, Minnesota, came in from Salt Lake City twelve minutes ahead of schedule. There had been a crew change there—Captain Milt Shirk, First Officer Seth Oberg, and Stewardess Joan Hollinger taking over the flight for the rest of the trip to Los Angeles.

The first passenger O'Brien had checked in, boarded Flight 39 with eleven other persons plus an infant. Once on the aircraft, he picked seat 9-A, in the next-to-last row on the left side, across from the lavatory.

The name Agent O'Brien had entered on the manifest was Binstock. Approximately seven minutes after takeoff, Saul F. Binstock, a sixty-two-year-old retired jeweler from North Hollywood, California, got out of his seat and went into the lavatory. In his pocket were four sticks of dynamite and a blasting cap.

Stewardess Hollinger didn't see him leave his seat. Three other passengers did but didn't mention to her the fact that he still hadn't come out of the lavatory twenty minutes later. Stewardess Hollinger had completed her cabin-service duties and had sat down in 10-D directly ahead of the lavatory bulkhead when it happened. The time was 3:33 A.M.

". . . I heard a horrible blast, a terrific gust of wind, and the cabin filled with a thick fog and an eerie light," she recounted later. "I put my hand to my head as I sat bolt upright. My hat was gone, and my hair was flying in my face. I was stunned, shocked. I thought this was the end for a minute . . . I knew there was a hole behind me, but I wasn't about to move. The window on my right was shattered."

At the moment of the explosion, Flight 39 had just reported passing a radio checkpoint at Daggett, California, flying at ten thousand feet. In the cockpit, Shirk and Oberg heard a loud noise, a kind of thump, from the rear of the Convair 240, and felt a slight jolt. All the instruments appeared normal; to Oberg, who was flying the plane, the noise was like that of a double-barreled shotgun fired just behind his head.

"Better go back there and see what happened," Shirk ordered the copilot. Oberg returned to inform the captain there was a large hole in one side of the aft cabin.

"Is Joan all right?" Shirk asked.

"My God, I didn't see her," Oberg confessed.

"Go back and make sure she's okay and help her. Move the passengers forward and have all seat belts fastened."

Oberg went back to check and returned in a few minutes to report the stewardess safe and to give Shirk a further report of damage. The captain decided to see for himself, turned over the controls to the first officer, and went into the cabin. He found a two-by-five-foot hole in the fuselage; the lavatory had disappeared along with the bulkhead. He returned to the cockpit and contacted Western's dispatch to advise that he was declaring an emergency and would land at George Air Force Base, less than forty miles away.

Flight 39 put down at George without further incident, and the Convair was put under military guard as soon as the shaken passengers deplaned. A head count disclosed that passenger Binstock was missing. A search along the flight path located his body later that day. The FBI began an immediate investigation of his background, discovering that a casual friend of his had purchased four sticks of dynamite for him—Binstock telling him he needed the explosives to demolish a mountain cabin he owned.

At Burbank, just before leaving for Las Vegas, the retired jeweler had bought two flight insurance policies totaling $125,000—$62,500 each—naming his wife as beneficiary. The strong circumstantial evidence against Binstock did not prevent his family from suing Western for damages, however. Renda, in turn, filed a countersuit seeking repayment for the $13,000 it cost to fix the Convair, and the family's legal action was dropped.

The bombing incident occurred in an otherwise rather tranquil year in Western's turbulent history. But 1957 also was the calm before the storm. Outwardly, things couldn't have looked better. The fleet was being modernized steadily—the last two DC-4s were phased out, and the DC-3 platoon was down to five aircraft, which Drinkwater planned to retire as soon as possible. To replace the all-coach DC-4s, Western increased its DC-6B orders again—from thirteen to eighteen, with four aircraft specially configured to carry eighty-seven coach passengers; by 1957, approximately 23 per cent of WAL's passenger revenues were coming from coach service.

The new Electra's first test flights were eye-openers. The plane had enormous reserve power and handled like a fighter—smoothly, docilely, responsively. It was fast, versatile, uncomplaining, and, for a large transport type, surprisingly forgiving of mistakes. Above all, it was a pilot's airplane. Today, when only one domestic trunkline (Eastern) still operates Electras on regular schedules, it is difficult to remember that it probably was the most pilot-loved airplane ever built. No one at that stage of the Electra's controversy-ridden career could foresee anything but a brilliant future for an aircraft that was a pilot's dream and a passenger's delight. At Western, the only doubts expressed were not technological but economic, the question being the wisdom of a $2.4 million outlay for a propeller-driven airplane with the jet age looming ahead. There were those at WAL who felt the Electra could be only an interim airplane, and Dom Renda was one of them. Drinkwater and Shatto considered it perfect for Western's then-existing route system, and Renda agreed. But Dom also thought nine Electras were too many, and he objected even more strongly later when Western upped its order to a total of twelve. Renda was on the equipment selection committee along with TCD, Shatto, and Jud Taylor.

"We're going to see the day when jets will be serving places like Las Vegas," Dom told Terry.

"You're nuts!" Drinkwater snapped.

About a year later, Renda found himself off the equipment committee. It was the first sign of serious dissension between Dom and the man who had once told him, "Of all the guys around here, you have the background, the capability, the opportunity, and the youth to someday take over my spot."

It is interesting to note that two of Drinkwater's favorites among Western's officialdom were the pair running the airline in its fiftieth year: Kelly as president and Renda as executive vice president. Drinkwater seems to have envisioned Kelly as a possible successor just as he did Renda; Alvin Adams says TCD once told him Art Kelly would make an excellent chief executive when it came time for Drinkwater to retire. He may have had similar thoughts about other top executives, of course, but he never voiced them; at that point in time he apparently didn't think of Shatto in terms of the presidency, even though his reliance on Shatto's judgment was increasing steadily, nor of Landes or Taylor.

Terry was genuinely fond of all his officers, much in the manner of a patriarch enjoying the antics as well as the skills of high-spirited sons. At one directors' meeting held in Banff, local college students put on a play for the entertainment of the distinguished visitors. Drinkwater attended, naturally, and settled back in his seat to enjoy the drama. Suddenly he bolted upright. Shatto, Landes, and Renda were in the cast.

Like all airplane executives, Terry had to mine some humor

out of adversity and minor setbacks or he would have been climbing walls. Then public-relations director Ken Smith furnished him the prize publicity goof of 1957 when a Hollywood photographer named Peter Gowland approached Smith with a request: He was doing a speculative magazine layout on a day in the life of a typical stewardess.

"I already have the model," he informed Ken, "but I need a Western uniform."

It was against company policy to loan out WAL uniforms to anyone but bona fide stewardesses, but Smith agreed after Gowland outlined his idea: a sequence in which a pretty girl is dreaming about a career as a flight attendant. Smith doesn't remember whether Gowland mentioned the magazine or magazines to which he was trying to sell the layout, but Ray Silvius—Ken's assistant at the time—recalls it was supposed to be *Coronet* or *Pic*. Silvius also says Western co-operated on the supposition that the piece would emphasize improved cabin-attendant training—Western had just opened its new million-dollar flight crew training center adjacent to the general offices, and Gowland's projected photographic article would provide nationwide exposure. That it did—nationwide exposure, not for the training center but for the model Gowland used, and not in *Coronet* or *Pic* but as the centerfold in *Playboy*, then only four years old.

The photographer had promised to furnish Western with a full set of the pictures he intended to submit for publication. He never did supply the ones he sent to *Playboy*, and for a very good reason—they included nude shots. The model turned out to be a girl who worked for United in reservations and couldn't resist the going rate for Playmates of the Month—a reported three thousand dollars in those days. There were some staid, harmless pictures of her working in uniform on a flight and posing with a flight engineer near a plane, but the centerfold was something else.

It appeared in *Playboy's* July 1957 issue, and Smith nearly had a coronary. There was no mention whatsoever of Western; the text merely said she worked for a major airline and that the photographer had met her on one of her flights. She was wearing a Western stewardess uniform, but nobody could have identified her as a WAL flight attendant even with a magnifying glass to examine her wings. Unfortunately for Smith, however, the flight engineer with whom she was posing in one shot was only too identifiable as Western—the Indian head insignia on his uniform cap was plainly visible.

Drinkwater saw the magazine before Smith did. Thanks to Terry's habit of getting to work earlier than most employees, when Ken came into his own office *Playboy* was on his desk opened to the centerfold.

"I knew Terry had put it there," Smith says ruefully, "and I knew I either had blown it completely or the old man was going to really dig it. I couldn't wait to find out, so I walked down to his office. He was sitting there with his feet propped up on the desk. He looked at me for a full minute, then started laughing.

"He sent me back to the office with instructions to buy up every copy I could find. I heard later he sent them to every person he knew in the industry. My first reaction was that I was going to be held responsible for what happened and then later, when Mr. D. didn't blow his stack, I started taking credit for it. For years everyone outside of the company assumed that Playmate was really a Western stewardess, and the word went around that Drinkwater fired her the day the magazine appeared on the stands. He couldn't have, of course—and I never did find out what United did to her."

Smith topped the centerfold coup with the annual report for 1957. Airline PR chiefs frequently are in charge of the annual report, which is simultaneously one of their most vital and cordially detested duties. To grasp the true significance of what happened to Mr. Smith's annual report for 1957, one must understand that all corporations regard this yearly publication with reverence and handle it with extreme care. A platoon of vice presidents nitpick over paragraphs, sentences, and punctuation. It has more censors than a Russian newspaper.

Western's biggest event of '57 was the inauguration of service to Mexico City, and the annual report for that year naturally featured WAL's newest and longest route. It was decided to devote both the front and back covers of the annual report to Mexico, and two photographs were selected: a shot of the ancient Hacienda Vista Hermosa bell tower on the cover, and on the back a picture of the modern skyscraper building housing Western's offices on Paseo de la Reforma in Mexico City—the old-vs.-the-new contrast so typical of the Mexican capital.

Copies were off the presses and distribution had started when Ken Smith got a call from a Western staff member who was laughing so hard Smith could hardly understand him.

"I just saw the annual report," he managed to gurgle.

Smith was nettled. "It may not be great literature, but it sure isn't anything to laugh at."

"Oh, no? Take another look at the back cover."

Ken did. At first he failed to see any cause for uncontrolled mirth. It was just a street scene, with usual cars and people, a glass-and-steel office building in the background. Then he noticed that every person across the street from the building was looking at something in the lower-right-corner of the photograph. Smith's eyes followed theirs—and it was near-coronary time again. What they were gazing at with interest ranging from avid to startled were two dogs copulating. The picture had been checked by at least a half-dozen persons and nobody had spotted what might be termed the first pornography ever to appear in a corporate annual report. Smith himself had selected this one shot over many others—without ever seeing the dogs.

His first thought was Drinkwater, his second was to compose a résumé for a new job application, and his third was a panic-stricken rush to call back every copy that had already been mailed out—mostly to the press, he realized with sinking heart. Getting it back from the news media would be like asking them to refrain from covering a fatal crash.

He did manage to recall a few. Undistributed copies were hastily trimmed in such a way that the dogs were eliminated from the scene. Naturally, most of those who had received the "first edition" were not only reluctant to surrender them, but also adamantly refused to do so—Western's 1957 annual report quickly became a collector's item.

Drinkwater was stunned at first—until he began to see the humor of it and locked away his own copies among his most valuable souvenirs. The following year he sent pictures of puppies to those possessing the original back cover.

Ken Smith's dubious reward would have come in the form of

Western's annual award for the biggest executive boner of the year if he hadn't won it the previous year for the *Playboy* episode. This honor, known as The Order of the Fur-lined Thundermug, was Drinkwater's idea. American used to have an annual Bonehead Award, which Terry had won in his last year there—for taking the Western job in the first place. He mentioned this once at a committee meeting where the yearly Christmas party for executives was being planned. Dick Ensign, Ken Smith, and Jack Slichter were on the committee, and Terry was recounting gleefully how he had earned American's lowest tribute.

"We ought to develop something like that for Western," he suggested. "Give it out at the Christmas party every year."

Ensign and Smith were entrusted with the task of designing and acquiring a suitable trophy. They went out and bought a child's toilet, lined it with simulated leopard skin, and got a jeweler to mount it on a base. Who specifically christened it has been lost in antiquity—the award was born in 1953—but it still is given out annually to some red-faced brass hat who performed far below the call of duty.

A few samples of Thundermug winners and/or nominees will suffice to explain why the trophy is one of the least coveted in any industry:

• John Good, director of cargo sales, for buying dog kennels made out of a material that was to a dog what catnip is to a feline: The dogs ate their way right out of the containers.

• Jud Taylor, for buying Western a one-hundred-year supply of mailing tubes for which nobody could figure out a use.

• Dick Ensign, for buying one November five thousand pairs of Christmas slipper socks that were still in a storeroom the following July; what really swung the selection committee in the direction of Ensign was the discovery that he had reordered another supply.

• Frank Vosepka, for installing a bird-repellent light in a hangar, which was promptly invaded by an estimated two thousand birds who perched on a freshly painted plane.

• Bert Lynn, for 250,000 timetables that listed a one-hour schedule for a flight between Los Angeles and Seattle that would have required a cruising speed of some nine hundred miles an hour, and also erecting a huge billboard on the fringe of Los Angeles International Airport that proclaimed open house in Western's new terminal—twenty-four hours before the terminal opened.

 • Norm Rose, for heading an on-time committee that set a record for starting its own meetings late.

 • Pete Wolf, for asking "Who's he?" when told in staff meeting that composer Meredith Willson had criticized the speaker system on the Electra.

 • Terry Shrader, in charge of encouraging attendance at the annual executive Christmas party at which he failed to show up himself.

 • Tony Favero, for supervising construction of a water fountain in front of the general offices that kept drenching everyone who tried to enter the building.

Considering the importance of the Los Angeles–Mexico City route, the annual-report incident was more of a tribute to Drinkwater's sense of humor than anything else.

The Mexico City inaugural meant a great deal to Terry and to Western. It added a 1,555-mile nonstop route to the system—not ideal for the DC-6B but within its capability—and culminated an 11-year fight to activate an award dating back to 1946. The Mexican Government had thrown enough roadblocks in its path to avenge the Cortés invasion, being understandably nervous about U.S. carriers dominating the nation's air commerce. Between 1945 and 1951, the United States and Mexico had held no less than five conferences on the exchange of reciprocal air service rights without reaching agreement. The Mexicans felt that the United States had violated their sovereignty by awarding certificates without Mexico's approval.

President Truman finally got tired of all the procrastination and in 1952 invalidated all the still-legal Mexico awards, including Western's Los Angeles–Mexico City authority. Western and other carriers, believing the White House action illegal, protested to no avail, but when Dwight Eisenhower took office in 1953, the skies began to clear.

Welch Pogue, whose Washington influence was no small matter, spearheaded the lobbying efforts to overthrow the Truman edict. They paid off on March 8, 1957, when President Eisenhower wrote the Civil Aeronautics Board:

> . . . on the advice of the Attorney General, I am recognizing the validity of the certificates issued in 1946 and hereby approve them and determine that they stand unrevoked.

On the same day the letter was sent, the United States and Mexico signed a bilateral air agreement effective June 5. Western was first out of the starting gate, inaugurating daily Los Angeles–Mexico City service on July 15. Eastern followed with New York–New Orleans–Mexico City flights, and American came in later with nonstop Chicago–Mexico City service.

Western's standing in Mexico today is virtually that of a community member, a friendly neighbor with sensitivity toward Mexican pride. WAL was the first airline to hire Mexican nationals exclusively for its Mexico operations—including Luis Pasquel, hired as a salesman and in 1966 promoted to vice president.

It was Pasquel who represented Drinkwater with an unusual dilemma. One of the Mexico City daily newspapers to which Western subscribed was conducting a raffle to stimulate circulation. Luis called TCD one day, sputtering with excitement.

"You aren't going to believe this," he announced, "but we won the grand prize!"

"What the hell *is* the grand prize?" Drinkwater asked.

"A six-unit apartment house. It's worth about a hundred thousand dollars."

Drinkwater groaned. "Luis, we can't keep it. It wouldn't be right."

"Perhaps we could raffle it off again, among employees," Pasquel suggested.

Terry hesitated. "Maybe, but I'd better come down there. I got an idea."

He flew to Mexico City and through Pasquel was given an appointment with Mexico's Secretary of Transportation.

"We don't really want the building," Drinkwater confessed. "We won only because we subscribed to the newspaper."

"It's legally yours, Señor Drinkwater."

"I know that. Look, you have an airline training school here—the only one in Latin America, as far as I know. Suppose Western gives the apartment building to the school."

"That would be most generous," the Secretary beamed.

"With one suggestion," Drinkwater added.

"And that is?"

"The income from the apartment house is to be used for scholarships to train Mexican nationals for the airline business."

"Accepted," was the immediate answer.

And *that* was pure Drinkwater—his belief that an airline has to be part of every community it serves. He held no patent on that creed, but he abided by it more faithfully than a lot of airline presidents. It *was* a generous gesture, but it also was a smart one; Western has enjoyed a mutually friendly relationship with its neighbors to the south ever since the inaugural flight two decades ago.

Another valuable if less spectacular inaugural took place late in 1957 with the start of service between San Diego and Denver via Phoenix, a route of almost nine hundred miles. Western's Phoenix routes, like the cutoff case, were won largely through the efforts of one man. Most of the major carriers were battling to get into the Phoenix market, with United and Continental working particularly hard to line up community support for their applications. But Western's Tom Murphy got there first and did a masterful job of enlisting the local backing needed for WAL to gain access to this important resort city.

The legs of the old Indian were getting longer—and profits correspondingly stayed healthy. Net income dropped in '57 to slightly over $2.4 million, a decline attributed almost entirely to a business recession that affected the whole industry. Yet Western paid a cash dividend to its 7,500 stockholders for the seventh year in succession and declared—for only the second time in its history—a second stock dividend in that same year. The year closed with a CAB announcement that WAL would be authorized to start Los Angeles–Phoenix nonstop service early in 1958—the Arizona metropolis that someone once called "San Francisco in a ten-gallon hat" was fast becoming a key point on a system now nearing the ten-thousand-mile mark.

There was one line in that famous 1957 annual report of vastly greater import than the capering canines. In discussing the successful completion of contract negotiations with four of the airline's seven labor unions during the year, the report added that "negotiations were under way with union representatives of the pilots, the mechanics, and the office and station personnel."

The last two were to be settled peacefully. The talks with the Air Line Pilots' Association were to collapse, culminating in one of the longest strikes in U.S. airline history. Western's pilots walked out on February 21, 1958, and operations did not resume until June 10—a 108-day shutdown of the entire system whose long-range effects transcended the immediate issues involved.

The basic issue at stake was simple: In addition to the usual wage and working-condition demands, ALPA sought a promise that the third cockpit crew member on the forthcoming Electras would be a qualified pilot instead of a flight engineer. It was the pilot union's first overt move toward eliminating the smaller, younger Flight Engineers' International Association (FEIA) by requiring jet-powered aircraft to be manned by an all-pilot crew. ALPA picked Western and National, two of the smaller carriers, as test cases for a policy it hoped to establish throughout the industry; the union's home office figured that if Western and National fell into line, the bigger carriers would have to follow along.

Faced with the same strike threat as Western, National reached a quick compromise agreement with its pilots—it added to a new contract a side letter promising that the "third man" issue would be put to arbitration when the Electras were delivered. Dom Renda, who had been put in charge of WAL's labor relations (in addition to his regular legal duties) in 1956, thought National's solution made sense and proposed that Western follow the same course. He had reason to believe the pilots would go along, but he ran into a stone wall in the persons of Drinkwater and Shatto.

Stan's responsibilities by then had been greatly enlarged—he was no longer merely vice president of engineering and maintenance, but since 1949 had also been vice president of operations —a corporate realignment that put the pilots under his jurisdiction. Renda may have been in charge of labor relations, but Shatto was the unofficial No. 2 man in the company, and TCD was listening to him more frequently than to Renda. There are some Western veterans who trace the beginning of deteriorating pilot-management relations to that year of 1949, when the entire operations department went into Shatto's bailiwick. Stan seldom took a direct part in contract negotiations, but his presence—and his views—were always felt. More important, whatever stand he took, Drinkwater usually was on the same platform. Renda found himself negotiating as much with Shatto and Drinkwater as with the pilots, and Terry became increasingly hard to budge as Shatto's influence grew.

Jud Taylor believes that Shatto's chief weakness in the delicate, mine-strewn field of labor relations was, ironically enough, one of his better qualities.

"Stan was an unusual man," Taylor says. "If he told you he'd do something, he'd do it. And he carried this principle to the extreme when he got into a fight with a union. When he said, 'This is my final offer,' he damned well meant it."

The pilots undoubtedly disliked Shatto, a blending of fear and distrust that gradually achieved the persistence of a dull, nagging toothache. Conversely, they were fond of Terry, but TCD didn't return the favor. He considered them, as a group, a bunch of spoiled, greedy prima donnas hopelessly and blindly biased against management to the point of total unfairness. He hadn't always felt that way, and there was some justification for his changed attitude. The image of any labor union, to the eyes of management, is reflected by a comparative handful of its most vocal, vociferous members; ALPA is no exception, and Drinkwater—perhaps unjustly but very understandably—viewed pilots through a distorted mirror. Drinkwater had a simplistic view of loyalty, anyway: If you were for him and Western, you were a great guy or a great group, and if you weren't, you were a bastard or a bunch of bastards. Once his attitude toward anybody or anything solidified, he was harder to move than a 747 mired in ten feet of mud. Combined with Shatto's unyielding toughness, the labor-relations atmosphere around Western was either icily frigid or boiling with anger, with seldom any intermediate temperatures.

Once Terry's antilabor beliefs hardened—toward all unions, not just ALPA—he made no effort to hide them. He was still capable of acts of kindness toward individuals, but as the unions grew in power, TCD's prejudices ballooned correspondingly. On more than one occasion, when some ALPA complaint or demand was laid on his desk, his shrill "those goddamned sonsofbitches!" could be heard three offices away. He ordered crew meals removed from all flights, and it was years before the pilots got them back.

But it was not a one-way street; the vendetta was mutual. Western had a small but effective nucleus of militant ALPA members who were intensely antimanagement. In this atmosphere of perpetual belligerence and mutual suspicion, labor relations became synonymous with labor strife. The only communication consisted of name-calling.

What Renda, a tough man himself but a reasonable one, inherited in the 1958 pilot negotiations was a can of worms. He was helpless to stop the strike from developing, and once it began, the attitudes of the contestants were frozen. Renda repeatedly asked the National Mediation Board to step in, but the Board might as well have been the League of Nations futilely trying to stop Japan from invading Manchuria. February, March, and April passed with no sign of settlement, not an iota of yielding on either side.

The strike continued until Renda himself broke it. He asked Drinkwater for permission to go before the Mediation Board and inform it that Western would start hiring new pilots to replace the strikers unless they agreed to go back into negotiations. Drinkwater, whose patience had been exhausted long before Renda's, couldn't say yes fast enough. Renda advised the Board of management's ultimatum, and the pilots returned to the bargaining table, where a new contract was agreed on—with the third-man issue tabled but not forgotten.

The day after the new contract was signed, Renda marched into Drinkwater's office.

"I like my job, Terry," he said, "but if you want someone to handle labor relations, go get yourself another boy."

He had taken the job at Drinkwater's and Shatto's request; previously he had confined his activities in the labor field to giving Shatto legal advice during contract negotiations. Renda's appraisal of Shatto as a labor negotiator is both candid and interesting.

"Stan was of the old school," Renda relates. "He was never able to accept what was happening in this country, the movement that was going on—changes in basic labor-management philosophy, the union shop concept, the tremendous increase in fringe benefits like paid holidays and vacations, pensions, and so forth. Stan was a hard negotiator. When he became involved in a labor matter, that's all he had on his mind all day and all night. It became an obsession with him . . . he lived with it.

"It served a useful purpose, his firmness, but in retrospect the Drinkwater-Shatto philosophy on labor went a little too far on the conservative side. There could have been more of a middle ground, certain compromises we should have made that would not have been too costly for the company. Being a small airline, we were in no position to pioneer, to take on some of these so-called national issues like the third man in the Electra."

It is equally interesting to note Shatto's own views on what kind of a negotiator he considered himself to be:

"I was never tough—I was firm but fair. I didn't believe in playing footsie with any union. They had their job to do. I expected them to keep their end up and so would we. But we never rolled over and played dead. I told the pilots once, 'You guys should be congratulated—you've outsmarted all the airlines. You made airline managements look like a bunch of idiots. You never got anything they didn't give you.'

"There should be some means of having people who represent unions at the bargaining table sign a binding agreement, instead of going back and getting the membership approval. Management gives its negotiators this authority but not the unions. They take a good contract back to their members and return to the bargaining table for second helpings. The unions know which guys panic. They're skilled at prolonging pressure tactics—often right down to the last minute in pure scare strategy. I favor compulsory arbitration and I've advocated this for years—the way it is now, it's a leap-frogging program with no end to it.

"Yeah, I know I was supposed to be the bad guy in Western's labor relations. But let me tell you something—not too long ago, an ALPA vice president came up to me and told me, 'I just want you to know, Mr. Shatto, that a lot of guys in ALPA think you were the best negotiator in the industry because the boys knew where you stood . . . they never got any bullshit from you.' "

No one will ever know for certain how much of WAL's labor policies at this time were mostly Shatto's, mostly Drinkwater's, or a combination of both. But what *is* known is that the long pilots' strike of 1958 left scars that were not healed for years, wounds that went deeper than the usual aftermath of a labor-management brawl.

Union-management differences congealed into seemingly never-ending bitterness on both sides. "Compromise" and "concession" became dirty words to management; "management" and "company" became epithets to the unions. And in this almost total breakdown of communications between employee and employer were sown the seeds of future intrafamily quarrels that were not only equally bitter but even more damaging.

The happy days were over, and Jud Taylor's ledgers showed only too clearly what the dispute did to Western's finances. The airline actually suffered a net operating loss of $120,000 for the year, despite a strong second-half comeback. Only the sale of surplus aircraft kept WAL in the black during 1958, the company winding up with a surprising profit of more than $1.5 million. Schedules did not resume immediately on the signing of the new contract—all pilots had to requalify on every type of aircraft. This included ground school and stringent flight checks, a reasonable requirement inasmuch as the best airman can get rusty after being out of a cockpit for more than three months.

The retraining program led to one of the few laughs that came out of the strike. A pilot named Wally Grigg was being checked out in Western's new DC-6B simulator—a regular cockpit hooked to electronic devices that re-create various types of in-flight emergencies. Grigg's check instructor was Bob Knowles (now in charge of Western's DC-10 training program), and he threw everything at Wally except an accusation of adultery. They "took off" in the simulator, and Knowles killed an engine before they broke ground. When the gear came up, Knowles killed an engine on the same side during the climbout. Wally was sweating but he was doing fine until warning bells began clanging and lights started flashing Knowles had pulled an electrical fire on him.

Grigg released the yoke, slid the simulator seat back, and started to leave the cockpit.

"Where the hell do you think you're going?" Knowles demanded.

"Home," Wally said calmly. "I couldn't handle that third emergency. Too many emergencies at one time."

He left the training building and walked briskly toward the parking lot, Knowles running behind him.

"Come on, Wally," he pleaded. "Let's go back and try it again."

"Nope," Grigg refused, "we just crashed. I'll see you tomorrow —if I've recovered from my injuries."

Humor was hard to come by in any department; both the airline and Drinkwater seemed snakebitten. Even route-expansion plans met a defeat, although admittedly it was one Terry didn't mourn. Western had applied for extension of its Los Angeles–Twin Cities authority to Chicago—mostly at the instigation of Renda and Brooder, who wanted badly to get the Indian head into the Windy City. Chicago was then, as it is today, a giant hub for connecting flights to and from every part of the nation.

Drinkwater, however, wanted no part of Chicago—it was too far East for him.

"It's the greatest traffic generating point in the world," Brooder argued. "We have to get in there, and Dom agrees with me."

TCD finally relented and told Renda to file the application— but he insisted on turnaround rights. This meant Western not only would have been allowed to fly between Los Angeles and Chicago via Minneapolis and other intermediate points, but also could have operated local flights between the Twin Cities and Chicago, turning westbound flights out of Chicago around at Minneapolis and heading them right back East again. This would have put Western in direct competition with Northwest and North Central, and Brooder knew the CAB wouldn't allow a third carrier into that local market.

Application was filed in 1957. The following year, Brooder informed Drinkwater the company could win CAB approval of the Chicago extension, but not with turnaround rights.

"I don't want Chicago without them," Terry said stubbornly.

"Terry, it will never go through the Board if you insist on those turnaround rights."

"The hell with them," Drinkwater growled. "The extension wouldn't be worth a damn to us without those rights."

Western's application to serve Chicago subsequently was rejected. Inexplicably, Terry blamed Brooder, who was justifiably upset.

"You know damned well why we didn't get in," Jerry said.

"Yeah," Drinkwater replied in almost a philosophical tone, "but you can rationalize anything, I suppose."

It was a tough time for Brooder. After he became a vice president in 1955, he flew to the general offices for staff meetings but steadily resisted Drinkwater's efforts to make Los Angeles his headquarters. He finally issued an ultimatum on the matter; he was at a meeting of WAL vice presidents, with Drinkwater presiding, and Terry suddenly announced:

"Jerry, we've been talking this over, and we all think the time has come for you to move your office here."

Brooder looked him right in the eye. "Terry, it's certainly been nice working for you."

Drinkwater, grinning, glanced around the room and sighed, "Well, I guess that takes care of that."

It was the last time Terry asked Brooder to pull up stakes—and it was just as well, because subsequent events wouldn't have allowed him to spend much time on the West Coast; before 1958 came to a close, Dom Renda had begun planning briefs for the longest route extension in Western's history: nonstop authority to Hawaii.

More than any other route application filed in the twenty-one years Drinkwater served as Western's president, the bid for Hawaii bore his personal stamp. It was more than just a dream to him; it became an obsession. He had lived in the Islands when he was a little boy; his father had been an Army surgeon stationed in Hawaii, and Terry loved the area. For almost thirty years, he had haunted secondhand bookstores for out-of-print Polynesian histories and missionary diaries, eventually owning more than two hundred books on various Hawaiian subjects. He became a living encyclopedia on the region, made many trips there even before Hawaiian application was filed, and once told a close friend, "When I retire, I'd like to live there and teach at the University of Hawaii."

Western sought not only Hawaiian authority but also became involved in two other complicated route proceedings, the first known as the Southern Transcontinental Case and a later one called the Pacific Northwest-Southwest Case. Renda strongly urged that the airline fight as hard for these key domestic routes as for Hawaii. Dom wanted to expand WAL's system from Seattle into Dallas and other southwestern cities, and then make Western a transcontinental carrier with a Miami–Los Angeles route through the Southwest; while Renda agreed it made no sense to move East by competing against United, TWA, and American, the Miami–Los Angeles route was practically virgin territory.

Renda to this day believes Western had a good chance to get excellent route awards out of either or both of the Pacific Northwest-Southwest and Southern Transcontinental cases if Drinkwater hadn't been so completely immersed in Hawaii. Hawaii was all he wanted, and nobody could dissuade him from almost total concentration on that single application. His former associates say he almost abdicated his day-by-day leadership of the airline, delegating immediate problems and devoting almost full time to Hawaii. He began making periodic trips to the Islands, establishing excellent contacts and making a lot of friends for WAL; his burly frame and bristling Prussian crew cut, so incongruous with that pixie smile and inevitable bow tie, became a familiar sight at the Royal Hawaiian Hotel, where he knew everyone from the manager to the busboys by their first names. It was great public relations—but while he was laying the groundwork for changing his dream into a reality, Renda, Brooder, and Tom Murphy fought the battle of the domestic route cases in which Terry was not nearly so interested. A CAB examiner recommended Western for Seattle–Denver–Dallas authority, but that was the closest WAL came to victory in these domestic applications.

The Hawaii bid was only one part of the CAB's much larger Transpacific Case, involving international routes throughout the Pacific and to the Far East. Renda tried to get TCD interested in moving beyond Hawaii to Tokyo, as well as gaining a foothold in Alaska as a springboard to Far East expansion, but Terry's ambitions stopped at Hawaii.

Renda found himself in the position of a general trying to fight battles for which his chief of staff seemed to have assigned rather low priority. He was disturbed further when Drinkwater, in his zeal to win Hawaii at all costs, moved outside the company and hired Stan Gewirtz away from the Air Transport Association as vice president of administration—with responsibility in the field of government affairs. His appointment cut straight across the lines of authority already set for Renda, and Dom wasn't happy even though he knew Gewirtz as a brilliant young man with wide airline experience. Gewirtz had once been James Landis' assistant when Landis was CAB chairman, worked for Al Adams' consultant firm briefly, and had been with National as well as ATA; he was an extremely close friend of Art Kelly's, but he was light-years away from Drinkwater's usual concept of an airline executive. Stan was his own man—rather cynical, sharp-tongued, and highly irreverent toward such corporate institutions as paternalism.

Having moved Gewirtz into Renda's and Brooder's bailiwick, Drinkwater's next move was to undercut all three. While he had assigned the chief responsibility of the Hawaiian proceeding to Renda, he also told Dom flatly:

"You are not to concern yourself with the White House."

It seemed to be clear that Drinkwater would handle the Hawaiian case himself as far as White House lobbying was concerned—a decision that Renda privately questioned although he followed orders, the result being that Dom never knew what if anything was being done at the White House level or who specifically was doing it. He assumed it was Gewirtz acting for TCD, but in actuality, Stan's job was one of generally bird-dogging the whole proceeding. Lack of influence at 1600 Pennsylvania Avenue was to prove a major factor in the controversial events that were to follow.

These were not easy times for Terrell Drinkwater. Just before Western launched its campaign to become the third California–Hawaii carrier, competing against entrenched Pan Am and United, Drinkwater's very rule at Western was challenged in a power play by a group that included two WAL directors.

One was William Bartman, a wealthy Los Angeles lawyer who had been named to the Board in 1956. The other was Wilford Gonyea, a timber magnate from Oregon, who became a director in 1957. Gonyea professed to be a great admirer of Drinkwater and his accomplishments at Western—Terry even threw him a big party held at Stan Shatto's house when Gonyea was elected to the Board. What TCD didn't know was that Gonyea already had joined forces with Bartman to seize control of the airline, the third party to the plan being Jay Pritzker, whose family founded the giant Hyatt House hotel chain; Gonyea seems to have been a front for Bartman, the lawyer's brother, and Pritzker—a kind of Trojan horse who, with the others, had acquired huge chunks of Western stock. Reportedly, Gonyea had bought some of his stock from Dudley Swim, although Swim was not in on the plan.

Drinkwater's first inkling of jeopardy came at a directors' meeting when Bartman asked for the floor, announced calmly that his group had sufficient stockholder commitments in their pockets to take over the company, and then demanded majority representation on the Board. Even Swim, no all-out Drinkwater supporter, was stunned, and Terry was almost speechless. He went into a whispered huddle with Welch Pogue.

"I think they're bluffing," Pogue told him. "They may have enough votes to call a shareholders' meeting but not enough to win a proxy fight at the meeting."

Drinkwater, at his best in this kind of scrap, glared at Bartman and barked, "We'll settle this at a stockholders' meeting if you think you've got enough votes to call one!"

Bartman demanded the shareholders' list—a dead giveaway that Pogue's bluffing theory was right. The meeting eventually was called, but Drinkwater was taking no chances; in a masterful display of counterstrategy, he changed the bylaws just before the meeting to abandon the usual practice of cumulative voting in favor of straight stockholder voting. In cumulative voting, each share of Western stock was entitled to fourteen votes—one could be cast for each of the fourteen Board members, or all fourteen could be cast for one director if the stockholder desired. Under straight voting, each share was allowed only one vote. With the latter method, the Bartman-Pritzker-Gonyea group had no chances of mustering sufficient votes to gain control and oust

Drinkwater. Bartman and Gonyea went off the Board, although the latter was to make one more futile attempt to overthrow TCD. A Board replacement was oilman Edwin Pauley, a Drinkwater choice despite some misgivings on the part of Pogue.

"What would you think of Ed Pauley as a director?" Terry asked.

"Well, I know him quite well, Terry," Pogue said cautiously. "If you have a specific reason for putting him on the Board, fine. But if you do, you're going to have to listen to Ed Pauley whenever he wants to talk, and you'll be listening to some ideas you won't like because he's pretty direct."

It was the same advice he had given Drinkwater about Dudley Swim, with identical results. At the first directors' meeting Pauley attended, he began asking questions about Western's fuel contracts; like Swim, he badgered and needled Drinkwater mercilessly as long as he served. But at least these two outspoken directors weren't after TCD's scalp, and having beaten back a serious challenge to his leadership, Drinkwater had no reason to fear the future as he guided Western across the jet-age frontier. By the end of 1959, WAL had inaugurated its long-awaited service to Calgary, taken delivery on the first six Electras, which went into scheduled operation that summer, installed the airline's first electronic reservations system, retired the last of its DC-3s, signed a contract for three Boeing 720 jetliners while leasing two 707s on an interim basis, and netted a record $5 million annual profit. The Electras right from the start surpassed all expectations in passenger appeal and operating efficiency, to such an extent that both Drinkwater and Shatto believed the propjet eventually could take over all routes except for the long-range ones served by a few jetliners.

What had happened on September 29, 1959, was just a small cloud on Western's rosy horizon—after all, the event involved another airline.

That was the night a Braniff Electra, cruising in good weather at fifteen thousand feet over the town of Buffalo, Texas, lost a wing and plunged to earth.

CHAPTER FIFTEEN

Hawaii—We Aren't Coming

The Electra had been Stan Shatto's choice—with no dissenting votes.

It was never meant to be anything but an interim airplane, a logical bridge between the DC-6B and the pure jets. As such, it was ideally suited for Western's route structure—economical to operate over short and medium-stage routes and yet versatile enough to serve the longer-haul schedules.

"We had no qualms about ordering the Electra at a time when the jets were just around the corner," Shatto reminisces. "We considered going straight from the pistons to the pure jets, but the decision to buy a turboprop was based largely on the fact that the only jets available then were the 707 and DC-8, which were too big. And the Electra was one hell of a flying machine— maneuverable and with more muscle than any other airplane flying."

Along with other Electra operators, Western was shocked at the Braniff accident but not unduly concerned. Shatto kept in close contact with Lockheed during the course of the investigation, which presented the CAB with a single, unpleasant fact —a wing had come off in level flight under good weather conditions—and numerous other facts that said it was impossible for that wing to come off in level flight with no weather problems. One by one, theories and hypothetical solutions were proposed and discarded: in-flight fire, collision with some object ranging from another plane to a guided missile, metal fatigue, sabotage, control malfunction, prop blade failure, and a sharp pullup from an unexplained dive.

The probers looked into every component and system built into the airplane, trying to uncover some weakness, failure, or malfunction that might have caused wing separation. They drew one blank after another; by March 17, 1960, the Buffalo, Texas, crash was about to be consigned to the unsolved file when—on this St. Patrick's Day—another Electra lost a wing and dove into the ground at 618 miles per hour near a small Indiana town called Tell City.

This was a Northwest flight bound from Chicago to Miami, and its fate was a virtual mirror image of the Braniff crash. What had appeared to be inconsequential or insignificant evidence at Buffalo became real clues when it also turned up at Tell City. On May 5, 1960, a Lockheed official stood up at a meeting of CAB and FAA officials and uttered six words that added up to solving two of the most mysterious crashes in aviation history:

"We're pretty sure it's whirl mode."

Whirl mode is a form of vibrating motion inherent in any piece of rotating machinery such as oil wells, table fans, automobile drive shafts—and propellers.

A propeller has gyroscopic tendencies; in simplest language, it will stay in a smooth, even plane of rotation unless it is displaced by some strong external force, just as a spinning top can be made to wobble if a finger is placed against it. The moment such a force is exerted against a propeller, it reacts in the opposite direction from which it is spinning. The result, if the mode is not checked, is a wildly wobbling gyroscope that inevitably begins to transmit its violence to the only outlet—the wing.

Whirl mode was not unknown on piston-engine aircraft, but it always encountered the powerful stiffness of the entire engine-nacelle structure and remained stable without spreading to the main wing area.

Why not in the Electra?

The answer lay in the No. 1 outboard nacelle structure on the Braniff Electra, and the No. 4 nacelle structure on Northwest's. Investigators found that the entire engine package on both these outboard engines had been wobbling before wing failure; whirl mode had spread to the wing unchecked. It was further discovered that the nacelle structure had to be in a weakened condition prior to the start of whirl mode—possibly through a previous

hard landing, sharp maneuvers, or turbulence. Such damage reduced the structure's stiffness to the point where a sudden jolt at
high speed, or a sharp upward movement, caused the propeller-
nacelle package to wobble crazily—a giant finger touching a
smoothly whirling mass, breaking its stride, and in seconds transmitting massive flutter into the wing.

In the 2½ months that elapsed between the Northwest crash
and the determination of whirl mode as a murderer, the Electra
had become an aviation Pariah not only feared but spurned by
air travelers throughout the nation. Western was no exception
among Electra operators hard-hit by the disgraced airliner. In
January 1960, WAL's Electra flights were averaging load factors
of nearly 80 per cent; in two months, they were down to less
than 50 per cent.

And more than just the public was affected by the anti-Electra
hue and cry. Northwest's Don Nyrop, badly shaken by the Tell
City disaster, in which thirty-three men, twenty-one women, and
eight children had died, actually asked Lockheed to take back
the Electras it had sold to NWA and return the old Boeing Strat-
ocruisers it had traded in on the new propjets. Nyrop was one of
the airline chieftains summoned by FAA administrator Pete
Quesada to Washington for an emergency meeting on the Electra crisis. Shatto represented Western at the dramatic session,
stunned along with virtually everyone else in the room when
Nyrop rose and announced he was grounding every Electra in
Northwest's fleet that very day.

The tough, brusque head of Northwest was almost in tears as
he told his fellow airline executives he didn't care what anyone
else was going to do: Northwest was through with the disgraced
airliner. Shatto, along with C. R. Smith of American and Eddie
Rickenbacker of Eastern, was among those who pleaded with the
distraught Nyrop to change his mind and finally succeeded,
pointing out that if Northwest grounded the plane, other Electra
operators would have to follow along—because it would be impossible to explain to passengers why one airline grounded its
Electra fleet and the others kept flying the plane. An interesting
side note, underlining Shatto's influence with Western, was that
he was one of the few officials present who was not president of
his respective carrier. He was there, with Drinkwater's full ap-

proval, to defend the airplane and express Western's faith in its inherent safety. And it came down to a defense that had to be made not only to the public and the government, but also within Western's own hierarchy—the Electra controversy had reached into WAL's Board of Directors, which met to discuss the propjet's tarnished image and sinking load factors.

It was a heated session, with several directors bluntly urging Drinkwater to sell the entire Electra fleet—the six already delivered and the remainder on order. Leading the anti-Electra fight among the directors were Harry Volk, who by then had left the insurance business to head the Union Bank of Los Angeles, and Robert E. Driscoll, a banker from Rapid City, South Dakota. Aside from the merits of the Electra case, their alliance symbolized the diversified nature of Western's Board—ranging from big-name financiers and industrialists like Pauley and Swim to small-town civic leaders like Alexander Warden, publisher of the *Tribune-Leader* of Great Falls, Montana.

Drinkwater and Shatto led the fight to save the Electra, first because they had faith in the airplane and second because TCD in particular wasn't ready to go all-out for the only alternative if the Electras were sold: big jets. With the DC-3s gone, Western was in the process of peddling its last four Convair 240s along with a DC-6B going to the Los Angeles Dodgers baseball team. WAL was about to become an all-four-engine airline, and Drinkwater was not ready to commit himself to large-scale jet purchases.

Welch Pogue joined Drinkwater and Shatto's defense of the embattled Electra. The vote on a motion to sell the fleet was deadlocked at six to six when Terry and Pogue cast their votes against the motion, and the Electra was saved—fortunately, it turned out, for once the aircraft's deficiencies were corrected, it became one of the finest transports the airlines have ever operated. Chronologically speaking, its timing was bad; the pure jets took over faster than anyone expected, and the Electra reached virtual obsolescence long before the normal lifespan of a good airliner.

"It was the last of the fun airplanes to fly," says one Western captain, speaking for all ex-Electra pilots to whom a sound became a memory—that muted, low-pitched snarl of the mighty

Allisons so peculiar to the Electra: a kind of rasping growl that bespoke hidden power and a belligerent defiance of the skies.

Western's earliest Electras were equipped with Lockheed-approved galleys, which earned the instant dislike of every stewardess assigned to an L-188 trip. Dick Ensign was the chief target for the stewardess complaints, and he rode enough trips to concede they had a point—several points, in fact; it required the muscles of a stevedore to work, the brain of an Enrico Fermi to figure out, and the patience of Job to live with.

"The problem was simple," Ensign admits. "The girls not only weren't mechanical engineers but their normal areas of reach were different than men—yet men had designed the galley to fit their own anatomical measurements."

The result was a decision to call in a dozen stewardesses to look at basic galley designs and actually work with mockups under simulated service conditions. Another decision coinciding with the Electra's new galleys was fleet standardization of galley equipment, especially in tray carriers. This innovation saved almost enough money to pay for the improved galleys—it meant continuity in service procedures, greater efficiency, and drastically reduced inventories. The latter was no small item, for on an airline each piece of equipment, from the airplane down to the serving trays, requires three separate inventories—one for equipment in operation, a second for equipment in overhaul, and a third for equipment going into or out of maintenance. Standardization is a magic word in the airline business, and Stan Shatto was one of its most faithful disciples; in years to come he would even order the Boeing 737 short-range jet with the same size wheels as the much larger 720-B, so tires would be interchangeable.

For a time, there was a strong suspicion that Drinkwater himself was willing to adopt the ultimate in standardization—one type of airplane—and there is some evidence to indicate that he at least was thinking about Western operating an all-Electra fleet. This was at the time TCD was getting static from within the company concerning the delay in ordering jets—most of it coming from Kelly and Renda. Art was concerned from a competitive standpoint, Dom because of the Hawaiian application.

"How the hell can we win our case unless by the time the

hearings start we can at least say we've ordered jet equipment?" Renda asked Drinkwater bluntly. "Everyone else with an application before the CAB is proposing some kind of jet service; we're the only exception."

Ed Pauley, too, brought up Hawaii when Drinkwater continued to procrastinate—while simultaneously extolling the virtues of the Electra.

"If you win Hawaii," Pauley told him, "you sure as hell aren't gonna fly the damned route with Electras."

Terry at first stubbornly refused to commit himself. His adamant stand was best illustrated by a remark he made at a travel agents' meeting in 1958—when every major airline in the country already had signed its first jet contracts with either Boeing or Douglas. Someone asked from the floor why Western hadn't ordered any yet.

"Would you buy the *Queen Mary* to sail across Lake Tahoe?" Drinkwater cracked.

In the end, it was Stan Shatto who swung the recalcitrant president into line. More than one WAL veteran still believes Shatto was as responsible as Drinkwater for the delay in buying jets, but the accusation is false; Stan allied himself with Renda and Kelly, forcing Drinkwater into the inevitable decision he was so reluctant to make. Shatto recognized the all-turbine airliner exactly for what it was: an air travel revolution. Where Kelly and Renda couldn't move TCD off dead center, Shatto could—joining them in pestering him and badgering him to the point where he finally growled, "All right, you guys, go ahead and do what you want!"

It was easier said than done; the decision had been delayed so long that any Western orders for the 707 would have put the airline far down the list in priority for delivery dates—and no one could be sure that Hawaiian authority wouldn't be granted before WAL got its first jets. Besides, Shatto didn't think the 707 was the right plane for Western, anyway—it was too big, and so was the DC-8, which already was trailing the Boeing entry in delivery times. The Convair 880 was considered, but Shatto thought it too small.

Boeing had a smaller, lighter version of the 707 called the 720-A. Seating slightly fewer passengers and with about 300 cubic feet less cargo space, the 720 appeared to be a good choice for Western's three long-haul routes—Los Angeles–Minneapolis/ St. Paul, Los Angeles–Mexico City, and the tentative Hawaii run. United had ordered a number of 720s, but Boeing was scrounging for additional customers and was more than receptive when Shatto flew up to Seattle for some down-to-earth negotiating. It was a typical Drinkwater/Shatto equipment purchase operation of those years—Terry would ask Stan what the airline needed, or Shatto would tell him Boeing was ready to make a good deal. Then TCD would nod and say, "Tell Jud to raise the dough." This informal method might be contrasted to Western's 1976 equipment purchase deliberations, which involve all senior officers and a five-year profit plan based on every conceivable factor from projected traffic growth to environmental considerations.

But the method worked in those days, for Shatto had an uncanny instinct for choosing the right airplane at the right time— and at the right price. He never played follow the leader in buying airplanes; he was not one of those smaller-airline executives who thought the major carriers were infallible in their equipment selections, and who tended to wait and see what the big boys were buying before making their own decisions.

So when he went to Seattle to talk to Boeing about buying jets, he was not influenced by United's choice of the 720-A; he didn't like its power plants, the same Pratt & Whitney JT3C-6 engines used on the early 707 models. The latter were the "water wagons," named for the water injection boosts that provided additional thrust on takeoffs. What Shatto wanted was the relatively new fan-jet engine, which weighed slightly more than the older engine but boosted thrust from twelve thousand pounds to eighteen thousand, with almost identical fuel consumption.

Thus was born the 720-B, a jetliner that combined a lighter airframe with a more powerful engine that turned it into a virtual flying hot rod. Western was the first airline to order the 720-B, whose takeoff, climb, and altitude capability made even 707 fan-jets seem stodgy. Until the 747 came along, for example, the 720-B was the only commercial jetliner able to climb to and cruise at more than forty thousand feet with a full load—an achievement made possible by the fact that the 720-B had the same wing and engines as its bigger fan-jet brother but a lighter structure.

The 720-B order didn't solve WAL's jet equipment problem—the three Western was buying wouldn't be delivered until sometime in 1961, and Renda kept warning that authority to operate the Hawaiian route might come while the new planes still were on the assembly line. Fidel Castro unwittingly solved the problem; Cubana Airlines had signed for two 707s, but when Castro overthrew the Batista government, Cubana was unable to take delivery. Shatto negotiated a leasing deal with Boeing for the two planes, and Western had its first jets—assigning them initially to the Los Angeles–Seattle and Los Angeles–Minneapolis schedules. They were too big, of course, but they were ready to serve Hawaii if that route award should come through; after fourteen months in domestic service, they were turned over to Pan Am.

The 720-B contract included an option for a fourth fan-jet and another option for five more scheduled for delivery in 1962 and 1963; Western exercised the first option quickly as confidence grew that the CAB would grant the Hawaiian application. Meanwhile, the maligned Electra gradually returned to the public's good graces.

Lockheed itself eradicated the whirl mode menace via a $25 million modification program. The entire nacelle structure was strengthened, doubling its stiffness, and as a precautionary measure the wings themselves were beefed up in key structural areas which the Braniff and Northwest accidents plus additional tests had disclosed to be adequate but not as strong as they could be.

The Electra's reign as the queen of Western's fleet was short-lived, but it continued to serve the airline faithfully and efficiently for another decade—WAL's last Electra would be retired in 1971, and its final task was a cargo run to Alaska. Although it began as the epitome of first-class luxury, it spent most of its dozen years in service as an all-coach transport—a configuration decision that caused some controversy within management. Shatto himself advocated the all-coach layout—which naturally included elimination of the rear lounge—and stirred up something of a fuss when he and Marv Landes decided on their own that the galleys should come out, too. They were removed before any protest could be organized—a frequent Shatto strategy.

This was anathema to Art Kelly and the rest of the sales department, but Drinkwater, who still insisted that the 1948 experiment of eliminating meals should have worked, upheld Shatto. In at least one market—Denver–Calgary—the galleyless Electras were a disaster; this was a route heavily patronized by affluent Texans making business trips to the Canadian oil fields, flying up from Dallas and connecting with Western at Denver. They were not only used to first-class travel but also demanded it, and their howls of protest reached the approximate decibel level of the "Remember the Alamo" battle cry.

The complaints reached such proportions that Drinkwater consented to discuss the situation at a staff meeting. Kelly and others made impassioned pleas at least to put back the galleys, and Renda asked Shatto: "Stan, how much would it cost to go back to the original configuration?"

"About $100,000 per airplane or $1.2 million for all twelve," Shatto announced.

Kelly groaned. "That's a lot of money to spend, Art," Drinkwater said. "Let's think about it."

Coming out of the meeting, Renda whispered to Kelly, "Funny how a guy's arithmetic can screw up a good idea."

"Arithmetic?" Kelly asked.

"Yeah. He put a decimal point in the wrong place—the correct cost is closer to $10,000 per aircraft."

There was no use reporting the error; TCD's mind had been made up, and changing it—poor arithmetic notwithstanding—would have been like reversing the earth's orbit. But while that incident is so typical of the Shatto stories still told around Western, it does not detract from his accomplishments in the area of his greatest skills: maintenance and operations. Some pilots may have hated his guts, for example, but he also had his supporters. Jack Slichter was on a flight once and got to talking to an official of the company handling Western's hull and liability insurance. Slichter mentioned that as far as he could find out, Western's insurance rates were below the industry average.

"They are," the insurance executive agreed. "And do you know why?"

"I'd be interested in your answer," Slichter said.

"Just two words. Cockpit discipline."

Western had officially entered the jet age on June 1, 1959, using one of the leased 707s between Los Angeles and Seattle and the other from Los Angeles to Minneapolis with a single stop at Salt Lake City. Inevitably, the advent of the jets generated a fresh collection of stories centering around the new jet crews, especially a young airman named Frank Ballantine.

Ballantine was assigned as a second officer on one of the first 707s to land at Salt Lake City, where the ground personnel weren't too familiar with the giant jet. While the captain and first officer went into dispatch for a weather check, Ballantine was busying himself with a walk-around inspection just as a fuel truck rolled up.

"How much fuel do you need, Frank?" the driver asked.

"Oh, fill 'er up," Ballantine said nonchalantly.

They did. With 130,000 pounds of kerosene for a flight that needed around 50,000 pounds, the latter figure including enough reserve fuel to hold over Minneapolis for two hours. The captain returned to find out that Ballantine's casual command would result in a delay of between one and three hours; the 707 couldn't legally take off from Salt Lake City with 130,000 pounds of fuel, and it takes far more time to empty a jet's tanks than to fill them.

Ballantine drew the redoubtable George "Knuckles" Ryan as captain on another 707 trip, and Jack Keyes was the copilot. They were landing at San Francisco on a Seattle–Los Angeles flight, and Ryan, always somewhat abrupt on the controls, pushed the rudder pedal a bit hard during final approach. Pilots seldom need to touch the rudder on a jet, and Ryan shoved hard enough to cause the tail to swing around. Both Keyes and Ballantine knew what had happened, but they went into an immediate act of suspecting that something abnormal had occurred.

"You feel that?" Keyes asked the flight engineer.

"Yeah. Wonder what it was."

"Inadvertent hard-over signal, maybe," Keyes theorized.

Nothing further was said until after they landed. "Frank, better go out and take a look at that rudder," Keyes suggested.

Ballantine, cued in as if he were reading the first officer's devious mind, nodded, put on his cap and uniform jacket, and left the cockpit—ostensibly to go outside and examine the tail section. Actually, he merely went back into the cabin, chatted with the stewardesses for a few minutes, and then returned wearing a frown of carefully controlled panic.

"The rudder's gone," he announced.

Ryan wheeled around, his face pale. "What?"

"Well, not exactly gone," Ballantine assured him. "Jack, what do you call those pins that hold the flutter tabs on?"

"Fratisan pins," Keyes said helpfully—knowing that one might have difficulty locating fratisan pins holding flutter tabs on the starship *Enterprise*, let alone on a Boeing 707. But Ryan was too shaken to realize that his leg was being pulled right out of its socket.

"The fratisan pins holding the top flutter tab are missing," Ballantine disclosed in the sepulchral tone he would have used if revealing that a wing had fallen off.

"Jesus," muttered the stricken captain.

An expression of hope fluttered across the copilot's face. "Wait a minute, Frank," Keyes said, "are you sure it's the top flutter tab? Not the bottom?"

"I'm not sure," Ballantine confessed gravely.

"Look it up in the MEL [Minimum Equipment List]," Keyes ordered.

Ballantine lifted the heavy 707 manual out of his bag and gave an excellent imitation of a flight engineer looking for *flutter tabs*. "Here it is," he finally declared. "Let's see—rudder . . . tabs . . . flutter tabs . . . fratisan pins."

"What does it say?" Ryan pressed desperately.

"It says," Ballantine proclaimed, "that you can operate with the top fratisan pins gone but not the bottom ones."

"Thank God," Keyes sighed.

"Yeah," agreed Ryan. "Frank, why don't you go out again and make sure it's the top one?"

It was years later, after Ryan had retired, that Keyes finally got around to telling him the Truth About Fratisan Pins and Flutter Tabs. Yet there is a kind of sadness about the story; the jets were taking something away from those Western pilots who had been weaned on 247s and DC-3s and in some cases even the old Fokkers, even as they added new dimensions of safety, speed, and comfort to passengers. It was evident in the way a crusty veteran like Ryan could fly a 707 as well as anyone else, yet really didn't grasp its complexity. It was evident in the changing relationships between pilots and stewardesses—an almost imperceptible change at first, but still a slow, gradual lessening of camaraderie and comradeship, reaching the point in the seventies when those relationships were to become casual and often impersonal.

With the lowering of such barriers as mandatory resignation upon marriage, the flight attendants found their jobs more of a career profession than a premarital avocation. And the pilots themselves matured under the far greater technical demands of the jet age—they had more buttons to push, computers became crew members, and electronic aids made flying easier as well as safer, but all these advantages also required more stringent training, stricter rules, and even greater responsibility; a captain was no longer a Greek god with four stripes and a father image, but a highly paid technician/businessman in charge of a multimillion-dollar office building with wings. On a jet, the captain's choice of cruising altitude can mean the difference between a profitable or an unprofitable trip.

Of all WAL's employees in the 1959–60 period, none awaited the decision on Hawaii more anxiously than the flight crews. Only a handful would be able to bid the Hawaiian trips, but as the more senior pilots and flight attendants grabbed the coveted schedules to the Islands, the more desirable mainland flights would have some vacancies. While the cautious Renda kept warning that CAB decisions were notoriously unpredictable, the general optimism around Western matched the confidence of Notre Dame playing Slippery Rock.

Western filed its Hawaiian application at about the same time Hawaii became the fiftieth state—the latter an event that became significant as well as coincidental. WAL asked for authority to provide nonstop service from Los Angeles and San Francisco to Honolulu and Hilo, plus one-plane service to the two Hawaiian cities from San Diego, Phoenix, Salt Lake City, Denver, and the Twin Cities. When Hawaii became a state, the Western application took on the status of purely a domestic route bid, but unfortunately—as it turned out—it was tossed into that vast, complex hopper known as the Transpacific Route Case.

Originally, the latter was not as complicated as it later became. Western's competitors for Hawaiian authority were Continental, Northwest, and Hawaiian Airlines. Continental sought authority to serve Hawaii from various inland points on its system, competing against Western between California and the Islands; Northwest also asked for California–Hawaii rights plus a central Pacific route, and Hawaiian requested only Hawaii–California.

Hawaiian Airlines developed into the most serious opponent in the first phase of the case. The CAB examiner assigned to the proceeding, Ray Madden, issued an initial decision awarding Hawaiian Airlines Los Angeles–Hawaii and San Francisco–Hawaii rights, denying it only San Diego–Hawaii. There was momentary panic at Western, but Renda counseled patience.

"We've still got the full Board to pass judgment," he told Drinkwater, "and I don't think they'll uphold the examiner. It'll be the Northeast situation all over again."

Renda was referring to a previous Civil Aeronautics Board decision letting tiny Northeast Airlines compete against Eastern and National over the lucrative New York–Miami route. The award was not one of the CAB's wisest, for Northeast wasn't operationally or economically capable of competing with two established carriers in a long-haul, highly competitive market. Northeast fell flat on its face, eventually merging with Delta. The Northeast experience was one of the major lines of argument Renda employed in trying to convince the Civil Aeronautics Board that it should overturn the examiner's initial decision.

The CAB's vote in the original Transpacific Case was three to two in favor of Western. But the Board's approval touched off an almost incredible cycle of events. First, the final decision was made on December 7, 1960, but for some undisclosed reason was kept under wraps until January 19, 1961—the last full day of the Eisenhower administration—when the official announcement of Western's award was issued.

It was a totally meaningless announcement, for with the decision came a temporary stay order that postponed WAL's operating rights to Hawaii pending further study. The CAB explained that its international route recommendations in the Transpacific Case had been disapproved by outgoing President Eisenhower because of its possible effect on U.S. relations with Japan. The Chief Executive, the Board went on, also had suggested that the CAB reconsider its Mainland–Hawaii award. The double-barreled announcement, giving Western Hawaiian authority with one hand and snatching it away with the other, was accompanied by the text of a White House letter outlining the President's position. After declaring that "our foreign relations would be adversely affected were we at this time to add second carriers on our major routes to the Orient," Eisenhower added these words fatal to Western's and Terry Drinkwater's hopes:

> Due to the advent of Hawaii as a State, the President, under law, no longer has jurisdiction over service between the Mainland and Hawaii. It would be my hope, however, that the Board would reconsider its decision to authorize additional service between the Mainland and Hawaii by a carrier which heretofore has not been engaged in service over the Pacific. At some future time it may be deemed advisable from every standpoint to add a second United States carrier on the California–Hawaii–Tokyo route. The carrier selected—which would be presumably a carrier customarily engaged in international commercial aviation in the Pacific—should also be authorized to carry local traffic between the Mainland and Hawaii. To do otherwise would be to handicap such a second carrier in terms of its ability to compete with the carrier now serving this route to the Orient, a carrier which already has full traffic rights between the Mainland and Hawaii and which is thus able materially to support its overall route to the Orient.

Obviously, the President not only had slammed the door on Western's Hawaiian dreams but had also padlocked it. In effect, he had illegally intervened in a domestic route case, formulating a policy which—if applied by the CAB in the future—would disqualify Western from flying any Mainland–Hawaii route, leaving

Pan American and United alone in the California–Hawaii market.

That controversial paragraph raised two questions:

1. Why was it written in the first place?
2. Why did the CAB abjectly accept unlawful White House intervention in a domestic route case, allowing what the President himself admitted had no legal standing to override the Board's own findings?

It is generally believed throughout the industry that Pan Am's lobbyists, extremely efficient at the White House level in those days, had a large hand in composing the letter that Eisenhower signed. But there is no plausible theory as to why the CAB itself did an about-face and literally surrendered its own jurisdiction over the domestic phase of the Transpacific Case, or why it deliberately withheld public announcement of Western's award forty-three days and then released it along with the countermanding stay order and the White House letter.

No one at Western even knew that the award had been made on December 7. Renda was in Drinkwater's office the following January 19, and Gewirtz still was bird-dogging the case in Washington when the news reached WAL via a phone call from Gewirtz. TCD was stunned—"so shocked he didn't know what to do," Renda recalls grimly.

On January 27, 1961, one week after John Fitzgerald Kennedy became President of the United States, Western Airlines filed a motion with the Civil Aeronautics Board to cancel its stay order and implement its decision awarding the carrier Hawaiian authority. The Board rejected the motion—thus touching off a battle that was to last nearly a decade and end in what amounted to no real victory for anyone. When Western finally won its Hawaiian route award nine years after the original award, it was hamstrung by restrictions and diluted by excessive competition —which might never have been imposed were it not for a series of events involving such supposedly unrelated factors as a nationwide labor dispute, a vengeful White House, and the single-minded adherence to principle demonstrated by Terrell C. Drinkwater.

This strange cycle began early in 1961, in the form of a sequel to the 1958 strike of Western pilots over the "third man" issue. The battle for cockpit representation began with the transition to turbine-powered transports, ALPA insisting that the third man in a jet cockpit had to be pilot-trained, and the smaller but equally belligerent FEIA arguing that the third man had to be a qualified flight engineer, requiring no pilot training or qualifications. Both unions cast a noble mantle of safety over their claims —ALPA saying that the complex, unforgiving jets needed a third pilot far more than it did a flight engineer, who really didn't have much to do on a jet except watch the gauges; FEIA claiming that any large airplane required the presence of an airborne "Mr. Fixit," a kind of supermechanic who knew the jet's components, systems, and structure to a degree no pilot could because of the flight engineer's specialized training.

It was an extremely touchy issue for all airlines. There was general realization that ALPA was trying to become the bargaining agent for all flight crew members, using safety as an excuse for a representation power play—yet there also was considerable agreement that the flight engineer's role in jet operations *had* diminished even as the need for a third pilot increased. Senior captains were bidding the jet schedules, and the chances for pilot incapacitation went up correspondingly. Balanced against this was the natural reluctance on the part of many airlines to give loyal and skilled flight engineers the shaft.

The first solution for this dilemma came from four of the biggest carriers American, Eastern, Pan American, and TWA. They signed contracts with ALPA agreeing to operate all four-engine jets with four-man crews—three pilots and a flight engineer. This compromise at best was temporizing and at worst extremely uneconomic; "featherbirding" was what it was called by new FAA Administrator Najeeb E. Halaby, whose own agency said flatly that a three-man complement was perfectly safe.

The fifth of the industry's giants, United, refused to go along with the four-man-crew concept. After fruitless talks with both ALPA and FEIA, the dispute was turned over to the National Mediation Board, which ignited the dynamite: It ruled that all members in a jetliner cockpit should have a single collective bargaining unit. This was a solar-plexus blow to FEIA, which stood no chance of winning any representation contest with ALPA; infuriated, the flight engineers struck seven carriers—American, Eastern, TWA, Pan Am, National, Flying Tiger, and Western.

WAL had begun contract negotiations with its flight engineers on December 28, 1960, with no apparent acrimony. A negotiating session had been scheduled for February 21, five days after the walkout was called. Stan Shatto heard about the FEIA strike plan less than two hours before it began, and he headed immediately for the airport, where he confronted the head of Western's FEIA chapter.

"What are you guys going to do?" he asked.

"We're going out."

"You're making one hell of a mistake," Shatto warned. He went into an immediate huddle with Drinkwater, urging a firm stand against an illegal strike.

It was exactly that—illegal under the terms of the Railway Labor Act, which forbade any strike while a current contract still was in effect and while negotiations for a new one were in progress. A further illegality was a ban against any walkout because of a labor ruling affecting another airline. Renda composed the text of the telegram being sent to 123 flight engineers, choosing his words carefully, as he explained later, "so if we had any litigation, we'd be on solid ground."

In addition to the telegrams, supervisors contacted the engineers individually, requesting them to report for duty and orally warning each one that his services would be terminated if he refused to work. Flight engineers on vacation or sick leave were told not to come back until their leaves had expired or they were off sick leave. With the exception of about twenty men, the flight engineers, in effect, told the company to go to hell. Two years later, they were to file a lawsuit against FEIA charging that they defied Drinkwater on the direct orders of the national union—which had not only called the walkout but had also paid strike benefits. FEIA, in turn, was to admit that the Western strike was illegal to begin with and to claim that the WAL engineers had walked off their jobs as individuals, with the union powerless to make them return.

Whether the national union or the chapter was at fault, the result was the same: Western's flight engineers cut their own throats. The strike began at 10:00 P.M. on Friday, February 17.

The next day, Renda sent an attorney, Don Hall, to the U. S. District Court, which issued an immediate restraining order against the strike. Only a handful obeyed—approximately a hundred men continued the walkout as Western's operations ground toward a total shutdown. On Monday, the company began sending telegrams to the strikers advising them they were fired, and Hall went back to court to get the restraining order dismissed; for by now, Drinkwater and Shatto had their respective bellies full of the third-man brawl. With the grounding of Western's last flight on Tuesday, February 21, they announced to employees and the federal government that Western had begun hiring and training replacements, and that as soon as sufficient new flight engineers were qualified, service would be restored first to those portions of its system where no other air service existed, and subsequently to the rest of the system.

Western actually had a small nucleus of pilots with flight engineer qualifications who needed only brief refresher courses. Other pilots, low on the ALPA seniority list, agreed to take flight engineer training, and there still were about twenty flight engineers available who hadn't gone out. This manpower was sufficient to resume partial operations in a week and full service within two weeks.

Drinkwater had taken swift, positive, no-nonsense action in a crisis and rightfully deserved plaudits. But his decisiveness was a virtual solo act; only Flying Tiger followed Terry's lead, and the other affected airlines were only too willing to let Uncle Sam solve the third-man issue.

The last thing John F. Kennedy needed at the start of his New Frontier was a major labor dispute crippling the nation's air transportation system. He acted as swiftly as Drinkwater, but in the direction of conciliation rather than confrontation. On February 21, with four of the five biggest carriers and three smaller ones shut down, JFK appointed a special presidential fact-finding commission headed by Professor Nathan Feinsinger of the University of Wisconsin to investigate the third-man dispute and report its findings to the White House. Coincidental with this announcement came a statement from Secretary of Labor Arthur J. Goldberg, who said he had met with representatives of six of the grounded carriers and received their assurances that their striking flight engineers would be taken back with no disciplinary action, while the Feinsinger commission deliberated.

Note that he mentioned *six* of the strikebound airlines; Western was not included, and in that omission were planted the seeds for Terry Drinkwater's clash with the President himself. Nowhere in all the records, files, clippings, and documents on the 1961 flight engineers' fight is there a satisfactory explanation of why Western wasn't invited to that crucial meeting in Goldberg's Washington office. It was an affront, perhaps inadvertent or maybe deliberate, which crystallized Drinkwater's attitude and gave him—in his own mind, anyway—justification for acting in the way he did. After it was belatedly pointed out to the White House that Western couldn't be expected to co-operate in a peace settlement when it had been excluded from the Goldberg meeting, Kennedy issued an executive order amending Order 10921 establishing the Feinsinger commission. His announcement merely said that Order 10921 "is hereby amended to include Western Airlines within the mentioned air carriers." No explanation. No apology.

TCD reacted as only he could: He refused to take back the fired flight engineers.

And by doing so, he set in motion a chain of events that was to result in near disaster for the Hawaiian route, the resignation of a trusted vice president, and the alienation of the man he had once considered for his successor.

CHAPTER SIXTEEN

One Strike—You're Out!

The first executive casualty in the Drinkwater-Kennedy clash was Stan Gewirtz.

He was something of a man in the middle to start with. A stanch Democrat, a firm believer in the New Frontier, and an admirer of Labor Secretary Arthur Goldberg (whom he refers to today as "the Henry Kissinger of his time"), Gewirtz was Terry's ace in the hole for dealing with the Administration TCD had defied.

That he probably was, but Gewirtz' effectiveness as a go-between was weakened by the fact that he didn't agree with Drinkwater's stand; he didn't try to sabotage it, but neither did he try to make any kind of a strong case for it among the men TCD was counting on him to influence. Although labor affairs were part of his myriad duties, he hadn't been consulted on the decision not to take back the striking flight engineers, and he made no secret of his opposition.

Gewirtz had gone home the afternoon of February 17—the Friday the strike was called—and went to the movies that night aware that there were rumblings of a walkout, but not knowing that the engineers actually were going out. When he walked into his house around midnight, one of his daughters told him Terry Shrader had been trying to reach him. Shrader, Western's director of labor relations, had been hired away from Eastern by Gewirtz himself. Stan called Shrader, who told him the flight engineers had struck.

"It's not all that bad, Terry," Gewirtz consoled. "You know what to do—we've discussed our strategy in a strike."

"Yeah, I know what to do—but Drinkwater didn't pay any attention to me. He fired the whole lot of them. Renda's already been told to come down to the general offices tomorrow and draw up the legal procedures. I wish you had been here when everything hit the fan."

"Terry, I couldn't have done very much about it."

"You might have been able to persuade him to take it easier," Shrader protested mildly.

"Look," Gewirtz said firmly, "I know Terry Drinkwater, and once he makes up his mind—and I assume in this case it was with the consent, approval, advice, and counsel of Stan Shatto—that's it. It's over, done with, and dead."

Gewirtz made no attempt to reach Drinkwater that night but went to the office early Saturday morning and talked briefly to Renda, who had started the legal machinery going. Over the weekend, developments reached the crisis stage—starting with the Goldberg meeting to which Western wasn't invited. By the middle of the following week, after this oversight had been corrected without altering Drinkwater's stance, the pressures began mounting to pull Western back into line with the other struck carriers. What Goldberg and other Administration officials feared was that no flight engineers would go back to work unless WAL hired back its men. It didn't happen that way, but all the White House could see at the time was a continued shutdown of all seven carriers directly attributable to Drinkwater's stubbornness.

The calls kept coming in. Two WAL directors, Welch Pogue and Ed Pauley, both urged TCD to reconsider—Pauley reportedly at the request of the White House. Goldberg tried to reach Drinkwater by phone, and when he failed, called Senator Warren Magnuson of Washington State and asked him to tell TCD that the Secretary of Labor wanted to talk to him.

"Arthur," Magnuson sighed, "what the hell am I supposed to do—call him and tell him to answer his phone?"

Governor Pat Brown of California got through to Drinkwater.

"Terry," he apologized, "it's embarrassing, but the White House asked me to call you."

Drinkwater was affable but unco-operative. "Pat, I understand, but it's none of your business."

Today, fifteen years after the event, a belief still persists that Drinkwater actually refused to take the call when President Kennedy himself called—the story being that TCD was playing golf and passed the word he was too busy to be bothered. It never really happened. What did happen was that Nathan Feinsinger flew to Los Angeles and met personally with Drinkwater and Shatto, pleading that they take back the fired employees.

"Nate, we can't," Drinkwater replied calmly. "We've already hired replacements."

"You're holding up the other airlines," Feinsinger said with a trace of anger. "Their engineers won't go back to work until Western's do."

"That's too damned bad!" Drinkwater retorted. "We took a 108-day strike by pilots because we signed an agreement with the flight engineers protecting them against ALPA's third-man policy."

Feinsinger then suggested that Drinkwater talk to JFK.

"Don't bother to have him call me, Nat," Terry said. "I'd hate to turn down the President of the United States, but that's exactly what I'd have to do."

Kennedy never did try to phone Drinkwater. CAB chairman Alan Boyd flatly refused to intercede with the Western president, but FAA administrator Najeeb Halaby did—and according to Drinkwater got very tough in the course of his phone conversation after TCD told him bluntly: "Jeeb, this is none of your damned business!"

Many of the pressure calls came to Gewirtz, who had the same answer for all of them: Nothing could be done. During this period, he himself couldn't get in to see Drinkwater. By this time, Terry was refusing to take outside calls which he knew were connected to the flight engineers' situation, and Gewirtz finally drove over to his house one night. Helen Drinkwater came to the door.

"Is Terry in, Helen? I have to see him."

"He's here, Stan, but I don't think it'll do you any good."

"I'll try, anyway."

She let him in and Gewirtz found Drinkwater lying on a couch, obviously in a bad mood.

"Don't bother me," he snapped. "I'm not gonna change my mind."

"Terry, all these guys have been trying to call you—Arthur Goldberg in particular."

"I'll talk to him in the morning," Drinkwater relented, "but don't give him any false hopes."

Gewirtz then reached Goldberg and said Western's president would talk to him the next day, adding, however, "It won't make a goddamned bit of difference."

There *was* a Drinkwater-Goldberg conversation, and it got exactly nowhere, just as Gewirtz had predicted. Drinkwater unfortunately got the impression the Labor Secretary was trying to threaten him; he told Gewirtz that Goldberg had said the Teamsters would shut down WAL if Drinkwater didn't take back the strikers. Goldberg denied this when he talked again to Gewirtz after his futile call to TCD.

"Stan, do you think the President should call Drinkwater?" Goldberg asked.

"Arthur," Gewirtz replied, "I don't think the President of the United States should ever call anyone unless he knows he's going to get the answer he wants. And he isn't going to get the answer he wants from Terry Drinkwater."

Some expected TCD to weaken when the only other carrier that had joined Western in refusing to take back its flight engineers—the Flying Tiger Line—caved in under Washington pressure. Shatto was the first to hear of the defection when a Flying Tiger official called him. "Stan, I hate like hell to tell you this, but we just went belly-up. We're taking our engineers back."

Shatto immediately notified Drinkwater, who held firm. But now uneasiness bordering on revolt was spreading within the ranks of his own executives and among a small bloc of directors headed by Pauley and Pogue. Not even Pogue could reach Drinkwater as the tension increased, reaching a climax when Terry phoned Dom Renda.

"I want you to be in your office tomorrow morning," he ordered. "I may call you and I may not, but don't move out of there."

Dom followed those instructions. When Pogue phoned, asking

THE ONLY WAY TO FLY

where he could reach TCD, Renda had to tell him, "I don't know where he is—and Stan Shatto isn't around, either."

"God, Dom," Pogue insisted, "you have to find him."

"All I know is that I've been told to stand by when and if he calls me," Renda said.

The call came, as Renda remembers it, early that afternoon, and it was from Shatto. He asked Renda to meet them at a restaurant on Pacific Coast Highway in fifteen or twenty minutes. Renda drove there and found Drinkwater, Shatto, and director Harry Volk waiting for him. Terry wanted to know what was going on at the general offices, and Renda told him about the numerous calls, including Pogue's. Drinkwater merely nodded.

"We've called this meeting to review a few things," Drinkwater announced. "We want to decide right here and now whether to take the flight engineers back. And what we need from you, Dom, is your legal opinion as to whether we can make these firings stick in court."

Renda hesitated, feeling he was about to jump off a corporate cliff, but he finally plunged ahead. "Terry, as you know, these are difficult cases, but I think we can sustain the discharges as within our rights. They walked off their jobs, and that's discharge for cause, and from a legal point of view that part can be sustained. I think they've violated the court injunction." Drinkwater looked relieved.

Renda swallowed hard and continued. "But Terry, there's more to this case than deciding it on the basis of the legal issue. I'd like to give all of you my views on how important this situation is to the Transpacific Case, and my opinion of how it would be interpreted by the Kennedy administration."

Drinkwater glared. "When I want your opinion on that, I'll ask for it! Today I just want your legal opinion, and I'm not interested in what your view on the other situation is."

Renda flushed. "I'm going to tell you anyway, Terry. As I size it up, the Kennedys are not going to forget. Anything that anybody does to this Administration, you'd better be prepared to answer for it!"

"That's a responsibility I'll accept," Drinkwater said curtly. He looked at the others. Shatto nodded agreement, and so did Volk.

Renda prepared Western's defense to lawsuits filed by the

flight engineers seeking court orders to force the airline to rehire them. WAL won every legal contest as each successive court ruled that the engineers had not been fired but quit, because the strike was illegal in the first place. In the fall of 1961, the Feinsinger commission dealt FEIA a fatal blow by ruling that the third man in jet cockpits had to be a qualified pilot. The commission recommended that all flight engineers be given pilot training and that those who failed to make the grade should receive generous severance pay or nonflying jobs. The commission also ruled against the concept of a four-man crew as completely unnecessary in terms of safety.

Thus ended the third-man issue. Western's flight engineers were the biggest losers, their discharged status eliminating any possibility of receiving the severance pay as recommended by Feinsinger and adopted by the rest of the airlines. As late as 1966, they were trying in vain to set up a meeting with Drinkwater to conciliate all differences, but by then the flight engineers who hadn't gone out, plus the new men hired and the pilots who took on flight engineer assignments, had formed a union of their own and won the right to bargaining representation. It was called the Second Officers' Association (SOA), and a few months after it was organized, its members voted to merge with ALPA.

But if WAL's engineers had lost the battle, Western came close to losing a far bigger war. Renda's warning that by defying the White House in the labor dispute, Drinkwater might be endangering the Hawaiian case, turned out to be only too true. There is nothing in cold print to confirm this, but the circumstantial evidence is overwhelming—one has only to look at subsequent chronological developments in the Transpacific Case to reach the conclusion that Western, in the words of aviation historian R. E. G. Davies, "must have had good reason for believing that the responsible civil servants and politicians kept on tossing the proverbial penny until it came down heads."

On July 27, 1961, the CAB reopened the international phase of the Transpacific Case but specifically excluded the domestic California–Hawaii phase.

On June 8, 1962, the CAB lifted its stay on the domestic phase but permitted other carriers to file petitions for reconsideration—which they did, in large numbers.

On November 8, 1963, the Board issued an incredible decision: By a three-to-two vote, it terminated both the domestic and international phases of the Transpacific Case, tossing out five years of briefs, hearings, and oral arguments covering nine thousand pages of transcripts, plus legal work involving millions of dollars in fees and expenses.

On November 29, 1963, Western asked the CAB to reconsider. More than a month later, the Board refused. WAL carried its fight for some kind of a decision on Hawaii to the U. S. Court of Appeals for the District of Columbia. After remanding the case back to the CAB three times for action on its findings that additional service was required, the Court of Appeals finally upheld the CAB after the Board changed its findings to deny the need for an additional Mainland–Hawaii carrier.

In 1966, the Civil Aeronautics Board reopened the Transpacific Case, with no less than eighteen airlines seeking various Pacific routes—including Northeast, the smallest of the trunks, which might as well have applied for authority to serve Mars via the moon. In 1969, Western got its Hawaiian route at long last—but it was an award tainted with restrictions and competition.

This, of course, is getting ahead of the Western story, but the chronology of continued frustration in obtaining Hawaiian authority originally granted in 1960 contains one significant fact: Every CAB decision against Western came out of a Board with a Democratic majority; Drinkwater's legally correct and morally justified chickens had come home to roost. Dom Renda, discussing this near-decade of apparent retribution, had a ringside seat throughout the proceedings and has this to say about what happened:

"In my considered judgment, there had to be some instructions from the White House to make sure Western did not get this route. We didn't sit on our hands. From then on, after the flight engineers' strike, Jerry Brooder and I had the responsibility of trying to patch everything up. We had support from strong people in Capitol Hill like Senators Mike Mansfield of Montana and Ted Moss of Utah. Alex Warden, who was on our Board, had meeting after meeting with White House staff members trying to convince the Kennedy administration it shouldn't hold the strike against us.

"In the second Transpacific Case, I think there was a sense of responsibility on the part of the Civil Aeronautics Board. When the CAB finally gave us Hawaiian authority, it was in cognizance that we had won the route originally. If we hadn't won it before, I don't think we would have gotten it, because by then Continental had become a real force. If you read the CAB opinion, you can see the tightrope it was walking—and why we got all those restrictions. Continental is unrestricted out of Los Angeles, whereas Western has to start all its Hawaiian flights from points east of California. I'm positive there were those on the Board who were in favor of not giving Western a goddamned thing.

"If Western had received its original 1960 award, at that time there were only two carriers to compete against—Pan Am and United. We would have started California–Hawaii service in 1961 as the third carrier, instead of having to start service in 1969 as one of six carriers. That 1961–69 period would have been a very fat profit time for Western, and we would have been placed in a solid position for eventual expansion into the Pacific.

"I think the decision Drinkwater made regarding the flight engineers may have been absolutely right at the time in terms of labor policy. But in terms of political knowledge, I think Terry was naïve, and it shocks me to think that with all the experience he had, he would all of a sudden have become so stubborn. Why did he? I'll tell you.

"Because by then there had been this change in him—from being the type of guy who welcomed and invited and entertained advice, like in that 1947–58 period—and I speak about him during that period with great love—to a man imbued with authority, who did not want opinion. It got so he acted as if he owned the company, lock, stock, and barrel. He lost that sense of responsibility to those who did own it—the stockholders. He went too far in taking away the independence of expression from his subordinates."

Renda stayed at Western for several years after Drinkwater openly ignored his advice and made it only too clear that Dom was no longer his fair-haired boy. To this day, Renda cannot recall the years following the flight engineers' strike without tears moistening his eyes.

Gewirtz, lacking Renda's deep emotional commitments to the airline and its president, didn't wait around for all this to happen to him. He had lost respect for Drinkwater, and he considered Shatto a bad influence. Along with Renda, he had the political savvy and foresight to realize the future import of Terry's defiant stand.

"He violated a fundamental rule in labor relations: Don't crawl out on a limb you can't crawl back from," Gewirtz says. "I was supposed to be the expert in this field, but he acted without even calling me. I would have told him you just don't fire an entire craft and class, not if you need them. Sure he was on solid legal grounds, but when he refused to go along with the other airlines, he screwed everything up. He totally antagonized Goldberg, who hates pretty good.

"On strictly principle, Drinkwater's position was right. But when he insisted on maintaining it, he refused to believe it was related to Western's getting the Hawaii route. I'm not going to say Goldberg gave me any firm commitment that if Drinkwater took the strikers back, it would assure us of Hawaiian authority. But there wasn't any doubt in my mind that there would have been substantial White House pressure on the CAB to give Western the route."

Soon after Western resumed operations, Gewirtz told TCD, "I want to get the hell out."

Drinkwater just looked at him in disbelief. "Go out in the desert and clear your head, Stan."

"I mean it, Terry. I want out."

"Okay, sonny, you've had a disappointment. We don't have to agree on everything. Go to Palm Springs, blow your nose, clear out your head, and come back."

Gewirtz didn't quit on the spot, and Kelly urged him to stay, but a few days later Gewirtz was in Sacramento where the Democratic Party's finance committee was holding a meeting. Gewirtz happened to be talking to Fred Glass, who had just been named chairman of the President's new task force on national aviation goals.

"You think you could find me a good vice chairman who'd be willing to do a lot of work?" Glass asked.

"I've got just the man for you," Gewirtz said quickly. "Me."

As soon as he returned to Los Angeles, he told Drinkwater he was leaving Western, TCD's reaction being a terse, "It's your decision." Gewirtz caught a plane East to see his father on the latter's seventieth birthday, returning on a Friday afternoon to inform his secretary he would be in the following Monday to clean out his desk.

"Hasn't Mrs. Gewirtz told you?" she asked.

"Told me what? I haven't been home yet."

"I think you'd better talk to her, Mr. Gewirtz."

He did. "A lot of your files are in our garage, Stan," she said.

"How would anyone know which files I'd want?" he asked.

"It beats me. Better ask your secretary."

He got the story from the secretary. Gewirtz was sharing an office with Renda at the time, and both their nameplates were on the door. The morning after he left for the East Coast, his secretary arrived at 8:00 A.M. to find Drinkwater unscrewing the Gewirtz nameplate. He looked up as she approached and barked, "Mary, get Mr. Gewirtz' stuff the hell out of this place!"

Gewirtz, at this writing a vice president of Pan Am, says he left Western still feeling that under Drinkwater, it had become the best-organized airline in the industry.

"His strengths were substantial," Gewirtz adds. "I could never understand why Shatto so dominated him—they weren't really anything alike. My theory is that Terry simply didn't understand the technology of air transportation. Yet he was so concerned about maintenance and operations, so convinced of their importance, that in his own lack of knowledge he placed undue reliance on Shatto's expertise. In the process, he developed a dependence on him that in my opinion proved to be unhealthy."

Drinkwater's change in personality, method of rule, and increasing stubbornness at this stage of Western's history were apparent to executives other than Renda and Gewirtz, but the other side of the coin was the airline's financial accomplishments. During the decade of the sixties, the same period in which his relations with some subordinates steadily deteriorated, Western kept making money—with a primarily regional route boasting only two long-haul segments. Only one other carrier with this kind of restrictive route structure matched Western in earnings —and that was Continental. Short-haul trunks like Northeast and Capital staggered toward bankruptcy, saved from this ignominy only through merger with larger, healthier carriers. Western, too, was a merger target in this period, but as a strong attraction, not an ailing fruit ripe for easy plucking. Continental's Bob Six made some tentative overtures to Western in 1961 through Ed Pauley, and in 1964 Eastern, Braniff, and TWA each approached Drinkwater evincing some interest in a possible merger.

Certainly WAL's continued profits, even in years when most airlines heaved corporate sighs of relief if they broke even, generated both envy and interest on the part of bigger carriers. From 1961 through 1968—the latter Drinkwater's last full year as president—WAL hung up this year-by-year record of black ink:

1961: $863,000 after a first-half loss of $1 million due mainly to the flight engineers' strike
1962: $5 million
1963: $9.3 million, a record
1964: $13.3 million, another record
1965: $12.1 million
1966: $16 million
1967: $12.2 million
1968: $8.4 million

And in some ways, TCD was the same old Drinkwater—a natural leader with the command aplomb of a Patton, possessing the inherent ability to dominate any kind of meeting, whether with a single person or a ballroom full of questioning stockholders. Typical was the April 27, 1961, annual shareholders' meeting held at the Los Angeles Ambassador Hotel. The tension was thicker than a coastal fog, for the session came while WAL flight engineers were still picketing, the Lockheed Electra remained under a cloud, and former director William S. Bartman was trying once more to make waves of the tidal variety.

Bartman introduced two resolutions, the first to rescind proxies obtained by directors for the annual meeting and the second to restore cumulative voting. Drinkwater ruled both motions out of order and thus ended Bartman's last effort to overthrow him. With what the Los Angeles *Examiner* called "a fine show of chairmanship," TCD either squelched or effectively answered all questions raised concerning management decisions.

The Hawaiian defeat stayed inside of Drinkwater like an undigested bowling ball. Ray Silvius, Western's public-relations chief, remembers the time he accompanied TCD to Hawaii where Drinkwater was to announce that Western was throwing in the towel on its original application for routes to Hawaii—this was after the courts had bounced the CAB's first decision back to the Board for a third and still unsuccessful review—and would file a new application for service across the Pacific. Silvius was along to set up a news conference in Honolulu, and he noticed that in the last hour of their flight Drinkwater was unusually pensive.

"I knew what he was thinking," Ray says. "We were on Pan Am, and he was wishing so very hard that it could have been Western—that this plane should have been our own."

A changed man Drinkwater was, with an inner sadness and disappointment that seemed to poison his attitude toward loyal executives like Renda. Each successive setback in the bid for Hawaii increased the friction between them, Drinkwater becoming more and more convinced—albeit unfairly—that Renda had to be held personally responsible. The inevitable break did not come for a long time, and in many ways the years immediately following the flight engineers crisis were relatively uneventful—highlighted mostly by expansion of the jet fleet even as route development stayed rather stagnant. Outside of the continuing drive to win Hawaii, Western's only other major route application in this period was involvement in the Pacific Northwest-Southwest Service Case, in which WAL sought a route stretching from various Texas points all the way to Seattle and Portland via Denver, as well as one-plane service from Texas to Calgary via Denver. The application was filed in 1964, but final Civil Aeronautics Board action did not come until May 1970.

"The case had Western written all over it," one WAL executive recalls, but once again the senior airline in the nation took its lumps from the CAB as new route awards went to Braniff, Continental, Eastern, Frontier, and TWA.

Route stagnation notwithstanding, Drinkwater was doing a 180-degree course change in his attitude toward jets. The Boeing 720-Bs were so successful that he took delivery on three more in 1962 and ordered another three. With coach travel steadily assuming major proportions, Western that same year converted all sixteen of its remaining DC-6Bs to at least partial coach configuration and instituted "Thriftair" between Los Angeles and San Francisco—a "no frills" service that brought back memories of the ill-fated Los Angeles–Seattle experiment. The difference this time, of course, was mushrooming public demand for lower-cost air travel, and as Western acquired more jets, the entire Electra fleet also began undergoing modification to all-coach seating. The airline needed more seats; in 1962, Western carried more than two million passengers for the first time.

By 1963, Drinkwater had Shatto looking around for the Electra's replacement on WAL's shorter segments. The latter, who had Favero as his top maintenance assistant and Dick Ault (formerly with Eastern and Lockheed) as his chief engineering aide, went to England to look at the BAC-111 but turned it down flatly as too small—a decision American was to wish later it too had made. Shatto liked the DC-9, generally speaking, but not its narrow cabin, with five-abreast seating, and decided to wait for the twin-engine Boeing 737, whose fuselage was the same width as that of the big Boeing jets. As usual, Drinkwater left the equipment selection problem entirely in Shatto's hands.

The annual report of 1964, Western's sixteenth consecutive profit year, cited one statistic that emphasized how far the airline had come. In that single twelve-month period, WAL boarded some 3.5 million passengers—more than it had carried in the first twenty-five years of its existence. And for the first time in its history, Western's stock was split.

The glowing financial reports had the effect of feeding Drinkwater's self-confidence, his mounting independence from the advice of former confidants. And in this time of success, the pain and frustration from the only area of failure Hawaii—increased accordingly, and so did his resentment toward Renda. He never blamed Dom directly, but he obviously had an irresistible urge to find some kind of scapegoat for the Hawaiian disappointment, and by his actions, the target unquestionably was Renda. In 1964, Drinkwater nominated Washington, D.C., attorney Howard Westwood and Jud Taylor to the Board of Directors. Renda had no objections to either man, but TCD had previously indicated to him that he probably would be picked to fill the next board vacancy. Renda considered himself as deserving as Taylor, and he already was having some serious doubts about Westwood's growing influence with Drinkwater.

Westwood was and still is with the law firm of Covington and Burling in Washington. Terry had known him since the days when Westwood was American's counsel in the nation's capital at the same time Drinkwater worked for C. R. Smith. They became fast friends, with a great deal of mutual respect.

Ironically, they were poles apart in a political sense. Drinkwater was an avowed conservative Republican, Westwood a real liberal who had once campaigned for Socialist Norman Thomas and all his life had been active in Legal Aid and other voluntary charity projects within the legal fraternity. He was the first Western director to show up at meetings with long hair—not an entirely unexpected coiffure for a man who, as the then-youngest partner in doggedly conservative Covington and Burling, used to walk down its staid corridors whistling the "Internationale." Love of books was one thing they had in common—Drinkwater with his deep interest in anything written about Hawaii, and Westwood whose passion is Civil War history. More important was their common ground of civil aviation.

Westwood served as counsel to the late Colonel Edgar Gorrell when the latter set up the Air Transport Association, in 1937, and actually helped him write the Civil Aeronautics Act of 1938, which created an independent CAB and established the basic structure of the U.S. airline industry as it exists today. Again collaborating with Gorrell, Westwood was instrumental in drawing up the pre-World War II plan for government acquisition of airline aircraft in a national emergency, and he also was the chief architect of the Universal Air Travel Plan—the first all-industry credit card.

With that kind of background, he was extremely well qualified to go on Western's Board and to give Drinkwater advice. There is some difference of opinion on how much he influenced TCD. Renda, who incidentally became good friends with Westwood, believes Westwood's influence was considerable—"about 110 per cent in the regulatory field," Renda adds. Art Kelly, on the other hand, doubts whether Westwood's influence was as great as many assume.

"Very few people had much influence on the fundamental decisions, attitudes, philosophies, and doctrines that Drinkwater formulated," Kelly declares. "Oh, he might ask for opinions or ideas, but in the final analysis he made up his own mind. He had his own opinions, his own principles, and his own standards—and in these areas he was almost inflexible."

Jud Taylor tends to side with Renda to some extent, agreeing that Westwood carried great weight with Drinkwater not only in regulatory matters but also in the area of equipment purchases, Shatto's major role notwithstanding.

"One reason Western got into overequipment problems in the sixties," Taylor expounds, "was the influence of Howard Westwood. He wanted to buy more jets than Western needed, long before we got a Hawaii route; I remember there was some strong language at a Board meeting, with Hugh Darling and myself arguing against Westwood."

Westwood went on WAL's Board as a replacement for Welch Pogue, who resigned to avoid conflict of interest when his law firm took on Eastern as a client. Westwood himself became eligible for a directorship after Covington and Burling ceased representing American, and Drinkwater's offer to join Western was doubly motivated: He wanted someone with a Washington background, like Pogue's, and he apparently needed to solidify his own security—Howard Westwood was the first of several close personal friends Drinkwater put on the Board.

The splurge in new aircraft ordered continued unabated in 1965—with Renda, Taylor, and Darling arguing futilely that WAL might be overextending itself. By the end of 1965, Western had eighteen Boeing 720-Bs in the fleet with four more on order plus the original twelve Electras and five DC-6Bs (eight of the now-obsolete workhorses were sold that year). And Western had signed a contract for twenty Boeing 737s with an option for five more that later was changed to ten. Renda didn't object to the original 737 order, but he urged that the option be dropped in favor of seriously considering the bigger, more versatile Boeing 727. Shatto disagreed, feeling the 737 was the better airplane for Western's routes, and his view prevailed—within two years, WAL had exercised all options, which gave it the second-largest 737 fleet in the world, runner-up to United, which bought seventy-five.

Western entered 1966—its fortieth anniversary year—with virtually an all-jet-powered fleet, consisting of eighteen 720-Bs, the same twelve Electras, and only five DC-6Bs still in service. And with the phase-out of these veterans also came a thinning in the ranks of the Old Guard. Marv Landes would soon go on a leave of absence and then retire. The so-called Young Turks, who had waged the battle of the budget with Drinkwater so often, were no longer middle management but at the vice-presidential level —Kelly a senior vice president, along with Taylor, Brooder, Shatto, and Renda.

In addition to Ensign, Peirce, and Lynn, five other department heads had been elevated to the previously closely held title of vice president. They included Charles J. J. Cox, Taylor's right-hand man; engineering's Dick Ault; Harold W. (Bud) Caward, flight operations; Tony Favero, maintenance; and Terrell Shrader, industrial relations.

Even the indestructible Jerry Brooder decided he had reached the end of the line. He had tried to quit in 1964, after buying some property near Phoenix, Arizona—an area he had always loved; he already was three years past the mandatory retirement age of sixty-five then, but Drinkwater wouldn't hear of his leaving.

"I want to live closer to my kids, Terry," Brooder explained patiently, "and they're in Arizona."

"So go ahead and move to Arizona, but your office goes with you."

That was all Brooder needed; he sold his house in Denver and bought a new home in Carefree, Arizona. His office was at Sky Harbor Airport in Phoenix, and he flew to Los Angeles for a staff meeting every Wednesday morning for the next two years. But by 1966, Brooder—like Renda—was fed up with Drinkwater's obsession for finding a scapegoat in the Hawaiian debacle. While

TCD tagged Renda with most of the blame, he felt Brooder had failed him too; his attitude toward Brooder changed just as it did with Renda—constant criticism, refusal to listen to advice or suggestions, and a generally frigid relationship instead of the warm friendship that had once existed. Brooder didn't mind so much for himself—he knew he was going to leave anyway—but he deeply resented Drinkwater's coldness toward Renda.

Brooder left Western on August 1, 1966. The man who missed him the most was Dom Renda, who was continuing to have his own problems with the president of Western Airlines—further dilution of his responsibility in the field of regulatory affairs. Jack Slichter had left WAL to become a vice president of the Air Transportation Association, but early in 1966—without mentioning it to Renda—Drinkwater rehired Slichter as vice president of a newly established government and industry affairs division; Dom knew nothing about it until an official announcement was made.

Renda had nothing against Slichter, who was a personable man with great ability and a dry wit; Slichter once was testifying at a CAB hearing, and the examiner finally remarked, "Mr. Slichter, I guess I don't have any more questions."

"That's fine," Slichter said, dead-pan, "because I don't have any more answers."

But Jack in his new Washington role was the equivalent of a fast halfback being asked to play defensive tackle. For one thing, it was only too clear that Howard Westwood was beginning to call the signals in Western's route cases, and Slichter's real forte lay in areas other than regulatory proceedings and lobbying. But if the assignment was somewhat unfair to Slichter, it also was another veiled insult to Renda and a further undermining of his position at Western. And Renda was to receive still another blow.

Drinkwater called him in one warm spring day in 1966.

"You're not going to like this," he began, "but I'm gonna tell you about it anyway. I'm putting two more people on the Board. One of them is James Garibaldi and the other is my brother-in-law, Dick Wright."

Garibaldi was a well-known California lobbyist; Wright, a Denver man, was executive vice president of the Montana States Employers' Council. Renda knew both and had no quarrel with either, but he was thunderstruck that he had been passed over again.

"Terry, I can't believe it," he said with intensity. "Of course I don't like it."

Drinkwater snapped something to the effect that choosing directors was his prerogative. He already had named radio and television personality Art Linkletter to the Board, and later was to nominate Leonard Firestone, president of the Firestone Tire and Rubber Company of California—replacing directors who had died or retired. The Wright selection increased the Board to fifteen members.

"Terry," Renda continued impassionately, "it's impossible to talk to you any more. We're heading for trouble. Real trouble."

"You just run your own shop and let me worry about everything else," Drinkwater replied airily.

Renda wasn't joking. His deep concern involved two areas: overexpansion in equipment, and TCD's own management policies, the latter demonstrating what appeared to Renda as an alarming proclivity for one-man rule. Unfortunately for Dom, his predictions of inevitable disaster took several years to materialize.

The flattering statistics being brought up on the occasion of the airline's fortieth anniversary seemed to indicate otherwise: a record $16 million in profits for 1966 and the eighteenth consecutive year of black ink; a payroll of 5,564 employees; almost as many flights a day (some 300) as Western Air operated in its entire first year; and a total of 4.4 million passengers carried—more than double the number flown only two years earlier. TCD even made a tacit admission of previous deficiencies in corporate planning—he hired, as vice president of a new economic planning division, Dr. John R. Summerfield, who had been with Douglas and the RAND Corporation.

Western's fortieth birthday found Fred Kelly I back on the payroll—hired to participate in several publicity activities starting in 1964, but the aging, ailing airman received his biggest assignment in 1966 when he was sent, along with Al DeGarmo, around Western's system to help promote the anniversary. They were the only survivors of the Four Horsemen; Jimmie James had died in 1964 of a heart attack. Kelly was seventy-five when he made the tour with DeGarmo, and in the few years remaining to him he was to enjoy the dignity of occasional promotional jobs and a monthly paycheck that made him feel he was still a part of the airline he helped launch.

There were those who shared to some extent Renda's gloomy misgivings, but with more of a vague uneasiness instead of specific fears. To voice such uncertainty at the summit of Western's forty years of progress would have stamped any doubter as an alarmist at best and a malcontent at worst. Renda, Taylor, and Darling were neither alarmists nor malcontents—they were men holding honest differences of opinion with a man whose trump cards included undeniable success. Art Kelly, somewhat isolated in a booming sales department, was not blind to the rapidly developing Drinkwater-Renda impasse, but he was in no position to do much about it. He had not experienced Renda's frustration with Drinkwater; on the contrary, Terry had shown refreshing openmindedness in the areas with which Kelly was most concerned—such as the champagne flights, Hunt Breakfasts, and the VIB campaign. And in this year ending WAL's first four decades, he was about to approve—with absolutely no hesitation whatsoever—one of the most daring, innovative customer-relations plans ever attempted by an airline.

This was the renowned "Flub-Stub" program—in essence, a willingness to tell more than four million passengers: "If we goof, we'll pay you for your inconvenience or dissatisfaction."

As with champagne flights, no single person can be given credit for thinking up Flub-Stubs; it was a combination of ideas from several officers, and at least part of its genesis was a feeling on the part of many Western stewardesses that the company wasn't giving them sufficient support. This complaint always has been an occupational hazard in the flight attendant's profession —a stewardess has the most contact with the public, and thereby becomes the most obvious, easily reached target for passenger unhappiness regardless of who or what was responsible for what went wrong.

Roger Gardemann, in charge of WAL's flight attendants and one of Dick Ensign's assistants, talked this problem over with Ensign, and the result was a survey to show the areas where Western was doing a much better—or much worse—job than other carriers. Ensign, in turn, discussed the situation with Bert Lynn. It was shortly after the survey results were in that a plan was suggested whereby passengers would be offered some kind of guarantee or warranty for certain basic services normally taken for granted but not always provided. This collided head-on with CAB rules against rebates of any sort, but Ensign and Lynn thought a small gift would circumvent that regulation.

The first suggestion was aimed at testing Western's advertised promise that any call to reservations would be answered within six rings. Lynn proposed that if reservations didn't answer within that prescribed time, Western would send the caller a dime.

"A dime seems kind of chintzy," someone objected. "How about making it a dollar? We answer 80 per cent of our calls within the six-ring limit, so we wouldn't have to pay out much dough."

A dollar was a more promotable amount, but it was generally agreed that limiting the payments to deficiencies in reservations' telephone responses wasn't going to do much about other areas of service. Specifically, what could Western promise of sufficient value to impress the public and yet not go broke trying to live up to its pledges?

WAL's advertising agency, Batten, Barton, Durstine & Osborn, sat in on preliminary planning and then came back with a complete package. One of the major decisions involved method of payment for an unkept promise: Should stewardesses or agents pay off right on the spot, or should they provide forms for passengers to mail? The agency finally settled on a plan to have stewardesses hand out prepared forms on the aircraft, and passengers could collect a dollar from any Western ticket counter. And the advertising brains came up with a name for the forms: Flub-Stubs.

Originally, the plan called for a dozen pledges, but BBD&O narrowed this list down to eight:

1. A smile and a genuinely friendly greeting from every Western Airlines employee you will meet.

2. If your ticket is supposed to be waiting at Will Call, it will be ready and waiting.

3. A stewardess to greet you with a smile at the door of your plane when you arrive and when you leave; and to treat you throughout the flight as you would a guest in your own home.

4. A special dietary meal if you order three hours in advance of your flight.

5. The best cup of coffee in the sky [not an impossible promise, for Western used a brand especially blended to its own specifications and always served fresh].

6. En route announcements from your pilot or copilot.

7. A clean plane with clean ashtrays and sparkling washrooms on all originating flights.

8. A sincere "thank you" whenever you call or visit a Western Airlines ticket counter or office.

At the bottom of the list was printed:

"Anytime we don't live up to one of these promises . . . or give you an immediate explanation why we can't . . . you get a Flub-Stub worth a buck." On the Flub-Stub itself, which resembled the paper money in the game of "Monopoly," was a cartoon of a blushing man with the motto "to err is human" written in Latin: *errare est humanis.* The last word should have been *humanum,* but in the first Flub-Stubs it was misspelled deliberately to see if anyone caught the mistake. A few did—and each received a dollar.

There were two serious objections raised to the Flub-Stub campaign before it got under way on May 9, 1966. One came from the stewardesses, who feared the stubs would be used to punish flight attendants and other employees. A stewardess had to sign each Flub-Stub she handed out, for example, and the girls at first expected recriminations; it would have been easy for WAL to keep records on which stewardesses were giving away the most stubs, as if this were a barometer of their performance. To allay their fears, the company sent teams of officers around the system to explain the purpose of the Flub-Stub project.

"They emphasized that no names would be noted nor records kept," Lynn says. "The only data we wanted from the stubs was a tabulation of which complaints were costing us the most money. We made it clear it was all in fun, almost tongue-in-cheek."

The second objection was raised by the faint of heart in the executive echelons. It was freely predicted that the Flub-Stubs would cost Western two hundred thousand dollars a month. Flub-Stubs lasted more than eighteen months, and in that time the airline paid out a total of around ninety thousand dollars. The highest monthly total was under eight thousand dollars, and the average per month was less than five thousand dollars. One unexpected development was the failure of many passengers to cash in their stubs; some wrote in to report they had theirs framed.

In its later stages, the Flub-Stub program was modified somewhat. First the eight pledges were pruned down to four—retained were Nos. 1 through 4, but space was made available on the back of the stub for passengers to list any deficiency they thought worth mentioning. The final stubs made no specific promise but invited all complaints, in a space following this message addressed to WAL: "You want to know how I got this Flub-Stub? Well, I'll tell you . . ."

The wide-open "write your own gripe" offer naturally led to some that were unreasonable and overly petulant. Kelly got the prize complaint. A woman had gone into an airport lavatory and found there was no toilet paper. She marched straight to Western's ticket counter, intending to claim a Flub-Stub dollar, but she had to wait in line behind a man who was complaining that his WAL flight didn't serve his brand of bourbon.

The agent ruled this a transgression worthy of a Flub-Stub payment and gave the man a dollar. The irate lady stepped up and demanded the same sum because of the absence of toilet paper in the airport lavatory.

"I'm sorry, ma'am," the agent explained, "but the rest rooms here are the responsibility of the airport, not Western."

A few days later, Kelly received a letter from the furious passenger.

"I will never fly Western or any other airline again," she wrote, "that considers bourbon more important than toilet paper!"

Over-all, however, the Flub-Stub was a unique and unprecedented airline marketing gimmick. As had the VIB, it provided a human, friendly image of an airline with the courage to break away from the usual cold impersonality of a large corporation.

The Flub-Stubs even overshadowed—in public interest, anyway—Western's obtaining nonstop authority from Los Angeles and San Francisco to the Twin Cities, increasing the economic importance of an already lucrative route and giving the 720-Bs some schedules more suited for their long-range capability. But the Flub-Stubs themselves had to play second fiddle to another event that occurred in the momentous fortieth anniversary year.

On October 26, 1966, Terrell Drinkwater—his own route-expansion plans stymied by a mixture of CAB procrastination and adverse decisions—moved in another direction.

To the north.

On that day, he signed an agreement to merge Western with Pacific Northern Airlines—extending the WAL system from Seattle to Alaska.

CHAPTER SEVENTEEN

The PNA Merger

The president of Pacific Northern Airlines was Arthur G. Woodley—a man of iron will, unimpeachable integrity, awesome profanity, a streak of sentimentality the approximate depth of Carlsbad Caverns, the liquor capacity of a 747 wing tank, and a hair-trigger temper.

He founded PNA as Woodley Airways on April 10, 1932, and was one of the pioneering Alaskan bush pilots who brought air transportation to the vast, virgin territory that was America's last frontier. Art Woodley was a New Englander and fell in love with Alaska when he visited his brother there in 1928.

Woodley had learned to fly as a cadet in the Army Air Corps at Kelly Field and was a reserve officer in 1931 when he received word that this brother, an Anchorage priest had been killed in a hunting accident. After the funeral, Woodley just stayed in Anchorage. He had flown a five-passenger Bellanca there all the way from New York, landing with one cup of gas in the tank, and this was the plane he used to launch Woodley Airways out of Anchorage—at the time a mere village, with only twenty-five hundred inhabitants. Woodley Airways fitted nicely with the minuteness of its home base; it consisted of President Woodley, pilot Woodley, mechanic Woodley, and salesman Woodley—a one-man airline with one airplane.

In its first year, it flew exactly fifty-three passengers; it was strictly a charter operation of the "Have plane—will travel" variety. Woodley would haul anyone anywhere in Alaska for such fees as $150 to fly from Anchorage to Nome. The price itself was attractive, because the only other way to go was by dogsled, which took a month (the Bellanca did it in 5½ hours) and cost $750. Then Woodley started a weekly trip from Anchorage to Kuskokwim, a hinterland mining and trapping area, and to Bristol Bay, a fishing center, which seems to have been the Alaska Territory's first scheduled air service of sorts.

As more business developed, so did the tiny airline—Woodley gradually acquiring more planes and pilots. Single-engine Travelaires, Wacos, and Fleetsters were followed by trimotored Stinsons, Woodley himself logging as many hours as his airmen. His payroll was as skimpy as his bank account, and about the only bargain-priced labor market he didn't try to tap was the polar bear population. One part-time employee was a priest, Father Dermot O'Flanagan, who succeeded Woodley's brother as the Anchorage priest and who later became bishop of Alaska. The young man of God and the young man of Alaska formed a deep if unlikely friendship; Woodley's temper, impatience, vocabulary, insoluble feuds, and living habits, added to the risks of his unpredictable profession, all made it highly possible that he would qualify for permanent wings long before he earned a halo. Father O'Flanagan gave up trying to reform him quite early in the course of their friendship and settled on what he loved best next to his religion—airplanes. He ran errands, cleaned the aircraft, and helped Woodley with maintenance. They were putting an engine back in the Bellanca one day, the priest holding it steady while Woodley was trying to tighten the bolts. Woodley couldn't get the bolt lined up because the engine was wobbling, and he yelled, "Damnit, O'Flanagan, hold it steady!"

"I am holding it steady!" the priest shouted. "We're having an earthquake!"

One of Art's first employees turned out to become a lifelong friend—Mary Diamond, hired as a secretary when she was twenty years old and working in an Anchorage drugstore as a bookkeeper. Woodley couldn't afford her full-time services but conned her into helping him out.

"You can bring the store's books right up to my office and work on them there, Mary," he told her. "Not much for you to do—just watch the office while I'm out." He neglected to tell her he would be out on more occasions than he would be in—either flying trips or, for example, waiting at the docks for steamship arrivals so he could solicit passengers. She agreed to this arrangement but quickly realized she had to choose between Bert's Drugstore and Woodley Airways, and she picked the latter—eventually rising to the post of assistant corporate secretary and staying with the airline until the Western merger.

She knew Woodley possibly better than anyone else in the world; he confided things to her he would not tell even his top officers. Yet she was not immune from his volatile temper. He once fired her because she had failed to put "Mr." in front of an addressee's name in a business letter. She stayed fired for four days while Woodley wallowed helplessly in the muck of office procedures that only she knew. He couldn't find anything, so he called her back. She walked into his office, glared straight into his eyes, and said icily:

"You sonofabitch—don't you ever do that to me again."

He didn't. She sold tickets, ran the office, and drove passengers to the airport in her own car to make sure they didn't miss their flights. It took her a while to learn the airline business itself, let alone the airline business Woodley-style. His tirades and tantrums made life interesting, to use an inadequate adjective. He walked in one day to find an office door painted pink; it was repainted an hour later. His own office had a window in the partition separating it from Mary's outer office. It was equipped with a venetian blind so he could peek out and see whoever was standing by her desk, asking to see the president. If it was someone he didn't want to see, he would press a red button on his desk, while a green button would signal her that he wanted to talk to the person seeking admittance. The system would have been foolproof except for Woodley's impatience—frequently he would hit the green button by mistake, berate the innocent victim who had been ushered in, and then roar at Mrs. Diamond for the mistake he had made himself.

She still remembers that day he threw a typewriter out of a six-story window. Yet conversely, he could be amazingly calm in a moment of crisis. The airline's hangar at Anchorage burned down some years ago while Woodley was out on a flight. She met his returning plane, sobbing out the bad news. He looked at her as if she had just told him they needed a few new light bulbs.

"Okay," he said. "Where's my load for the next trip?"

These were the days, of course, when flying in Alaska wasn't much of a guarantee for longevity. Yet Woodley right from the start of operations installed some iron-clad safety rules for himself and anyone who flew for him. His airline went thirty years before suffering a crash that involved passenger fatalities; prior to that, it had lost a Stinson with only a pilot aboard.

"I had told him you couldn't fly that plane with an outboard engine out," Woodley says. "The center one couldn't be used to swat flies, but the poor guy didn't believe me."

There were no aircraft radio ranges in Alaska while Woodley was developing his operations. The pilots lacked weather forecasts; Woodley himself used to judge the wisdom of taking off by whether he could see the mountains around Anchorage from Merrill Field—if they were visible, he'd tell Mary Diamond to "get the load ready." A few amateur radio stations comprised the territory's early aviation communications network, supplemented by the Washington–Alaska Military Cable & Telegraph System. Paved runways were virtually unknown until World War II. One unusual hazard existed for a time at Dawson, where the owner of the field hated pilots so much that he laid railroad ties down his dirt runway. The majority of early bush pilot operations were conducted with float planes using Alaska's many lakes and rivers, ski gear being employed when there was snow on the ground. The first manmade runways were the mine tailings.

Many of Woodley's flights were strictly mercy missions, dropping food and/or medical supplies to marooned prospectors and trappers. Woodley added to this category occasional trips to Eskimo villages, where he'd drop candy for the children. But as Alaska grew, so did air travel; the routes Woodley Airways had begun serving mostly on a sporadic basis—from Anchorage to Kodiak, Bristol Bay, and Kuskokwim—became fixed air routes under the Civil Aeronautics Act of 1938.

World War II interrupted the expansion of civil aviation in Alaska, Woodley himself being chosen as a special pilot for Army Intelligence, flying a number of secret missions. And his airline stayed in operation, transporting military personnel and supplies between Alaskan defense bases. The end of the war found Woodley Airways ready to become the leader in the territory's air transportation future. It already had acquired a few Boeing 247s, and these were replaced by three new DC-3s; never before had any Alaskan carrier operated a brand-new airplane. Woodley himself flew the delivery flight of the third aircraft—the last time he was to serve as a working pilot. Coincidental with the prestige and pride of a modernized fleet went a change in name—from Woodley Airways to Pacific Northern Airlines, which, incidentally, left Braniff as the only U.S. scheduled carrier still operating under the name of its founder.

Pacific Northern was not Art's first choice. He preferred Alaska Airlines as a name, and at one time had filed an application in Juneau to register that name. Through an attorney's oversight, he failed to accompany the application with the required fifteen dollars registration fee, and a rival airline operator, Raymond Marshall, quickly grabbed "Alaska Airlines" for his own company, much to Woodley's outrage. He disliked Marshall intensely, and from then on it was open war between the two companies.

Woodley was a great deal like Terry Drinkwater in his attitude toward people; both tended to put everyone in a friend-or-foe category, with no exceptions allowed. Each used a whipping-boy device—once they made a "bad guy" out of somebody, the individual was consigned permanently to the doghouse, and anything bad that happened had to be his fault. Bob Kinsey, Woodley's assistant at PNA, remembers that Woodley got down on one of his officers in this fashion—to such an extent that when Kinsey confessed authorship of some blooper, Woodley refused to believe him and blamed the other man.

"He didn't do it, Art," Kinsey protested. "I just got through telling you it was my idea."

"You go down there and tell him I want to see him," Woodley growled. "I'll give him hell!"

His personal idiosyncrasies had to be forgiven if not forgotten in light of what he accomplished for an airline that literally grew up with the area it served so well. PNA was the first Alaskan carrier to develop its own communications system, the first to operate multi-engine aircraft, the first to utilize instrument flight procedures, and the first to be certificated by the CAA as a scheduled airline. By 1947 it was flying fifty-five-passenger DC-4s, and three years later it won the CAB's permission to operate from Seattle/Tacoma to both Anchorage and Juneau—the latter having been added to PNA's routes in 1947 along with Cordova and Yakutat. Service on the Seattle–Alaska routes was not inaugurated until 1951, however, because it required presidential approval, and with the White House okay came the addition of Portland as a coterminal with Seattle/Tacoma.

By now PNA was not only a well-established carrier but a fairly prosperous one, enough so to purchase a small fleet of Lockheed Constellations. Gone were the days when Woodley admittedly was cutting a few regulatory corners to keep his limited fleet in the air—although never to the degree exercised by another Alaskan carrier. Faced with a CAA order to install deicing boots on the leading edges of the wings, it painted the leading edges on all its aircraft black so CAA inspectors would think boots had been put on.

The Seattle–Anchorage route was PNA's way out of the era of shoestring operations. As early as 1947, the Seattle area was furnishing 70 per cent of PNA's total revenues—a sufficient volume to warrant establishment of the airline's financial and sales offices in Seattle years before Woodley began serving the Pacific Northwest metropolis directly. With the new long-haul routes and general growth came the development of an able executive staff to help Woodley run what had been a one-man operation for so many years. There was Felix Aubuchon, PNA's Anchorage-based vice president; Harold Olsen, vice president of marketing and sales; the aforementioned Bob Kinsey; Gerald O'Grady (a feisty little Irish lawyer who had first met Art in the early 1940s when O'Grady was on the Civil Aeronautics Board's legal staff), PNA's Washington representative; Hal Foster, Pacific Northern's longtime vice president of maintenance who also was acting head of operations; and Clarence Nelson, secretary/treasurer.

They each shared an unusual attribute: Not one of them was afraid to argue with their explosive boss. If there had been tape recordings of their frequent clashes, a listener would have had to conclude that PNA's executive atmosphere was homicidal.

Woodley's stormy relations with his top management corps overflowed into the lower echelons as well, and there was enough left over for the rank and file. Art was not one to believe in the smooth, glossy practices of modern management, as evidenced by the time his director of personnel came in to complain about the worsening labor situation at Homer, Alaska, one of PNA's smallest stations.

"We have a 100 per cent labor turnover at Homer," he reported—neglecting to mention that Pacific Northern's entire work force at Homer consisted of a single agent.

"And what do you think we should do about it?" Woodley growled.

"We can't keep good men at the salary levels we've established. As a matter of fact, Mr. Woodley, we should be increasing salaries for all employees."

"What the hell for?"

"For morale."

"To hell with their morale!" Woodley shouted. "What about *my* morale?"

Yet, as so often happens with strong leaders, Woodley commanded tremendous loyalty throughout Pacific Northern. His personality was a two-sided coin; he was belligerent, profane, ruthless, and incessantly demanding, yet he also could be kind, considerate, and generous—a pushover for any employee with a hard-luck story. He used language that went with the territory, so to speak, but when one got to really know him, it was apparent that behind this rough façade was a brilliant mind and high principles. Kinsey says of him:

"Like most Alaskans, he worked harder and played harder than normal men. You never needed his signature on any document—his verbal promise was sacred. I don't know anyone in Alaska whose word was as good as his. He never defaulted on anything he pledged."

A big man with a build of a Kodiak bear, Woodley was extremely dependent on companionship. His chief interests in life were his three sons, the Catholic Church, and the airline. A judge had awarded him custody of the three boys in a divorce suit that Woodley does not like to discuss; to a man who always had been and always will be devoted to Catholicism, the breakup of his marriage was the most traumatic experience of his life. PNA officials and employees saw the tender, compassionate side of this unusual man through the way he raised his sons. There was Woodley, the hell-raising, hard-drinking extrovert. And there was Woodley, the devoted father, who loved to take his boys hunting and fishing and tried valiantly to compensate for their lack of a mother.

With such men, a dual personality generates love-hate relationships in extremes. In Woodley's case, the grudge he bore against Alaska Airlines reached almost paranoic proportions. He turned purple at the very mention of that carrier or one of its presidents in particular, Charles Willis. Anyone who worked for Alaska Airlines and anyone who ever did anything for Alaska Airlines was, in Art Woodley's frequently expressed language, "a crooked sonofabitch," but Willis occupied a very special niche—it was a tossup whether Woodley loathed Willis as an individual or Alaska Airlines as an institution the most. Art was lunching with Kinsey one day and, as usual, much of the one-sided conversation consisted of Woodley's daily diatribe on the subject of Willis.

Kinsey listened patiently and resignedly to one slanderous statement after another. When Woodley finally paused for breath, Kinsey soothingly remarked, "Don't worry so much about Charlie Willis, Art—he's his own worst enemy."

"Not while I'm alive!" Woodley roared.

O'Grady once took Woodley to the Civil Aeronautics Board's offices so he could meet the Board members personally. The fifth and final stop was to visit Chairman James Landis—"It's purely a courtesy call, Art," O'Grady reminded him, "so don't get into any arguments with him. He's up for reappointment and we can't afford to antagonize him."

Woodley just grunted. They were ushered into the chairman's presence, O'Grady shaking Landis' hand and then introducing Art. "Mr. Chairman, I'd like you to meet the president of Pacific Northern, Art Woodley."

"It's a pleasure, Mr. Woodley," Landis smiled, offering his hand, which Woodley blithely ignored. O'Grady paled; he had a strong suspicion of what was coming, and he didn't have long to wait for confirmation.

"Landis," Woodley roared, "I think you're crooked. You're in bed with that goddamned Alaska Airlines."

Landis, noted for his own temper, unloaded a few choice expletives in Woodley's direction. O'Grady finally coaxed his steaming boss out of the office and Woodley calmed down.

"Well, I guess we told the bastard off," Woodley said with obvious satisfaction. "Where do we go now?"

"To church," O'Grady replied. "I think we'd better say a few 'Hail Marys' to make sure he isn't reappointed."

Woodley, like any good airline executive, considered "status quo" dirty words; he knew a carrier never could stand still and continue to prosper, not when potential competition always was lurking around the corner, anxious to move in on any monopoly route making money. Early in PNA's existence he had tried to extend south to Los Angeles, just before Western got authority to compete with United in the Los Angeles–Seattle market. The CAB rejected PNA's bid to become the third carrier, figuring two were enough. In 1949, Woodley spent two days with Juan Trippe in Seattle, attempting to convince him he should sell Pan Am's Alaskan routes to PNA.

"That's all we did—talk," Woodley says. "After every third olive, Trippe would say, 'I want to buy PNA,' and I'd come back with, 'I want to buy your Alaskan routes,' and neither of us got anywhere."

Pacific Northern struck out in virtually every route case it entered; not even O'Grady, an exceptionally able advocate in PNA's behalf, could overcome the CAB's persistent refusal to let the airline broaden its system. Woodley's own unpopularity within government circles may have been a factor, but most of the anti-PNA prejudice seemed to stem from its size; despite its dominance of Alaska and its demonstrated ability to operate the long-haul Seattle–Alaska route, the CAB evidently felt that Pacific Northern couldn't hack it in any elevation to major airline status.

Woodley waited until 1961 to make the jet plunge, and when he did he became the first airline president in history to borrow the equivalent of his gross annual revenues so he could finance the purchase. PNA ordered two new Boeing 720-As and borrowed $11 million for financing; Pacific Northern's gross that same year was $11 million. Advance word of the purchase somehow leaked to the Seattle *Post-Intelligencer*, so the official announcement was something of an anticlimax. When PNA public-relations director Howard Clifford set up a news conference in Seattle, the only reporter present was veteran aviation editor Bob Twiss of the Seattle *Times*.

Woodley, Kinsey, and Olsen were there to answer questions, but noting the one-man attendance, they adjourned the press conference to a restaurant where the three PNA officials began briefing Twiss on further details during prelunch cocktails.

"Getting down to business, Art," Twiss said, "I'd like to know where you'll operate the Boeings."

"Seattle–Anchorage and Seattle–Kodiak," Woodley replied promptly.

"Not Kodiak," Olsen corrected him. "Ketchikan and Juneau."

"Over my dead body you'll fly 'em into Ketchikan and Juneau!" Woodley shouted. "I said Kodiak."

"That's silly," Olsen argued stubbornly. "We can't ignore Ketchikan and certainly not Juneau—for Christ's sake, Art, that's the capital of Alaska."

"I don't give a damn! I said Kodiak, and furthermore, Olsen, you . . ."

The argument went on for a half hour, Twiss and Kinsey completely ignored.

"It was," Clifford wryly recalled later, "a typical Art Woodley press conference."

The new Boeings worked out so well that later in the year, Woodley bought a third 720-A from Braniff at a bargain price. It was painted brown, one of those attention-grabbing paint schemes Braniff had introduced after Harding Lawrence had come over from Continental to assume the presidency. It needed more than a new paint job, however; Woodley remembers that the interior "looked like it had been through World War II." The cabin carpet was so worn that the fuselage metal could be seen, and the upholstery was in equally bad shape. About a month after Pacific Northern acquired the plane, Woodley bumped into Lawrence at a party.

"How do you like that Boeing we sold you?" Harding inquired.

"I don't know," Woodley replied. "We haven't finished rebuilding it yet."

Although the Boeings made money, they failed to resolve Woodley's concern over the airline's future. The year 1965 was the best in Pacific Northern's history, PNA netting $2 million on a record gross of $30 million; it carried, for example, more passengers between Seattle and Alaska than Northwest, Pan Am, and Alaska Airlines combined. But Woodley was interested in prognosis as well as profits. Not even PNA's first jets could quell his growing conviction that the long-range outlook was poor.

And he himself was tired. The long years of struggle against mammoth odds, the constant need for economizing in order to make any kind of profit, the drumbeat of CAB rejections—all these were eroding his will to keep fighting and struggling.

"I figured the day of the small airline was over," is the way he describes his mood at the time, "and there was just no way to expand nor any way to get further financing for the additional jets we needed for the routes we already had. We ordered four 727s in 1965 and then had to cancel the contract because no one would loan us the money."

Woodley looked over the prospects for a possible merger. He considered Braniff and Continental, but his first choice right from the start was Western—WAL's system could be linked directly to PNA's at Seattle and Portland. Western had historical identity in Alaska, too, from the wartime sourdough days and from promotional tie-ins with PNA. He had a few preliminary conversations with Drinkwater, the last one held just before Drinkwater headed East to Washington on a business trip. All that was certain at this point was their mutual desire to merge if an acceptable deal could be worked out, and they appeared to be fairly close even at this stage.

In Washington, Howard Westwood was hosting a luncheon at the Metropolitan Club for Drinkwater, Slichter, and Neil Stewart —the latter an ex-Navy pilot who had worked for WAL in Seattle for twenty years and was now one of Slichter's assistants. TCD called Stewart, a Mormon, "Bishop." The three Westerners were in the men's room where Drinkwater suddenly began peering under the stall doors. "Got something to tell you guys," he explained to his mystified companions, "and I wanna make sure nobody can hear us."

Satisfied that no spies were present, Terry confided, "I'm about to close a deal that'll merge Western with Pacific Northern. I'm going from here to San Francisco to meet Art Woodley. Then we'll meet in Seattle with his top officers. I've made Woodley a pretty good offer, and I think he'll go for it."

"Neil might be a help to you in Seattle," Slichter suggested. "He knows that whole PNA crowd from the days when he was sales manager at Seattle—Harold Olsen and Bob Kinsey, for example, and Woodley himself."

Drinkwater turned to Stewart. "Might be a good idea, Bishop."

The momentous meeting was held October 26 at the Hyatt House near the Seattle airport. Representing Western were Drinkwater, Shatto, and Taylor, with Stewart on hand to assist if needed. Woodley was accompanied by Kinsey and O'Grady—Woodley hadn't asked Olsen to attend because the vice president of marketing and sales already had expressed vitriolic objections to any merger. The negotiations were friendly, and at times the participants appeared to be spending more time telling off-color jokes than working out a multimillion-dollar corporate marriage; they were so loud that guests in adjoining rooms asked the hotel to move them off the third floor where the WAL-PNA officials were meeting.

Despite the jovial atmosphere, there also was considerable haggling. When Drinkwater made what he insisted was his final offer, Woodley said it wasn't quite good enough. Drinkwater stood up.

"We've got an appointment over at Boeing to look at some airplanes," he said brusquely. "We're not gonna give you a goddamned cent more, Art, so make up your mind while we're gone."

When the Western contingent returned, Woodley announced he would accept Drinkwater's terms—basically, an exchange-of-stock deal giving PNA stockholders one share of WAL stock for every two shares of Pacific Northern. As of the day the merger was consummated, there were slightly over one million shares of PNA common stock outstanding, with Woodley holding a fair-sized bloc. Under the terms of the agreement, he became Western's largest stockholder. Woodley would later be elected to

WAL's Board along with appointment as vice president—Alaska. Harold Olsen ultimately became vice president of Western's cargo sales, and O'Grady became vice president of properties and facilities. Also absorbed into Western was Kinsey, who was named vice president and assistant to Drinkwater.

The following morning, however, a collection of king-sized hangovers, plus the sobering realization that an airline had just died, dampened some of the previous enthusiasm. Most affected were Drinkwater and Woodley, who began snapping at each other as soon as they met that next morning. Both had agreed to hold a joint news conference to announce the merger. Neil Stewart working with PNA's Howard Clifford in making the necessary arrangements—this was around 4:00 P.M. of the previous day, and the call to set up a press conference was the first inkling the veteran PNA public-relations man had that a merger was even being discussed. Woodley hadn't told him about the negotiations; only Mary Diamond knew of the preliminary talks, and only Olsen, O'Grady, and Kinsey, plus Mary, were aware that an agreement had been reached.

For a couple of old fire-eating rugged individualists, Drinkwater and Woodley were surprisingly cold and stiff at the news conference. The only light moment came when they were asked for head shots of themselves. Drinkwater gave out some recently taken photographs he had with him, and Woodley supplied one of himself that must have been thirty years old—it showed him with all his hair, and by 1966 he was almost bald. Drinkwater sneaked a look and objected.

"I looked pretty damned good in *my* high school annual, too!" he protested loudly.

It was the only time Woodley displayed much animation during the proceeding. He obviously was having second thoughts, although he had given his word and would never reneg. There was no question but that his conscience bothered him a lot more than his hangover did; he was compassionate enough to realize the merger's effects on PNA employees—their airline was *not* the surviving carrier, and he knew that their reactions would range between disappointment at best and outright anger at worst. PNA had 830 employees at the time of the merger. A reporter asked Woodley how many people he had working for him.

"Oh, I would guess about half of them," he replied.

Woodley had done his best to protect their interests. He obtained from Drinkwater a pledge not to dismiss a single Pacific Northern employee. He also claims that Terry gave him a promise not to transfer anyone who didn't want to move from his or her PNA station.

Drinkwater denies making any such promise, and Kinsey, genuinely fond of both men, believes Woodley misinterpreted what TCD actually did promise: that no one would lose their job but that some would have to be transferred—"in other words," Kinsey explains, "jobs were assured but not locations."

Art Kelly strongly urged that Western run PNA as a full-fledged regional operation, at least for a time, pointing to the chaos that resulted when United absorbed Capital in the early sixties; instead of operating Capital as a separate airline until the voluminous merger bugs could be worked out, UAL combined both systems immediately, and it took a couple of years to straighten out the mess. Operating PNA as a kind of independent subsidiary certainly would have resolved most of the labor problems, such as touchy seniority questions and transfers, but Drinkwater didn't think the WAL-PNA merger paralleled United and Capital. Both the latter were larger than Western itself, and some of their premerger routes overlapped. He decided to absorb Pacific Northern immediately, employee resentment toward mandatory transfers notwithstanding. There were individual cases that Drinkwater tried to arbitrate fairly, and one of them concerned a veteran PNA official who *wanted* a transfer. That was Felix Aubuchon, the Anchorage-based vice president of operations, whose wife was suffering from the effects of a stroke and badly needed a balmier climate.

Kinsey, aware of the problem, did what Aubuchon hesitated to do: He went to Drinkwater and told him about Felix's dilemma. At a party to introduce the Western executives to PNA employees in Anchorage after the merger agreement was signed, Drinkwater and Shatto called Aubuchon into a side room and told him he was going to Los Angeles to work as a regional specialist in Slichter's government and industry affairs department. It lacked vice presidential status, but Aubuchon couldn't have cared less.

Aubuchon's reprieve, however, was one of the rare exceptions to the rule: PNA employees were to go where they were told or resign. Many did the latter; the defections were particularly high in Seattle, where hundreds of Pacific Northern people owned homes and had established deep-seated roots. Quite a few women employees had husbands working for Boeing and simply refused to leave the Seattle area.

There was surprisingly little industry opposition to the merger, even though it was in apparent conflict with the CAB's record of rejecting mergers between healthy carriers. Both Western and PNA had just come off the most profitable year in their respective histories, but the CAB announced its approval anyway, on June 2, 1967—one of the few times the Board had given Arthur G. Woodley what he wanted.

Woodley retained his office in Seattle to go with his new title, but unfortunately Drinkwater didn't give him much to do with either the office or the title.

The inactivity got to him, and he retired in February 1971—retaining, however, his place on Western's Board; at this writing, he is a director-emeritus. Every former PNA officer or employee remembers him with a mixture of affection, admiration, and a touch of awe. He was one of the most forceful, commanding men ever to head an airline, as illustrated by an incident that took place immediately after the Alaskan earthquake of March 27, 1964. And the eyewitness was none other than then-Governor Walter Hickel, who was in Seattle when news of the disaster reached him.

Hickel and his wife rushed out to the airport to catch the first available flight to Anchorage—a PNA 720. As Hickel recalls it, there were about a thousand people trying to get space on a 122-passenger airplane. Into the midst of the confusion strode Arthur G. Woodley, who stood on the top of the besieged Pacific Northern ticket counter.

"Now, folks, just quiet down and listen to me," he bellowed. "I'm Art Woodley, president of PNA, and it's perfectly obvious everyone can't go on this flight who wants to go. We've set up a priority system I think is fair. Those who have immediate families in Alaska will be boarded first. Those who have property in the area of the quake will board next. Then we'll take newspapermen and photographers who have to get to the earthquake scene as part of their job. After these three categories are boarded, we'll take as many others as we can get on the airplane. And don't try to put anything over on us because I'll be at the boarding gate asking questions."

He was, too. He tossed every confirmed reservation into a figurative wastebasket, and on the basis of personal interviews at the boarding gate passed judgment on who deserved a seat. He undoubtedly made some mistakes and succumbed to a few sob stories, but there was a noticeable absence of complaints after he took command of the situation.

Woodley always took pride in one of PNA's major contributions during the earthquake crisis. The killer quake had wrecked the FAA control tower at Anchorage, but flights were handled by controller personnel operating from a Pacific Northern Constellation parked on the battered ramp.

PNA's six Constellations were turned over to Western in the merger, along with the three 720s—they were the older "water wagon" models—and a single DC-3 known to all PNA employees as *Old Queenie*. Drinkwater was happy to get his hands on three jets, but he made no bones about disposing of the piston airplanes as soon as he could. Shortly after the merger was consummated, someone asked Terry what he intended to do with *Old Queenie*.

"Sell the sonofabitch," he growled unsympathetically.

He had a similar low regard for the Connies, suggesting on one occasion that "we oughta take them down to Kodiak and make crab traps out of them." As a matter of fact, nobody got overly fond of the three water wagons with their relatively antiquated engines and correspondingly higher operating costs. And then came the day several years later when the ex-PNA 720s created a minor crisis involving Art Woodley.

They were sold to Alaska Airlines.

When Alaska agreed to buy the three jets, Kinsey expressed frank concern as to the effects of the transaction on Woodley.

"Unless he's told about it in advance of the announcement, he's liable to have a heart attack or decide to take a bar apart," Kinsey told other Western officers. Art Kelly agreed to call

Woodley and break the news. Much to everyone's surprise, his reaction was fairly mild.

"Why the hell couldn't you find anyone else?" he grumbled, but that was about the extent of his protest.

In retrospect, the merger was a good deal for Western. Jud Taylor, who handled most of the financial negotiations, believed WAL paid "a little bit too much" largely because Woodley was an excellent horse trader. But Western acquired some prime new routes, capable rank-and-file personnel, and excellent executive blood. O'Grady eventually rose to his present position as senior vice president of legal affairs and corporate secretary, and Kinsey is now senior vice president of corporate planning. The man who had begged Woodley not to merge, Harold Olsen, served Western for only two years but did so with distinction; he died unexpectedly in mid-1969.

For Terry Drinkwater, acquisition of PNA marked the apogee of his Western regime. He stood at the pinnacle of personnel and corporate success in 1967, and there was no reason to believe he could be pushed off the peak to which he had so laboriously and courageously climbed. The Transpacific Case had been reopened, and Drinkwater clung to his conviction that Western was going to get Hawaiian authority. His over-all optimism was such that he signed tentative contracts for three different types of jetliners, two of them aimed squarely at the Hawaiian route.

The new planes included five long-range Boeing 707-300Cs, the intercontinental version of the 707, and six Boeing 727-200s, stretched models of the well-proven trijet. The third plane was the first of the wide-bodied "jumbos"—the magnificent 747; Western reserved two places on the assembly line although no binding contract was signed. Finally, Western exercised its options on an additional ten 737s, bringing the "Baby Boeing" fleet to thirty aircraft delivered or on order. Of the twelve Electras WAL was operating, five were turned over to Lockheed for conversion into mixed passenger/cargo configuration and three more into all-cargo aircraft.

This massive equipment plunge was accompanied by what Terry considered additional insurance for obtaining a Hawaiian route. He reopened Western's Washington office, putting it in charge of Henry deButts, an experienced attorney who had served as administrative assistant to two CAB chairmen.

One side benefit of the Pacific Northern acquisition was the opportunity to expand Western's bid for Hawaii, for now the airline also was able to seek Anchorage–Hawaii authority. Ironically, this was something Art Woodley had been wanting for years, and his interest had been sparked by Governor Hickel. Hickel, now a WAL director, was to see his dream of direct Anchorage–Hawaii service come true, but for Woodley it came too late.

The first and only president of Pacific Northern received a deserved honor on May 2, 1975, when Western's remodeled and enlarged transportation center in Anchorage was dedicated as the Arthur G. Woodley Transportation Center. Woodley and Mary Diamond, along with many other former PNA employees, attended the dedication ceremony, the former close to tears as Art Kelly unveiled a bronze plaque at the entrance of the $2.2 million building and read the inscription:

> This facility is dedicated to Arthur G. Woodley, pioneering Alaska bush pilot and founder of Pacific Northern Airlines. His vision and courage built a one-plane air service into an enterprising jet airline that became part of Western in 1967.

Momentous indeed was the word for 1967—but there are times when momentous can be synonymous with sad. One of the major events occurring that year was not mentioned in the annual report for 1967, except by omission. The list of top company executives did not include the name of Dominic P. Renda.

On the day before the annual executive Christmas party, he had gone into Drinkwater's office and told TCD he was leaving Western. And what Dom told him to his face that grim day contained the reasons why his own days at Western were numbered.

CHAPTER EIGHTEEN

"The Purpose . . . Is Investment"

Dom Renda had made up his mind to leave Western after much soul-searching and painful inner conflict. His brain told him to get out of an impossible situation, and his heart told him to stay.

He was not lacking for opportunities elsewhere. First and foremost was a chance to go with aggressive, prosperous Continental. Bob Six began wooing him in earnest late in 1966, but Six had been dropping coy hints long before that. Renda had never argued a case before the CAB without Six coming up to him later and complimenting him on his performance. The 1966 approach was direct if not specific, Six merely telling him, "Dom, I'd sure like to have you on our side." It is interesting to note that Six was particularly impressed by the way Renda handled himself in the difficult, frustrating Hawaii proceeding—the same case that caused Drinkwater to sour on him.

Late in 1967, Six met Renda in Washington where the latter was arguing a case.

"I'd like to talk to you when we get back to California," Six said. "I've got something in mind."

The "something in mind" wasn't laid right on the table at first. Six, one of the industry's finest recruiters of executive talent, approached Renda by circling him cautiously in the early stages —inviting him over to his house on several occasions, where they'd discuss industry affairs and problems. Obviously, he was sizing up Renda. In late December, he made his move—offering him a job as senior vice president of international affairs, with the initial responsibility of organizing Air Micronesia, the tiny

Continental subsidiary that would be CAL's foot in the door for future Pacific expansion. This really intrigued Renda—a chance to pioneer a new route in an area he had long felt was ripe for development.

"The Washington office will report to you," Six said. "You'll have charge of our regulatory affairs and community relations to start with—but what I need first is to get Air Micronesia off the ground and as soon as possible have it operating with a permanent certificate."

Renda was tempted but also torn. One of the factors he considered was Six's age—the fiery leader of Continental was going to have to retire eventually, there hadn't been an heir apparent since Harding Lawrence left CAL to head Braniff, and Renda was a comparatively young man whose credentials as a possible successor were as good as anyone else's and better than most. Furthermore, Dom liked and respected Six. Renda had heard stories that Robert F. was impossible to work for or with, but on the other hand, Jerry Brooder had always told Renda that Six, for all his explosive idiosyncrasies, was fair, enormously competent, and a man who always kept his word. The fact that Brooder was genuinely fond of Six was a point Renda took into careful consideration; Jerry Brooder seldom made a mistake in judging a man.

Of major consideration was the fact that Renda would be president of Air Micronesia and its chief executive officer. What Six was offering him was an opportunity to actually start up a new airline and pioneer a new route across the Pacific, not to mention the chance to work with the colorful Six himself.

The financial arrangements and fringe benefits Six proposed were more than generous, yet Dom faced a real emotional tug-of-war when it came to leaving Western. He didn't confide in anyone except his wife, and even there he wasn't seeking advice —he knew he had to make the decision himself. The only other person who realized Renda was close to jumping Western was Hugh Darling; shortly before Six made a definite offer, Dom had told Darling, "I don't know how much longer I can stand this— I'm ready to leave."

With the cool logic of the good lawyer he is, he weighed the pros and cons carefully. Six had set an informal decision deadline of January 1, 1968, telling Renda, "I want to finalize this thing by January." The day before the traditional Christmas party for the WAL brass, Renda phoned Drinkwater in his office. "Terry, I'd like to see you."

"Hell, I'll see you at the party."

"This is personal and important. I want to talk to you now."

The few yards separating Renda's second-floor office from Drinkwater's third-floor headquarters seemed like a ten-mile elevator ride to the tall lawyer whose first job at Western two decades before had been the negotiating of airport leases. Drinkwater said "Hi, Dom," in friendly fashion, but his welcoming smile was to be the last time he would be even civil toward Renda.

"Terry," Renda began, "I've made a decision and you're going to be the first to hear about it. I've decided to leave Western. I'm most grateful for all the opportunities you've given me in the past, but you know what's happened here in the last couple of years. You know how our relationship has deteriorated. I don't like the direction in which the company is moving—I see nothing but problems ahead. It's becoming difficult to communicate with you in some of these areas, and I've made up my mind I want to be released from my contract. I don't want anything from you, Terry. If, out of the goodness of your heart, you think I merit any severance pay or the deferred compensation I've earned, fine—but I'm not asking for it. I just want out. Period."

"You must be crazy!" Drinkwater blurted. "I don't believe you. I'm not going to act on this, Dom. You'd better think about it."

"Terry, I've done my thinking. I'll give you all the time you need, up to thirty days if necessary. I'll stay on for another month, clean everything up, do whatever you want. If you want me to leave today, I'm ready to leave today. I've reached the point of decision, and this is it."

Terry did what he did so often in any time of crisis; he called Shatto, who went over to see Dom with open reluctance and some embarrassment: TCD wanted him to talk Renda into staying.

"I'm not going to try to talk you out of it, Dom," Shatto said quietly. "I'm sure it's something you thought about before you decided."

After Christmas, Renda—who hadn't heard a word from Drinkwater since their meeting—called him.

They quickly agreed on a phasing-out program, Renda recommending that Gordon Pearce—assistant corporate secretary—succeed him as secretary. That was the last verbal contact between two men who had been the closest of friends. Renda had to forfeit his accumulated deferred compensation, because of a clause in his contract specifying that he was ineligible if he quit before the contract expired. And he departed without so much as a thank you or good luck from Drinkwater. From that day on, Terry refused to speak to him.

"I've made the gesture many times," Dom says. "Like in the Transpacific Case when I was representing Continental. I was sitting with Bob Six during oral argument. I walked over to Terry and in the presence of everyone in that room, I put out my hand. He walked away from me. He still comes into Western's offices and visits a lot of his old friends, but if he sees me coming down the corridor, he'll duck into a room so he won't have to face me.

"I don't carry any animosity toward him. In fact, I feel sorry for him. What happened to him, and to a lesser degree to Stan Shatto, should not have happened. Those two men dedicated their whole lives to Western. When I look back on the great times we had and the wonderful relationship we had, it hurts to realize how everything deteriorated to the point where I had to do something about it.

"It would be so much easier for him if he'd just step into my office one day and say, 'Hi, Dom.' I've seen him on the street while I was driving home—we live only a block apart—and I'd honk my horn. He'd look and then turn his head. I guess it was traumatic for him when I left—he finally had someone level with him, look him right in the eye, tell him what was wrong, and still be willing to pay the price I had to pay. And make no mistake about it—I paid one hell of a price by leaving."

As it turned out, so did Terry Drinkwater; for the Western Airlines that Renda left behind him bore the flush of a dangerous fever almost everyone mistook for the glow of corporate health.

More than anything else, 1968 was a year of major equipment developments—electronics, ground facilities, and airplanes. Reservations and communications became fully computerized with the introduction of Accu-Res, a $9.2 million system requiring the installation of 625 visual inquiry sets, the training of 2,700 agents, and the linking of 23,000 miles of communications lines between two huge IBM computers and WAL reservations, sales, and airport offices in 12 states. A $1 million 737 flight training simulator went into service, and a 727 simulator costing $1.25 million was ordered in anticipation of the delivery of the new trijets.

The company also shelled out $12 million for various new ground facilities—a Transportation Center at San Francisco for maintenance and training, a similar building at Denver, an all-purpose structure at Anchorage, and a six-story warehouse at Los Angeles International. These were the first major ground facility projects since the 1964 opening of the new general offices on Century Boulevard, just around the corner from the old general offices on Avion Drive. The design of the new G.O. seemed to have been a bit impromptu; it actually was built not only to furnish more office space but also as a façade for Western's mammoth hangars located directly behind the new building. Someone who noticed that the fourth floor of the new general offices was empty for more than a year asked TCD why the building had to be four stories high.

"Because the damned hangar was four stories tall," Drinkwater explained simply.

The biggest chunk of company spending in 1968, however, involved aircraft. The Electra conversion program cost $4 million, and more new planes were incorporated into the fleet than in any single year of Western's history—22 jetliners consisting of 5 Boeing 707 Intercontinentals and 17 Boeing 737s. The stubby 737s were quickly dubbed "Fat Albert" after the Bill Cosby character; they carried 107 passengers in an all-coach configuration, and their delivery ended the age of the piston on Western's routes south of Alaska. All Electras went either into all-cargo use or into service in Alaska, while the former PNA Constellations and the three remaining DC-6Bs were sold.

"Fat Albert"—a nickname frowned on by Western's officialdom but adopted quickly and affectionately by every crew member—proved to be a superb airplane but one with an added

operating cost factor that wasn't the 737's fault. It had been designed specifically for a two-man crew, and there wasn't much
space in the cockpit for a second officer/flight engineer. But
WAL, along with other 737 operators, was victimized by a successful ALPA fight to fly the smallest of the Boeing jets with
three-man crews, even though both the DC-9 and BAC-111 were
being flown by two-man crews.

Shatto was one who thought the 737 was the best two-engine
jet ever built, although he bemoaned the fact that Boeing didn't
decide to produce it until the DC-9 was far ahead in orders and
well established in the short-haul field.

"It would have backed the Nine off the board if Boeing had
started it sooner," he says. "The added cost of the third man
wasn't as much as some people would have you believe, but it
still was expensive and it still was nothing but featherbedding.
One thing is for sure: Western didn't anticipate operating it with
three men."

The only place for a 737 second officer was in a jump seat located between and just behind the two pilot seats. Western's
crews promptly dubbed the third man "GIB"—for Guy in Back.
Like "Fat Albert," the monicker was strictly unofficial and its
public use discouraged, particularly after someone happened to
come across the word "gibcat" in a dictionary. It means castrated
tomcat.

The additional cost of the three-man 737 was just one of many
financial pressures beginning to build up like ominously gathering thunderclouds. Training costs for the new twinjet of necessity had to be high—of such magnitude that it was decided to
defer more than $1 million in these costs for future amortization
of the 737 equipment. This was a departure from Western's tra-
ditionally conservative accounting procedures, which frowned on
deferment of current expenses in an amortization program, and
this was another ominous indication that the company was getting deep into a fiscal morass.

There was no such deferment in regard to the five Boeing Intercontinentals joining the fleet. The long-legged 707s were the
biggest airplanes Western had ever bought, with a 151-passenger
capacity. They went into service between Los Angeles–Mexico
City and Los Angeles–Minneapolis, both good traffic markets,
but 1,500-mile routes that were too short for an aircraft in the In-

tercontinental's 5,000-mile range. Drinkwater had ordered them in anticipation of the Hawaii award, but the CAB's decision in the second Transpacific Case still was pending when the quintet of giant jets was delivered and put on routes for which they were ill adapted.

Inflationary pressures, reflecting a worsening national economic situation, were mounting, too. Increased expenditures for fuel, landing fees, wages, and other inescapable costs of doing business were added to the ugliest word in the airline industry: overcapacity. Historically, Western had established an anti-inflation formula, which simply meant boosting productivity by means of larger, more efficient aircraft; in the past this had meant lower seat mile costs, or, in simplest terms, what it cost WAL to move one passenger one mile. In 1968, however, seat mile productivity (capacity) jumped to such an extent that not even a 15 per cent increase in revenues was enough to offset climbing costs. That 15 per cent boost was swallowed by a 21 per cent hike in expenses.

Finally, there were some rumblings of discontent within management, climaxed by the resignations of two vice presidents whose talents would be missed in the days of crisis ahead. Terry Shrader, the labor relations expert Gewirtz had hired away from Eastern, was the first; Shrader left Western to accept Braniff's offer to become its vice president for industrial relations. The second was John Summerfield, vice president of economic planning, who resigned a few months after Shrader. Both were said to have clashed with Shatto—Shrader over labor policy and Summerfield over equipment purchasing. Shrader's replacement was Larry Lee, now vice president of in-flight service, but like Shrader he faced Shatto's dominant influence in that sensitive field. Summerfield's slot was to be unmanned for another four years.

With all of Western's proliferating problems in 1968, the airline managed to keep its head above water for much of the year, and not all the developments were unfavorable. While Drinkwater waited impatiently for the Transpacific decision, the CAB lifted restrictions that had required WAL to operate one- or two-stop service on several key routes. The result was new nonstop authority on such segments as Denver–Calgary and Twin Cities–Phoenix, Las Vegas and San Diego. Operating revenues hit

$221 million, highest in the company's history; nearly 5.7 million passengers flew WAL's 14,000-mile system; and the payroll nudged the 9,000 mark.

There were signs of impending trouble, however, as the fourth quarter began with losses that were still being incurred by the end of the year. They weren't heavy enough to wipe out the profits of the first three quarters, but combined with the over-all financial picture, they were cause for alarm. Western's long-term debt mushroomed in 1968—from around $80 million to $184 million.

Drinkwater remained optimistic and confident even as the picture continued to blacken. Western offered two of its new 707s to the Military Airlift Command for Vietnam contract flying, but the MAC contract that the government proposed didn't call for enough volume to make it profitable. Aside from the Los Angeles–Twin Cities and Mexico City regular schedules, the only meaningful utilization of the big planes came in the form of extra sections flown to the 1968 Olympic Games in Mexico City. Terry wasn't worried—he figured there would be plenty of use for the 707s when the Hawaii award came through. A CAB examiner already had recommended WAL for Hawaiian authority.

It was going to come through—in January 1969. But even as Terrell Drinkwater's dream was about to be realized, his twenty-two-year-old role at Western Airlines was challenged. On Monday, December 9, 1968, there appeared in the financial sections of the Los Angeles *Times* and other major newspapers an advertisement covering almost the entire half page—4 columns wide, 17½ by 7 inches in dimension. In large black letters at the top ran this announcement:

OFFER TO PURCHASE 1,500,000 SHARES OF CAPITAL STOCK OF WESTERN AIRLINES, INC.

Its opening paragraphs:

1. The undersigned will purchase any and all shares tendered up to a maximum of 1,500,000 shares of Capital Stock of Western if duly tendered prior to termination of the offer. If more than 1,500,000 shares are tendered on or prior to December 19, 1968,

the undersigned will purchase 1,500,000 shares on a pro-rata basis.

2. The undersigned will purchase Western Capital Stock at $45 per share net to the seller in cash.

Farther down in the advertisement was assurance that "the purpose of the undersigned's proposed purchase of Capital Stock of Western is for investment."

"The undersigned intends to seek representation on the Board of Directors of Western for the shares acquired through this offer," the ad continued, "but does not presently intend to seek to change the present executive officers of Western. The undersigned does not have any present plans or proposals to seek to liquidate Western, to sell its assets or to merge it with any other persons, or to make any other major change in its business or corporate structure."

At the bottom of the advertisement was this concluding paragraph:

> Since 1966, the undersigned's principal occupation has been that of an officer and director of Tracy Investment Company ("Tracy"), all of the outstanding stock of which is owned by the undersigned. Tracy is the principal stockholder of International Leisure Corporation, a Nevada corporation which through subsidiaries owns and operates the Flamingo Hotel in Las Vegas, Nevada, and is in the process of constructing a second resort hotel in Las Vegas. For the period from November 1958 until March 1969, the undersigned served as Chairman of the Board of Trans International Air Lines Corporation, a supplemental airline of which he was the founder and principal stockholder. The undersigned's business address is 3111 Joe W. Brown Drive, Las Vegas, Nevada.

The name of the undersigned followed.
Kirk Kerkorian.

He was the personification of the American dream, a real-life reincarnation of the rags-to-riches Horatio Alger legend—he

[30] Leo Dwerlkotte, who ran Western during the Coulter regime — president in all but title.

[31] Art Woodley, president of Pacific Northern.

[32] Dom Renda, key figure in Western's turbulent history.

[33] Fred Benninger, Kerkorian's right-hand man, is Western's Board chairman.

WESTERN AIR EXPRESS, INC. 1926

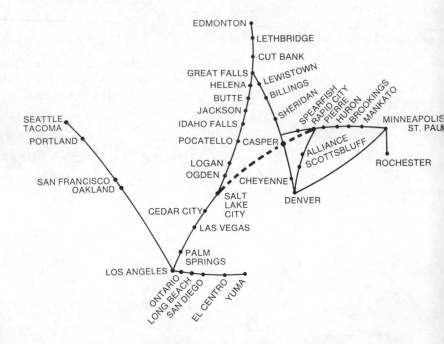

Casper Cut-Off — 1953

These three maps tell the story of Western Airlines. [34] At the top, left, the original CAM-4 route, which began operating in 1926. [35] Bottom, left, the famed Casper cutoff route, which gave Western a final link in an East-to-West route — the dotted lines representing the leg that closed the last gap. [36] Below, Western's present system.

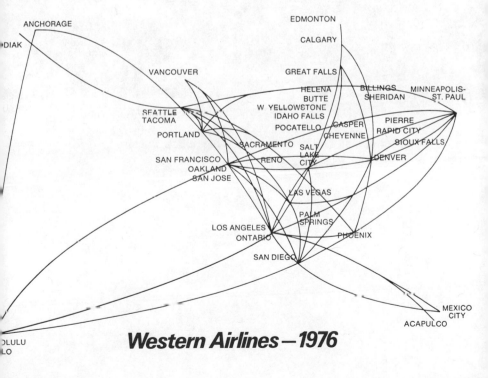

Western Airlines—1976

[37] Feebly but proudly down the steps comes Fred Kelly I, assisted by Dom Renda. The old pilot was in tears as Western paid him this honor only a few months before he died.

started out in the early thirties steam-cleaning engines for used-car dealers, and at the time he made the tender offer for Western's stock, his personal fortune was valued at some $200 million. En route to that stratosphere of affluence, he had parlayed a single-engine monoplane into a world-girdling supplemental airline, built an $80 million resort hotel, and was second only to Howard Hughes in the value of his Las Vegas real-estate holdings.

Kerkor Kerkorian was the last of four children born to Ahron and Sushon Kerkorian, who migrated to the United States in 1905 from Harput, Armenia, now a part of Turkey. When Kirk (the Americanized version of Kerkor) was sixteen, he had to quit trade school and went to work to help support the family. He spent a year with the Civilian Conservation Corps in the early days of the New Deal, keeping $5.00 of the $30 a month he earned and sending the rest home. After the CCC, he worked at odd jobs—one of them at MGM, where he earned $2.60 a day moving rocks; some thirty years later he was to hold controlling interest in the studio.

He then set up his first business—steam-cleaning automobile engines while boxing a little on the side. The engine-cleaning business evolved into buying used cars, reconditioning them, and selling them for a small profit. But in his spare time, Kerkorian took flying lessons—paying for them out of extra money earned milking cows and pulling weeds. By 1941 he had his commercial license, and when the United States entered World War II, he became an Army flight instructor and later a ferry pilot for the Royal Air Force.

He was too hooked on the magic and excitement of flight to give it up at war's end. He bought a single-engine Fairchild 24 monoplane for $5,000 and began teaching instrument flying. From this modest start he went into the used-airplane business, latching onto a war-surplus C-47 first and selling it in South America, where he soon had established a thriving market. In 1947, he launched his own airline—Los Angeles Air Service, one of the numerous postwar nonscheduled operations in which there were twenty bankruptcies for every success.

His fleet consisted of a couple of DC-3s and a Cessna, which was used for charter flights to Las Vegas. The Korean War gave him his first break when he wangled a government contract to fly personnel and material to the war zone. In 1959, he changed the airline's name to Trans-International, and it prospered—hanging up total revenues of $3 million in 1967, at which point he sold it to the Studebaker Corporation. A year later the venerable auto manufacturer was on the ropes and sold TIA back to Kerkorian for a lot less than it had paid him originally. By 1967, the airline was netting $5 million annually on a gross of $32 million, and more than one investment conglomerate was beginning to eye it covetously. At this point, the diversified financial giant that is Transamerica Corporation offered Kerkorian nearly 2 million shares of its stock, worth about $90 million, for his 58 per cent interest in TIA. He agreed to sell 780,000 shares of Transamerica stock, netting him $37 million in cash, and was still left with enough shares to make him the giant conglomerate's largest single stockholder. In effect, he had run up an initial investment of $12,000—the price he paid for the Cessna in 1947—into $90 million in stock and hard cash.

His next venture was in Las Vegas property, where he bought the Flamingo Hotel for $12.5 million and spent another $2.5 million modernizing and expanding it. Also under the Tracy Investment Company's banner (the holding company was named for Kerkorian's daughter) went 40 acres of land on the Strip; it became the site for Caesar's Palace. He paid $5 million for 63 acres on a road just off the Strip—and on this land he built the huge International Hotel, which for a time was the biggest in Las Vegas.

These activities would have been enough for the average man —or even the average multimillionaire—but Kerkorian had acquired a love of the airline business in his TIA days and began looking around for a good investment in that area.

"Aviation had always been my first love," he was to explain later. "Western's potential attracted me. They stood in a strong position to get a Hawaiian route, and I was convinced that leisure travel was virtually an untapped market. I did look at other carriers, but Western was always my first choice."

It may have been Kerkorian's first choice, but his enthusiasm wasn't entirely shared by the man who was Kirk's chief adviser and one of his closest friends—Fred Benninger, former executive vice president of the Flying Tiger Line, who had known

Kerkorian since 1948 and had been his top associate for two years. Kirk asked Benninger if he thought WAL was a good investment.

"From what I know, it's a good little airline with potential," Benninger said cautiously. "But Kirk, if I were you, I wouldn't buy any airline at this time."

Rarely did Kerkorian go against Benninger's advice, yet Kirk still was his own man—a gutty gambler who played for high stakes and blamed no one but himself for a mistake in judgment. At this stage, he had formed no set-in-concrete opinions of Western's executive personnel, from Drinkwater on down; he knew a few WAL officers casually and so did Benninger, but what influenced him the most was the airline's record of consistent profits with primarily a leisure-oriented route structure and a pretty good chance of obtaining Hawaiian authority. Like a cool crap shooter with a thick roll of bills, he rolled the dice.

It was midafternoon on Friday, December 6, three days before the tender offer was made public.

Alden W. Clausen, vice chairman of the Bank of America, which was Western's chief lending institution, called Drinkwater.

"Terry," he said, "Kirk Kerkorian wants to see you this weekend. Do you know him?"

"I know of him. I don't know him personally."

"Well, I've raised Kirk from a pup. He's a nice guy and he wants to see you about something important."

"I'll see him Monday," Drinkwater said impatiently. "I'm busy this weekend."

"He wants to see you right away."

"What about?"

"I can't tell you."

Drinkwater snorted. "Well, if you can't tell me, then it'll have to wait until Monday."

With that curt dismissal, TCD had driven the first nail into his own coffin. His had been a natural reaction; he didn't know Kerkorian, he had no inkling of why Kirk wanted to see him, and he wasn't the kind of man who pussyfooted around. But it is interesting to speculate what would have happened if he had met

Kerkorian as the latter requested. As it was, the totally unexpected tender offer did much to harden Drinkwater's attitude toward Kerkorian.

Drinkwater heard the news on his car radio while driving to
the office the following Monday morning. Just behind him in the
usual Los Angeles rush-hour traffic jam was Bob Kinsey, who
also was listening to the radio. They chatted briefly in the parking lot after arriving at the general offices, and Kinsey thought
Drinkwater seemed surprisingly calm. Kinsey remembers that he
went to Terry's office with him, but Drinkwater says that before
he saw any WAL officer that morning, he called the Bank of
America official who had asked him to meet with Kerkorian.

"I was furious," TCD says, "not so much at Kerkorian—hell, I
didn't even know him—but at Clausen. The minute I got to my
office I called him."

It was a classic Drinkwater tirade.

"Ever since Western's been making money, every bank in California has been after our business," he yelled at Clausen. "I told
them Bank of America was our bank and our chief lender and
we'd stay loyal to them. Now you guys come along and try to cut
our throats. I'll bet you've loaned him God knows how much to
make a corporate raid."

"It's not a raid, Terry," Clausen insisted. "Kerkorian is acquiring the stock as a good investment."

"Bullshit!" Drinkwater barked, and hung up.

That same afternoon, Kerkorian came over to Western accompanied by his chief legal adviser, William Singleton, after phoning from Las Vegas and asking for an appointment with Drinkwater. Kinsey, as TCD's assistant, was present when they met
and was impressed by Kerkorian's frank but friendly demeanor.
Physically, Drinkwater towered over the wiry, tanned Armenian,
but one has a compulsion to forget height differences in
Kerkorian's rather commanding presence. He exudes a kind of
cold electricity; there are coiled steel springs under the rich, casually handsome sports jacket he invariably wears. Usually he
prefers turtleneck jerseys or open-collar shirts, but for this occasion he had on a tie.

"I'm Kirk Kerkorian," he greeted the frowning Drinkwater.
"I'm sorry I couldn't get in touch with you prior to the offer, but

now it's been made, I'm sure you want to know who I am, what I'm like, and what my interests were in making this investment. We have many friends in common and you can check me out through them."

Drinkwater, who had been sitting quietly with Kinsey for more than an hour apparently in full control of his emotions, reacted violently. He went into a rage, opening with "you dirty sonofabitch!" and continuing a torrent of abuse and invectives. His verbal flaying of Kerkorian lasted about fifteen minutes and might have gone on longer if Singleton, desperately seeking a common ground for calmer discussion, hadn't asked TCD about his collection of Polynesian masks on the walls of his office.

Almost magically, Drinkwater cooled off and rather proudly explained the symbolism behind each mask. It was as if he had suddenly purged himself of all anger in the process of hurling expletives, and he became actually pleasant.

He asked Kerkorian, "By the way, do you play golf?"

Before Kirk could answer (actually, he prefers tennis), Drink-water opened a drawer and took out two boxes of golf balls that had "Western—the Only Way to Fly" imprinted on the covers. He handed them to his visitors, and the rest of the session was amicable. Drinkwater suggested that Kerkorian send him a letter or telegram confirming that he was investing in Western, not taking it over—"We want to allay any apprehension on the part of officers and employees," Terry explained. Kerkorian agreed, and when he finally mentioned that they had to get back to the airport, Drinkwater asked if they had a car.

"No, we took a taxi over here," Kerkorian replied.

"Bob will drive you over," Terry offered, nodding in Kinsey's direction.

Kinsey dropped them off, declining Kerkorian's invitation to inspect his luxuriously furnished private DC-9. After Kinsey drove off, Singleton looked at the gift Drinkwater had given them.

"Well, now we know where the profits have been going," he said jocularly. "They've been buying these damned golf balls."

It was an uncertain yet promising start to the Drinkwater-Kerkorian relationship, but the friendly gesture of the golf balls was the last Terry would make toward the man who suddenly had become WAL's biggest stockholder. They clashed bitterly at the second meeting they had a few days after the session in TCD's office, when Drinkwater brought Shatto, Taylor, and Kelly in to meet Kerkorian and his own top aides. By that time, it was apparent that the Las Vegas financier's $67.5 million bid to control Western was going to succeed—he hadn't acquired all the 1.5 million shares he hoped to buy, but he had enough early takers to quell any doubts as to its happening. Nor had he made any secret about asking for representation on WAL's Board; that had been mentioned in the tender offer announcement, and he repeated it to Drinkwater at the first meeting. Yet when TCD introduced his three top executives to Kerkorian, Drinkwater already had determined to keep Kirk or any of his associates off the Board.

Why—when Kerkorian obviously held all the aces? Neither Taylor nor Kelly urged him to fight Kerkorian, and Shatto, too, knew opposition would be futile. Kinsey believes the decision was made jointly by Drinkwater and Howard Westwood, mostly TCD but with Westwood encouraging him. Drinkwater's motive was simple: He considered Kerkorian an inteloper, a corporate raider, a pirate trying to grab what Drinkwater had built himself over twenty years of struggle and adversity.

In the midst of the gathering storm came a surprising new development: On December 15, Pacific Southwest Airlines, a moneymaking intrastate carrier operating largely between Los Angeles and San Francisco, announced it would buy *all* Western stock for $53 a share—a $261 million offer. On the face of it, the bid seemed ridiculous; Western was several times larger than PSA, and as well heeled as the latter's owners seemed to be, it would be a case of the minnow swallowing the whale. Fred Benninger, when he heard about the PSA offer, expressed his opinion in considerably more colorful terms.

"It would be awfully hard for a flea to rape an elephant," Benninger drawled.

Western's common stock on the Friday before Kerkorian made his tender offer was listed at $36.75 on the New York Stock Exchange. By the next Monday, it had jumped to $42, and was up to $44.25 on the day PSA got into the act.

The PSA bid never really got off the ground, mostly because it was never officially tendered; when the airline went to court to obtain a list of Western's stockholders for solicitation purposes, it was turned down on precisely those grounds: Press announcements are not official tender offers. And by that time, Kerkorian had a firm grip on Terry Drinkwater's airline. Kerkorian actually had obtained control without going into his own vast financial holdings; the Bank of America had given him two unsecured loans totaling $73 million just at the stage when WAL stockholders began to accept that $45 per share offer. By the end of December, Kerkorian had acquired nearly 1.4 million shares, or about 28 per cent of the outstanding stock.

He didn't have that 28 per cent when he, Benninger, and Singleton met with Drinkwater and TCD's three top executives at the Century Plaza. It was an uncomfortable, somewhat awkward session, each side trying to size up the other; Drinkwater didn't help matters any when he coldly rejected Kerkorian's request that he and his two associates go on Western's Board. Terry's obstinance was against the advice of Hugh Darling and Art Woodley, the latter having known Kerkorian for years.

Woodley, when he headed PNA, had bought an airplane from Kerkorian—a DC-4, sight unseen. PNA's maintenance chief called Art after the plane was delivered. "Art, let's get this goddamned thing out of Seattle—it's leaking so much it's a fire hazard."

Woodley rushed over to where the plane was parked and found that the complaint hadn't been exaggerated one bit. The mechanics were afraid to even run a tractor around it for fear a backfire might ignite the leaking fuel. They finally got it towed to a far end of the field, and Woodley called Kerkorian with a Woodley-type suggestion as to where Kirk could put that DC-4 with all four props revolving.

"Art, so help me, I didn't know it was in that kind of shape," Kerkorian apologized. "I'll give you back your dough."

He did, promptly, and earned a place on Arthur G. Woodley's rather abbreviated "Honest Businessmen I Have Known" list.

It was Shatto, however, who came closest to being a tempering factor in the Drinkwater-Kerkorian dispute. He was as close to Terry as sweat is to skin, yet he also had respect for Kerkorian; they had played golf together and were on a first-name basis.

Stan told Drinkwater, "I don't know anything bad about him, Terry—he seems to be an honest, capable guy, and people who've had dealings with him say he's straightforward." Kirk had phoned Shatto the day before the tender offer was made public, trying to locate TCD.

But for once, Terry wasn't listening to his first lieutenant, and Shatto's rather tenuous peace-making chances foundered when it became apparent that Kerkorian wanted Benninger to keep close tabs on Western. Stan had no love for the ex-Flying Tiger official, referring to him on more than one occasion as "that damned hatchetman." Feeling as he did about Benninger, Shatto's mild mediation efforts diminished in direct proportion to Benninger's rising influence. If open war had been declared between Drinkwater and Kerkorian, the Shatto-Benninger feud amounted to a second front.

Thus did Western come to the end of 1968—a year that had begun with so much hope and ended with upheaval, uneasiness, and unhappiness. The new year opened on a high note of promise: On January 4, 1969, President Johnson confirmed a Civil Aeronautics Board decision awarding Western routes between eleven Mainland cities and Hawaii, including Anchorage–Honolulu. But while Drinkwater himself hailed it as "the most important route award in the forty-three-year history of the company," the Hawaiian authority actually came almost ten years too late to deserve that accolade. First, it suffered from the restriction that forced WAL to operate all Los Angeles–Hawaii service from points east of California, thus preventing the origination of flights from Los Angeles. Second, whereas the abortive 1960 decision would have made Western the third carrier in the Los Angeles–Hawaii market, the 1969 Transpacific Case ruling added Continental as a fourth carrier—without any restrictions out of Los Angeles—plus TWA and Northwest as the fifth and sixth. Third, not content with turning the Los Angeles–Hawaii route into a competitive free-for-all, the CAB gave American, TWA, Northwest, and Braniff limited Mainland–Hawaii authority—glutting the market with eight carriers. The Board apparently had tried to please everyone and ended up pleasing nobody—except, perhaps, TCD.

Drinkwater was overjoyed. Shortly after the Hawaiian award

was announced, he placed orders with Boeing for twelve new jets—three 747s, five additional 707 Intercontinentals, and four more stretched 727s. The contracts were conditional on Western's obtaining lender approval and satisfactory financing arrangements. The three 747s replaced the two assembly-line positions previously agreed on.

With this plunge, however, Drinkwater had committed the disastrous error of overextending the airline's already stretched resources. The trio of jumbo jets were easy to justify—they were scheduled for delivery starting in October of 1970, and Terry was not alone in believing that Western had to have wide-bodied aircraft to compete in the Hawaii market; Pan Am, United, and Continental all had ordered the 747. But the orders for the additional 707s and 727s were tough to explain, particularly the former. Western already had five Intercontinentals available for Hawaii service and could have supplemented these with some of its twenty-seven Boeing 720-Bs until the 747s were delivered. And the decision to increase the 727 order from six to ten was equally puzzling, inasmuch as Western in 1969 would be putting another thirteen 737s into service. The entire equipment-purchase program added up to making an existing overcapacity situation worse.

Kerkorian would shortly view this proliferation with concern, particularly in view of Drinkwater's persistent refusal to allow him the Board representation Kerkorian thought essential. Under those circumstances, Kerkorian had no choice but to act.

His first move, through a series of private market transactions, was to increase his holdings in the belief that 28 per cent ownership wasn't quite enough muscle to budge Drinkwater from his "no representation" stand. Terry's only gesture of compromise came when he offered Kerkorian one seat on the Board, which Kirk angrily refused. On January 27, Western's Board met in San Francisco and voted a compromise: The Board would be increased from fifteen to eighteen members, and the three new directors would be Kerkorian, Benninger, and Singleton. It was an uneasy truce that collapsed as Kerkorian's quiet acquisition of additional stock continued. On February 12, Kerkorian disclosed that he now held in the neighborhood of 31 per cent control, mainly through the purchase of some $6.1 million worth of convertible debentures. Two weeks later, Kerkorian asked Drink-water to call a special meeting of the Board; he wanted five seats on the Board, with himself as chairman.

With that bombshell came three additional demands: Kerkorian asked for Western's list of stockholders so he could so-licit stockholder proxies in advance of the annual shareholders' meeting scheduled for April 24, he insisted that Western's officers provide him with their plans for financing the aircraft or-dered earlier in the year, and he requested that purchase of any new equipment be delayed until he had a chance to review the financing arrangements.

Drinkwater's initial reaction was unmitigated fury and, as it turned out, ill-advised defiance. He flatly rejected all three demands, and Kerkorian promptly filed suit to obtain the list. On March 20, TCD counterattacked by asking the CAB to void Kerkorian's acquisition of control on the grounds that it was ob-tained without Civil Aeronautics Board approval in violation of Section 408 of the Federal Aviation Act—a provision requiring anyone who already is engaged in any phase of aviation to seek CAB permission before buying control of an airline.

He also actually attacked on the legislative front. The Senate Commerce Committee was considering a bill that would require CAB approval if noncarrier interests acquired control of an air-line. Howard Westwood appeared before the Commerce Com-mittee to urge that the bill be made retroactive back to Decem-ber 1, 1968—which would have included Kerkorian's purchase of WAL stock. The lawyer never got to first base with this strata-gem, and the main offensive was waged at the CAB.

Drinkwater based his claim of illegal acquisition of control on (1) Kerkorian's ownership of stock in Transamerica, which con-trolled Trans-International Airlines; (2) Kerkorian's ownership of Tracy Investment, which among other things operated an air taxi business, and (3) Tracy Investment's status as majority stockholder in International Leisure Corporation, which, in turn, owned the Flamingo Hotel—an enterprise that chartered air-planes and derived 18 per cent of its income from these flights.

The counterattack failed. On April 3, the Board declined to order an investigation into Kerkorian's acquisition of control. William Lundin, acting director of the CAB's Bureau of Enforcement, said there was no indication that Kerkorian was engaged in any phase of aeronautics when he bought into Western. He said Kerkorian held less than 4 per cent of Transamerica stock and in no way controlled its Trans-International subsidiary. As for Tracy Investment, Lundin added, it had surrendered its air taxi certificate before Kerkorian purchased any WAL stock. And the Flamingo Hotel, he ruled, was not engaged in any aviation business.

A second request for a full-scale CAB investigation also was turned down, and Drinkwater suffered a new defeat when Western was ordered by the courts to give Kerkorian its stockholder list. The April 24 shareholders' meeting loomed as a donnybrook; by now, the angry Kerkorian was seeking nine seats on the eighteen-member Board, and Drinkwater—in an impassioned letter to stockholders mailed a week before the meeting—reminded them that "they would be in a position to select the officers of your Company and to determine Company policy."

Kerkorian would have been the first one to agree with that warning; he *did* want a voice in how Western was going to be run, mainly because he didn't like what he had seen thus far. Almost on the eve of the April 24 showdown, Drinkwater surrendered to the inevitable. He was to say later that he gave in in order to avoid a proxy fight, but there wasn't much doubt he also knew he didn't stand a chance in a proxy fight; Western's officers and directors, including Terry, owned only 3.5 per cent of the stock, and Drinkwater wasn't even sure of their 100 per cent support. The executives were in a painful position, torn between loyalty toward Drinkwater and realistic appraisal of their own status in an airline being ripped from his once-iron grasp.

The directors were caught in the same emotional tug-of-war. Loyal to Terry, they didn't share all his feelings toward either Kerkorian or Benninger. In truth, some had been more impressed by Kerkorian's attitude—one of friendly co-operation and a sincere interest in Western's welfare—than by Drinkwater's anchored-in-concrete hostility.

TCD already had evidence of eroding support among the directors themselves, despite Terry's angry contention that a man holding about 30 per cent of WAL's stock didn't deserve 50 per cent representation on the Board. When he asked Woodley for his proxy vote, Art snapped, "I'll vote my own shares, Terry!"

Relations between Drinkwater and Woodley were never good once the PNA-Western merger was consummated, and they deteriorated further when Kerkorian came on the scene. Woodley phoned Kirk after the tender offer to congratulate him, and Drinkwater found out about the call. He let Woodley know he didn't like it, and Art's reply was a curt "I'll talk to whomever I damned please."

The shareholders' meeting was just a few days away when the opposing forces were drawn together by a third party with a large stake in the dispute—the Bank of America, lenders to both parties. The bank representative suggested that if Western reduced its pro-Drinkwater directors by three, it might lay the ground for an agreement and avoid the proxy battle.

Drinkwater turned purple, but just as he opened his mouth to reply, Shatto cut in. "Terry, before you answer that, I'd like to ask Mr. Clausen if he'd permit you, myself, Jud, and Art to step out in the hall for a few minutes." Clausen nodded.

Once outside the room, Shatto got to the point quickly. "Now there are three directors here, not counting Terry. I'm willing to resign and maybe you two guys will and we can get this thing settled."

Taylor and Kelly agreed instantly, but Drinkwater at first protested that it wasn't fair to any of them—Kelly, for example, had just been named a director and was immensely proud of that status. TCD finally gave in, however, and they returned to the meeting where Shatto presented his compromise proposal. This time it was Kerkorian who balked.

"I appreciate what you're trying to do, Stan," he said quietly, "but I won't go along with any of you resigning from the Board."

Apparently they were back where they started, but the resignation offer gesture at least had the beneficial effect of clearing the air. After some haggling, a compromise was reached: The Board would be increased from eighteen to twenty-one members, with all nine Kerkorian-named nominees going on. Three outside directors would be removed, and Drinkwater himself would choose which ones.

Included in the Kerkorian slate was Leo Dwerlkotte. Kirk had heard he was living in Las Vegas and wrote him, expressing a desire to meet him personally. Leo had never even heard of Kerkorian and was somewhat skeptical, but they did meet, and Dwerlkotte was impressed with Kirk's confidence. The upshot was Leo's agreeing to be nominated as a director on Kerkorian's proxy list and thus gained his measure of revenge.

Admittedly, the compromise amounted to giving Drinkwater a face-saving out of the impasse, and Terry wisely sensed it was a take-it-or-else ultimatum. The three men he asked to leave the Board were Ed Pauley, Leonard Firestone, and Howard Westwood. Pauley, who was named director emeritus, didn't care one way or another. Firestone, to quote TCD, was "madder than hell," but Westwood was delighted.

The proxy fight had been averted, but in the wake of the settlement lay an ugly smog of ill will that was never to be dissipated.

The toboggan slide had begun—for Terrell Drinkwater personally and for Western as that almost mystical entity so symbolic of the airline industry, an impersonal corporate machine that somehow has had life breathed into it by the loyalties, skills, and dreams of those who form the sum of its human components.

Dissension ran yapping at the heels of each successive misfortune, criticism marched in step with every setback, a gremlin seemed to be riding herd on whatever well-meant decision was made. Not even the coveted Hawaiian award was exempt from the assorted afflictions that plagued the suddenly staggering airline. Four days after taking office, President Nixon deferred all Transpacific awards, including Western's, pending further review.

The CAB's original decision carried an effective date of March 5, 1969, and Western had geared its preparations to inauguration of service on April 27. But Nixon's deferment order resulted in one additional delay after another; not until July 25 did WAL commence serving Hawaii with flights from the Twin Cities and Phoenix to Honolulu via Los Angeles. The succession of postponements cost Western dearly; to handle both the influx of new aircraft and the introduction of Hawaiian service, the airline had boosted its payroll more than 12 per cent—to a record 10,026 employees by summer. The arithmetic was devastatingly simple: Payroll expenses and aircraft ownership costs soared while the Hawaiian route lay dormant.

When the Pacific operations finally got under way—and WAL managed to beat all other transpacific contenders with inauguration of service—the Hawaiian routes were flown by the five 707s and featured an "Islander" theme with a Polynesian atmosphere that embraced ground services as well as in-flight services. It was tasteful, imaginative, and effective, but it fell short of what Art Kelly's team of sales and service hoped to accomplish. Kelly was the innocent victim of Drinkwater's increasing irascibility, understandable in light of the Kerkorian situation but unfortunate in that it made TCD almost impossible to work with.

Quite early in the Hawaiian planning stages, Terry told Kelly, "Don't appoint any personnel or lease space in Honolulu, Art— I'll handle all that personally." He undoubtedly meant to, but beset by all his difficulties with Kerkorian and the airline's oversupply of various troubles, TCD left some things undone. Even with all the delays, Western wasn't totally ready to start Hawaiian service when the time did come. The "Islander" motif was fine as far as it went, but Kelly wasn't the only WAL executive who thought it had to be better than anyone else's, not just as good—Western was invading a new market served both by established carriers like United and Pan Am, and new competitors with marketing ingenuity like Continental.

Art went into Drinkwater's office one day prior to start of service and made as strong a pitch as possible for in-flight movies. He was startled at Terry's reaction, not merely negative but angry.

"Absolutely not!" TCD snarled. "There will be no movies on our flights. We don't need them."

That arbitrary decision jolted Kelly, who already was disturbed over Western's having to butt heads against the 747 in the Hawaiian market; for hardly had Western started service to Honolulu, than it no longer had a wide-bodied jet on order—a development directly attributable to the unyielding stand of Fred Benninger, who much to the annoyance of Drinkwater and the undisguised resentment of Stan Shatto, was now calling not just a few shots around Western.

Benninger, a tall, forceful man with a deceptively benign appearance, occupied a unique role at WAL—a kind of unofficial *ombudsman* representing the interests of not just Kerkorian but also all stockholders. He never wanted to get deeply involved at Western; he had his fill of the airline business after spending twenty-two years at Flying Tiger. Benninger was a certified public accountant, and one of his first jobs after his discharge from the Air Force following World War II was auditing the cargo carrier's books. When the audit was finished, he was asked to stay on a couple of more weeks helping the accounting department—and suddenly found himself hired as a staff auditor. He had risen to executive vice president of Bob Prescott's airline when he became acquainted with Kerkorian—Flying Tiger did maintenance for Kirk's old Los Angeles Air Service.

In 1967, Kerkorian—on the verge of getting into the Las Vegas hotel business—asked Benninger to join him. Kerkorian's timing was perfect, for Benninger was looking around for a nonairline venture; neither knew anything about the Vegas jungle, but they were tough, experienced businessmen, and they complemented each other—Kerkorian a canny gambler, Benninger more cautious but equally decisive once he had judged the odds. It was Benninger who advised Kerkorian to buy the Flamingo Hotel, partially as a real-estate investment but also as a training ground for operating the giant International Hotel; when Fred went with Kerkorian, the latter already owned the land on which the hotel would be constructed, and architects had been hired to draw up preliminary designs.

In many ways, the relationship between the two men was much like that between Drinkwater and Shatto—mutual respect and total trust. It was typical that Kerkorian gave Benninger the task of overseeing construction of the $60 million project, even though Benninger's previous experience with hotels had been the rather universal process of occasionally checking into one. It also was typical of Benninger that he accepted the job; with his Germanic thoroughness (he still speaks with a soft trace of a German accent), he learned with incredible swiftness.

While the big hotel was going up, he was trying to tell an architect some ideas he had for a magnificent staircase sweeping from the lobby to a second level. Unable to express what he wanted in technical terms; he finally told the architect, "Hell, I'll build you a model to show you what I mean."

A craftsman in woodwork, he produced a carved miniature staircase and then created tiny chandeliers out of glass and beads to get across some of his lighting-fixture recommendations. After the staircase and the chandeliers were re-created in full-size scale in the International, Benninger decided there was no point in letting his exquisite miniatures gather dust. He proceeded to build a French château dollhouse and furnished it with Louis XIV furniture, which he also made himself. The château reproduction offers a side of Benninger few Westerners know—including some of the officers who are familiar only with his no-nonsense, clipped efficiency and questioning mind.

When things began to go bad at Western, Kerkorian gave him his orders. Benninger wasn't happy about them, but he was a crack executive officer to a ship's captain; Kerkorian had told him, "Well, I guess you're elected—see if you can straighten things out," and Benninger had taken him at his word.

Western's equipment problems came up at the first eighteen-man Board meeting held after the near-proxy brawl. Benninger asked bluntly why WAL wanted to buy the giant plane, and listened quietly to various officials defending its purchase—the chief justification being that it was needed for competitive reasons. When all the pros had been enunciated, Benninger demolished them with a single con: "Listen," he said, "as long as I'm a director of this company, I'll vote against the 747."

There were protests—Drinkwater and Shatto were enraged, and Kelly, although he agreed with Benninger's gloomy analysis of Western's financial situation, still was concerned about competing against the magnificent new jumbos with narrow-bodied 707s. It wasn't much of a contest, however; most of the new Kerkorian-picked directors knew virtually nothing about aviation and went along with Benninger, not only in his opposition to the 747 but also in his suggestion that Western temporarily abandon equipment expansion until it got back to a more solid financial position.

The result was cancellation of the agreements for the three

747s, five 707s, and four 727s. The six 727s contracted for in 1968 were delivered in 1969 but under a lease arrangement instead of outright purchase. The two men who showed the most resentment over Benninger's display of managerial strength were Drinkwater and Shatto—neither ever forgave him and from then on displayed nothing but hostility toward him. They regarded Benninger as their enemy to a far greater degree than they did Kerkorian. Benninger concedes he was a natural target for their open hatred.

"Drinkwater didn't like me because I was always asking questions and challenging," he says. "Nobody could bulldoze me because I had been in the airline business a long time. I guess he also felt I was going to take over his job. There was ill feeling right from the start, and as Kirk's alter ego I had to take the brunt of it.

"The organization seemed demoralized. One thing I noticed was that one individual was afraid to talk to another individual. If you were in one department, you didn't communicate with anyone else outside that department. As for Drinkwater, he spent more time hating than paying attention to his business, to do something about Western's problems. Even some of the older directors felt he had changed.

"Personally, I had no ambitions to take anybody's job at Western. I didn't want to come in here. I had enough of the airline business, and I was too involved with other things. So I told both Drinkwater and Shatto, 'Look, if I can help you, if I can improve things, fine.' But there was no give on their part."

The dispute over the 747 was the first major policy collision Benninger had with TCD and Shatto, and from then on it was undeclared war. There was a second clash of almost equal bitterness concerning the Electras—Benninger voiced the opinion that the company had wasted $4 million converting them to all-cargo operations and flying them in that configuration up and down the West Coast.

"Christ, get rid of the damned things!" Benninger finally exploded. "You're just losing your fannies and draining away assets because there's no way you can make money even if you flew every Electra with a 110 per cent load factor."

Benninger later traded verbal punches with Shatto over a plan to reinstate the on-time committee composed of various department heads ranging from maintenance and flight operations to sales and ground services. Western's on-time performance, which had improved sharply when the committee was established in 1964, had slumped, and Benninger wanted to resume the practice of having the key departments get together at 8:00 A.M. each weekday morning, discussing all delay factors frankly and if possible pinpointing any causal patterns that could be corrected. But Shatto objected.

"It's a waste of time," he argued. "Why the hell should I have to listen to the sales department? They're a bunch of goddamn idiots. Or why should I have to sit there with the flight department? I know why delays happen."

The on-time meetings began again and were highly successful —in fact, they still are held daily—and, Shatto's misgivings notwithstanding, they helped WAL climb to a consistent first or second place in on-time performance. But Shatto simply refused to attend, an attitude Benninger duly noted and one that increased in petulance in direct proportion to Benninger's rising influence. The latter wasn't running Western, he wasn't formulating policy, and he wasn't invading management prerogatives, but he *was* there to guide, caution, and counsel—a kind of corporate hair shirt.

An unusual man, Fred Benninger—pragmatic yet with a wry sense of humor, tough at times but possessing a thick vein of tolerance and a willingness to discuss issues. He developed his own views as he grappled with a problem that interested him, and it never bothered him to have someone raise strong opposition. In most differences of opinion, he was far more likely to say, "Okay —you know how I feel, but you're running the company and I won't impose my views on you." Only in extreme cases did he resort to a flat "This is the way it's going to be." He didn't mind anyone pulling the rug out from under him, provided the man doing the yanking had a strong case. To Benninger, losing face was an exercise in futile ego.

Western's executives, except for Drinkwater and Shatto, gradually began to like Benninger as well as respect him. Benninger, in turn, soon discovered that the airline's management corps was a lot more capable than WAL's sagging fortunes would indicate.

He admired Jud Taylor tremendously, for example—their accounting backgrounds provided natural charisma. He saw in Art Kelly not just a good salesman but also a leader of considerable skill. And significantly, he began to get a pretty good idea of what Dom Renda had meant to the company and the circumstances under which he had left.

At first, Benninger didn't know anyone at Western very well and would ask a lot of questions. Those dropped into Shatto's lap usually were ignored. He once asked Shatto about some federal regulation and Stan sent him an entire file on regulations with a note that said, in effect, find it yourself. Someone told Shatto one day that Benninger had questioned a new color scheme proposed for an aircraft interior.

"Who's going to listen to that goddamned accountant from Flying Tiger?" Stan growled.

What the other officers considered Benninger's constructive criticism and helpful advice, Shatto interpreted as blatant interference with management. Stan was fond of reminding close friends that Kerkorian, when he bought control of Western, had said the airline possessed the finest executive operating team in the industry and that he had no desire to change it. But Shatto never seemed to grasp that in opposing, needling, and feuding with Benninger, he also was striking at Kerkorian himself. One of the major mistakes Shatto made was to underestimate Benninger in virtually every way—his closeness to Kerkorian and corresponding authority at Western, and his very capability. The man Shatto so disparagingly referred to as "that goddamned accountant from Flying Tiger" was the same man who built the colossal MGM Hotel for Kerkorian in Las Vegas, acting as his own contractor for erecting the 2,000-room edifice in the record time of 14 months—and saving between $6 million and $10 million in the process.

Uppermost in Shatto's mind was his never-ending loyalty to Drinkwater, and to Stan's credit he never wavered—even though Terry's grip on the airline was loosening visibly with each new setback. The delay in starting Hawaiian service was just one of several unfavorable developments on the battlefront of routes. Especially disappointing was Western's bid to win a Seattle–New York route via the Twin Cities and Milwaukee, which would have made WAL a transcontinental carrier. A CAB examiner recommended against Western in 1969, and his decision would be upheld by the full Board the following year; Western did get Seattle–Minneapolis/St. Paul authority out of the case, which it didn't particularly want.

Equally damaging was the CAB's awarding nonstop authority to Northwest between Los Angeles and the Twin Cities, ending WAL's monopoly in what had been its bread-and-butter route.

By far the most crippling blow came only four days after inauguration of service to Hawaii. On July 29, 1969, Western's mechanics began what would be an eighteen-day strike—a walkout that cost the airline an estimated $18 million. With all its difficulties, WAL might have made money that year except for the strike; losses in 1969 totaled $12 million, and much of the red ink was directly attributable to the effects of the walkout. The dispute was mainly over the issue of who would control the mechanics' pension and medical benefits funds—the company or the Teamsters Union. Union negotiators actually accepted management's final contract offer, but the membership turned it down and the strike erupted after the union failed to resume bargaining. Benninger was to comment later that "it was a hell of a time to take a strike—right in the middle of summer traffic."

For Terry Drinkwater, it was more than just another labor fight; it meant the end of the line as far as the presidency of Western was concerned. The strike made a fourth-quarter comeback in 1969 virtually impossible, and Kerkorian was fed up with the way his investment had turned out—not to mention his being fed up with Drinkwater's stubborn rejection of all overtures toward co-operation. Terry himself believes his ouster as president primarily resulted from another factor: TCD had been talking merger with American Airlines and was hell-bent for concluding a deal Kerkorian didn't think was good enough. There is reason to believe this was, indeed, a major factor, but it wasn't the only one. Western simply wasn't big enough to hold both Terrell Drinkwater and Kirk Kerkorian—a couple of strong-minded individuals, neither of whom was used to playing a subordinate role. It might have worked out, at least for a time, if the airline hadn't run into so many financial problems and caused Kerkorian to take strong measures for protection of his huge investment. It might have worked out if Drinkwater hadn't regarded both Kerkorian and Benninger as rank interlopers instead of honest men seeking the same goals as TCD. As it was, circumstances and events, combined with Terry's own uncompromising personality, dictated otherwise.

Shatto got the first word one day in October 1969—from Fred Benninger, who called Stan into his office and informed him that Kerkorian was going to call a special directors' meeting for the purpose of firing Drinkwater. Benninger added that what Kirk really wanted was for Terry to move up to chairman of the Board, but was convinced that Drinkwater would never agree to being kicked upstairs. Outright dismissal, Benninger said quietly, seemed to be the only alternative.

When Benninger said the special meeting would be held the next day, Shatto asked him to postpone the showdown.

"I don't know how you arrived at the conclusion that Terry would never accept the chairmanship," Shato said—"maybe it's true and maybe it isn't. But I'd like very much to do this if you and Kirk agree: Give me forty-eight hours to see if I can't get Terry to agree that he'll step aside for a new president and become chairman of the Board himself."

For probably the only time in their stormy relationship, Benninger and Shatto faced each other on a common ground: the desire to avoid humiliating the man who had guided Western to greatness.

"I'll certainly agree to that, and I know Kirk will," Fred said softly. "In the meantime, we'd better start thinking about his successor as president."

Kerkorian already had broken the news to Drinkwater; TCD had met Kirk in the latter's suite at the Los Angeles Beverly Hilton to fill him in on the merger talks he had been having with George Spater, president of American Airlines. When Terry had urged him to accept the merger terms Spater was offering, Kerkorian tersely refused and suggested that Western should have a new president.

"Fine," Drinkwater had snapped. "I'll send you some names to consider and you send me your own list."

Drinkwater's list of prospects was in Benninger's hands when he met with Shatto; curiously, it did not include the name of

Stanley R. Shatto, probably because TCD figured Stan stood no chance whatsoever of being accepted by Benninger or maybe even Kerkorian. But several names were discussed between Benninger and Shatto, with neither man reaching any conclusions nor agreeing on specific recommendations.

"Do I still have those forty-eight hours you promised?" Shatto asked again. "That's what I'll need to swing Terry over. It'll be better for employees, stockholders, directors, and everybody else if we can avoid a fight—and keep the presidency inside the company instead of picking someone from the outside."

"You have my promise," Benninger assured him.

Shatto went immediately to Drinkwater's office and began his sales pitch.

"They're going to call that special meeting, Terry," he warned, "and they wouldn't have gone that far if they weren't sure of the votes against you. If you become Board chairman without surrendering any of your rights and privileges under your contract, it seems to me we can at least keep this thing on the tracks. You'd have three or four more years to go under the contract and you still could be helpful to the airline."

"Would you mind if I called Jud and Art in?" Drinkwater asked in a tone of calmness that belied the turmoil boiling inside him.

"Sure," Shatto said, "I think that's a good idea."

When Taylor and Kelly arrived, Shatto briefed them on the situation—repeating what he had just told TCD about Kerkorian having the votes to oust Terry anyway, and the necessity of choosing his successor from within the company.

"Look," Drinkwater finally sighed, "I'll let Kerkorian kick me up to the chairmanship on one condition: if one of you guys will become president. I'll start with you, Stan. Would you accept the presidency?"

"No way, Terry. I'm perfectly satisfied with the contract I have."

"How about you, Art?"

"Hell, I don't have the financial background yet," Kelly answered honestly.

"Jud?"

It was strictly up to J. Judson Taylor, who had started with

Western thirty years before as chief accountant and whose presidential ambitions were about as potent as distilled water.

His reaction to Drinkwater's question reflected not just uncertainty but also a semblance of unwillingness. He refused to make any firm commitment and admitted he wasn't even sure he wanted to be president.

"Anyway," he added, "I'd have to talk with my wife about it."

"Would you let me call Benninger and tell him you're at least thinking about it?" Shatto asked. Taylor nodded, and Shatto put in a call to Benninger at the latter's Las Vegas office. Stan used one phone and both Kelly and Taylor got on extensions. Stan informed Benninger that both of them were listening to the conversation.

"We've talked to Terry," Shatto said, "and he'll go along with the chairmanship provided he doesn't get hurt financially in any way. We're agreed that Jud should become president but he wants to think about it for a little while. And if he does accept, we think Kelly should have a contract. Also, we recommend that you become vice chairman of the Board."

This suggestion came as a complete surprise to Benninger, who said he'd have to think *that* one over himself.

"Talk to Kirk about all this," Shatto urged. "If he doesn't buy this, Fred, I don't have any more suggestions for you."

"Okay, I'll talk to Kirk," Benninger replied. "Can you, Taylor, and Kelly come over to Las Vegas?"

The trio agreed, and the next day they met with Kerkorian, Benninger, and Singleton. The previous night, Taylor had discussed the offer of the presidency with his wife.

"Somebody's got to steer the boat," he had told her. "We're all on it and we can't get off."

When the Western executives walked into Kerkorian's office, however, Taylor still hadn't made any commitment. He asked a couple of questions and Shatto tossed in one of his own. "How much authority would Jud have—full authority to hire or fire anyone as he sees fit?"

Benninger and Kerkorian nodded.

Taylor's jaw tightened. "I'll accept with this understanding: Fred will agree to come to Los Angeles and spend one day a week at Western."

Benninger said that was fine with him and also agreed to accept the vice chairmanship. It took only a few minutes to arrange a contract for Kelly, and in less time than a WAL jet consumes flying from Los Angeles to Vegas, Jud Taylor had become Western's fifth president.

There is some disagreement as to whether Taylor had any serious outside competition for the WAL presidency. Director Harry Volk says flatly that William "Bill" Boyd of Airlift International, a Miami-based supplemental carrier, actually was Kerkorian's and Benninger's initial choice to succeed Drinkwater. According to Volk, both he and Hugh Darling were worried over an outsider being picked as the new president and bluntly informed Benninger that Boyd was unacceptable.

Darling says he suggested Jim Austin, former president of Northeast, as an interim presidential possibility if they just wanted to hold the airline together; Dom Renda and Al Adams were other names Darling tossed into the conversation.

Kelly remembers getting a call from Boyd himself after Taylor had been named president—a conversation that began with Boyd's saying, "Did you know I almost became president of Western?"

Says Benninger:

"Several people were considered. Boyd was just one, and we didn't consider him seriously—he was never No. 1 or No. 2, for example. Actually we looked at four or five individuals, including a guy from Overseas National and also the ex-president of Trans-International. But I told Kirk, 'Looking at the company and the people in this company, before we take a chance on someone from the outside, unless I know he's a top-notch man, I'd rather try the inside.' And I finally convinced Kirk this was the way to go."

It was at least a peaceful if not entirely happy ending to the latest Drinkwater-Kerkorian confrontation. As chairman of the Board, Terry retained all the materialistic trappings of authority —his big, plush office, his presidential salary, and numerous fringe benefits. What he also retained, however, was his dislike of Benninger and his distrust of and bitterness toward Kerkorian. And this was in direct conflict with what he could *not* retain:

power. In this kind of executive Twilight Zone of his own creation, he committed his last and fatal mistake:

He tried to force Kerkorian prematurely into a merger between Western and American.

CHAPTER NINETEEN

To Merge or Not to Merge . . .

The possibility of an American-Western merger first arose in December 1968—and American was the instigator.

One week after Kerkorian made his tender offer, President George Spater of American telephoned Drinkwater and without much preamble asked if Western would be interested in a merger.

"You're not the first airline president to make that inquiry," Terry chuckled. "I'll be honest with you, George—I'm not interested in discussing merger with anybody at this time. We're on the hot seat with our Hawaiian application, and I don't want to do anything to upset it."

The matter rested there for several months. Drinkwater hadn't been kidding Spater about Western being wooed by other carriers, either—one of them was Northwest, whose president, Don Nyrop, reportedly had been envisioning a three-way merger involving NWA, WAL, and a third airline.

Spater's interest in an American-Western marriage was in no way lessened by Drinkwater's rebuff. In March 1969, he contacted Kerkorian through American's investment banking firm, Lazard Frères, trying to find out what Kerkorian really intended to do with his WAL stock—keep it or sell it? Two Lazard Frères representatives met with Kerkorian in Las Vegas, but Kirk seemed lukewarm at best. He told the two emissaries that he believed Western had excellent profit potential if better operating efficiency could be achieved.

"I wouldn't rule out merger possibilities," he added, "but I'd have to show a substantial profit on my shares."

THE ONLY WAY TO FLY 425

That cooled off Spater as far as approaching Kerkorian was concerned. He decided to go back to Drinkwater again once the upper-echelon waves caused by Kerkorian's acquisition of control had subsided. On June 11, 1969, Spater and Drinkwater met in Los Angeles and for the first time got down to some serious merger discussion. The atmosphere seemed favorable enough for Spater to see Kerkorian the very next day, with Bill Singleton present.

Spater repeated what he had asked Kirk the first time: Would he be interested in a merger? Kerkorian repeated what he had answered the first time: He still believed Western could be made profitable, but he'd be willing to sell his stock at a profit.

"How much profit?" Spater inquired bluntly.

"I paid an average of $47.25 a share," Kerkorian replied, "and my selling price is $60 a share."

Spater shook his head doubtfully. "It's too high," he allowed. Spater left the Beverly Hilton disappointed but convinced that so long as Drinkwater seemed interested, American still had a good shot at acquiring Western. Spater bided his time, waiting until August to see TCD again—visiting him at Western's general offices while en route to Australia. They talked mostly about Spater's unsatisfactory discussions with Kerkorian.

On September 27, Spater booked space on a Western flight from Los Angeles to Honolulu, and Drinkwater came out to the airport to see him off. Their conversation was casual and friendly, but Spater made the point that merger was impossible unless Kerkorian came down in his asking price.

"I don't see how we can offer more than a share-for-share exchange," he declared, "and that's about half the price Kerkorian is demanding."

At this point, Terry was sold completely on the share-for-share formula as fair and reasonable. He told Spater that as far as he was concerned, American had a deal and he would talk to Kerkorian about it. Drinkwater then took a long memorandum to Kirk's suite at the Beverly Hilton, filling him in on the negotiations he had been conducting with Spater and fervently recommending that Kerkorian take the share-for-share exchange. It was more a collision than a business discussion, for Kerkorian not only rejected any merger on that basis but was openly angered at Drinkwater's conducting the negotiations virtually solo.

"You have no right to deal with Spater," Kerkorian charged.

"I'm chairman of the Board and I have every right," Drinkwater retorted.

TCD, it must be said, felt strongly about the necessity for merging with American. By his own admission, he had been thinking about it long before he ever heard of Kerkorian, and the more he thought, the more it made sense. First, TCD didn't believe the smaller airlines had much of a chance with the expensive wide-bodied jets coming along—a single 747 represented a capital investment of some $23 million, which happened to be the total amount of cash Western had on hand as of the end of 1969. Second, if merger was to be the only way out, American—in Terry's eyes—was the obvious choice. His admiration for American had never slackened in all the years that had elapsed since he worked for C. R. Smith's airline.

The very existence of merger talks, however tentative and thus far unsuccessful, was a terrible burden to place on the shoulders of Drinkwater's successor. Keeping them from airline employees is about as easy as hiding pregnancy, and Western was no exception. Almost from the day Taylor took over the presidency, he faced a morale situation that steadily worsened as merger chances progressed from long-shot odds to stark reality. It wasn't too bad in the early stages—vague rumors at first, with most of the concern centering around the more immediate crisis of WAL's financial status.

The most pressing problem was the Hawaiian market, into which WAL had poured so much manpower and material resources. And this was where Art Kelly and his team came through—once Kelly knew there was no chance of getting a wide-bodied fleet for a long time, he drained the utmost out of what tools were on hand. With Drinkwater's veto power eliminated, Kelly got Taylor to approve in-flight movies. An even more important move was a decision to avoid the small lounges that had been proposed by other carriers for Hawaiian service. Eliminating the lounges made it possible for Western to go to thirty-eight-inch pitch seats through the coach section, giving passengers the equivalent of first-class legroom no matter where they were sitting.

To Willis R. "Bill" Balfour, then vice president of agency, interline, and group marketing went the task of building new Hawaii-oriented markets in the cities Western served. The restriction requiring all Los Angeles–Hawaii flights to originate east of California turned out to be a blessing in disguise; it gave Balfour a chance to stress to tour operators the advantages of using Western's one-plane service to the Islands from such inland cities as Minneapolis/St. Paul, Phoenix, and later Las Vegas, Salt Lake City, and Denver.

The fleet serving the Hawaiian market was a hybrid affair, mixing 707s later with 720-Bs converted to overwater configuration. The latter proved more economical to operate than the bigger Intercontinentals and a lot more reliable than the 747s, which started flying the Hawaiian routes in 1970. The jumbo's early engine-reliability problems didn't involve safety, but they did cause delays and even cancellations—in sufficient proportions to dilute much of the giant jet's early passenger appeal. Various engine difficulties were responsible for some 40 per cent of delays affecting 747 schedules to and from Hawaii in 1970. Unexpectedly, Western began picking up an impressive number of passengers who preferred schedule reliability to wide-bodied luxury, and the effectiveness of WAL's advertising campaign— "Western: First in Space" and "You've Got First-class Legs"—did much to offset the admittedly greater spaciousness of the 747.

By mid-1970, Western had gained its beachhead in Hawaii, achieving a market penetration second only to the dominant carrier—United. Market share, it must be said, however, was never the name of the game at WAL; it scheduled for profit, not share of the market.

Slowly, Western battled its way out of the twin traumas of 1969's setbacks and the overthrow of Drinkwater. It was almost a kind of healing atmosphere, and under those conditions there was no more effective leader than Jud Taylor. Inherently kind and considerate, with absolutely no pretensions yet possessing a streak of toughness, probably his greatest asset was his own belief that he was more or less an interim president—someone to guide the airline back to stability, at which point he was perfectly willing to turn over the reins to someone else.

Perhaps with this in mind, he called an old friend and colleague, Dom Renda, and it was no casual conversation. To quote Renda: "He contacted me and he wanted me to come back to Western. He told me he was going to consolidate a number of departments, and his thinking was that eventually I'd move up because we always understood each other. I wasn't interested. First, it was too soon. I had responsibilities and a five-year contract with Continental. Second, I loved what I was doing. I was committed to get a permanent certificate for Air Micronesia. So I thanked Jud but told him no."

One of the first things Taylor did when he became president was to write a letter to each of Western's nine thousand employees, earnestly seeking any suggestions, advice, or ideas anyone might have to help him pull WAL out of its spin. The response was so good that Taylor later established a suggestion program, with a system of monetary awards for money-saving ideas, the first the company had operated in many years.

Taylor cared little about the trappings of the presidency. He once flew into Washington, D.C., accompanied by another Western official, marching quickly to the baggage-delivery area, where he picked up his own luggage and started to walk out of the terminal.

"Jud, where are you going?" his companion asked.

"Gonna find that airport bus that goes downtown," Taylor said.

He had to be talked into taking a taxi.

"Jud Taylor," another Western officer recalls fondly, "was about as polished as a piece of raw coal. Like the way he'd borrow money for the airline. Any other president would have prepared for him elaborate charts, traffic forecasts, complete financial data, and all the rest of the usual rigmarole. Jud would walk into the bank with a few figures scribbled on a piece of paper. But it always worked, and in many cases the bank was prepared to give him more than he asked for because they trusted him."

A financial reporter was interviewing Taylor one day and asked a question about WAL's long-term debt. The newsman, who had interviewed quite a few other airline presidents, leaned back and waited for Jud to pick up a phone and ask some subordinate for the required figures. Taylor got out of his chair, walked over to a shelf from which he took a thick volume, and laboriously looked up the information himself.

His forte was never speech-writing nor speech-making, but whereas virtually all airline chief executives utilize the professional skills of their public-relations personnel, Taylor hated to bother anyone in Western's PR. Came the day when he had to address his first shareholders' meeting as president and, typically, he decided to compose the opening remarks himself. He sent them over to Hugh Darling and Bob Kinsey for approval and/or criticism. Darling expressed no approval whatsoever but a lot of criticism and suggested that he supply Taylor with another speech. Jud winced, but called Kinsey in for his verdict.

"Well, Jud," Kinsey began hesitantly, hating to hurt Taylor's feelings, "I know what you're trying to get across, but maybe . . ."

"Don't bother telling me," Jud interrupted. "Darling's already seen what I wrote. He's writing me a new speech."

A few days later, the president of Western rose to address the shareholders. He opened the looseleaf notebook he always carried around with him—and blanched. All he had in front of him were his original remarks; he had forgotten to put in Darling's revisions. Somehow, he stumbled through considerable ad-libbing, extemporizing, and occasional snatches of what he could remember from Darling's prose.

One of Taylor's earliest tasks was to repair at least some of Western's tattered communications between labor and management. He took labor relations away from Shatto, "mainly because there was so much bitter feeling and division on the executive level," Taylor explained later. He didn't reorganize to the extent Kelly urged, for Art was 180 degrees away from Shatto in their thinking on how to deal with labor. Kelly wanted everything to run smoothly, and he was willing to listen to the unions, to compromise on divergent views. Taylor placed himself somewhere in the middle of Kelly and Shatto, and by and large his relations with labor during his brief regime were fairly good. At least there were no strikes in that time, except for a five-hour steward-ess strike shortly after Taylor became president.

The most visible change to occur at Western while Jud Taylor served as president was a completely new corporate image—and the abandonment of the old Indian head as Western's symbol. The project got under way in 1969, prodded mostly by Kelly, Lynn, Ensign, and a new WAL official—Don Drews, an archi-tect hired originally as an airport and facilities planner. What they were seeking is technically called a corporate identity pro-gram; as Drews explains it, "people like Kelly and Lynn wanted a common thread, something in design either through color or graphics or the way a logo is put on . . . a consistency of theme so we could begin to look like the company we are.

"Too many people evaluated Western as a small outfit, and we really weren't. We needed a new approach, which was what a lot of experts were trying to tell us. They said we were trying to say a lot of different things to a lot of different people but we didn't have a central theme. The Indian head was the strongest visual image we had, but all it did was establish recognition of Western as a regional carrier, strictly a western outfit."

Western's design committee established as its first "new look" task a new logo. Western went to an outside firm for aid in this most drastic version of the new look, choosing the New York firm of Lippincott & Margulies to come up with a new corporate vis-ual symbol. The design committee itself was divided on whether to drop the Indian head entirely, and there was open opposition on the part of many WAL veterans, officers and employees alike.

A few officers insisted that maybe the Indian head itself could be modernized, but Kelly, Lynn, and others fought for an en-tirely new approach and won. Lippincott & Margulies submitted about two hundred separate designs, virtually all of them focus-ing on the letter W. There was no attempt to try for a new logo like the TWA and Pan Am globes, for example. From the origi-nal list of two hundred, the design committee sifted down to a dozen choices, then narrowed the list to three, and finally picked what might be termed a "flying W"—the symbol that represents Western today, leaving the Indian head a memory of the past's troubles and triumphs. The decision was made with no input from Drinkwater, who privately thought the whole business of a new corporate image wasn't terribly important—a view, it must be admitted, that some of the older officers and directors shared. But TCD's indifference, unlike many of the veterans, was not one of nostalgic affection for the old Indian insignia; he had become obsessed with what he sincerely believed was the only course for the airline he had once governed: merger with American. And *only* American.

He concentrated on that single subject just as he had once devoted all his interest and attention to Hawaii—but with one important difference. As president and chief executive officer, he could do whatever he wanted to in the Hawaiian case. As chairman of the Board, an empty title in his case when it came to any real authority or power, he was skating on razor-thin ice trying to continue his own negotiations with Spater. He had defied Kerkorian once on that issue and it had cost him the presidency. Now, dealing from a far more vulnerable position, he kept up his pressure on Kerkorian for the American merger.

It came close to being an act of deliberate self-destruction. Drinkwater had plenty of warning that he was pushing Kerkorian too far—not just with the merger but also with his attitude toward the tough-minded Armenian in general, his belligerence toward Benninger, and his undisguised contempt for both these men he believed had robbed him of his airline. Bob Kinsey, who admired and likes Kerkorian and Benninger tremendously yet has maintained an unceasing friendship with TCD, was a personal witness to what Drinkwater was doing to himself. On more than one occasion, Kinsey says, he heard Kerkorian actually plead with Terry not to push him too far.

"You know what I'm going to have to do," Kerkorian had warned, "and you know I can do it. I don't want to but you're forcing me to."

Even before Terry lost the presidency, Kerkorian told more than one close associate that Drinkwater was forcing himself out. After Drinkwater was kicked upstairs, presumably to a spot where his wings of influence had been effectively clipped, TCD refused to accept the reality of defeat. He was a Napoleon, exiled to a corporate Elba, but still with dreams of regaining power. It would not be too farfetched if one grasps the extent of his stubbornness, the enormous residue of pride and confidence stored up in two decades of rule. Power never corrupted Terry Drinkwater, but it did blind him. He had defeated every previous attempt to take Western away from him, and he seems never to have really grasped that Kerkorian actually had accomplished what no one else could.

When Jud Taylor first became aware of the merger talks and realized how badly Drinkwater wanted a deal with American, he told TCD, "Terry, you can't force Kirk into a merger—you have to convince him first it's a good idea." But Drinkwater continued his contacts with Spater.

They met at Los Angeles International Airport on February 26; Spater was there in connection with American's upcoming 747 inaugural flight four days later, and filled Drinkwater in on the failure of two previous talks he had had with Kerkorian earlier in the year. He had met Kerkorian in New York on January 31, a session at which Kerkorian indicated he might be willing to come down slightly from his asking price of sixty dollars a share. Spater stuck to the one-for-one exchange, and a subsequent telephone conversation between them on February 25 produced no progress whatsoever.

Western's annual shareholders' meeting was scheduled for April 23 at the Beverly Hilton. On April 21, Spater phoned Drinkwater, who asked in the course of the conversation if American still was interested in the one-for-one deal.

"We definitely are," Spater assured him.

The roof blew off at the shareholders' meeting.

All went smoothly, with Jud Taylor presiding after Drinkwater had made a few introductory remarks, until Taylor threw the meeting open to questions from the floor. A stockholder named Flint Rainey rose and lit the fuse to the dynamite.

"Mr. Taylor," he began, "my name is Rainey. I am a stockholder. I speak for my mother, mother-in-law, and wife, who also are stockholders. Published articles in *Fortune* and the Los Angeles *Times* have suggested that American Airlines is willing to merge with Western on a share-for-share basis and that the stumbling block for such a merger is Mr. Kerkorian."

Fred Benninger's face darkened.

Rainey sailed on. "It seems to me this would be a very good merger for Western at this time or sometime this year, because American is profitable and Western is not. American pays a dividend and Western does not. American stock is about twenty-five dollars and Western's is about 50 per cent lower, at thirteen dollars. American Airlines possesses the ability to modernize their fleet of aircraft to compete in today's market and Western apparently does not.

"For these reasons, a merger between the two would seem very logical to Western stockholders, who have seen their investment drop about 70 per cent since Mr. Kerkorian's tender offer at forty-five dollars in December 1968. If Mr. Kerkorian is the stumbling block here—and that's been reported in the press—then I think he is gambling not only with his own money, which is fine with me, but also with the investments of the other 70 per cent stockholders in Western, and I think that's wrong for him to be doing if that's what he is doing. I would like to ask several questions.

"The first: What is the present attitude toward a merger with American or some other airline on the part of Mr. Taylor, Mr. Drinkwater, and Mr. Kerkorian or one of his representatives? That's the first question."

Taylor was the first to answer, in a calm voice that managed to hide his distinct feeling that this was not going to be a routine session.

"At the time of my election last fall," Jud said, "the Board of Directors authorized me to make a statement that no mergers were then contemplated. Since that time and to the present time, I have had no discussions of any kind whatsoever concerning a possible merger between Western and any other airline. That does not mean to rule out the possibility of a merger if it should be in the best interests of the stockholders, obviously. It only means there have not been and there are no current discussions going on, so far as I am concerned, with any airline. Furthermore, under our charter and bylaws, any merger will require the affirmative vote of two thirds of the shareholders.

"Unless we were convinced that a merger would be for the

benefit of the shareholders or had a reasonable chance of being approved by the shareholders, it probably would not be to the interest of Western Airlines to propose a merger that would not be successful."

Taylor promised to explore any merger that looked promising, but cautioned that no merger route was easy—not only requiring overwhelming stockholder approval but also CAB sanction and possibly facing opposition from the Justice Department.

"I can only say," he concluded, "that I am not necessarily opposed to a merger if I think it is in the interest of the shareholders, and that we will continue to explore the matter, but we have no announcement to make this morning on the subject."

That didn't satisfy Mr. Rainey.

"Could Mr. Drinkwater comment?" he asked.

Drinkwater could and did—simultaneously signing his own execution order.

"Well, I no longer speak for the company," Terry remarked in a rather wistful tone, "and I don't know that it is appropriate for me to comment at this time . . ." For his own sake, he should have stopped right there, but he kept writing on that figurative death warrant. "But in all honesty, I must say that I recommended to Mr. Kerkorian, while I was chief executive officer, that the proposed merger under which Western would receive one share of American for one share of Western was, in my judgment, a sound, progressive arrangement. I said it had a very good chance of being approved."

Benninger was glaring openly at Drinkwater, but Terry barged right ahead. "I thought it was a sensible merger which would involve no competition of any consequence, and I recommended to Mr. Kerkorian that we proceed on that basis. Mr. Kerkorian would not agree to that, and obviously Mr. Kerkorian holds 28.4 per cent of the shares outstanding, which for all practical purposes would give him enough stock to block that merger."

The huge ballroom of the Beverly Hilton was still with unspoken tension. Rainey's voice broke the silence. "Mr. Benninger, could you comment or someone else for Mr. Kerkorian?"

The tall figure of Fred Benninger uncoiled from his seat.

"I would like to clarify a few statements made here," he said tersely, his anger undisguised.

"No. 1: Insofar as the fact that American Airlines made an offer of a certain number of shares for a certain number of shares of Western, to my knowledge, unless something happened that I don't know of, American Airlines has never made any offer to Western Airlines or Mr. Kerkorian for any exchange of stock at any price. That's true for any other airline.

"Secondly, speaking on behalf of Mr. Kerkorian, and speaking on behalf of myself as a director of Western Airlines, we would still consider any proposal from any airline which is to the advantage of the stockholder. Mr. Kerkorian is a large stockholder of Western Airlines. He has the same interest as the stockholder who has a hundred shares of Western Airlines. If a proposal may come along which is to the advantage of the stockholders of Western Airlines, I will vote for it and Mr. Kerkorian will vote for it. But until such time as a proposal comes along, there is nothing that can be done.

"Thirdly, my personal opinion is this: Any time that you are merging or trying to merge with a company, you must merge from strength, not from weakness. So therefore, as far as Western is concerned, the first thing we have to do is turn around!"

The shareholders burst into applause. Taylor interjected at this point an explanation of why the share-for-share proposal had never been disclosed to stockholders. He said when he heard Drinkwater had been discussing merger with American's top official, he sought legal advice as to whether preliminary talks warranted such disclosure. Western's general counsel, Hugh Darling, Taylor emphasized, investigated the matter "and determined that the discussions were sufficiently preliminary in nature and had not blossomed into any actual offers to the extent that a further disclosure was required on the part of the company.

"Am I correct, Mr. Darling?" Taylor asked the general counsel.

"Yes," Darling confirmed. In effect, Taylor had supported Benninger's contention that American had never made a formal merger offer based on the one-to-one exchange ratio and that Drinkwater was out of line implying that a specific, official offer had been made.

Stockholder Rainey wasn't satisfied. He proceeded to read a

paragraph from an article in the March 1 edition of the Los Angeles *Times,* which was entered into the meeting minutes:

> American confirmed last October that very tentative merger talks had been held with Western. Informed sources said American had offered to exchange one share of stock for each share of Western, but that Las Vegas financier Kerkorian, who owns 28 per cent of Western's shares and effectively controls the airline, was simply holding out for considerably more. "I will be glad to renew discussions if anyone else wanted them," Spater says now.

"If Mr. Kerkorian does not want a merger with American Airlines," Rainey inquired after reading the clip, "what else is he doing to prevent Western from going bankrupt, Mr. Benninger?"

There was some applause at the question, but Benninger kept his cool, his dry wit coming to the rescue.

"Perhaps we should have waited a little bit before we invested in Western Airlines," he remarked as the audience laughed, "but that is beside the point. . . ."

"I wish I had sold my stock to you," Rainey broke in, amid more laughter.

The tension eased somewhat, Benninger continued in a sober vein. He praised Western's officers for "doing a good job" in trying to turn the airline back to profitability, but again reminded the stockholders that significant improvement would take time.

"I for one, as far as the directors are concerned, do not recommend at this point that we sell out to anybody at any price that may come along, and I feel very strongly about that," Benninger added as the stockholders applauded again.

It is a matter for honest debate as to whether Drinkwater was really off base by claiming that a firm merger offer had been made; it was almost a question of semantics. What was more to the point was that TCD thought the offer, firm or too vaguely tentative as the case may be, should be accepted immediately. Benninger in effect called him a liar for implying that the one-for-one exchange represented a tangible "merger proposal" virtually ready for consummation. But what infuriated Benninger even more was Terry's bid for stockholder support of what Benninger considered a terrible deal to begin with. He felt at that particular point in time it was dangerous for employees to think a merger definitely was in the works; their own concern over their future was only too likely to slow down efforts to get the airline back in the black.

Fred was further enraged at Drinkwater's claim that Kerkorian single-handedly had blocked a supposedly good merger, for if Western's self-recovery efforts were to fail, Kirk would be held responsible for having turned down the deal with American. Benninger also believes, and so does Darling, that Drinkwater or someone close to him planted the question Rainey asked, in a deliberate attempt to force the issue by bringing it before the stockholders.

"Drinkwater had brought up the American offer at a Board meeting prior to the shareholders' meeting," Benninger relates. "He recommended that we take up the one-for-one exchange, but the directors didn't even act on it. How the hell could they? Drinkwater hadn't given us anything specific or detailed to consider—he gave us the impression it had been discussed between himself and Spater like chatter in a cocktail lounge. I thought it was a poor deal—I had gone through a merger between Flying Tiger and Slick, and I personally was against any merger. I didn't think we needed one to survive. Then when he got up and told the stockholders an offer had been made and that Kerkorian had blocked it, I was furious. Kirk wasn't against merger—he was against merging right away on American's terms.

"It kind of pushed me over the hill, so to speak, concerning Terrell Drinkwater's future with the company. Anyone can make a mistake, but I knew he was just being vindictive and would go to any lengths to carry on a vendetta against Kerkorian. That's when I realized he had to go—there was no sense in keeping him. In his own mind, I will say, he was absolutely convinced that the only way this company could exist was to merge with somebody."

Benninger informed Kerkorian of what had transpired at the Beverly Hilton, and they mutually agreed on the next move Shortly after the shareholders' meeting, Drinkwater left for Japan—leaving in his turbulent wake a fuming Kerkorian. Hugh

Darling learned of his fury when Kerkorian's lawyer, Bill Singleton, phoned him.

"Hugh, Kirk's calling a special Board meeting as soon as possible," Singleton advised. "I thought you might as well know why
—he's throwing Drinkwater out."

Darling was not surprised, but his immediate reaction was one
of protest. "He can't do that when Terry's out of the country,
Bill. At least wait until he gets back. The company's in no position to have its dirty linen aired, and there could be some internal litigation."

"Yeah," Singleton agreed. "I know Terry has a contract. Look,
if you have any alternatives, I'll be glad to relay them to Kirk."

"My idea is to wait until Drinkwater gets back," Darling
suggested. "As far as I'm concerned, no officer should go against
the wishes of the company's owner, and to all intent and purpose, Kirk is Western's owner. But to fire him when he's not here
to defend himself just isn't right."

Singleton relayed Darling's feelings to Kerkorian, who proposed that the three of them might have lunch to discuss the
matter. At the luncheon, Darling reiterated that while he wasn't
against ousting Drinkwater, it wasn't fair to give him the ax *in
absentia*.

Kerkorian was pleasant enough about it at first. "Well, Hugh,
if you feel that keenly, I'll put it off until he gets back."

Darling, thinking he had at least spared Drinkwater some humiliation, relaxed to enjoy his lunch, but Kerkorian began having
second thoughts. Just before dessert was served, he turned to
Singleton. "Bill, I don't think this company can hold both of us
any longer—go ahead and call that meeting!"

Darling, stunned, made a final pitch. "Well, will you do this,
Kirk? Will you talk to Harry Volk this afternoon? He's a sensible
guy. Just talk to him, please. Because if you hold that meeting
now, I'll vote against you. If you wait until Terry gets back, I'll
vote for whatever can be worked out in an acceptable fashion.
I'm not opposed to firing him because I don't think he should be
taking a contrary position to yours."

Kerkorian relented once more, but that night Singleton called
Darling again. "Hugh, Kirk has another idea. He wants to in-

crease the Board by two members who'd go along with his views."

Kerkorian obviously was worried that Drinkwater might have enough of a loyal following among the directors to prevent his final ouster. In truth, the Board at this juncture was fairly well split, and a vote on such a controversial issue as Drinkwater's outright dismissal could go either way. Darling, in fact, suspected that his might be the swing vote.

"Bill, you can't do that," Hugh told Singleton. "You've just had an annual meeting. If you call another one and increase the size of the Board again, the SEC [Securities and Exchange Commission] is going to be down your throat before you can turn around."

"I suspect you're right," Singleton sighed. "I'll get back to you. You gonna be there?"

"I won't budge," Darling assured him.

Singleton phoned again in about an hour. "Kirk says you win."

The brief but tense confrontation between Darling and Kerkorian achieved only a delay in Drinkwater's inevitable destruction. Darling reached TCD in Honolulu, where he had stopped over with his wife and the Richard Wrights en route to Tokyo, advising that Kerkorian had called a special Board meeting and asking him to return with Wright immediately.

"The hell with it," Drinkwater told his brother-in-law, "I won't go back."

"I've got to," Wright said soberly, "and I think you'd better, too, Terry."

On May 29, 1970, Terrell Croft Drinkwater walked into the Charles Russell Room (named for the famed painter of the old West) at Western's general offices and faced his peers. A resolution reportedly had been prepared demanding TCD's ouster as chairman but was not officially read into the minutes; Terry insists that one was drawn up and that Howard Westwood saw a copy of it in Darling's office. No formal resolution was necessary, at any rate, for Terry knew why he was there. He had brought Westwood with him to help him salvage what he could from the ashes of defeat.

The execution was neither merciful nor quick; under the circumstances, it couldn't have been. After some terse discussion,

Drinkwater stood up—a George Armstrong Custer surrounded, defeated, but defiant to the last.

"I know you guys have enough votes to fire me," he said with undisguised contempt. "There's no question about this, but if you fire me you're breaking my contract. I'll sue the company and I'll sue each of you individually. This won't be good for anybody—Western or you directors. I'm willing to compromise and I'd like to have my lawyer come into this meeting so we can talk about it."

Benninger demurred, suggesting instead that a compromise could be discussed without Westwood's presence, but that Drinkwater was free to leave the room and consult with his attorney at any time during the proceeding.

After much hassling and argument, Drinkwater finally came up with a concrete formula for settling the bitter quarrel.

"I'm willing to surrender my stock options, waive the remaining three years on my contract, and resign," he offered, "if you'll give me my deferred compensation and a contract as a consultant for twelve years at fifty thousand dollars a year. Otherwise I'll go ahead and sue."

He was asked to leave while the directors discussed this proposal. Terry went across the hall to his office—he had kept it even after Taylor became president—and sat there with Westwood waiting for the "jury" to decide. The "jury" was split, the older directors leaning strongly toward acceptance of Drinkwater's terms, the newer, pro-Kerkorian Board members considering the proposed settlement somewhat overgenerous. The Western officers on the Board—Taylor, Kelly, and even Shatto—stayed neutral. Someone asked Taylor how much money TCD would get if the Board paid off the remaining three years of his contract.

"About the same as he'd receive under the consultant contract he wants," Jud replied. "The difference is that if we paid him off in a lump sum, he'd take a bath from Internal Revenue."

"Let him take the bath," one director murmured.

"It's obvious he won't be doing much consulting," Taylor conceded, "but I don't think we should subject him to an IRS clobbering. And by spreading it out with a consultant's contract, we'll avoid a lawsuit."

Darling and Volk, who seemed to be the spokesmen for the older directors, argued sturdily for acceptance of Drinkwater's demands, and the general sentiment swung that way. Kerkorian himself moved that the Board accept TCD's resignation, and Terry was called in to discuss final settlement terms, mostly involving the consultant contract. This resulted in renewed bickering, with Terry running back and forth between the Russell Room and his office to confer with Westwood. Darling finally snapped, "You're getting to the point where there's going to be no contract at all," and an agreement was reached. Westwood got Darling to one side and informed him, "Terry wants it signed today—out of the oven by this afternoon."

Darling had the pact typed up, and accompanied by Taylor, he took it to Drinkwater's office late that afternoon, already executed by the appropriate company officials. Terry signed it without comment and shook hands with Jud. Darling stepped up to Drinkwater's big desk and reached across it, offering his hand.

"Terry," he said soberly, "after all these years, I'm sorry it had to end this way."

Drinkwater turned his head away, ignoring the outstretched hand, rose, and walked to the rear of the room. To this day, he has never spoken again to Hugh Darling; as he blamed Renda for the Hawaiian defeat, he also blamed Darling for his forced resignation as Board chairman. In Terry's book, Darling betrayed him by not siding with him against Kerkorian—a judgment that Hugh regrets far more than he resents.

Terry Drinkwater's resignation was effective May 31, 1970, and he took about a month to clean out his office—whether he procrastinated out of sentimental reluctance to leave or simply to bug Benninger is something known only to Terry. Taylor finally had to tell him, "You can stay here the rest of your life if it were up to me, but Fred's on my back and wants you out of here." Drinkwater then finished his packing and departed; the biggest single item he took from his office was his easy chair. He asked Taylor to let him keep the company-owned black Lincoln Continental assigned to TCD for his personal use; Jud had to refuse but sold him the car for three thousand dollars, considerably under its actual value.

There arose the inevitable matter of a farewell party for the man who had given so many years to Western. TCD professed not to want anything elaborate, and his old cohorts took him at his word. They had a small gathering at the Airport Marina Hotel and gave him a handsome watch as a going-away gift. Years later, Terry was to cite that party as one of the reasons for his bitterness.

"One of the things that hurt me most was my own farewell party," he recalled. "It was just a small cocktail party at the Airport Marina—I think only about twenty people were there. They gave me a beautiful watch, but it was no big deal. Not when I think of the years I spent with Western. Not when I think of what I did for Western. Shatto, too. He did as much or more than I did. Brilliant guy, Stan. Never finished his second year of high school, but he's smarter than I, and I've got three degrees."

For Shatto, Drinkwater's departure meant the beginning of the end for him also. It didn't have to be that way, but once Terry left Western, the bitterness he felt over his forced resignation seemed to infect Shatto like a virulent disease. Under Taylor, he continued to hold the same title Drinkwater had bestowed on him: executive vice president of transportation. Shatto's wings had been clipped in terms of authority and influence, particularly in the field of labor relations and flight operations. But there seemed to be no disposition on anyone's part, from Kerkorian on down, to make him suffer Terry's ignominious fate. In his own area of expertise—maintenance and engineering—he was still considered to be as good as there was in the industry, and even Benninger, fully aware that Shatto disliked him intensely, thought Stan could make a major contribution to the airline's recovery.

Shatto's actions and attitude throughout the Drinkwater crisis had surprised many of his fellow officers. He had performed the almost impossible task of remaining loyal to TCD without alienating Kerkorian or Benninger; he had helped ease Drinkwater out of the presidency without breaching his own friendship with Terry. As of May 31, 1970—the day Drinkwater's employment at Western ended officially—Shatto not only had survived the bloodletting but apparently along with Taylor and Kelly was considered part of the trio Kerkorian believed capable of achieving WAL's comeback. The only thing wrong with this surmise was that no one could perceive the corrosive effects of the Drinkwater tragedy on Shatto until it was too late; for part of Shatto went with Terry—a chunk of managerial skill that in the past had reacted to challenge and thrived on decisiveness. The part that was left included most of his faults—irascibility, resistance to co-operation, petulance toward other officers and departments, and rudeness to subordinates and fellow executives alike. He was to stay at Western for almost another four years, but Stanley R. Shatto really left the airline the same day as Drinkwater.

TCD still is held in respect around Western, as befits a man who was so much a part of the airline for more than twenty of its first fifty years. At one directors' meeting, Phil Peirce was delivering a report, and director Art Linkletter asked a question concerning a certain statistic.

"Well, Mr. Linkwater," Peirce started out—and the room was filled with hearty laughter. Someone told Drinkwater about the incident.

"Yeah, I guess they still remember old Terry," he rumbled, pleased. "Some of them do, anyway."

That they undoubtedly do. But much of the nostalgic affection and genuine appreciation his former colleagues feel is accompanied by the belief that he largely caused his own downfall.

The irony of Terrell Croft Drinkwater's unwilling departure was that it was a mere prelude to a fresh crisis; for the very thing that had cost TCD his job and his airline—the proposed merger with American—was far from dead.

CHAPTER TWENTY

Changing of the Guard

Jud Taylor's first full year as Western's president—1970—contained enough troubles, trials, and tribulations to make him curse the day he had accepted the office.

The ledgers showed he did not only a creditable job but also an almost incredible one, considering the atmosphere in which he had to work—the debris of the Drinkwater departure, sagging morale amid merger rumors, lack of wide-bodied jets on the crucial Hawaiian route, a nationwide economic slump that staggered virtually the entire airline industry, an increasingly sullen Shatto, and the always present shadows of Benninger and Kerkorian, the latter becoming Board chairman when TCD left.

Admittedly, he got little static from Kerkorian, who depended heavily on Benninger to keep tabs on the airline, and who by mid-1970 was embroiled with serious merger negotiations.

Taylor actually preferred a healthy two-way argument with Benninger to some of the far quieter sessions he had with Kerkorian. Kirk could be a conversational enigma, most willing to listen to a point of view but seldom providing the slightest clue as to what he thought of the expostulator's stand. Jud went to Las Vegas once to take a strong position with Kerkorian on some issue, the nature of which Jud has long forgotten. He returned to Los Angeles late in the day, and Kinsey asked him how he had done.

"It's a funny thing," Taylor chuckled wryly, "but I talked for almost an hour. When I got through, I couldn't tell whether he had agreed with me, whether he had disagreed, or whether he was even listening."

Not the least of Jud's troubles was his failure to get some of the senior officers working together harmoniously—Kinsey recalls that the staff meetings were more dogfights than meetings. Jud got along best with a fast-maturing, increasingly knowledgeable Art Kelly, who realized that Taylor's forte was finances and that he badly needed all the help he could get in other areas. Gradually, almost imperceptibly, Kelly was assuming the status of a potential heir apparent; the embittered Shatto, although he was to retain his title as executive vice president for another eighteen months, had abdicated that role.

Even though Taylor consulted with Benninger frequently, he managed to stay his own man—not an easy accomplishment for someone who didn't want the presidency to begin with. There were tough decisions to make—including one to drop service temporarily at a number of small Alaskan points by turning over WAL's short-haul routes west of Anchorage to Wien Alaska Airlines. Taylor's own accountants told him Western was losing a million dollars a year serving these communities—which was true except that the accountants were judging them solely on the basis of current losses instead of possible future profits.

Art Woodley begged Taylor not to abandon the short-haul Alaskan routes. "Wait about six months and see what happens," he urged, "because one of these days you're going to have a hell of a boom when they develop Alaska's coastal oil reserves."

Kelly agrees with Woodley that Western gave up too soon. "We were pencil-screwed out of those routes," he said later. "We simply lost control of several potentially profitable points because they weren't showing an immediate profit." The temporary transfer became part of the CAB's Alaska Service Investigation, and Western was to be hoist on its own petard. When the CAB finally decided the case in 1971, it made transfer of the short-haul routes permanent but also suspended WAL's authority to serve Ketchikan and Juneau for seven years in favor of a subsidized carrier, Alaska Airlines. Those two points had generated 3 per cent of Western's total 1971 revenues and earned some $1 million before taxes.

Over-all, Jud Taylor made few errors in judgment He not only turned the airline around financially but also in the sensitive area of labor-management relations. He had a genuine interest in employee problems; he lacked communications polish, but in his own way he did much to heal the wounds of the Drinkwater/Shatto regime. By year's end, he could point with pride to a modest but significant profit of $600,000. It looked awfully good after 1969's showing of a $27 million loss before taxes and a $12 million deficit after taxes, and it also put WAL into the position of being one of only four trunk carriers to finish in the black that year; Continental, Delta, and Northwest were the others. Yet Western's comeback had conflicting side effects. It whetted American's merger appetite but simultaneously weakened the chances for CAB approval of the merger. It also convinced the majority of WAL executives that their airline didn't need a merger to survive, even as the internal pressures for merger built up.

And the pressure *was* rising. With the Drinkwater needle out of his side permanently, Kerkorian became far more amenable to serious negotiations. In the June 3-to-October 30 period of 1970, there were ten separate contacts between Western and American officials—most of them in person, but a few via telephone—in which merger terms were discussed. Kerkorian himself met four times with Spater and/or Donald Lloyd-Jones, American's senior vice president of finance, during this time span, in which American started sweetening the pot.

On August 19, American tentatively proposed a share-for-share exchange plus a three-year, thirty-five-dollar warrant—the latter meaning that any Western shareholder could purchase one share of American stock at the fixed price of thirty-five dollars per share, provided the warrant was exercised within a three-year period. A month later, Kerkorian informed Spater that these terms were acceptable but only if Western was permitted to issue a 20 per cent stock dividend before the merger was consummated. Spater said no, but negotiations continued, with Kerkorian next suggesting a 10 per cent stock dividend before the exchange. Spater said he'd think this one over.

Kerkorian had something special going for him throughout the merger haggling—American had plenty of competition for Western's hand in marriage. In mid-1970, four other carriers approached WAL with merger offers ranging from speculative to specific, including: Alaska Airlines, Braniff, National, and Continental.

Bob Six made the most serious pitch of all, with talks extending far beyond the mere exploratory stage into frequent meetings between WAL and CAL personnel, and exchange of operational data.

Kerkorian had a deal with Continental on the back burner through the most critical phases of his negotiations with American. He had known Six for years, and even before Kerkorian had bought control of Western, Six had made some vague merger gestures in the direction of the old Indian head—mainly through Ed Pauley. It was when Dom Renda joined Continental that Six got the idea a WAL-CAL merger was no impossible dream. From the day Renda went to work for Six, they talked about merging the two airlines.

"He always felt it never could be accomplished while Terry Drinkwater was there," Renda recalls. "I found out that their so-called feud was more on Terry's part than Bob's. Terry used to say terrible things about Six, but I never heard Bob Six say one thing against Drinkwater—in fact, he used to talk about Terry's good points."

In the course of their discussing a possible merger with Western, Six brought up the latter's disastrous 1969 showing and asked Renda if he thought a merger still was a good idea.

"Despite what they're reporting in losses," Renda told him, "it's the best goddamned system around if you could get your hands on it and run it right."

That was all Six needed. He placed Renda in charge of a merger project, Dom putting together what was called "the little green book," listing all the advantages of linking the Continental and Western systems. Six contacted Kerkorian, who passed the matter down the chain of command—first to Benninger, Fred then asking Jud Taylor to work with Renda. A joint WAL-CAL merger study had been in progress for about a month when Benninger called Renda one day in mid-August.

"I've been hearing some good things about you," Benninger declared. "We've never met and I wonder if you could fly over to Vegas so we can have a talk."

"About what?" Renda asked.

"About your returning to Western," Benninger said bluntly.

"I'll have to call you back," Renda said. His immediate reaction was one of wariness—he was not going to jeopardize his relationship with Six by going behind his back for any talks with Western. So he informed Six of Benninger's call.

"Hell, go talk to the guy, Dom," Six advised. "Maybe this can be worked into a part of a merger deal."

So Renda and Benninger met for the first time—a session in which a strong friendship was launched. Benninger said the airline needed a capable No. 2 man who could eventually take over when Taylor retired. Renda refused to commit himself but a few days later met with Kerkorian and Singleton on the same subject. On Friday, August 14, Kerkorian asked Renda to meet him the following day at his home. Continental's complete study of a CAL-WAL merger had just been delivered to Western's officials, and Renda figured Kerkorian wanted to discuss it. He didn't—he wanted to talk about Renda's coming back to Western.

"Look," Dom said, "I consider it quite an honor and an opportunity, and I'm interested. But first, only if you have no intention of merging Western with any other company—that we'd try to run it alone because I still think it's one damned good company. Second, if you're interested in merger, it would be with Continental or some smaller company. If you have plans to merge Western with American, I'm definitely not interested."

"I'd like to know why you're opposed to a merger with American," Kerkorian said quietly.

"Mostly because I think it would be impossible to obtain either CAB or White House approval."

Kerkorian nodded, not in agreement but in acknowledgment of Renda's frank views. They parted amicably, but Kerkorian made no further attempt to corral Renda again. Taylor did, however; in October, he told Dom he was under pressure to name an executive vice president and potential successor. "Would you consider coming back in that role?"

"Yes," Renda replied instantly. "But only if there are no plans to merge with American. I want no part of going back to an airline that's about to be swallowed up."

"Well," Taylor sighed, "I honestly can't give you any reassurance on that score."

On October 30, 1970, Western and American signed a tentative agreement to merge. Prior to this accord, Kerkorian and Spater had indulged in some old-fashioned horse-trading. Spater said American wouldn't go along with a 10 per cent premerger stock dividend but would approve a 5 per cent dividend. Kerkorian said maybe—but only if the duration of the warrant be extended from three to five years. Kirk also asked for "downside protection"—some provision that would protect Western stockholders if the price of American's stock should fall.

The terms of the October 31 agreement called for:

• Declaration of a 5 per cent stock dividend by Western.

• A one-for-one exchange of Western and American stock, plus one warrant to purchase a share of American (the surviving carrier) at a price of $35 a share good for five years from the date of merger, for each Western share.

• Downside protection via a provision that if American's stock should decline below $16 a share, American would have to issue additional stock or distribute cash to Western shareholders so that the value would be restored to the $16 figure.

As of October 29, American's stock had closed at $19.25 per share. Combined with an estimated warrant value of $5.90 per share, the merger terms added up to a $152 million deal.

Just before agreement was reached, Six wired Western a counteroffer: Continental would exchange 1.75 shares of its stock for each share of Western. It wasn't quite enough to cause Kerkorian to waver, and both American and Western agreed to convene their Boards of Directors on November 18 and 24, respectively, to vote on the merger pact. Six promptly came in with a new offer: 2 shares of Continental for 1 share of Western, plus a five-year warrant to acquire 1 share of the surviving corporation at $12.50 a share. In mid-November, he increased the ante with an offer of 2.3 shares of Continental for each share of Western, plus 1.5 warrants per share. And just before the scheduled November 24 meeting of WAL's directors, Six made what turned out to be his final offer: the same terms as his November proposal, but with an extension of the warrants from five to ten years.

It was obvious he meant business, and for the first time, Western paused in its headlong rush toward American's willing arms. The directors, acting on Hugh Darling's advice, postponed consideration of the merger agreement so Continental's offer could be studied. And the November 24 Board meeting was put off, first until December 7 and then to December 16. Darling was a powerful force in the delaying action; he was dead set against merging with American. As a member of Western's planning committee, he had told his colleagues: "I don't think doom is around the corner—if we can hold together, if we fly our own flag until we get stronger, we'll be in a much better bargaining position in any merger situation."

Continental's offer intrigued Darling, largely because he felt a CAL-WAL merger would be a true marriage and not the end of Western. Darling had talked to Six about combining the two carriers as far back as 1947, when Drinkwater first became president; even then, Six was enthusiastic. And when Six suddenly interjected specific and surprisingly favorable merger terms into the almost consummated negotiations with American, Darling turned to none other than Western's second president, Alvin Adams, who at the time was in the aviation consulting business, for advice. In a phone call, Darling confided that both Continental and American had made merger offers.

"We'd like to retain you to study both offers and make your own recommendations," Darling said. "I've already talked to Jud Taylor, and he'd very much like your views."

"How much time do I have?" Adams inquired.

"Four days."

"Four days? How the hell can I do it in four days?"

"That's all the time we can give you, Al," Darling apologized.

In four days, Adams completed a study of the two proposals and submitted his recommendations—which happened to be in full agreement with Darling's own opinions. He mailed in a six-page report, the gist of which said that Western shouldn't merge at all, but if it had to merge with somebody, Continental was the best choice.

On December 16, Western and American went back to the negotiating table and came up with a brand-new agreement:

• The five-year warrant was eliminated.
• American upped its 1-for-1 exchange to 1.3 shares of American for each Western share after a 10 per cent stock dividend. The downside protection was altered, requiring American to issue only additional stock and not cash to restore its stock price to $16.

The revised terms were valued at $178 million, $26 million above the October 31 figure, and they were too much for Six. He was later to be asked at a Senate hearing on airline financial problems why he bowed out of the bidding.

"I just ran out of chips," he answered laconically.

On January 20, American's Board of Directors approved the new merger agreement, and five days later Western's directors followed suit.

In the spirit of historical accuracy, it must be reported that within Western, the man who played the most active role in the merger negotiations was Kirk Kerkorian himself. He had taken a terrible shellacking on his WAL stock, and he saw in the merger his only chance to recoup. No one could honestly blame him; the national recession of 1970 had hurt him on a massive scale. He was short of cash, the value of his enormous holdings had shrunk, and he had poured a considerable chunk of his resources into purchase of MGM. At the time the American-Western merger was submitted to the Civil Aeronautics Board, Kerkorian's obligations were close to equaling his assets—he was hard pressed enough to put his beloved DC-9 up for sale. At no time did he panic; good gamblers don't panic, and Kerkorian was not just good but superb. His Western stock, however, was one of the financial weapons in his dwindling arsenal, and he was forced to use it as he saw best.

Conversely, some of Western's hierarchy was opposed to the merger—and that included Fred Benninger. Kerkorian trusted no man in the world more than he did Benninger, as a friend as well as an adviser. Kerkorian had consulted with Fred before accepting American's final offer, and Benninger, as usual, was not afraid to tell him something he really didn't want to hear: The merger was a bad idea. Patiently but firmly, Benninger listed his objections.

First, the company could survive easily on its own—the comeback from 1969 was an accomplished fact, not a hoped-for dream. Second, Benninger knew the headaches involved in any merger—the effects on the loyal officers and employees of the nonsurviving carrier, the problems of consolidating union seniority lists, and the unpredictable costs. Third, he had the strongest of hunches that the CAB would never approve a merger between two healthy airlines.

He told all this to Kerkorian, who listened carefully before making the decision of a born gambler.

"Well, you never know," he said softly. "Let's try it anyway."

Kerkorian, naturally, looked at the merger from an investor's standpoint. He had never been as close to Western's day-to-day operations as Benninger, who not only took a jaundiced view of mergers in general but also appreciated how many of Western's executives and employees felt about what had to be eventual dismemberment of their airline. To a man, the officers backed the merger 100 per cent publicly—or rather, they backed Kerkorian 100 per cent, as did Benninger once the decision had been made. There was absolutely no attempt to sabotage it; the executives made every effort to sell the merger to the employees, and they kept their private opinions mostly to themselves, knowing that many of them were heading for transfers, demotions, or even dismissal once American absorbed WAL.

One vice president was having dinner with Spater—a pleasant, extremely likable man—after the agreement was signed.

"Tell me," American's president asked, "how would you feel about moving to New York?"

"I'd rather move to Poland!" the WAL official snapped. Spater's jaw dropped.

"I'll move to any place my job takes me," the vice president continued grimly, "but you asked me the question, and those are my feelings."

A handful of directors weren't happy, either—Darling, Pauley, and Woodley in particular. (Pauley had returned to the Board in

July 1970.) At one Board meeting where the merger was being discussed, Woodley called it "nonsensical."

Not a few members of the WAL brass-hat corps preferred Continental if some kind of merger had to be consummated. First and foremost, there would have been no surviving carrier as such—it would have been a true merger, not an acquisition. In fact, Renda says if Six's plan had gone through, the consolidated airline would have been called "Continental-Western Airlines."

Considering their real feelings toward the merger with American, many of Western's officials—Benninger included—did a remarkable job in fighting for it. As Kelly puts it, "Sure I felt bad about it, but discipline in corporate circles requires that when a decision is made, you support it." Several WAL executives toured the system, meeting with employees to explain the merger but also to discuss plans for new service, new promotional ideas, and the new corporate image. The latter was akin to selling a terminally ill woman patient on the necessity for wearing brightly different makeup, but strangely enough, this epitome of contradiction seemed to work. It had the effect of giving employees a fleeting, wispy sliver of sunlight amid the advancing thunderheads of an unwanted merger; it provided a tenuous ray of hope in an otherwise bleak future.

The timing for the corporate image changeover couldn't have been worse. It had been announced as a definite project in July 1970, and the merger agreement came in October; the lone 720-B painted in the new colors and with the new insignia seemed like the final, defiant waving of a battle flag just before surrender. Yet it was an important symbol, in some ways as constructive as it was futile—a kind of visible, tangible security blanket.

"It seemed to be telling employees to stay with it," Don Drews remembers. "That if the merger didn't go through, we'd be doing things. One of the new image's original goals was to instill a spirit of progress throughout the company, an extremely difficult task when merger appeared to be almost inevitable."

Unquestionably, employee loyalty expressed in terms of performance under trying circumstances helped defeat the merger in the end. Before the 1969 mechanics' strike, Western had more than 10,000 employees; by the end of 1970, the payroll was down to 8,800. But with fewer employees, Western's revenues increased from $240 million in '69 to almost $300 million the following year. One reason was higher productivity, the key to corporate profits. And the fact that Western made money in 1970 (conversely, American ran deeply in the red) just about demolished the "we must merge to survive" argument on which so many hats had been hung. It also was hard to apply the "failing carrier" doctrine to a company that ended that year with nearly $65 million in cash and short-term securities on hand—one of the better figures in the industry. No airline can both make and save money unless its employees are doing their damndest to help it prosper. But while an "all for one and one for all" spirit did exist in sizable proportions, there were exceptions.

The old ALPA-management feud flared up again, even with Shatto out of the negotiating picture. The pilots' contract became amendable about two months before the merger agreement was signed, and what had been fairly smooth bargaining suddenly turned into a thorny dispute. ALPA and Western had been close to a new pact, based largely on what United had just given its crews. But WAL's pilots didn't like the way UAL had been administering some of the provisions and wanted some changes. Western, jittery because of the merger, began resisting.

The union's response was to call a slowdown—the polite term being "work to the rules." Not many Western pilots liked the strategy, but ALPA insisted it was the only way to pressure management into an agreement without calling an actual strike.

"A slowdown's just dirty pool," one veteran captain says. "It may be a good union tactic, and an alternative to what nobody wants—a strike—but it's not fair to the public. Why the hell should a passenger have to suffer a phony delay because a pilot decides to return to the ramp so a couple of bug spots can be cleaned off the windshield? Our own union leaders claim that a slowdown doesn't affect on-time performance but merely hurts the company because it adds to operating costs. That's bunk—Western's on-time performance percentages dropped through the bottom during that '71 slowdown."

Actually, Western's pilots feared the merger with American more than any other single group of employees. American's flight crews had pulled out of ALPA and formed their own union—the Allied Pilots' Association (APA)—which WAL's airmen would have had to join after the merger; Western's pilots were outnumbered three to one, and ALPA stood no chance in a bargaining representation election.

"We were afraid of merger," Captain Seth Oberg, head of ALPA's 1970–71 negotiating team, explains. "We saw what had happened to Trans Caribbean pilots when American absorbed TCA—APA walked all over them with company approval. Their senior pilot's date of hire was 1945, but he was four hundred numbers down on American's seniority list. We badly wanted a good contract with Western before the merger."

Obviously, they wanted it badly enough to pull the slowdown, and Oberg subsequently was fired along with another pilot. Taylor and Benninger had to enter the hassle personally before a contract agreement was reached and the two dismissed pilots were reinstated as part of the settlement. It was a particularly trying period for Jud, beset by the twin problems of employee morale and a deep sense of responsibility toward Kerkorian's merger plans. Taylor was bothered by the knowledge that as Western's president, he represented the last hope of those who wanted to oppose merger and couldn't. He had told Kirk he could live with either merger—American or Continental. Kerkorian kept asking him if Western could survive without any merger.

"I can't give you that guarantee," he always responded.

And without that guarantee, Kerkorian set his course.

At the CAB's hearings on the merger, virtually the entire industry lined up in opposition—Continental and United leading the pack. Unions representing Western and other carriers who would be competing against the merger-created giant, the Department of Justice's antitrust division, and the CAB's Bureau of Operating Rights all testified against it. Only the Department of Transportation supported merger, and the handwriting was on the wall when a CAB examiner issued an initial decision recommending against merger. Much of the antimerger strategy was mapped by three former Western officials who knew the strengths and weaknesses of WAL's system—Renda and Jim Mitchell (WAL's former director of research), who were part of the CAL team, and John Simpson, ex-director of law, representing Hughes Air West.

The promerger forces tried their best—Kerkorian was an excellent witness, impressive with his staccato, clipped answers. But the climate simply was wrong; Western too obviously was a healthy carrier and, in fact, was beginning to look decidedly healthier than American.

The CAB's final disapproval didn't come until July 28, 1972, but by this time it was strictly an anticlimax. Even Kerkorian had given up most hope by then, and Western already was embarked on a steady go-it-alone course.

"We felt the merger was good at the time," Kirk says today, "but we were wrong. American had many problems later that we hadn't foreseen."

Western was not just climbing but even zooming back to the comfortable cruising altitude of profits, the specter of merger fading rapidly as CAB disapproval became more and more of a certainty.

Officially, merger remained company policy throughout 1971, but even the conservative, cautious language of the annual report for that year had a kind of "if it doesn't go through, the hell with it" bravado.

". . . your company has worked vigorously to obtain approval of the merger with American Airlines," the report assured stockholders. "Despite opposition from various parties to the case, we continue to believe that the merger is in the public interest and that it should be approved. While awaiting the final decision of the Civil Aeronautics Board and the President, however, we are moving ahead with plans that are designed to continue the company's growth and enhance its financial strength."

Western still was the only carrier competing in the California–Hawaii market that was not operating wide-bodied jets, although it continued to maintain a good share of the traffic. Its five 707s were being converted to the "wide-bodied look"—a $2.75 million program involving installation of overhead bins instead of the old-fashioned racks, new seats, and improved lighting. More important were the first steps taken to acquire the magnificent McDonnell Douglas DC-10 for the Hawaiian routes

—a jetliner somewhat smaller than the 747 and with three engines instead of four for greater operating economy. The DC-10 was more to Fred Benninger's liking; flying between Hawaii and the Mainland, it used 19 million fewer gallons of fuel yearly than the 747—a savings of $6 million annually for each aircraft at 1975 fuel prices.

Inability to finance wide-bodied jets was one of the key arguments advanced in favor of the merger. Pleading poor mouth may have been perfectly truthful in the early stages of the merger efforts, but as Western's financial posture steadily improved even as American's worsened, it became obvious that WAL couldn't delay a wide-bodied program much longer. And its implementation was made possible by a clause in the merger agreement.

American had exercised an option for four DC-10s subject to the CAB's approving the merger. Western in turn agreed to assume the contract if the merger fell through and to reimburse American for its $24 million down payment on the four aircraft valued at some $90 million, including spare engines and parts. The whole deal underlined lack of confidence on the part of both companies in the merger's chances; American wouldn't have exercised its options unless it knew Western was ready to pick them up, and Western wouldn't have given such assurances if it hadn't been able to arrange financing. For that matter, the very activation of the DC-10 option provision further weakened the case for merger; obviously, WAL could and would finance acquisition of a wide-bodied fleet.

The 707 modernization and the DC-10 orders represented only part of a revitalized equipment program that had been dormant for two years. Western also signed for three new stretched 727s for delivery in the spring of 1972 and a bit later ordered two additional 727s. It was a far more harmonious, closer-knit, and balanced Board of Directors that approved these heavy but essential commitments.

Slowly at first, then at an accelerated pace, Western moved toward a new independence. The image revolution didn't get into top speed until the merger had been defeated officially, but one by one the newly painted aircraft began joining the fleet. The rate was one aircraft per month to start with, and the face-lifting job went on despite unexpected litigation from an unexpected source—Winnebago, manufacturers of motorized homes and campers.

Western, of course, had made quite a publicity smash with the pictures of the 720-B that bore the new Flying W markings. They drew a lot of attention, most of it favorable, but not in the case of John Hanson, president and Board chairman of Winnebago. Hanson, through his attorneys, informed Western that the new insignia plagiarized Winnebago's corporate symbol.

Litigation dragged on for four years and ended with a court ruling in Western's favor—another example of the legal jungles through which airlines have to trod their wary path.

It was no wonder that Jud Taylor, even in the flush of Western's fast-moving recovery, began his personal countdown to the time when he could retire. Lawsuits were just one of the unsavory items on the menu of every airline president. Hijackings were another, and Taylor's presidential years coincided with the development of "skyjacking" as a monumental industry problem. Western suffered through three—including the longest hijacked flight in history. On June 2, 1972, a black man and his white female companion commandeered WAL 701, a Boeing 727, while en route to Seattle on a flight from Los Angeles. The 727 first was flown to San Francisco, where some passengers were released and others herded aboard a four-engine Western 720-B, which the hijackers ordered to New York. There everyone in the cabin was let off except for the volunteer flight crew, headed by Captain Bill Newell, which had boarded in San Francisco. After a short delay the aircraft was flown to Algeria. Officials there took the hijackers and $500,000 in ransom money into custody and permitted the aircraft to be flown back to the United States.

Taylor waited a month for the ransom to be returned, and after some high-level State Department negotiations cleared the way, he dispatched Bob Kinsey to Algeria, where he picked up $487,300 of the $500,000 that WAL had paid.

The loss of a 720-B on a training flight, with no survivors among the five pilots aboard, was the unhappiest event of 1971 but one that galvanized the FAA into finally modifying its check ride requirements. For years, pilots and the carriers alike had been warning the government that it was too dangerous to practice engine-out procedures at low altitudes; such maneuvers, they argued, could be done just as easily and efficiently in simulators or at higher altitudes.

In the case of the ill-fated WAL flight, one engine had been reduced to idle thrust for a descent and missed approach at Ontario [California] International Airport to simulate an engine malfunction in bad weather. Fate picked that particularly crucial second to throw a real emergency at the crew: As the aircraft pulled up on its go-around, the rudder actuator support fitting failed, causing a complete loss of rudder control, and the pilots ran out of control, altitude, and time simultaneously. At a higher altitude, they probably could have regained control. In a simulator, there would have been no actual emergency. Western's was the fourth such fatal training accident—each a needless tragedy.

Lost in the crash were Captains Dick Schumacher, Ray Benson, Henry "Bud" Coffin, and Howard McMillan, and Second Officer Kent Dobson. McMillan wasn't even supposed to be on the flight but decided to tag along at the last minute because he was preparing to become a 720-B check pilot.

For all their troubles with management, sometimes the fault of the company but at other times the result of their union's intractability, Western's pilots have provided the airline with a priceless asset—a reputation for safety second to none in the industry. WAL's exceptionally low accident rate was achieved on a route system that has few "milk runs"—much of it is over mountainous terrain, and the weather conditions encountered involve frequent low visibility. The explanation lies in policy—one that has existed since the days of Drinkwater and has never been altered. Western has a smaller than usual corps of check pilots, and they are picked for their ability not just to fly an airplane but also for their guts, their willingness to call a spade a spade—they can and will crack down, even on close friends.

Bob Johnson, a veteran line pilot who is now vice president of flight operations, goes a bit farther. His explanation:

"The company isn't afraid to spend money on training and safety. We had a 727 simulator when we had only eight 727s—most airlines would have to have at least twelve to justify the cost of a simulator.

"Pilot attitudes have changed drastically in the past few years

—the guys aren't as antagonistic as they were. It's had a definite effect on on-time performance, and it's largely due to the way they're operating the airplane. We've developed more practical, realistic union representatives. A bigger percentage of men like these are coming out of the woods. The new MEC [Master Executive Council] chairman is a first officer—Martin Tynan."

One of 1971's highlights was a major on-time-performance reversal. The record was poor in January and February, but in six of the next eight months Western ranked first in the trunkline industry and finished the year in second place; it was to maintain high rankings from then on. It also finished the year with a profit of almost $6.5 million; under Jud Taylor, the self-professed interim caretaker, the airline had completed its turnaround and was soaring into what was to be his final twelve months as president.

The only discordant note came from the direction of Stan Shatto. Never a patient man and inherently brusque, he took on the disposition of a bear with ulcers. What had been fierce independence turned into defiance. His virtue of single-minded concentration on any problem in his own area of expertise changed to almost total indifference toward anyone's problem, including those involving officers he had worked with for many years. Everyone from Benninger on down sought his counsel, but Shatto was not the consultant type. He didn't like being asked for advice; even when he was Western's second-in-command, he used to tell subordinates: "Make your own decisions—if I have to make it for you, I don't need you."

Typical was his attitude toward the man who, in 1972, became senior vice president of operations—Arthur F. Gardner, a veteran line captain. Gardner had come a long way from the time he was a young Marine lieutenant and one of the two survivors aboard the WAL DC-3 that had crashed shortly after taking off from Salt Lake City in 1942; he was not only one of Western's most respected senior captains but also a model of civic responsibility. Gardner was president of the Los Angeles Board of Education, had served as chairman of the ALPA Master Executive Council, and was well liked by pilots and management alike. A real solid citizen, Art Gardner, and it was Kelly who proposed his name to Benninger.

Shatto wanted Tony Favero to head operations, and Favero actually was also Kelly's and Taylor's first choice, except that they didn't think Benninger would agree to diluting Favero's maintenance responsibilities. When Benninger accepted their recommendation of Gardner, Shatto not only objected strongly, on the grounds that he didn't think Gardner qualified for management, but also refused to co-operate with him in any way. When Gardner—in a gesture of good will—invited Stan to play golf with him, he got an abrupt refusal.

Benninger pleaded in vain with Shatto to give Gardner some aid. "Look, help him out when he needs it—if he has problems, if he needs information. You don't have to be working for him. Just be available." Gardner, it turned out, was miserably unhappy at a desk job. A man who loved flying and somewhat of a physical fitness buff (for years he had peddled a bicycle to the airport), he was ill prepared for front-office duties that were too confining and beyond his limited administrative experience. He went back to the line after less than two years as a senior vice president.

For Shatto's sake, it was too bad he didn't accept his lessened authority more gracefully, for Western could have used his knowledge, experience, and technical astuteness as it prepared to enter the age of the wide-bodied jets. He was too busy feuding with Benninger and ignoring everyone else. When Art Kelly sought Shatto's advice on the DC-10's interior configuration, Shatto snapped:

"I didn't have a goddamned thing to do with buying that airplane! Go talk to Benninger. He didn't ask my opinion when he ordered it."

Fred personally asked Shatto to help out with the DC-10 program. Shatto merely grunted—and talked to no one. Just as Drinkwater had forced Kerkorian into removing him, so did Stan force Benninger into doing what he really did not want to do—kicking him upstairs to vice chairman of the Board.

"What we tried to do was put him in a position where he still could contribute something to the company," Benninger says. "He had the knowledge, he had the ability, so we put him where he at least couldn't sabotage the operation. But it got so bad that we finally induced him to take early retirement."

Stanley R. Shatto's career at Western came to an official end on December 31, 1973. He was given a farewell party of somewhat larger proportions than Drinkwater's sendoff, and he also was allowed to keep his company-owned Continental—a decision made by Art Kelly, who also insisted on amortizing the rest of Stan's contract payments to ease the tax bite.

"He never thanked me," Kelly muses. "He was just too bitter to even realize that we had done more for him than for Terry."

Stubborn, brutally frank, and above all honest, Shatto left more friends and admirers behind him at Western than he knows —fellow executives who in their admiration for his integrity and ability regretted his faults that much more.

Shatto's real ambition was to serve, not rule. He made no apparent effort to become Drinkwater's successor in the 1969 purge; true, Benninger probably would have opposed him, but Shatto still had an outside chance what with Kerkorian liking him. Shatto was to remark later that he didn't take the job "because I thought I'd be stabbing Terry."

There is a decided ring of truth in that statement. Renda, closer to Shatto than any other Western officer, remembers Stan once saying to him:

"God, Dom, I hate going to these cocktail parties and receptions and shaking hands with all those people. I just want to do my job, run the airline, and get the planes out on time."

Western continued to progress in 1972, chalking up more than $11.2 million in profits—a 74 per cent increase over 1971's net earnings. Significantly, the black ink went hand-in-hand with two other achievements: the best on-time record of all trunklines, and the fewest consumer complaints filed with the CAB of any trunk carrier.

In response to the growth of consumerism, Western established an office of consumer affairs in 1972 to replace the older customer relations department. No matter what the title, those who work in this touchy area are an airline's unsung heroes, for nobody knows what the public is liable to come up with in the form of gripes, complaints, or criticism.

There was, for example, a woman who saw a stewardess taking cold drinks to the cockpit on an exceptionally hot summer day and promptly wrote Western that she had personally seen her serve "alcoholic beverages to the pilots." Wayne Lichtgarn, now assistant vice president of consumer affairs, interviewed her because of the seriousness of the charge.

"How did you know the drinks had alcohol in them?" he asked.

"The flight was very rough," she explained indignantly, "and the turbulence showed they had drunk so much they couldn't handle the airplane properly."

Lichtgarn got one letter from a woman threatening to sue Western because she had contracted a bad cold on a WAL flight. This complaint he investigated personally because of her theory on how she caught cold.

"The passenger sitting next to me left his window open all the way to Hawaii," she wrote.

Actually, she was easier to handle than a man who wrote a letter containing numerous technical questions. It took Lichtgarn several days of research to compose a three-page, single-spaced epistle with all the answers. A few days later, he received a reply.

"I never want to see one of your damned form letters again!" the passenger wrote angrily.

Lichtgarn shrugged this off, just as he philosophically regarded a response from a passenger he had written explaining Western's reservations system, the reasons for occasional over-sales, and numerous other points on which the customer had queried. Wayne's reply would have passed the requirements for a masters' thesis in detail and length; the acknowledgment he got back was a single word scrawled at the bottom of the last page of Lichtgarn's masterpiece:

"Bullshit!"

One of the most embarrassing incidents involved the stringent airport security measures that went into effect in 1972 to overcome the hijacking menace. Western's security department decided to test a new metal-detection device and put a gun, brass knuckles, and other forbidden items in a briefcase, which was sent through the screening apparatus at a WAL gate. The device worked perfectly, but while the security officials were congratulating themselves, a passenger by mistake picked up the test briefcase and boarded a flight to San Francisco.

After landing, he decided to take a helicopter over to Oakland and went through security again before boarding the 'copter. A detection device spotted the arsenal, and police immediately grabbed the passenger for questioning.

"That's not my suitcase," he pleaded.

"That's what they all say," an officer scoffed.

He was questioned for two hours—during which time Western, realizing what had happened, tried frantically to contact him. The airline finally located his wife by opening the briefcase he had left behind in Los Angeles and obtaining some identification. By the time they reached the passenger himself, he was a very irate gentleman who also happened to be a lawyer. Fortunately, he had retained enough of his sense of humor to let Western off easily—a five-hundred-dollar settlement.

With Jud Taylor's retirement drawing near, the time had come to pick his successor. Hugh Darling told both Taylor and Benninger he thought they had only two choices, which presented something of a Solomon-like dilemma.

"One is Art Kelly," he said, "and the other is Dom Renda—if you can get him away from Continental. Dom would be my first choice simply because he has had broader experience, while Art's been primarily in sales. I'd like to make this suggestion: Art's my boy and he'd make a great president, but we need Renda, too. Get Dom back and name him the No. 2 man. They'd make one hell of a team."

"I'm not sure Dom would want to come back under that arrangement," Taylor said thoughtfully. "He has a chance to become president of Continental one of these days, so why should he accept the No. 2 spot here?"

"Because he's always had a soft spot in his heart for Western," Darling replied. "He would have returned long ago if it wasn't for Drinkwater."

"I'd like to talk to Renda," Benninger said. "Meanwhile, I agree that Kelly also would be an excellent choice, and I know Kirk feels that way, too. I don't think we have to decide immediately between them, but I'd be in favor of naming Art executive vice president before a decision is made."

Early in the fall of 1972, Benninger did call Renda concerning Western's presidency.

"I've been authorized to approach you," he informed Dom. "I'll be frank: It's between you and Art Kelly, and we're planning to make Art executive vice president in October. Whether he'll go on to the presidency isn't a certainty at this time because we'd like to look at both of you."

Renda expressed cautious, noncommittal interest. In October, Kelly was named executive vice president, and shortly after the announcement Benninger phoned Renda again. This time he made it clear that Western wanted him back in the No. 2 spot, under Kelly but with the understanding that Renda would be given more authority than is normally accorded even executive vice presidents. As far as Dom was concerned, Benninger's offer —which had Kerkorian's approval as well as that of the Board— was not only fair but "made me feel really wanted." He felt he had accomplished his primary tasks at Continental—getting Air Micronesia off the ground, obtaining a permanent certificate for a five-thousand-mile route extending from Honolulu to Okinawa, and laying the groundwork for further expansion to Tokyo. He had no great desire to leave Continental and the feeling at CAL was mutual, but—as Darling had said—his heart was still at Western.

Renda had to go through the traumatic experience of telling Six he was leaving Continental—which was like a man confessing infidelity to his bride while still on their honeymoon. Six, however, was surprisingly decent about releasing Dom from his contract, and Renda says Six was especially fair in terms of a monetary arrangement. He did tell Renda he thought he was making a mistake and, Dom concedes, "maybe he was right—I was bouncing around between the two companies and the opportunity for the future was also there at Continental."

So Renda returned to Western on January 1, 1975, his official promotion to executive vice president following one month later as the Board of Directors chose Taylor's successor.

On February 1, Arthur F. Kelly became WAL's sixth president —one of the few sales executives ever to attain that rank. He brought to the job thirty-five years of experience, an unsuspected talent for administration, uninhibited enthusiasm toward innovations and fresh ideas, and a rock-hard determination to end once and for all the dog-vs.-cat belligerence that had for so long marked the airline's labor-management atmosphere.

As Darling had predicted, Kelly and Renda formed a unique team that had no precedent in airline history. The closest any carrier had ever come to their relationship was the Six-Lawrence combination at Continental, and even this was not quite comparable. Lawrence had been CAL's president in everything but title; Kelly and Renda literally took the massive areas of responsibility inherent in running a major airline and divided them up between them. Art never relinquished command authority, but up to a point he delegated much of it to Renda, particularly in Western's day-to-day operations. Renda quickly became more of an assistant president than an executive vice president, and this was with Kelly's wholehearted approval. Kelly admitted there were some areas in which Renda had broader knowledge and more experience—regulatory matters and finance, for example. And Renda knew that in marketing and sales, Kelly had few equals in the entire industry.

Jud Taylor left the presidency with the gratitude of nearly ten thousand employees, the admiration of every fellow executive, and absolutely no regrets. Kerkorian and Benninger had asked him to stay on a little while longer, but Taylor flatly said no. He told friends that on his first night as ex-president, he enjoyed the first good sleep he had had for more than two years.

Kelly proved to be a stronger president than many expected. In a sense, he had come close to training himself for the job. Since 1949, he had never missed a major policy meeting. Even when he was Drinkwater's assistant and fairly low on the management totem pole, TCD wanted him present to observe or answer questions. As Kelly rose through the ranks, Terry permitted him to attend Board meetings—something for which Art always will be grateful. Drinkwater was a master at training young executives, deliberately exposing them to the decision-forging process, like interns being allowed to watch skilled surgeons, and Kelly was one of the star pupils. In listening, watching, and learning, he absorbed leadership qualities; he acquired self-confidence without also developing arrogance.

"The smartest guy in the world," he is fond of saying, "is the one who says 'I don't know but I'll try to find out.'"

He wasted no time in establishing a *modus operandi* with Fred Benninger. Kelly abhorred the demands Western was making on Benninger's time; one day a week would have been fine, as Taylor wanted, but Benninger found himself working at WAL three days a week—often digging up answers on his own to questions others should have been able to handle. Kelly sat down to have a frank talk with the chairman of the Board.

"First, I don't think you should be bothered with internal affairs," he told Benninger. "We'll have a discussion between you and the senior officers on all this homework you've been having to do. They'll be doing that homework from now on. Every question you ask will get the highest priority."

What Kelly did, originally to ease Benninger's burdens but subsequently as a regular corporate practice, was to establish a senior officers' staff meeting every Friday morning, with Fred present. In effect, it amounted to a weekly session between top management and stockholders, for Benninger in reality represented the interests and views of all shareholders, from Kerkorian on down.

Of all he has done since becoming president and chief executive officer, these regular sessions rank near the top from the standpoint of personal pride. "Mini-annual meetings," Art calls them.

He assumed the presidency already cognizant of two major weaknesses in Western's corporate structure:

1. There was little planning toward a more efficient future—neither in recognition of need nor in selection of a man to implement such planning.

2. Labor-management communications.

One of Art's first moves as president was to talk over corporate structure with Renda. To a large degree, they instituted some restructuring of their own when they mutually agreed to divvy up certain areas of responsibility—Kelly, for example, retaining a direct line of authority over relations with directors and internal corporate affairs. But he knew that Western's rather creaky, outmoded structure needed far more than what he and Renda could work out between them. Out of their discussion of the problem came agreement on a vital point: The man in charge of planning would be as important as the concept itself.

"The guy I've been thinking about," Art told Renda, "is Bob Kinsey. He was assistant to Woodley, to Drinkwater, and to Taylor. He's been underused and also underestimated."

The basic deficiency in Western's corporate setup was that nothing much had been done in the way of future planning since 1969 because of merger uncertainties. The weakness, in fact, dated back long before the merger when TCD became so engrossed with Hawaii that what future planning existed was aimed mostly in that direction—and on something of a make-shift, piecemeal basis.

Overordering on the 737 was an example of lack of planning—the 727 would have been a better airplane for many of the emerging markets the 737 served. The mistake was symptomatic of Western's principal problem: The various divisions were engaged in policy-making decisions independently. There was no corporate structure that allowed marketing, for example, much of a say in what aircraft were ordered.

All this was changed under Kelly. A corporate planning unit was established under Kinsey—one of five major groups reporting to the president through Renda; the others were legal, finance, operations, and marketing. The latter in itself was the result of restructuring—it was a combination of sales and service. Into the corporate planning unit went four subgroups headed by some of the company's most experienced professionals: H. S. "Hap" Gray, financial planning; Carl Anderson, economic planning; "Chuck" Fisher, schedule planning; and Eugene Olsen, data processing. Kinsey's new department involved a structural revolution, for it crossed divisional lines throughout the airline. Computers (data processing) were taken away from finance, scheduling was removed from marketing, and economic planning went out of route development, to cite a few examples.

The whole purpose was to provide companywide input into decisions affecting future policy—there would be no repetition of excessive aircraft commitments, as there had been with both the Electra and the 737. And the second major corporate reorganization move was to decentralize Western, establishing ten regional vice presidents to put more decision-making capability into the field. This necessitated the creation of a new post in upper echelons—vice president of field management—and the job went to Jack Slichter; he was the choice of Renda, who had felt for a long time that Slichter's talents were being misused in government and industry affairs.

Decentralization was not a Western first; United had accomplished it earlier, much to the surprise of critics who said that decentralization would never work in the airline industry. UAL did make it work, thanks mainly to Edward "Eddie" Carlson—significantly, like Kelly, a marketing man who had gone into United's top post with an extensive background in the hotel business.

Carlson had one more thing in common with Art Kelly: the ability to communicate with employees. This was Art's second principal target for reform and a more difficult one to accomplish than corporate restructuring—not labor-management relations, for this by its very nature had to have inherent differences, but rather labor-management communications. As of this writing, Kelly still hasn't achieved his goals in this area, but progress has been made.

"The problem is simple," Kelly says, "namely to let people know that the company is as concerned about them as any outsider, including their own unions. Most of the industry is deficient in this respect.

"It's one of the reasons employees look to labor for leadership. It bothers me that some of our executives don't try to communicate with employees, don't take the time to even talk to them. I walk through a terminal and it takes me five times longer than it should because I *do* stop and talk to people.

"We sit there with thirty-five top officials discussing and solving our problems, but how much of that trickles down through the ranks? I'll never be satisfied until the ship cleaners, the telephone operators, the agents, pilots, flight attendants, and everyone else knows what the problems of this company are. There are about five different echelons you have to penetrate, peel your way through layers of suspicion, prejudice, and cynicism built up through years of indifference on management's part."

Kelly put his deeds where his mouth was. A visitor heading for lunch with him one day was startled to see him leave his office lugging two huge boxes of candy. He went first to the telephone switchboard complex, where he dropped off one box with a cheery "Happy Valentine's Day, girls," and then marched to the cafeteria, where he presented the other box to the women working behind the counter.

"Just want to make sure they know somebody is thinking about them," he explained to the visitor.

A small gesture, one might say, maybe even a bit ineffective—but at least a start toward what he had determined to do the day he became president: create an atmosphere of mutual trust among all levels within Western. He began showing up at pilot recurrent training sessions, talking earnestly to each group about the fuel situation, WAL's financial status, and the company's most pressing problems. It was not a sales pitch but rather an obviously sincere attempt to *share* those problems, to explain and ask for help.

Some of his appearances happened to coincide with negotiations for a new WAL-ALPA contract. A few of the more cynical pilots were betting that Kelly would stop showing up at recurrent training once the contract was signed. They were wrong; a contract was signed, and Art kept making his appearances. He went even farther: when it was decided to start a Management Club, captains were invited to join.

His attitude softened even the hard-bitten ALPA negotiators and officers like Seth Oberg.

"There has been a definite change in ALPA-company relations," Seth admits. "Things started to improve with Taylor and they got even better when Kelly took over. We have the feeling that Western wants to come up with a top-notch contract for its pilots, but because of size, they can't match what the bigger airlines can give. Quite frankly, we've got working conditions about as tight as we're gonna get for some time."

Kelly came a cropper at one meeting with the pilots. He had been telling each group about Fred Kelly II being the epitome of a great airman—namely because he was so cost-conscious.

"Once, it was suggested that he give passengers a good view of Boulder Dam by taking a little sightseeing detour," Art related.

"And do you know what Fred said? He said, 'Hell, no, it costs too damned much money.'"

After the meeting, Tony Favero came up to Kelly. "Art, I wish you'd go a bit easier when you're praising Kelly for saving the company so much dough."

"Why?" Art wanted to know.

"Because the sonofagun used to cost us a fortune blowing out engines—he was always trying to beat schedule by flying full throttle."

Optimist though he is, Kelly never expected to score an immediate success with his communications campaign.

"Anyone can be a successful marketing man or a chief executive if he bats .333," Art philosophizes. "It means you strike out twice and get one hit. It's an average that gives you not only a sense of humility but also a chance to improvise, to be daring, to innovate, to be unafraid of taking an opposite side, because you're not afraid to make some mistakes.

"This applies to communicating with employees, too. I don't mind an occasional or even a frequent setback. If a little orchid or a box of candy for a girl dishing out food gives her a purpose for her job, a change of pace, a touch of dignity, that helps make up for some of the times we can't communicate. The biggest problem in the airline industry is not equipment obsolescence but personnel obsolescence. Hell, we can take a 720-B and modernize it, or build a new hangar when we outgrow the old one. But when you get into human obsolescence, it's a different situation—you don't get productivity out of a skilled individual who has lost both his dignity and his desire."

Kelly became aware of a gray area within Western's employee ranks—supervisors who are at the first level of management. He pushed through raises for this group, about seventy persons, comparing them to corporals in the Army.

"We spend no time with the people at this level," he explains. "You make one a boss. He does one of two things—he either becomes buddy-buddy with his subordinates, and maybe plays favorites, or he becomes so damned hard-nosed that he alienates himself completely from those working directly under him. He can be an efficient supervisor, but he's completely uninformed about his company. He doesn't have the slightest idea, for example, that a penny a gallon increase in the price of fuel costs Western $3 million a year. We've got to get, through him, down to the eight guys under him."

Kelly's first two years in office marked the most successful in Western's history. Net earnings in 1973 topped $20.3 million and soared to $24 million in 1974, but it was no gravy train; the profits were achieved at a time of nationwide inflation, recession, and generally adverse conditions for the entire industry—of which skyrocketing fuel costs were only one factor. That WAL could set profit records under these circumstances was solid evidence of the new management team's ability.

Kelly and Renda began conferring daily to discuss the developments of the previous day and the problems of the day ahead —the *team* concept again. In his contracts with other carriers, Kelly had observed that to get a flat, definite answer on any problem, one had to bypass platoons of vice presidents and talk to the chief executives of the airline involved. An interviewer once asked Art if it wasn't true that a president can delegate authority but never responsibility.

"That's bull," Kelly snapped. "When I delegate authority I also delegate responsibility. That's why Dom works so effectively. The only thing I ask is that I be kept informed so I can supply my own input."

Kelly turned out to be that kind of chief executive. Shortly after he became president, he asked the design committee if there was anything he could do for the new freed-from-merger corporate image program.

"We could use your personal endorsement," Don Drews suggested.

"The hell with just that," Kelly replied. "I want to be part of it."

Under the Kelly-Renda combo, Western seemed to take on more than just a new corporate image—it acquired a stability, a maturity, a sense of independence, a professional efficiency blending skill with pride. The inauguration of DC-10 service in May 1973 symbolized the new Western, as the gleaming red-and-white giant began flying the skyways of America's senior airline.

Western's pilots loved the big new bird, although its size awed some of them. The neighbor of a captain just assigned to DC-10 training happened to walk by the latter's house one afternoon. The pilot was sitting on the roof.

"What the hell are you doing up there?" the neighbor inquired.

"Practicing taxiing," the captain explained.

It had been decided to lease two of the four DC-10s acquired via the merger pact, but two more DC-10s were ordered that year for delivery in 1974 and 1975, respectively, along with seven more stretched 727s. Simultaneously, WAL began to reduce its surplus aircraft fleet; seven 720-Bs and three 737s had been sold by the end of 1974.

It was typical of Art Kelly that he made sure a certain guest was aboard the day the first DC-10 was flown from its Long Beach hatchery to Los Angeles International Airport. And when Fred Kelly I walked down the ramp stairs to the ramp there was loud applause—and not a few tears.

"What do you think of the DC-10?" a reporter asked the old pilot.

Kelly I smiled. "It used to take us all day to get to Salt Lake City, and you got blown around a lot getting there."

He turned to stare up at the huge jetliner, shook his head, and laughed, like a child gleefully discovering a wondrous, incredible new toy.

EPILOGUE

The pastel shades of a California dawn are the silent reveille for another day in the life on an airline that has seen some 18,000 dawns.

It is a morning in May 1976—a rather typical morning in that five decades of technological progress are taken for granted both by the airline and the people it serves.

Within the next 24 hours, some 70 jetliners will fly approximately 22,000 passengers more than 243,000 miles. Those 70 planes will make more than 400 landings (which will cost about $25,000 in landing fees) involving 181 individual scheduled flights to more than 40 cities in the United States, Canada, and Mexico. They will be manned by some 450 pilots whose longest flight will cover 2,776 miles (Honolulu–Anchorage) and whose shortest leg will be only 30 miles (Oakland–San Jose).

The 70 jets will consume 865,000 gallons of fuel costing approximately $.32 a gallon. Aboard them will be nearly 1,000 flight attendants who, before the day is over, will serve 403 pounds of filet mignon, 242 pounds of roast beef, 315 pounds of chicken, 665 pounds of lettuce, 578 pounds of potatoes, 462 pounds of vegetables, 3,276 eggs, 131 pounds of sausage, 7,500 soft drinks, and 15,000 pounds of ice.

The 22,000 passengers will pay Western $1.2 million for air transportation this day, but WAL itself will be shelling out $499,000 in wages, salaries, and assorted employee benefits, $48,000 in federal and state taxes, and $17,000 for interest on aircraft loans on this same day. It will handle 33,000 pieces of luggage. It will carry 234 tons of cargo, for which it will be paid $76,000. It will board people, freight, and mail at places ranging from Los Angeles (population, 8.9 million for the metropolitan area) to Pierre, South Dakota (population, 10,300).

Its switchboards will field more than 33,600 calls just for reservations. Into P. O. Box 92005 at the World Way Postal Center in Los Angeles will come some 15,000 letters, about 250 of them from passengers either complaining or praising.

In the cavernous hangars located on the fringe of the sprawling Los Angeles International Airport complex are two 720-Bs undergoing their 26,000-hour overhauls—a job that takes 28 days and costs $180,000 per aircraft; that happens to be the same amount the Guggenheim Foundation loaned Western to buy its first three Fokker F-10s 50 years ago. Six other jets are in various stages of "sample structural inspection," a procedure in which maintenance is performed in regular stages so that the extensive 26,000-hour overhaul has been eliminated for the newer aircraft.

The biggest hangar of all is the new $6 million structure built for maintenance on the DC-10. The $6 million represents about 5 days of passenger and cargo revenue for the airline; Western's *accumulative* profits during the first 20 years of its existence fell $2 million short of that figure.

A single DC-10 tire costs $900 and lasts only 45 days, the equivalent of about 1,000 road miles on a car. Each of the jet's General Electric CF6 engines is priced at $1.1 million, the same sum Western used to pay for an entire DC-6B. The lower lobe DC-10 galley carries a $76,500 price tag, and one first-class seat runs $1,500—which is five times more than WAL paid for all 12 seats on an F-10. To feed more than 7 million passengers a year, Western spends around $20 million—a far cry from the $1.25 sandwiches it gave to a handful of passengers on the Model Airway.

It is nearing 8:00 A.M., and the tempo at Western's terminal is picking up as passengers stream aboard the early-morning flights. They march somewhat self-consciously through the various metal-detection devices, and put their luggage through a new X-ray machine that costs $47,000—$12,000 more than the previous model but one that is far more dependable, with a lower rate of false alarms.

In the bowels of the terminal, Norm Rose's flight control group wrestles with last-minute problems, hitches, and mild emergencies—such as an inoperative antiskid device on a 737 that is supposed to leave Minneapolis/St. Paul as Flight 541 for Denver and Phoenix. A 2-hour, 20-minute delay is posted, and later this is extended another hour while WAL mechanics finally try to borrow a replacement part from another airline. They strike out, and flight control co-ordinator Glen Mack, a tall, distinguished man who looks like Central Casting's version of a U.S. senator, is faced with two alternatives: fly a new part from San Francisco to the Twin Cities, or cancel 541. The former would stretch the delay to six hours, so Mack decides to cancel.

This sets a chain reaction exploding through the system. Passengers aboard 541 already have been placed on protecting flights, but there are 20 persons holding Denver-to-Phoenix space on 541. These must be put on a Frontier flight or a later Western trip. At the same time, it's decided to cancel Flight 218, Phoenix to Denver to Twin Cities, which is the return portion of 541—"to balance equipment," is the official explanation. This necessitates phoning the 58 passengers in Phoenix booked on 218 and another 26 holding space from Denver to Minneapolis.

Mack and ground services co-ordinator Allen McRae are doing some fast juggling. They discover that Flight 700, operating from Los Angeles to San Diego, Phoenix, Denver, and the Twin Cities —a 727—has only 79 passengers booked out of Phoenix to Denver. This leaves 43 seats available for 218's load, and only 15 passengers to be protected on other flights. Reservations is alerted to start calling the Phoenix-to-Denver passengers booked on 218, advising 43 of them that space will be available on 700, which leaves 55 minutes earlier than 218.

Crisis over—until the next one. And the swift inproximising will show up at the on-time committee's meeting the next morning, where department heads will review in excruciating detail what went wrong with 541 and the nine other WAL flights that failed to depart or arrive on schedule on the previous day.

In Wayne Lichtgarn's "office of onions and orchids," the assistant vice president of consumer affairs ponders the first batch of mail, which includes a letter from a customer demanding that Western eliminate all smoking from its aircraft. Lichtgarn remembers when the smoking issue first came up, in the early 1970s, and WAL went to Boeing to find out the most efficient, practical way of establishing smoking and nonsmoking areas in the cabin. Boeing's research showed the best method was to put smokers on one side of the aisle and abstainers on the opposite side—a jet's ventilation is such that the interior airflow is forward to aft rather than from side to side. Western tried it briefly but too many passengers complained; the very sight of a smoker sitting across the aisle from a nonsmoker was enough to cause discomfort, even if it was imagined.

In one corner of a hangar sits what was once the pride of Western's fleet—a Douglas M-2 mailplane. Restoring the old bird was a labor of love for such retired Westerners as Ralph Deeter, G. B. Smiley, Bill Oliver, and numerous other mechanics, machinists, and even a pilot from another airline. Retired Captain Ted Homan—in charge of the M-2 project—was to fly it from Los Angeles to Salt Lake City in a fiftieth anniversary re-enactment of the April 17, 1926, inaugural, but on the very morning of the scheduled flight, high winds that hit the Los Angeles area damaged the restored M-2 during a pre-takeoff taxiing test. Even without that ceremonial trip, however, the ancient biplane still symbolizes the first fifty years—a kind of time machine whose fragility, inadequacies, and deficiencies stir poignant pride. There is a little bit of the M-2 in every Western jet flying today.

The history of an airline can be likened to a stage drama—it tells of heroes and villains, principals and spear carriers, laughs and tears, triumph and tragedy. Unlike the fiction of the theater, however, history has no real ending; to paraphrase Shakespeare, the past is merely a preamble to the future. The airline and the industry of which it is a part go on, even as those who have guided their destinies for better or for worse become mere footnotes to the stories still being written. Their moments of glorious victories and painful defeats are for history to record, posterity to judge, and memory to please or pain, depending on the individual.

That bitterness is so prevalent among Western's leaders of the past is regrettable, yet perhaps inevitable. It is an inescapable residue of corporate Armageddons, Drinkwater being the prime example. Terry, who certainly earned a retirement of contentment and security, has built for himself a prison of bitter memories and apparently incurable resentment. He was never the type to stagnate into idleness; he serves as a director on the Boards of five different corporations and works hard at those jobs. He and his wife fly frequently to Hawaii—"at least they didn't take away my pass privileges."

"I'm not really bitter," he insists, "just disappointed in some ways. I don't miss Western a whole lot. I still visit the old place every couple of weeks or so—it's like old home week when I come back. I keep telling the guys, 'Don't let 'em catch you talking to me or it's your ass.' I keep busy. I play golf three times a week and I do my homework for the meetings of the Boards I serve on."

Stan Shatto's ill feelings are channeled almost exclusively in the direction of Fred Benninger, although, like Drinkwater, he professes no real bitterness. "I'm glad I'm out of it," he declares. "The fun has gone out of the airline business. It's strictly for dollars now—all computers instead of people."

Shatto, too, manages to keep himself occupied. He operates a small antique shop not too far from Drinkwater's home in the Brentwood area of Los Angeles. He is no mean expert on antiques, a hobby he took up when he was with Western and one that became a vocation after he retired. He runs the store by himself, and one is struck by the contrast between this tiny, quiet world of the past and the hectic airline empire whose rule he once shared with Drinkwater.

Leo Dwerlkotte has led a lonely life since his wife died several years ago. He resides in Las Vegas and attended Board meetings faithfully until his retirement. He travels a lot, always alone, seems to have no close friends in Las Vegas, cooks his own meals, and on rare occasions will dine at a Vegas hotel by himself before wandering around the glittering casinos, watching the gamblers.

Al Adams also lives alone in a Manhattan apartment that resembles a natural-history museum. It is crammed with mementos and specimens from his big-game hunting trips, including magnificent skins from big African, Indian, and South American cats. The second president of Western has never left aviation and still is active as the North American representative of the French firm that builds the big A-300B airbus—which he has been trying to sell to WAL for a long time. He has changed little since the days of his presidency—gregarious, sharp-tongued, and with a youthful alertness and interest that belie his age.

Tom Wolfe also remains active in aviation; retired and living in the Los Angeles area, he has become involved with a project to revive lighter-than-air transportation. Jerry Brooder lives in Carefree, Arizona—as beloved a figure around this mecca for senior citizens as he was, and still is, at Western. Marv Landes and Jud Taylor both are in Palm Springs and have remained close friends.

The old pilots who once flew the routes of the Indian head are dying off. Their dwindling ranks are minus one name in particular: Fred Kelly I. He was hospitalized in Medford, Oregon, in late April 1974, and Al DeGarmo went from his farm in Oregon to see his comrade for the last time. DeGarmo, accompanied by a friend, walked into Kelly's hospital room, but the first of the Four Horsemen didn't seem to know him.

"Hi, Fred," DeGarmo said softly.

Kelly stared at him, still with no sign of recognition.

"I think we'd better get out of here," DeGarmo said to his friend. "He's dying. It's too hard for him to breathe."

DeGarmo started to leave the bedside, but Kelly suddenly reached out and took his hand, squeezing it gently.

"Good-bye, Fred," DeGarmo muttered.

Kelly's sister called him the next day and said Fred had passed away shortly after DeGarmo's visit.

The date was May 7, 1974, three weeks after Western had started its forty-ninth year of service.

For Western, the Golden Anniversary year of 1976 mixed pride in the past with a gnawing concern for the future. It was no cause for celebration when not only America's senior airline but also the entire industry was and still is trying to survive in an anti-aviation, antitechnology climate that threatens to tear down the air carrier structure with no blueprints for a replacement. At this writing, a White House plan to gradually deregulate the airline industry stands a fair chance of becoming grim reality. It is a plan with great appeal to that potent new political force known as consumerism, for it would allow indiscriminate fare cuts of up to 40 per cent over the next five years without CAB approval. It also would open the door for virtually uncontrolled invasion of established route authority. To the airlines, the proposed legislation can be likened to a pitchman's advertisement, with succulent promises in large black type, and the fine-print drawbacks scarcely discernible without a magnifying glass. How can any airline break even in a government-ordered fare war (inevitable without regulatory restraints) when there is no corresponding government plan for corking the rampaging genie of inflation-fed costs?

The airlines don't like bloated fares any more than the public —every reluctant tariff increase carries the risk of compressing the air travel market by pricing the product out of reach. Western has a tradition of catering to budget-minded passengers—91 per cent of its 75-plane fleet capacity is configured for coach or economy transportation—but as with all scheduled carriers, reducing fares with no lid on spiraling costs is an engraved invitation to financial disaster and possible nationalization. Compounding this factor is a CAB decision that allows the supplemental airlines to provide point-to-point charter service in high-density travel markets where scheduled carriers already operate. Western is a case in point: Its handful of prime long-haul routes literally subsidize service to the majority of the smaller cities on its system.

WAL celebrated its fiftieth anniversary at least holding its own in this atmosphere of repression and criticism. It finished 1975 with net earnings of $12.3 million despite a second-quarter loss of $1.3 million—a creditable showing under an avalanche of adversity. As it had done so often in the past, it managed to recoil from each setback with the resilience of a carrier basically secure and strong.

It seemed only fitting that in the Golden Anniversary year, Western received two major route awards. It won Vancouver–Hawaii authority and only a month before the anniversary itself,

the Civil Aeronautics Board made WAL a transcontinental carrier for the first time in its history by granting its bitterly
contested application to operate nonstop between Los Angeles
and Miami.

The latter was something of a personal victory for Dom
Renda, who had never given up on his conviction that a Los Angeles–Miami route would be of enormous importance to Western's future. Drinkwater's priority for Hawaii had helped stymie
the first attempt, but when Renda rejoined Western some years
later, Kerkorian one day asked him what new route would help
the airline the most.

"Los Angeles–Miami," Renda said firmly.

Ironically, Kerkorian wasn't much more than an interested
spectator when the California–Florida route award came through.
In mid-January 1976, he moved to sever his ties with the airline
he had wrested from Terry Drinkwater. Kerkorian's holdings already had been reduced from 30 per cent to 17 per cent—about
2.5 million shares—and these he put up for sale in a bloc.

Western itself acted swiftly, agreeing to purchase all 2.5 million shares for $30.3 million, part in cash and the rest in sinking
fund debentures to Kerkorian. In a sense, this was bringing the
airline full cycle in its Golden Anniversary year—control of its
destiny was back in its own hands as it had been in the days
when a small group of men invested their hopes and their dreams
in an airline and in an industry.

It has come a long way since that windy spring day at Vail
Field when an airline was born. That it shares the industry's
serious problems and precarious future must be equated with the
fact that it also shares the industry's historical ability to overcome awesome odds. Many of the dangers that lurk in the airlines' future stem from the well-meaning but misinformed views
and deeds of those who have never truly appreciated the progress of commercial air transportation, nor its present role in the
life of this 200-year-old nation.

The reformers—ecological and economic alike—either have
never looked at the record or refuse to acknowledge its very existence. They don't have to read it all; they need but glance at
this story of one carrier—which started out with a lumbering

biplane hauling 256 pounds of mail some 500 miles and now flies more than 7 million passengers a year over a 25,000-mile system.

It is a story of technological advancement, but it also is a story of people who fused dreams, courage, ingenuity, personality, and determination into an inanimate corporate body. An airline *is* people, at Western and at every carrier. If there has been bitterness, bruised egos, and personal tragedy during Western's first 50 years, there also has been self-sacrifice, comradeship, and dedication to the cause of aviation's progress. For every mistake, there have been a thousand miracles—and only those who have played a role in an airline story, presidents and ship cleaners alike, can appreciate the accumulative extent of those miracles.

In July 1975, Art Kelly received a letter from the commanding officer of the Naval Air Station at Dallas, Texas. He wrote that he had heard Western intended to fly its restored M-2 over the original Los Angeles–Las Vegas–Salt Lake City route. He informed Kelly that he would like to fly the M-2 "in a completely nonpay status" during the Golden Anniversary because his father had been a Western Air Express pilot.

"My father continued to closely watch the progress of Western over the years long after he was working elsewhere in the aviation industry," the Navy captain added. "A very large part of [him] always remained with Western Airlines."

The letter was signed C. N. James, Jr.

He is Jimmie James' son.

On April 22, five days after the fiftieth anniversary, the Board of Directors of Western Airlines elevated Art Kelly to chairman of the Board and chief executive officer. At the same time, on Kelly's recommendation, the Board elected Dominic P. Renda the seventh president and chief operating officer of America's senior airline.

Thus did Western begin its next half century under leadership with roots in a proud past, but with a vision of an even greater future.

ACKNOWLEDGMENTS

A book, like any single airline flight, is the product of many people and the culmination of co-operative effort.

Two people deserve to share the byline: Ray Silvius, vice president of corporate affairs, and Linda Cole, manager of corporate information. Without their help, the book could not have been written, and it seems almost inadequate merely to express gratitude.

To Mary Lou Hendrickson of WAL, who typed—and frequently retyped—the manuscript, my heartfelt thanks.

For my wife's patience and tolerance during the many months of preparation, including long absences from home, I offer both thanks and love. It was no more than I expected, however—she once wore the wings of Western with great pride.

I must also single out Walter I. Bradbury of Doubleday, editor and friend, whose co-operation and encouragement is appreciated not only by the author but also by the men and women of America's senior airline.

The following, listed alphabetically, warrant my heartfelt appreciation for interviews, courtesies, and help in a hundred ways, all aimed at making *The Only Way to Fly* an objective account:

Alvin Adams	Jerry Brooder	Nancy Chauncey
Syd Albright	Dick Brown	Howard Clifford
Art Beggs	Sheila Buterbaugh	Barbara Cooks
Fred Benninger	Maude Campbell	Hugh Darling
Mary Bowser	Pat Carlson	R. E. G. Davies

Sandy Dawn
Henry deButts
Ed Deeter
Al DeGarmo
Mark Dennett
Mary Diamond
Don Drews
Helen Drinkwater
Terrell Drinkwater
Leo Dwerlkotte
Richard Ensign
Anton Favero
Charles Fisher
Joe Fogarty
Stan Gewirtz
Tom Greene
Don Hall
Terri Halverson
Dave Hatfield
Jack Hereford
Peggy Hereford
Les Holtan
Ted Homan
Larry Hyland

Bob Johnson
Mark Johnson
Art Kelly
Fred Kelly I
Kirk Kerkorian
Jack Keyes
Bob Kinsey
Irving Krick
Marv Landes
Jim LeBel
Sandy Levy
Wayne Lichtgarn
Bert Lynn
Glen Mack
Mason Mallory
Marina Marrelli
Allen McRae
Forrest Mulvane
Beverlee Nelson
Seth Oberg
Gerald O'Grady
Phil Peirce
Dick Peterson
Welch Pogue

Dom Renda
Margaret Rippy
Norm Rose
Eunice Ruch
Ruth Ann Schlick
Ed Schuster
Stan Shatto
Mike Simpson
William Singleton
Jack Slichter
Ken Smith
Ursula Brown Sperry
Neil Stewart
Jud Taylor
Al Tellez
Sloss Viau
Harry Volk
Les Warden
Howard Westwood
Tom Wolfe
Art Woodley
Willard Wright
Duane Youngbar

R